I0130198

Caribbean Reasonings

The Thought of New World

The Quest for Decolonisation

Other Titles in the Caribbean Reasonings Series

After Man, Towards the Human: Critical Essays on Sylvia Wynter

Culture, Politics, Race and Diaspora: The Thought of Stuart Hall

George Padmore: Pan-African Revolutionary

Caribbean Reasonings
Series Editors
Anthony Bogues
Rupert Lewis
Brian Meeks

Caribbean Reasonings

The Thought of New World:
The Quest for Decolonisation

edited by
Brian Meeks and Norman Girvan

Ian Randle Publishers
Kingston . Miami

First published in Jamaica, 2010 by
Ian Randle Publishers
11 Cunningham Avenue
Box 686
Kingston 6
www.ianrandlepublishers.com

Introduction, copyright selection and editorial material
© 2010, Centre for Caribbean Thought, University of the West Indies, Mona

While copyright in the selection, introduction and editorial material is vested in
the Centre for Caribbean Thought, University of the West Indies, Mona, copyright
in individual chapters belongs to their respective authors and no chapter may be
reproduced wholly or in part without the express permission in writing of both
author and publisher.

National Library of Jamaica Cataloguing-in-Publication Data

Caribbean reasonings : the thought of new world : the quest for decolonisation /
edited
    by Brian Meeks and Norman Girvan

    p. : ill. ; cm. – (Caribbean reasonings)

ISBN 978-976-637-401-3 (pbk)

1. Caribbean Area – Intellectual life – 20th century   2. Caribbean Area – Critical
thinking
3. Caribbean Area – Politics and government – 20th century   4. Thought and
thinking
5. Decolonisation
I. Meeks, Brian   II. Girvan, Norman   III. Series

320.509729   dc 22

The cover design includes a photograph of the *New World Quarterly*, vol. 11 no. 3, The
Guyana Independence Issue, 1966, edited by George Lamming and Martin Carter.

Cover and book design by Ian Randle Publishers
Printed in United States of America

In memory of
Lloyd Best,
George Beckford and
David de Caires

From left to right: Lloyd Best, Alister McIntyre, Roy Augier and
David de Caires at the 2005 New World Conference

Table of Contents

PART THREE: REMEMBERING

Acknowledgements

I am thankful to my co-editor Norman Girvan, whose knowledge of the events and personalities surrounding New World and its times is, perhaps, unmatched by anyone alive. Without his boundless energy, encouragement and keen editorial eye, this volume might not have seen the light of day. My colleagues and friends in the Centre for Caribbean Thought, Rupert Lewis and Tony Bogues were their usual generous selves in supporting and helping to organise the New World Conference and in gently pressing for the timely completion of this collection. Kari Polanyi Levitt and Norman Girvan read the original typescript of the interview with Lloyd and gave invaluable comments and information as to people, places and events that helped shape the final version. Eleanor Williams had the typically disagreeable job of keeping in touch with contributors and helping to copy edit and shape the final version, which she did with aplomb. I wish to specially thank the myriad of people at Mona who helped organise the Conference, particularly the members of the student-based Marcus Garvey Movement, whose voluntary help as liaison officers was invaluable. Finally, a special debt is owed to the late Lloyd Best and Sunity Maharaj Best, for entertaining Tony Bogues, Norman Girvan and I at their home on Tunapuna Road, Trinidad in January 2005 and for allowing that remarkable interview that appears as the third and final part of this volume.

Brian Meeks
Mona, March 2010

Introduction:

Remembering New World

Brian Meeks

In June 2005 the fourth Caribbean Reasonings Conference was held in Kingston, Jamaica, under the theme 'The Thought of New World: The Quest for Decolonisation.' After hosting three annual conferences dedicated to honouring and critically exploring the work, respectively, of Sylvia Wynter, George Lamming and Stuart Hall,[1] we in the Centre for Caribbean Thought felt the need to change gear for the fourth. Instead of focusing on the work of a single significant Caribbean thinker, we decided instead to engage with the collective contribution of an entire movement.

The New World Group[2] emerged and grew as a distinct, if multi-faceted intellectual trend in the Caribbean from the early 1960s until the early 1970s. As such, it fit neatly into the narrow space between the collapse of the West Indies Federation and the period of radicalisation of Caribbean politics, culminating in the fall of the Grenada Revolution in 1983. This interregnum, spanning the first post-independence decade in the Anglophone Caribbean, with all its promises and expectations of a better future, ended, however, with frustration, rebellion and disappointment. At its apogee, New World exceeded in conceptual and geographical scope any other Caribbean intellectual venture tried before its time or since. A quarterly journal of critical ideas was published in Jamaica; a fortnightly in Guyana; numerous pamphlets appeared on important social economic and political issues of the day; groups were formed in North America and throughout the archipelago, including Puerto Rico; and in Trinidad, New World moved from being a small circle of thinkers to approach the scale of a pre-party political formation. Its young membership, composed at the core of newly recruited faculty of the University of the West Indies, was trans-disciplinary in nature and held heterogeneous perspectives. However, it is fairly easy to define in this healthy mix of ideas an inner core of commonly held 'New World' positions. These included a general assertion of sovereignty over the resources of the

Caribbean region, the placing of 'the people' at the centre of the project of national and regional development and, despite the collapse of the federal experiment, the reassertion of the Caribbean as the broader canvas over which sovereignty should be exercised. In the cultural and psychological spheres this was mirrored in the affirmation of a Caribbean identity and the insistence that the Caribbean should legitimately be at the centre, both as a subject of research in its own right and more widely, as a project for development.

Yet, this early flowering and extraordinary potential for further growth, turned out to be temporary and somewhat ephemeral. By 1970, with the collapse of the Trinidad organisation under controversial conditions discussed elsewhere in this volume[3] and with a growing insurrectionary wave, New World lost momentum and eventually ceased functioning. Some supporters went with New World's founder Lloyd Best into the Tapia House Movement, while others turned to James Millette and his United National Independence Party (UNIP); many of the younger supporters cleaved to the burgeoning mass movement and joined the Black Power street demonstrations led by the National Joint Action Committee or one of the myriad of small movements that emerged out of the popular upwelling that is commonly known as the 1970 Black Power Revolution. In Jamaica, *New World Quarterly* continued for the first few years of the 1970s as an insightful and important publication from academics at the Mona campus of the University of the West Indies but, as Norman Girvan indicates in his chapter, the Jamaican segment too was overwhelmed by the growth of popular mass politics. With Michael Manley's election in 1972 and the subsequent radicalisation of Jamaican politics, the key New World players either drew closer to the Peoples National Party (PNP) or gravitated to the Marxist left, which had its own distinct constituency on the Mona campus. In Guyana – the other significant pole of concentration – New World also faded away and concerted resistance to the dictatorial trends inherent in Burnhamite paramountcy, beyond Cheddi Jagan's People's Progressive Party (PPP), would mainly occur with the return of Walter Rodney and the growth of the Working People's Alliance (WPA) in the mid to late 1970s.

However, the rise of the radical left was to turn out, in the sweep of history, to be equally fleeting and ephemeral. Walter Rodney was assassinated in June 1980; the Manley regime was ignominiously defeated by Edward Seaga's rightist Jamaica Labour Party (JLP) in the violent, near civil war election of October 1980; and, most damaging of all, the Grenada Revolution, the ultimate effect of the radicalised politics of that decade, devoured itself with the brutal killing of Prime Minister Maurice Bishop and a number of his closest associates by his own soldiers, followed immediately by the US-led invasion of Grenada in October 1983. This, as Norman Girvan eloquently asserts, was one of the final nails in the coffin that signaled the end of the experimentation with radical and alternative avenues to decolonisation, and the consolidation, simultaneously, of the neo-liberal paradigm.

For three decades, neo-liberalism, with its assertions of systematic individualism, negative freedom and market fundamentalism, dominated the region and the world at the levels of politics, policy and thought. Few governments, with the notable exception of Cuba and more recently Venezuela, sought to question these philosophical arguments and the requisite policy implications of structural adjustment, devaluation and privatisation. Most recently, however, neo-liberalism has also revealed itself to be a false prophet of social and economic salvation. Beginning with the collapse of the United States housing bubble in 2007, leading to the specifically US and then unprecedented world financial crisis of 2008, the outwardly sound structures of the neo-liberal house have all but crumbled. Indeed, not only are the specific tenets of the neo-liberal project in tatters, but increasingly, the undergirding foundation of the globalised, late capitalist system, is being called into question.[4] Spurred on by revelations that the present crisis was precipitated by speculation gone wild, that in turn was facilitated by the deregulation and marginalisation of the state, a significant movement in opposition to capital is rapidly coalescing. Once again, though under the peculiar post-Cold War conditions of the early twenty-first century, a window for a free and imaginative questioning of the contemporary economic order and the place and role of the Caribbean in it, is opening. There is no more appropriate moment than the present, therefore, for a critical review of the New World Group, which attempted to answer similar intellectual questions at an earlier time of open investigation of the Caribbean condition and of the place of the Caribbean people in the world. The chapters that follow, drawn in large measure from the 2005 conference, seek, collectively, to begin that necessary and urgent process of renewed and reinvigorated evaluation.

The volume is divided into three parts. In the first, *Reflecting*, former members and associates of the New World Group critically examine its philosophical tenets, explore little known formative dimensions of the movement and evaluate its significance in the context of a radically altered global and regional political economy. In the second, *Imagining*, scholars largely drawn from the generation after New World, engage creatively with its legacy of ideas in order to help jump start the relative stasis in Caribbean political and economic thought. New approaches to understanding and critically appreciating New World are combined with the beginnings of alternative proposals for the future direction of Caribbean political and economic policy. In part three, *Remembering*, Lloyd Best takes the floor. In early 2005, Best invited Tony Bogues and I to interview him at his fabled home on Tunapuna Road in Northern Trinidad. Norman Girvan accompanied us, and contributed significantly to the discussion that followed. In an unforgettable conversation which lasted the better part of two days, Best, in tracing the pivotal moments of his remarkable life, leapt with alacrity from London to Kingston, Paris to Georgetown, Montreal to Port of Spain and back to Kingston again. In between, he sketched the origins of New World, its conflicts, casualties and the personal and institutional continuities with the present.[5] More than giving a mere history of events and personalities, Best elaborated his philosophy, approach to life and his own perception of his far from inconsequential role in the political affairs of the modern Caribbean. Often witty, at times infuriating, but always provocative, Lloyd Best, as evident in this interview, is a voice that could never be ignored during his colourful lifetime and will resonate and continue to be heard long beyond his passage in 2007.

Notes

1. See Anthony Bogues ed. *After Man, Towards the Human: Critical Essays on Sylvia Wynter,* (Kingston: Ian Randle Publishers, 2006); George Lamming, *The Sovereignty of the Imagination,* (Kingston: Arawak Publications, 2004); Brian Meeks ed. *Culture, Politics, Race and Diaspora: The Thought of Stuart Hall,* (Kingston: Ian Randle Publishers, 2007).
2. There has been a notable revival of critical literature on the work of New World in the past two decades. See, for instance: Kari Levitt and Michael

Witter eds. *The Critical Tradition of Caribbean Political Economy: The Legacy of George Beckford,* (Kingston: Ian Randle Publishers, 1996); David Scott, 'The Vocation of a Caribbean Intellectual: Interview with Lloyd Best,' *Small Axe* No.1, (1997): 119–39; Dennis Pantin and Dhanayshar Mahabir eds. 'Plantation Economy Revisited,' *Marronage* vol.1 no.1, September 1998; Selwyn Ryan, *Independent Thought and Caribbean Freedom: Essays in Honour of Lloyd Best,* (Trinidad: Sir Arthur Lewis Institute for Social and Economic Studies, 2003); Kari Polanyi Levitt, *Reclaiming Development: Independent Thought and Caribbean Community,* Kingston: Ian Randle Publishers, 2005 and Lloyd Best and Kari Polanyi Levitt, *The Theory of Plantation Economy: A Historical and Institutional Approach to Caribbean Development,* (Kingston: The University of the West Indies Press, 2009). The entire collection of *New World Quarterly* is now being considered for publication as a single volume.

3. See in this volume, James Millette, Kari Levitt and the interview with Lloyd Best for differing positions on this still hotly contested moment.

4. Much of this debate and the paradigm shattering character of the moment have been captured in the tone of the headlines and articles of mainstream news magazines as they sought to come to terms with the unfolding events. Thus, the indomitable *Economist* of October 18, 2008, recognises, in its unforgettable cover picture of a wounded lion brought to ground, the reality of 'Capitalism at Bay;' the left of centre *Harper's* of November 2008, leads with a cover and a feature discussion on 'How to Save Capitalism;' and the headline of *Newsweek*, February 2009 is 'We are all Socialists Now.'

5. Best has always insisted, with justification, that the *Trinidad and Tobago Review,* his remarkable journal of Caribbean affairs, is the direct intellectual descendant of *Tapia*, the newspaper of the now defunct Tapia House Group and before that of *New World Quarterly* and *New World Fortnightly*.

PART ONE

Reflecting

1 | *New World and its Critics*

Norman Girvan

This chapter is part narrative, part analytical, part critical and part reflective. First, there is a personal account of the origins and early history of the New World Group from the standpoint of the author's own participation. Next comes an analysis of the content of New World thought and of its applications to various spheres of Caribbean life. I then examine critiques of New World thought made by contemporaries and discuss the reasons for its eventual loss of influence and the decline of the New World Group. Finally, I reflect on the legacy of New World thought and its relevance in the era of globalisation. The paper focuses on the 1960s–70s but the broader context is that of the postcolonial experience in the English-speaking Caribbean as a whole.

Origins

I was a student on the Mona Campus of the University (then University College) of the West Indies between 1959 and 1962. I remember it as a time of great excitement, tremendous ferment and heated debates. Imagine what it was like to be in a Caribbean populated by the likes of Norman Manley, Eric Williams, Cheddi Jagan, Grantley Adams and C.L.R. James; Frank Worrell and Garfield Sobers; Arthur Lewis; Vidia Naipaul and Roger Mais; Fidel Castro and Che Guevara, and the ghost of Marcus Garvey; moreover, in a world populated by the likes of Nehru, Nasser, Nkrumah and Nyerere; Tito, Sukharno and Mao Zedong.

A debate was raging over what form the West Indies Federation should take and what economic policies it should follow. The Jamaica Referendum was looming on the horizon. In Trinidad, Williams was campaigning for the return of the US Naval Base at Chaguaramas to be the site of the Federal Capital, pitting the symbol of West Indian nationhood against the symbol of Anglo-American imperialism. James was campaigning for Worrell to become the first black captain of the West Indies Cricket Team – cricket decolonisation. In Guyana, ideological cleavage had sharpened and ethnic conflict was simmering. The Cold War cast a long shadow over the region. Lewis had just come to the University and the Faculty of Social Science was being established. The Rastafarians were raising hell in Jamaica and Fidel Castro was raising hell in Cuba.

Repatriation and Revolution!

The burning issues of debate were West Indian integration and identity, imperialism, decolonisation, racism, socialism, democracy, mass party, and economic development. There was a widespread sense that the emerging postcolonial order was in crisis. The question was – what course should national independence take?

Late in 1959, the University had organised a series of Open Lectures on the future of the West Indies. C.L.R. James had spoken and had lit the place afire. After each lecture, staff and students would retire to the Common Rooms of the Halls of Residence to continue the discussion. This became the template for the group of young West Indian lecturers and politically aware students in the social sciences and arts, that later began weekly meetings on Lloyd Best's veranda at College Common. I attended these meetings from the start. I believe they began in late 1960 or early 1961. The group later adopted the name of the West Indian Society for the Study of Social Issues (WISSSI).

The first thing I remember Lloyd Best saying was that 'the current political leadership in the region is intellectually bankrupt, with the possible exception of Jagan.' This was a totally outrageous thing to say at a time when Jamaican students believed that Norman Manley was God and Trinidadians felt the same about Eric Williams. It was a provocative statement, challenging you to think about regional politics and economics in a different way. I recall that the dominant themes in discussions were the prevalence of crisis; the need for decolonisation in the economy, society and political culture; and the need for popular participation in the postcolonial reconstruction of West Indian society. Along these lines, papers were prepared by students in the group[1] on the economics, sociology and politics of colonialism and of independence.

4

Lloyd Best gave a lecture on this subject just before his departure from Mona in October 1961, which established him as the *enfant terrible* of West Indian academics.[2] By the time he arrived in British Guiana the following year, inter-ethnic violence was raging. He was there as a U.N. Economic Adviser to Jagan's Administration. He, however, soon decided that Jagan, too, was intellectually bankrupt – a victim of Cold War 'ideologising.'[3] This was the background to the formation of the New World Group in Georgetown in 1962 and the publication of the first issue of the journal *New World Quarterly*. The New World Group subsequently spread to Trinidad, Jamaica, Montreal and New York.

In 1962–65 I was a graduate student at the London School of Economics and my thesis on foreign investment in Jamaica was directly influenced by discussions in the WISSSI and by the teaching of Alister McIntyre who, as a young faculty member, was one its members. As I was finishing up in London, Lloyd invited me to join the team of economists working on studies of regional economic integration to contribute a case study of the bauxite industry. At the same time, McIntyre recruited me to come and lecture at UWI St Augustine, to which he had moved. So it was natural that when I eventually returned to Mona to teach in 1966[4] I would gravitate to the New World Group, which was by then active there. I served as Chairman of the Mona Group from 1966 to 1968. My work on bauxite, multinational corporations and dependency was strongly influenced by New World and the plantation school. In its own modest way, it made a contribution to the intellectual movement. I continued to be a regular contributor to *New World Quarterly* until it ceased publication in 1972.

Seven Theses in New World Thought

I will now summarise my understanding of what New World thought was about. This is my interpretation – others, both within the movement and outside it, will have their own. New World never had a manifesto; it was not an organisation in which members formally subscribed to a set of codified beliefs, principles and practices. It was an intellectual movement with varying tendencies; and its thinking evolved over time. My summary will focus on questions of philosophy, cosmology and epistemology, political economy, and social theory.[5] In distilling the ideas, I will refer mainly to two kinds of sources: the publications of the Group, in particular *New World Quarterly*; and intellectual spin-offs from New World, particularly regional economic integration, the plantation school, dependency and multinational corporations. I summarise the ideas in the form of seven theses.

First was the necessity for independent thought.[6] It held that the root of the Caribbean's problems lay in the colonial cast of mind, to epistemic dependency, to flawed conceptualisations based on 'imported' formulations. This was true for the economics, the politics, the society and the culture – all elements of an interconnected whole.

It followed that the first step in addressing the Caribbean problematique would be to conceptualise our own reality from within. It would mean observing the economy, the society, and the politics without reliance on preconceived models derived from the experience of others. It would mean close study of our own historical experience and locating our reality in the context of that history. It would mean drawing on the insights of writers, artists and other cultural workers, and then and only on that basis, developing concepts and theories that are appropriate to us.

Second, there was a theory of change that gave the central role to ideas. Ideas were asserted as the foundational step in effecting social transformation; and indigenous ideas were seen as the only sure way to escape from the colonial condition. According to Best '...social change in the Caribbean has to and can only begin in the minds of Caribbean men....[T]hought is the action for us.'[7] In similar vein, Beckford insisted that the transformation of plantation society begins with the psychological liberation of the intellectual classes from their colonised minds.[8] Related to this too was McIntyre's notion of 'functional' dependence – the dependence that arises not from the constraints of size or structure but from the policies that West Indian governments pursue.[9]

Third was the conceptualisation of the Caribbean as a plantation system.[10] I believe that this was New World's distinctive contribution to Caribbean social theory. It drew from the work of historians, sociologists and cultural anthropologists, especially from Wagley's notion of 'plantation America.'[11] What New World did was to turn the plantation into a basic paradigm for Caribbean society – a framework by which to interpret the past and the present, the economics, the politics, the society and the culture. New World's Pan-Caribbeanism, therefore, stemmed from a cosmology in which all the islands and the adjacent mainland were the frame of reference of regional identity.

The fourth thesis related to economic dependence and the fifth to plantation economy.[12] The economies were characterised as structurally dependent, meaning that governments had limited ability to influence economic activity by using the standard tools of monetary and fiscal policy. Dependence was attributed to the dominance over the key sectors of the economy by plantations and multinational corporations. The multinational corporations of the twentieth century were held to be similar to the Joint Stock Trading Companies in the era of Mercantilism – they controlled initiative, organisation, capital, technology and marketing for Caribbean economies.

From this followed the theme of 'continuity with change;' the terms 'Old Mercantilism' and 'New Mercantilism;' the concept of 'Plantation Economy' and its three versions or 'models:' 'Pure,' during slavery; 'Modified,' in the post-Emancipation period; and 'Further Modified' in the modern period. The plantation economy was held to be the underlying factor in economic dependence, boom-bust cycles, adjustment without transformation, persistent poverty and social inequality.[13]

The sixth thesis derived, for the Caribbean, a theory of plantation society from its base in the economy. The contemporary social structure and race and class relations were held to be products of the legacy of the plantation system – that is, what had been instituted by the slave plantations and modified over time by indentureship, by the rise of the peasantry, by urbanisation, migration, and by the rise of new export staples.[14] These modifications were believed not to alter its fundamental character.

Here we should note that there were at least two versions of the theory of plantation society with regard to the treatment of race and class and the applicability of Marxist class analysis. Best consistently maintained that the Marxist notion of class is derived from the special case of nineteenth century industrial Europe and has limited relevance to the contemporary Caribbean.[15] In the context of Trinidad and Tobago, he has argued that 'tribal' identities based on ethnicity and/or religious affiliation are the primary foci of group solidarity. Beckford critiqued the classical Marxist analysis for ignoring the race question in the Caribbean; but in his later work he analysed plantation society as an integral part of the international capitalist system and proposed '...a synthesis of how race and class make plantation society a sort of "special case" in the history of social formations.'[16] His analysis of race in plantation society is evidently influenced by Marxist methodology:

> When I say the 'plantation system' I am not talking about agriculture and the planting of food, I am talking about the planting of labour as the critical element...the labour regime is based on race...this labour is not homogenous in the classical sense...and therefore not deriving classes in the classical system of Marxist analysis. What I am trying to suggest is that race is instituted in both the mode of production and the mode of exchange.[17]

Beckford argued consistently that the cultural legacy of plantation racism is the major factor frustrating the potential of Caribbean people. Thus there is a sense in which, ultimately, race trumped class in his perspective.

The seventh thesis relates to Best's theory of 'Doctor Politics.' This holds that the practice of politics and governance in the Caribbean is a derivative of the culture of the plantation and of Crown Colony Government,[18] resulting in the excessive centralisation of personal authority in the office of Prime Minister. Best contrasted this with the civilised discourse and true participation in decision-making that he regarded as the essence of democratic politics.

To summarise: at the core of New World thinking was the need for epistemic sovereignty,[19] a belief in the power of ideas to effect change, and a view of the Caribbean condition as legacy of the pervasive effects of the plantation system.

The Rise and Fall of New World

Overview

New World thinking passed through several stages in its relations with the Caribbean intelligentsia. Its early days can be characterised as a period of insurgency. At this time – roughly in the early 1960s – it operated on the intellectual fringe, critiquing current orthodoxies, waging a kind of intellectual guerrilla warfare through its publications and outreach activity. The next stage I characterise as that of co-existence. At this time New World thinking achieved some degree of academic respectability and was accepted as one of several possible interpretations of Caribbean reality. From the mid-1960s, young West Indian UWI faculty began to publish regularly in *New World Quarterly* and the journal was widely read in intellectual circles. By the end of the decade, New World thinking had established a position of near dominance in the Caribbean social sciences, with a noticeable impact on the public consciousness and the political climate of the region. In 1971, Trevor Munroe was to write:

> For almost a decade, the New World and its associates were the most influential force amongst the progressive intellectuals primarily inside but also outside the University of the West Indies. In Kingston, Port of Spain and Georgetown the ideas of the group, embodied primarily in a quarterly journal, occasional pamphlets and public forums, had a deep influence on the thinking of students, university lecturers, high school teachers, journalists, publishers, artists, lawyers and others who wanted to develop a better understanding of West Indian society in order to contribute to its 'progressive' transformation.[20]

Other ideological currents feeding the radicalisation of the late 1960s/early 1970s were Rastafarianism and Black Power, socialism, and Third World economic nationalism. New World's contribution was to provide a rapidly growing body of Caribbean-grounded theoretical and empirical material, readily available in published form, on which radical scholars and political activists could draw. Similarly, its impact on the social sciences at UWI was widely acknowledged by contemporary scholars.[21] In the words of Carl Stone, it had '...filled a fundamental vacuum in analysis of the relationship between the dominating imperialist interest and those employed by that interest.'[22] New World's mission of epistemic decolonisation also appealed to a generation of young scholars infused with nationalist and regionalist ideologies and a sense of their generational mission to take over from foreign white academics.

Paralleling this stage, however, was one of intense critique and contestation of New World thought. Around the same time, the New World Group itself experienced internal convulsions. Paradoxically, it self-destructed while at the very height of its influence. The Trinidad

Group imploded in 1968; the Jamaican Group died quietly in 1969–70; bereft of their points of reference, the Groups in the Diaspora ceased functioning. *New World Quarterly* ceased publication in 1972. Although the intellectual influence continued through the 1970s, these developments signaled the onset of the final stage – that of dethronement and demise.

What accounts for the decline of New World, after such a promising start and impressive scholarly achievements? To this question, several answers may be offered. Here, one should make the distinction between what happened to the New World Group and what happened to New World thought.

The New World Group

The New World Group died principally as a result of internal disagreements over the relative emphasis to be given to direct political activity vis-à-vis intellectual work. In Trinidad, Lloyd Best led away a faction of the Millette-led New World Group to form Tapia; leadership rivalry was evidently also a factor in this episode.[23] Both Millete and Best founded popular newspapers, *Moko* and *Tapia* respectively, and both went on to found political parties that contested national elections. In Jamaica, after the Rodney Riot, George Beckford gave up the editorship of *New World Quarterly* and I, the chairmanship of the Jamaica New World Group, to join the Abeng collective, which published a radical black nationalist weekly newspaper. In the 1970s, we were both involved in support of Michael Manley's Democratic Socialist experiment in Jamaica.

The debate over 'thought' vs. 'action' was source of permanent tension within New World. Best's celebrated 1967 paper, 'Independent Thought and Caribbean Freedom,' was written partially as an answer to the demands of the younger members of his generation for greater political activism on the part of New World. Its widely quoted dictum, 'Thought is the action for us,' only temporarily resolved the simmering disagreement. In the years when the movement was struggling to gain acceptance of its ideas, the tension could be accommodated. At the moment of its greatest popularity and appeal, however, the pressures for, and temptations of, direct political action proved impossible to resist. Therein lay its undoing as a movement that was both intellectual in character and Pan-Caribbean in scope.

To begin with, the loss of several of its principal figures robbed the Group and its journal of much of the intellectual vitality underlying its initial appeal. In the second place, once New World scholars turned to political involvement, they could hardly escape the logic of national politics. The collapse of the West Indian Federation and the procession to national independence of the individual territories had unleashed a dynamic of insular nationalism, which increasingly constricted the space allowed for regional politics.[24] In the Rodney Riot in Jamaica in 1968 and the Black Power Revolt in Trinidad in 1970, governments of the two principal UWI campus territories signaled to Caribbean non-nationals their non-acceptance of involvement in national politics. Similar developments took place in Barbados.

Furthermore, the expansion of employment of professionals in national institutions and of separate campuses of the University of the West Indies led to the emergence of new educated elites with a vested interest in insular statehood. As these dynamics gained momentum, national development took divergent paths; and the climate became less conducive to the sustaining of regional political consciousness and organisation. Regional politics became passé.

New World Thought

The course of New World thought took a somewhat different trajectory. As it gained academic legitimacy it became increasingly part of the mainstream in the social sciences, its models and texts being incorporated into the curricula and its many of its personalities assuming positions of administrative leadership in the UWI. Inevitably, this had the effect of undermining the movement and the journal. Staff seminars in the social sciences replaced New World Group meetings as a discussion forum on burning problems of Caribbean development. ISER monographs and the ISER journal *Social and Economic Studies* became an outlet for the publication of the new thinking. The downside of this was the progressive loss of the disciplinary cross-fertilisation that had characterised New World's early activity, as the social sciences drew away from the humanities[25] and the disciplinary departments became self-contained academic enclaves.

New World thought – principally in the form of the plantation school and dependency – continued to exert a significant influence in the social sciences through the 1970s. However, 'New Worldism,' in its original incarnation as an aspiring system of indigenous thought, proved incapable of sustaining its intellectual dynamism and influence. By the late 1970s, it was being displaced by orthodox Marxism on the Left and by resurgent neo-liberalism on the Right. I attribute the terminal decline of New World thought to the weight of unresolved critiques that were made of its theory and methodology, to which I now turn.

The Critics and the Critiques

Overview

I group the critiques of New World thought into four thematic areas:

i.   philosophy and epistemology,
ii. theory of change and political praxis,
iii. economic methodology and social theory, and
iv. the policy dimension.

They came from two main sources: the Marxist left and the non-Marxist mainstream in the social sciences. Here I insert two caveats. First, the Marxist left in this context refers mainly to the Trevor Munroe-led Workers' Party of Jamaica (WPJ), which espoused an orthodox brand of Soviet Marxism.[26] The second caveat is that over time, both the critics and New World thinkers themselves shifted their positions in response to the debate and to wider developments in the region and globally.[27] One should, therefore, be careful not to box particular individuals into given positions, but rather locate positions in a specific temporal context and trace the evolution of thinking over time.

Philosophy and Epistemology

Many scholars objected to what they perceived to be New World's wholesale rejection of 'imported' knowledge. The Marxist critique on this subject was made in a seminal paper by Trevor Munroe in 1971 that characterised New World thinking as a form of 'Bourgeois Idealism.' This critique held that Marxism could not be rejected as an alien ideology since Caribbean society is capitalist, and hence that the Marxist method of historical materialism is as valid in the Caribbean as anywhere else, needing only to be applied to the concrete conditions of the region. Munroe's paper became the basic reference document for Caribbean Marxists on New World thinking and marked 'a closure to intellectual inquiry on this matter for the Jamaican left.'[28] Thereafter the tendency was for many younger scholars to fall under the influence of orthodox Marxist thinking.

From the mainstream, several scholars had difficulty with the New World position on 'independent thought.' The most serious charge came from George Cumper, then Professor and Head of the Department of Economics at Mona. Cumper charged that New World economists had rejected one particular kind of Western economics while ignoring the existence of other schools of thought, that they had overstated their case for political purposes, and that their real agenda was to take political power, impose intellectual closure to the outside world and establish a totalitarian political order.[29]

More broadly representative of the emerging view of the academic community was Stone's comment that the 'attempt at nationalising social science concepts (may have) reached an excessive point.'[30] The occasion for this observation was a 1975 seminar on the Caribbean social sciences organised by the ISER and attended by the region's leading scholars.

Box 1. Participants at the I.S.E.R. Seminar on Problems of the Applied Social Sciences in the Commonwealth Caribbean (Turtle Towers Seminar) June 1975

George Beckford, Compton Bourne, Erna Brodber, Barry Chevannes, Bernard Coard, Susan Craig, Alfred Francis, Eddie Greene, Marshall Hall, Don Harris, Edwin Jones, Elsie LeFranc, Vaughan Lewis, Louis Lindsay, Leslie Manigat, Joycelin Massiah, G.E. Mills, Maurice Odle, Carl Parris, Peter Phillips, Selwyn Ryan, Carl Stone, Dwight Venner, Rosina Wiltshire, Michael Witter and David Wong

Source: Conference Report, Lindsay (1978)

A notable feature of this event was the vigorous debate that took place over the relative merits of 'New Worldism' vis-à-vis Marxism in the analysis of Caribbean society. According to the Conference report, the consensus reached was that:

> ...while there are indeed ideographic or unique features in the Caribbean situation, these features do not in themselves justify the need for either a distinct Caribbean methodology or an autochthonous Caribbean theory.[31]

The seminar marked a turning point in the status of New World thinking and signaled the onset of its waning influence. However, the issue raised in the above passage was never adequately addressed. Did New World in fact argue for both an 'autochthonous Caribbean theory' and a 'distinct Caribbean methodology,' or does advocacy of the first necessarily imply proposal of the second? On the whole, neither New World scholars nor their critics drew an explicit distinction between theory and methodology. Such a distinction might have been useful in identifying the points of divergence and of coincidence in their respective positions and in advancing the debate.

New World scholars could not have subscribed to a position of absolute knowledge independence, for their texts show ample acknowledgement of their use of non-Caribbean scholarship. Their rejectionist stance was directed against what was considered to be inappropriate imported theory. However, the absence of an extended debate on the underlying methodological and epistemological issues left the matter unresolved and prejudiced the further development of the task of appropriate theory-building. The discussion became polarised around the contending claims of 'New Worldism' and Marxism, rather than proceeding in terms of an exploration of what constitutes appropriate theory and useful method.

Theory of Change and Political Praxis

New World was accused of political naivety in its argument that 'independent thought' could be the key factor in effecting political and social change. The critics argued that intellectual activity could not be divorced from its social basis and would need to be combined with leadership and political organisation. The critique came from both

Marxist and non-Marxist positions.[32] The eventual involvement of New World scholars in political activism appeared to validate this critique. Yet, as argued previously, it was a major reason for the disappearance of the New World Group. Paradoxically, this development confirmed both the critique of the thesis and the original thesis itself.

During the 1970s and the 1980s, significant political reversals were experienced both by former New World leaders and by the Marxists. Best's Tapia and Millette's UNIP were unsuccessful in electoral politics; the Michael Manley-led PNP, that had been supported by George Beckford and by the present writer, was heavily defeated in the 1980 election in Jamaica; while the implosion of the PRG in Grenada discredited the Caribbean Marxist left. One consequence of these developments was a process of introspection and reassessment of positions on the part of many of the protagonists in the debate. In 1990 Best was to declare:

> The central epistemological question in all times and all places is: how do people learn?...How do they apprehend reality?...The related political question is: how do you achieve mobilization?... [the] answer is quite simply that we do not know the answer to either of these questions. The only lesson you can learn from history is that there is no lesson you can learn from history.[33]

There is far less certainty here about the decisive role of ideas as a catalyst for change than is the case in 'Thought and Freedom' 23 years earlier. The Caribbean Marxist left, for its part, came to adopt a position on 'Thought and Freedom' that was diametrically opposed to that taken by Munroe in 1971. In the words of one of the movement's leading scholars (on the occasion of a Lloyd Best testimonial conference in 2002):

> Best walks tall in the political graveyard of the Caribbean left, whose death knell was the fall of the Grenada revolution...[he] challenges us...to an epistemic probing about how and what we understand about the contemporary Caribbean...[he] challenges received wisdom of both the left and the right, exposing the limitations of perception mimicked on models and ideas developed in Moscow, Berlin, London, Paris and Washington....

In Munroe's (critique of Best) lay some of the epistemic problems of the radical movements, and the dogmatism that characterized the exchange of ideas and helped shape political organization and practice. These issues had significant consequences for the lives of many people throughout the region, and this was brought to a tragic end in Grenada in 1983.[34]

What is common to both the above statements is the absence of certainty. A similar observation would apply to the present writer's comments on nationalisation. Hence, the issues raised by both New World and its critics on the goals of change in the Caribbean and the methods of bringing it about are as current as they ever were.

Economic Methodology and Social Theory

A recurring criticism of the plantation school by mainstream economists was the absence of clearly specified causal relationships and of empirical or quantitative analysis in its 'models.'[35] According to Levitt, detailed empirical work on the plantation economy models was carried out but not published. She opined that 'much misunderstanding might have been avoided had this work been available to critics.'[36] Here, too, however as in initial debate with the Marxists, there were unresolved issues of methodology. New World scholars argued, in effect, that there is a legitimate role for conceptual discourse supported by 'stylised facts' at a stage prior to formal theory-building and empirical testing. To arrive at their conceptualisations they employed a method that has been characterised as 'historical/ structural/institutional'[37] or as 'historically-based empiricism.'[38] Hence, Beckford, in presenting his seminal work *Persistent Poverty*, declared:

> The general approach is exploratory. More questions are raised than answered...I do not mind being charged with over-generalisation and under-documentation. This is an 'ideas' book. What we need most are studies pregnant with ideas, not studies full of sterile detail.[39]

Similarly, Best responded to the critics by explaining that:

> The models of plantation economy were put forward as an aid to discerning the Caribbean predicament as a legacy of history, as a simple tool for grasping complexity and as a partial formulation meant to focus on the whole.[40]

Best was also quite unapologetic in going beyond the social sciences to generate insights into the Caribbean condition. In one of his later statements he drew on the world of the poetic and literary imagination;[41] speaking about giving play to the 'curious imagination' and about 'light, sound, and landscape,' about invoking the context: historic, geographic, environmental, social, economic, cultural, above all about 'locating ourselves at the centre of the universe.'[42]

What was lacking in the discourse, as I have previously argued, is explicit engagement on questions of philosophy, epistemology and methodology – what is reality, what is truth, and how are they to be arrived at? As a consequence, the exchanges tended to assume the character of the proverbial 'dialogue of the deaf.' The resulting hiatus is to be regarded as an unfinished business of Caribbean thought, which awaits the attention of a fresh generation of scholars.

Regarding social theory, the kinds of questions raised included: whether does the plantation paradigm provide a social theory of Caribbean society as well as economic? Besides being a specific mode of economic organisation, is the plantation a satisfactory means of characterising an economy, a society, a polity and a culture? If so, does this hold equally true in the twentieth century as it did in the eighteenth? Does the plantation school overemphasise continuity and understate change? Due to limitations of space, we cannot address these questions in this paper. Some of these questions are addressed in Girvan (2006).[43] I must turn next to the critiques made of the policy dimension of New World thinking.

Policies

New World political economy advocated regional economic integration, land reform and localisation of ownership as the antidote to small size, foreign domination and dependency. Much of this was uncontroversial. The controversies arose out of the policies of nationalisation and economic self-reliance advocated by people like myself,[44] George Beckford and C.Y. Thomas[45] and their association with statist policies followed by governments in Jamaica and Guyana in the 1970s. The economic decline and political degeneration of these 'radical' projects in the Caribbean condemned New World political economy to a form of 'guilt by intellectual association.' Notable critics were Carl Stone, who pointed to Southeast Asia, and Courtney Blackman,[46] who pointed to Barbados, as evidence that orthodox export-oriented economic strategies were more successful than state-directed delinking from the international capitalist system.

The fact that New World writers themselves came to adopt a critical position on these radical experiments would have served to validate these criticisms in the eyes of the critics. Beckford denounced the vacillation of the Michael Manley administration in Jamaica;[47] C.Y. Thomas, drawing on the Guyanese experience, assailed the rise of the 'authoritarian state' (1984). The present writer, a strong advocate of nationalisation of mineral industries in 1971, was critical of the nationalisation experiences of the 1970s:

> ...the lessons of the 'radical options' show that the expansion of state activity is not merely a matter of political choice or will. The shortage of management and technical manpower imposes severe constraints in the short and medium term....This implies careful consideration of timing and sequencing in the expansion of state activity.
>
> Second, in the context of West Indian political culture, state activities have shown an almost universal tendency to become politicised – used by the governing part or group as an instrument of patronage, or even worse, as a means of consolidating its hold on power....
>
> A third, and related, tendency is for the management of and employees of state activities to adopt a bureaucratic attitude towards the society at large...as a consequence, there is strong undercurrent of distrust and often resentment on the part of the public towards state enterprises and state activity in general....[48]

In 1990 Best was to declare that:

...since 1976 I have been the most vehement critic of the New World and Marxist policies...the more faithfully (these) strategies...have been followed, the more disastrous have been the consequences for the common people.'[49]

It is a moot point whether the policies followed by the Burnham and Manley Administrations in the 1970s were those that were actually advocated, or intended, by the New World Group. What mattered is the perception that they were. The status of the ideas became linked to the status of regimes that were perceived to be putting them into practice.

The international intellectual and political climate was also changing. Dependency thinking, with which New World was associated, was critiqued on theoretical grounds, and for failing to admit the possibility of capitalist industrialisation in the periphery.[50] By the 1980s, 'Development Economics' – which was based on the premise that developing countries required an economics *sui generis* – was being displaced by neo-liberalism, which claimed universal validity across all countries. Finally, the tragic implosion of the Grenadian Revolution in 1983 completed the discrediting of the radical project in the Caribbean.

In summary, the demise of New World can be attributed to the accumulation of unresolved political and epistemological issues that led eventually to the breakup of the Group and to the loss of dynamism and of influence of the intellectual movement. Ideologically, New World was outflanked on the left by orthodox Marxism and later, on the right by neo-liberalism. Global developments also created a climate that was, by the end of the 1970s, far less receptive to New World's message of national economic self-reliance than it had been a decade earlier.

Rediscovery and Re-evaluation, or Where do We Go from Here?

From the 1980s, New World began to be treated as a significant chapter in the intellectual and political history of the region. The evidence is to be seen in a series of conferences and reviews of the leading texts, the leading ideas and the leading personalities of the movement.[51] Several articles, books and edited collections on the contribution of New World, 'plantation,' and 'dependency' have been published.[52] Various models have been proposed to evaluate the contribution. Bernal, Figueroa and Witter (1984) treat it as part of the

NEW WORLD AND ITS CRITICS

'critical tradition.' Benn characterises it as an 'ideology of economic decolonisation.'[53] In broader historical terms, New World thinking can be viewed as part of a process of the 'creolisation of thought,' following the model proposed by Gordon Lewis.[54]

My preferred model is the one proposed by Sankatsing (1998), who locates New World as a form of resistance within the periphery to Eurocentric thinking, 'the globalisation of the local experience in the Occident' that began 500 years ago. Sankatsing credits New World with 'remarkable feats in a search for indigenisation of the social sciences in the region, reluctant to uncritically accept dominant paradigms and theories.' I am in agreement with him when he says that the dissolution of New World, put 'an abrupt end to the scrutiny of the genesis of our societies,' leading to negative developments in the Caribbean social sciences including 'unwillingness to look for comprehensive explanations of our own reality,' 'moving away from theory,' 'blind empiricism,' and 'even scientific journalism.'[55]

Sankatsing's assessment challenges us to revisit the approach of New World and to reflect on its relevance to the world of today. A world where the Cold War is no more and there is a single super-power with no rivals. A world in which the dominant ideas are those of globalisation, market fundamentalism, market triumphalism, post-modernism and neo-liberalism; while Marxism and other forms of anti-systemic thought have been ghettoised. A world where national development is regarded as an obsolete goal, self-reliance as fantasy, and socialism as lunacy. A world where, however, scholarship has been engendered and progressive politics is the politics of feminist empowerment, civil society mobilisation and environmental activism.

The position that I hold is that the Caribbean-centred cosmology and the critical methodology that lay at the heart of the New World project are as necessary in this world as they have ever been in the past. In the 1960s, the choices we were being offered were Western capitalism and Soviet communism. Today we are offered the choice of joining capitalist globalisation or being condemned to marginalisation. We are offered one model for our societies: market-led integration into the global economy; on terms defined by capital and by the governments of the rich and powerful countries. We are told that we must cede our economic sovereignty, political sovereignty and intellectual sovereignty.

We are told that must cede our right to think for ourselves and this is unacceptable.

In the 1970s, the Third World was agitating for a New International Economic Order – the NIEO. By the 1990s we had a different kind of NIEO – a New Imperial Economic Order. It is represented by the WTO, the Washington-based International Financial Institutions, the transnational corporations, and the impersonal forces of global capital markets. Together with this is a New Imperial Political Order, not unlike that established by the Great Powers in the nineteenth century. NIEO and NIPO have a joint central committee; it is called the G8.

Consider the result of the meeting held at Gleneagles in June 2005. The G8 leaders declared that their countries would write off the debts owed to them by the poorest countries in the world, provided that these countries practise good governance and clean up corruption. One cannot question the need for good governance and clean government in our countries. My question is: by what authority do the leaders of the G8 sit in judgment upon our countries, setting up eligibility criteria and certification procedures, in the practice of good governance and honest administration? What is their track record in telling their truth to their own populations, for example about the reasons for going to war, their track record in respecting international law, their track record in the observance of open and transparent procedures for the award of contracts, their track record on respect for human rights? What does the history of the last 50, 150 or 450 years tell us about their record on democracy, human rights, or the practice of the most elementary principles of humanity? What are their qualifications for tutoring and examining the countries of the South in those subjects, besides the possession of military and economic power? It is nothing but a piece of impertinence and imperial arrogance.

These countries are telling the rest of the world that we have no choice but to open up our markets to their goods and services and their corporations and to surrender the sovereign rights of governments to regulate our economies, to protect the livelihoods of local farmers and local business, to regulate foreign corporations, to control the flow of short term capital which has destabilised countries as big as Brazil and Russia, all in the name of giving free play to market forces and levelling the playing field. The playing field is level when a few hundred giant corporations control a large slice of the world economy and when a few hundred billionaires have more wealth than billions of people living in the poorest countries. That level playing field is the New Imperial Economic Order and the New Imperial Political Order.

Packaged with this is a New Imperial Intellectual Order. Its purveyors are the northern universities, the visiting experts, the aid agencies, the World Bank and the IMF. They define the agenda. They tell us what our problems are and what the solutions are. They tell us what to think about ourselves. The World Bank has the biggest concentration of 'development professionals' in the entire world, some ten thousand of them, which is probably more than in the rest of the world put together.

Let me give you just one example. In May 2005, the World Bank published a report on the future of the Caribbean in the year 2020 whose title was Time to Choose.[56] What does it say about our condition when a Washington-based organisation is challenging us to choose? The report is 260 pages long and covers every aspect of Caribbean economic policy. In almost every area of Caribbean life, it purports to give both diagnosis and prescription. That is an example of the New Imperial Intellectual Order.

Caribbean scholars should be deconstructing and critiquing this document. We should be uncovering the hidden agenda: what it says and what it does not say, and why. We should be monitoring how far and how fast the language of this document enters the official discourse of officials and academics. The document talks about the need for governments to negotiate an 'orderly dismantling of preferences.' Do not the United States and the European Union give huge subsidies to their own farmers, $30,000 per farmer per year? Is this not a form of preferences? It talks about the need for transparency in government procurement. This is very necessary, and what does the World Bank have to teach us about that? A recent book tells how in Indonesia the World Bank pumped in $25 billion in loans and grants after the 1965 coup paved the way for a massacre of 500,000 people – in recognition of the country's exemplary human rights record, no doubt – and tolerated the theft of between $5 and $7 billion of this by the President's cronies because he was anticommunist.[57] They have a very good experience in fighting corruption in Indonesia that they can share with us.

It is we in the Caribbean who must put issues of governance and corruption on the agenda – and we are doing so – not because an international organisation tells us that it is bad for growth. It is we who must work out the most effective means of addressing it, not relying on others to provide the solutions that embody their own cultural assumptions, their own interest and their own agenda. Are we free and independent or are we not?

My point is that the New World mission of intellectual decolonisation is more relevant than ever because intellectual colonisation is alive and well and living in Mona and St Augustine and Kingston and Port of Spain. The methods of intellectual colonisation are the conditionalities of the international lending agencies and donor countries, their financial surveillance, their technical reports on our education system and our health system and our agricultural policy and public sector reform. The methods are the daily bombardment from the global media, it is scholarships and fellowships and travel grants that do us the favour of assimilating their worldview, and it is consultancies given to scholars where they define the terms and we do the work.

We need to take a close and candid look at the effect of consultancies on the sustaining of critical and of independent thought. What have been the effects on the academy of the economic difficulties of the 1980s–90s and the commercialisation of knowledge? I fear that it turned most of us in the social sciences at the UWI into hustlers for foreign consultancies. I could never oppose consultancy – it is often a necessity of survival and I engage in it myself. Yet as social scientists, we also have to stand back and see the bigger picture of which we are a part. The fact that you are working for a plantation does not make it any less of a plantation!

In Asia and Africa there is now a debate going among scholars on consultancies as 'colonised research.'[58] One African scholar has argued that there, the new division of labour in research mirrors the old colonial division of labour in economy.[59] The issues, the questions and the data categories are set by the agencies of the North that sponsor the research. They sub-contract the job of data collection to African institutions and researchers. The information is semi-processed and exported to the North, where the finishing takes place – the interpretation, conclusions and policy advice. That's the 'value added' in the production of knowledge. Then it is returned to the country of origin and consumed. The Global South is paying for its own intellectual recolonisation!

Is it any different in the Caribbean? Are we setting the agenda? Are we questioning the concepts that are handed to us and adapting them to fit out history and culture and cosmologies and inventing others when none of them fit? Have we lost the boldness and the audacity to think for ourselves and invent models of our own? We cannot afford to lose that capacity and I daresay we have not lost it. The question is, do we have the will to exercise it?

So that fact that the world has changed since the 1960s does not mean that it has not also remained the same. We have a different world from the world of New World but it is in many respects the old world that New World opposed. The fact that New World made mistakes and had contradictions certainly does not make what is now on offer inherently superior.

Economic globalisation does not have to mean a globalisation of the mind that detaches one from the specificity of local history and time and place and experience. It does not change the fact that Columbus lied when he said that he had discovered the West Indies, because, as the Calpysonian, Shadow, pointed out, he had only discovered some Indians who had discovered him.[60] Columbus was the purveyor of his own truth; we have to discover and purvey ours. It does not mean that Bob Marley was not right in his call to emancipate ourselves from mental slavery, for only we ourselves can free our minds.[61] Bob was singing a 'Song of Freedom;' New World was a Song of Freedom and long may we continue to sing it.

Notes

1.   Walter Rodney, Orlando Patterson, Richard Fletcher and myself.
2.   Among other things, Best enraged followers of Norman Manley by declaring that he could not lead his people to Independence 'wearing a waistcoat.' To my knowledge, Best's 1961 lecture was never published, but many of the ideas are contained in his later published writings.
3.   Lloyd Best, 'Economic Planning in Guiana,' in F.M. Andic and T.G. Matthews eds. *The Caribbean in Transition: Papers on Social, Political and Economic Development: Proceedings of the Second Conference of Caribbean Scholars, Mona, Jamaica, April 15–19, 1964* (Rio Piedras, Puerto Rico: Institute of Caribbean Studies, University of Puerto Rico, 1965).
4.   I lectured at St Augustine in February–July 1966 and took up an appointment at Mona as lecturer in Economics in August 1966.
5.   Not covered by this account is 'New World thinking' in literature and the humanities, which formed a significant portion of the publications of the Group.

6. New World Associates 'The Long Term Economic, Political and Cultural Programme For Guyana,' in N. Girvan and O. Jefferson eds. *Readings in the Political Economy of the Caribbean*, (Mona, Jamaica: New World Group, 1971) 224–66. Best, 'Economic Planning in Guiana.' Lloyd Best, 'Independent Thought and Caribbean Freedom,' in N. Girvan and O. Jefferson eds. *Readings in the Political Economy of the Caribbean* (Mona, Jamaica: New World Group, 1971) 7–28. George Beckford, *Persistent Poverty: Underdevelopment in Plantation Economies of the Third World* (London: Oxford University Press, 1972).

7. Ibid, 'Independent Thought and Caribbean Freedom.'

8. See Beckford, *Persistent Poverty* (1972, 6).

9. See Alister McIntyre, 'Some Issues in Trade Policy in the West Indies.' In Norman Girvan and Owen Jefferson eds. *Readings in the Political Economy of the Caribbean*, (New World Group, 1971).

10. See Best, 'Independent Thought'; Beckford, *Persistent Poverty*; and George Beckford, 'The Plantation System and the Penetration of International Capitalism,' in L. Lindsay ed. *Problems of Applied Social Science Research Techniques in the Commonwealth Caribbean*, mimeograph, (working paper no. 14, Institute of Social and Economic Research, Mona, Jamaica, 1978), 23–27.

11. See Charles Wagley, 'Plantation America: A Culture Sphere,' in V. Rubin ed. *Caribbean Studies: A Symposium* (Mona, Jamaica: Institute of Social and Economic Research, University of the West Indies, in association with the Research and Training Program for the Study of Man in the Tropics, New York, Columbia University, 1957) .

12. See New World Associates, 'The Long Term Economic, Political and Cultural Programme For Guyana;' Best, 'Independent Thought;' Lloyd Best and K. Polanyi Levitt, *Externally Propelled Growth and Industrialization in the Caribbean*, 4 vols., with A. Brown et al, mimeograph (Montreal: McGill Centre for Developing Areas Studies, 1969); Kari Polanyi Levitt and Lloyd Best 'Character of Caribbean Economy,' in G.L. Beckford ed. *Caribbean Economy: Dependence and Backwardness* (Mona, Jamaica: Institute of Social and Economic Research, University of the West Indies, 1975), 34–60; Beckford, *Persistent Poverty*; George Beckford ed. *Caribbean Economy: Dependence and Backwardness* (Mona, Jamaica: Institute of Social and Economic Research, University of the West Indies, 1975) 77–92; Norman Girvan, 'Multinational Corporations and Dependent Underdevelopment in Mineral-Export Economies,' *Social and Economic Studies* 19, no. 4, (1970): 490–26; Norman Girvan ed, 'Dependence and Underdevelopment in the New World and the Old,' *Social and Economic Studies* special edition, 22, no. 1 (1973); N. Girvan and O. Jefferson eds. *Readings in the Political Economy of the Caribbean*, (Mona, Jamaica: New World Group, 1971).

13. See Lloyd Best 'A Model of Pure Plantation Economy,' *Social and Economic Studies* 17, no 3, (1968): 283–326 ; Best and Levitt, *Externally Propelled Growth and Industrialization in the Caribbean*; Levitt and Best, *Character of Caribbean Economy*.

14. See George Beckford and K. Polanyi Levitt, *The George Beckford Papers: Selected and Introduced by Kari Levitt*, (Mona, Jamaica: Canoe Press, University of the West Indies, 2000).

15. See Best, 'Independent Thought and Caribbean and Caribbean Freedom'

16. I am indebted to Kari Polanyi Levitt's excellent introduction to *The George Beckford Papers* (Levitt 2000, xlix–l) for its account of Beckford's treatment of the race question. See George Beckford, 'The Future of Plantation Society

in Comparative Perspective,' in G.L. Beckford and K. Polanyi Levitt, *The George Beckford Papers: Selected and Introduced by Kari Levitt*, (Mona, Jamaica: Canoe Press, University of the West Indies, 2000), 336–46. In the same passage referred to, Beckford critiqued his earlier analysis of this question as having 'several weaknesses...specifically, its handling of the class question was overshadowed by the emphasis on race....' (2000d).

17. See George L. Beckford, 'The Plantation System and the Penetration of International Capitalism' in *Problems of Applied Social Science Research Techniques in the Commonwealth Caribbean* ed. Louis Lindsay (working paper no. 14, mimeo, Mona: Institute of Social and Economic Research, 1978), 24

18. See Selwyn Ryan,'From Picton to Panday: Doctor Politics in Trinidad and Tobago,' in S. Ryan ed. *Independent Thought and Caribbean Freedom: Essays in Honour of Lloyd Best*, (St Augustine, Trinidad and Tobago: Sir Arthur Lewis Institute of Social and Economic Studies, University of the West Indies, 2003), 185–210.

19. The term is suggested by Bogues. See Anthony Bogues 'Lloyd Best and the Politics of Epistemic Decolonization,' in S. Ryan ed. *Independent Thought and Caribbean Freedom: Essays in Honour of Lloyd Best*, (St. Augustine, Trinidad and Tobago: Sir Arthur Lewis Institute of Social and Economic Studies, University of the West Indies, 2003), 145–62.

20. Trevor Munroe, 'Bourgeois Idealism and Commonwealth Caribbean Intellectuals,' In Trevor Munroe *Jamaican Politics: A Marxist Perspective in Transition*, (Kingston: Heinemann Publishers Caribbean, 1990), chapter 5.

21. See Denis Benn, *The Caribbean: An Intellectual History 1774–2003*, (Kingston, Jamaica: Ian Randle Publishers, 2004); See Denis Benn 'The Theory of Plantation Economy and Society,' *Journal of Commonwealth and Comparative Politics* XII: 3 (1974): 249–60; See Richard Bernal, Mark Figueroa, and Michael Witter 'Caribbean Economic Thought: The Critical Tradition,' *Social and Economic Studies* 33, no. 2, (1984): 5–96; J. Edward Greene, 'Challenges and Responses in Social Science Research in the English Speaking Caribbean,' in H. Goulbourne and L. Sterling eds. 'The Social Sciences and Caribbean Society (Part 1),' special issue, *Social and Economic Studies* 33, no. 1, (1984): 9–46; D. Harris, 'Notes on a Marxist Methodology for Social Science Research in the Caribbean' in L. Lindsay ed. *Problems of Applied Social Science Research Techniques in the Commonwealth Caribbean*, mimeograph, Working Paper No. 14, (Mona, Jamaica: Institute of Social and Economic Research, 1978), 14–22; Carl Stone, 'Some Issues in Caribbean Social Science Research,' in L. Lindsay ed. *Problems of Applied Social Science Research Techniques in the Commonwealth Caribbean*, mimeograph, Working Paper No. 14, (Mona, Jamaica: Institute of Social and Economic Research, 1978): 1–13.

22. Stone, 'Some issues in Caribbean Social Science Research,' 4–5

23. See James Millette, (2003) 'Millette and the Rift in New World,' 'Lloyd Best and the Politics of Epistemic Decolonization,' in S. Ryan ed. *Independent Thought and Caribbean Freedom: Essays in Honour of Lloyd Best*, (St Augustine, Trinidad and Tobago: Sir Arthur Lewis Institute of Social and Economic Studies, University of the West Indies, 2003), 175–84; Ryan, *From Picton to Panday*; and Brian Meeks 'Lloyd Best: The People and the Road not taken in 1970' in S. Ryan ed. *Independent Thought and Caribbean Freedom: Essays in Honour of Lloyd Best*, (St Augustine, Trinidad and Tobago: Sir Arthur Lewis Institute of Social and Economic Studies, University of the West Indies, 2003), 71–88.

24. This point was made by Lloyd Best in delivering the C.L.R. James Memorial Lecture in 2004. No written or published text is available.
25. Notably, the journal *Savacou* commenced publication around the same time that *New World Quarterly* ceased publication.
26. The clarification is important, in that in fact some New World thinkers like Beckford and Girvan, and Caribbean dependency theorists like C.Y. Thomas adopted what I call a type of 'Third World Marxism' influenced by the Dar Es Salaam socialist school and the work of scholars including Walter Rodney, *How Europe Underdeveloped Africa*, (Dar es Salaam: Tanzania Publishing House, 1972); Andre Gunder Frank *Capitalism and Underdevelopment in Latin America*, (New York: Monthly Review Press, 1967); Samir Amin, *Accumulation on a World Scale*, (New York: Monthly Review Press, 1974); and Immanuel Wallerstein *The Capitalist World Economy*, (Cambridge: Cambridge University Press, 1979).
27. This is evident from a reading of the evolution of the thinking of Beckford, *Persistent Poverty*; George Beckford 'The Plantation System and the Penetration of International Capitalism,' in L. Lindsay ed. *Problems of Applied Social Science Research Techniques in the Commonwealth Caribbean*, mimeograph, Working Paper No. 14, (Mona, Jamaica: Institute of Social and Economic Research, 1978), 23–27; Norman Girvan, *Foreign Capital and Economic Underdevelopment in Jamaica* (Mona: ISER, UWI, 1971); Norman Girvan, 'C.Y. Thomas and the Poor and the Powerless: The Limitations of Conventional Radicalism,' *Social and Economic Studies* 37, no. 4, (1988): 253–74; Lloyd Best, 'Independent Thought'; Best 'Independence and Responsibility: Self-knowledge as an Imperative,' in K. Polanyi Levitt and M. Witter eds. *The Critical Tradition of Caribbean Political Economy: The Legacy of George Beckford*, (Kingston, Jamaica: Ian Randle Publishers, 1996), 3–18; as well as that of the Marxist critics of New World discussed below.
28. See Rupert Lewis, 'Lloyd Best and Epistemic Challenges,' in S. Ryan ed. *Independent Thought and Caribbean Freedom: Essays in Honour of Lloyd Best*, (St Augustine, Trinidad and Tobago: Sir Arthur Lewis Institute of Social and Economic Studies, University of the West Indies, 2003), 89–102.
29. Strictly speaking, the charge was made against the 'dependency school' rather than New World as such, and Cumper's critique was written in response to a Conference paper by the present writer, subsequently revised and published as Norman Girvan 'The Development of Dependency Economics in the Caribbean and Latin America: Review and Comparison,' *Social and Economic Studies* 22, no. 1, (1973): 1–33. See George Cumper 'Dependence, Development and the Sociology of Economic Thought,' *Social and Economic Studies* 23, no. 3 (September 1974): 465–82.
30. Stone, 'Some issues in Caribbean Social Science Research,' 1978, 5.
31. See L. Lindsay ed. *Problems of Applied Social Science Research Techniques in the Commonwealth Caribbean*, mimeograph, Working Paper No. 14, (Mona, Jamaica: Institute of Social and Economic Research, 1978), vii.
32. See for example Trevor Munroe, 'Readings in Government and Politics of West Indies' (Department of Government, University of the West Indies, 1971) and Denis Benn, *The Caribbean: An Intellectual History 1774–2003* (Kingston: Ian Randle Publishers, 2004).
33. The statement was made in 1990, at a conference held in tribute to George Beckford.
34. R. Lewis 'Lloyd Best and Epistemic Challenges,' 90.
35. See for example see CY Thomas 'Pure Plantation Economy: A Comment,' *Social and Economic Studies* 17, no. 3, (1968): 339–48; Steve DeCastro

'Export-Propelled Economy: A Comment,' *Social and Economic Studies* 17 no. 3, (1968): 349–65; G.E. Cumper *Dependence, Development and the Sociology of Economic Thought*, (Mona, Jamaica: Institute of Social and Economic Research, University of the West Indies,1974), 477; Adlith Brown and H. Brewster 'A Review of the Study of Economics in the English Speaking Caribbean,' *Social and Economic Studies* 23, no. 1, (1974): 48–68; and the critiques of Sudama, Farrell and Pantin referred to by Best 'Outlines of a Model of Pure Plantation Economy (After Twenty-Five Years),' 27–40, in D. Pantin and D. Mahabir eds. 'Plantation Economy Revisited,' special issue, *Marronage* 1, no. 1, (1998): 32–3.

36. Levitt further explained, in a conversation with this writer in February 2005, that the plantation economy models were meant to be used as a planning tool to aid government policy for economic transformation.

37. See Norman Girvan 'The Development of Dependency Economics in the Caribbean and Latin America: Review and Comparison,' *Social and Economic Studies* 22, no. 1 (1973): 12.

38. See Denis Benn, *The Caribbean: An Intellectual History 1774–2003* (Kingston: Ian Randle Publishers, 2004), 124.

39. See Beckford *Persistent Poverty*, vi–viii.

40. Lloyd Best 'Outlines of a Model of Pure Plantation Economy (After Twenty-Five Years),' 35.

41. In particular, the writers Kamau Braithwaite and Wilson Harris.

42. See Lloyd Best, 'The Economy of the British Commonwealth Caribbean: An Overview,' in *West Indies-Canada Economic Relations, Selected Papers* (July 1966): 5–6.

43. See Norman Girvan, 'Caribbean Dependency Thought Revisited.' In *Canadian Journal of Development Studies* 27, no.3 (September 2006): 330–52.

44. See Norman Girvan, *Foreign Capital and Economic Underdevelopment in Jamaica*. (Kingston: ISER/UWI, 1971).

45. See Beckford, *Persistent Poverty*, chapter 8; and C.Y. Thomas *Dependence and Transformation: The Economics of the Transition to Socialism*, (New York: Monthly Review Press, 1974).

46. See Carl Stone, *Understanding Third World Politics and Economics*, (Kingston, Jamaica: Earle Publishers, 1980); and Blackman, cited by Best in 'Outlines of a Model of Pure Plantation Economy' 34.

47. See George Beckford and Michael Witter, *Small Garden – Bitter Weed: The Political Economy of Struggle and Change in Jamaica*. (London: Zed Press, 1982).

48. See Norman Girvan, 'C.Y. Thomas and the Poor and the Powerless: The Limitations of Conventional Radicalism,' *Social and Economic Studies* 37, no. 4 (December 1988): 269–70.

49. To avoid confusion, it should be noted that Best in this comment distinguished Thomas's position from that of the New World Group, whereas the present review treats both as dependency thought and distinguishes them from orthodox Marxism. See Lloyd Best 'Independence and Responsibility: Self-knowledge as an Imperative,' in K. Polanyi Levitt and M. Witter eds. *The Critical Tradition of Caribbean Political Economy: The Legacy of George Beckford*, (Kingston, Jamaica: Ian Randle Publishers, 1996) 3–18.

50. On this, see Bill Warren, 'Imperialism and Capitalist Industrialisation,' *New Left Review* 1, no. 81, (September–October 1973); and G. Palma, 'Dependency: A Formal Theory of Underdevelopment or a Methodology

for the Analysis of Concrete Situations of Underdevelopment?' *World Development* 6, no. 7/8, (1978): 881–924.

51. Examples are the symposium at UWI Mona in honour of George Beckford 1990; establishment of the George Beckford Chair in Caribbean Economy at the Department of Economics, UWI Mona and of the Annual George Beckford Memorial Lecture in the early 1990s; Conference of the Association of Caribbean Economists (ACE) in Memory of George Beckford 1991; establishment of ACE George Beckford Award for contribution to Caribbean Economy, 1991; Publication of the *George Beckford Papers* (Beckford 2000a); Conference on 'Plantation Economy Revisited' to mark the twenty-fifth anniversary of the completion of Plantation Economy studies, Department of Economics, UWI St Augustine, 1993; Kari Levitt, Festschrift, Montreal, 1997; Conference in tribute to Lloyd Best, UWI St Augustine, 2002; and the Centre for Caribbean Thought Conference on the Thought of New World, June 2005.

52. Notably see Michael Witter and L. Lindsay 'Introduction,' in K. Polanyi Levitt and M. Witter eds. *The Critical Tradition of Caribbean Political Economy: The Legacy of George Beckford*, (Kingston, Jamaica: Ian Randle Publishers1996), xxi–xxvi; D. Pantin, and D. Mahabir eds. 'Plantation Economy Revisited,' special issue, *Marronage* 1, no. 1, (1998); Bernal, Figueroa and Witter, *Caribbean Economic Thought*; Glenn Sankatsing, *Caribbean Social Science: An Assessment*, (Caracas: UNESCO, 1989); M. Blomström and B. Hettne, *Development Theory in Transition; The Dependency Debate and Beyond: Third World Responses*, (London: Zed Books, 1984) chapter 5; Benn, *The Caribbean: An Intellectual History 1774–2003*, chapter 5; Denis Benn, *The Growth and Development of Political Ideas in the Caribbean 1774-1983* (Mona: ISER, UWI, 1987); 'Kari Polanyi Levitt and the Theory of Plantation Economy in Contemporary Perspective,' in Marguerite Mendell ed. *Reclaiming Democracy: The Social Justice and Political Economy of Gregory Baum and Kari Polanyi Levitt* (Montreal: McGill-Queen's, 2005), 92–101.

53. See Benn, *The Caribbean: An Intellectual History 1774–2003*, chapter 5

54. See Gordon Lewis *Main Currents in Caribbean Thought*, (Kingston, Port-of-Spain: Heineman Educational Books Caribbean, 1983), 26–7.

55. See Glenn Sankatsing, (1998) 'The Caribbean: Archipelago of Trailer Societies,' available online at http://www.crscenter.com/Trailer.html, accessed September 15, 2005.

56. On this, see 'World Development Report: A Better Investment Climate for Everyone' at World Bank (2005).

57. See Sebastian Mallaby, *The World Bankers: A Story of Failed States, Financial Crises, and Wealth and Poverty of Nations* (Penguin Press, 2004), 186.

58. On this, see 'Annual Report 2004 – Progress Report by the Director at United Nations Research Institute for Social Development,' 10–1.

59. Contribution by Adebayo Olukoshi to Panel Discussion at the UNRISD Conference (UNRISD 2004:11).

60. This a paraphrase of a line from the calypso 'Columbus Lied,' composed and sung by Winston 'The Shadow' Bailey.

61. The reference is to Bob Marley's 'Redemption Song.'

2 | The New World Group: A Historical Perspective

James Millette

I ask you to reflect on the fact that today, by day if not by date, is the twenty-fifth anniversary of the assassination of Dr Walter Rodney which took place on Friday, June 13, 1980. As a result of that act, the Caribbean lost one of its most fertile and creative intellectuals and one of its most important socialist and anti-imperialist figures in the region. Walter Rodney, as you will see, was very much a part of the New World story, even if he never belonged to the Group.

Admittedly, the problem with writing about the history of the New World Group is that very little has been written about that history. There has been much more attention paid to the issues raised by the Group and the Group's ideological position compared to the ideological position of other intellectual and political formations that have emerged in the Caribbean since the Second World War. There is, for example, the very critical assessment done by Dr Trevor Munroe some years ago about New World ideology;[1] and there is a very impressive recurrence of epistemological and epistemic studies of New World thought done by other luminaries in the social sciences like Dr Rupert Lewis and Dr Anthony Bogues.[2] Yet there is little or nothing on the history of the movement. If there are histories attempted or written, then I know nothing about them; and I very much doubt that credible histories could be written without taking my views into account. Also I say this not out of any excess of immodesty, but simply because, like Lloyd Best, I was one of the early important participants in the Group's activities. What is more, I am perfectly willing to have my participation in those activities scrutinised by researchers, but such scrutiny has so far not materialised.

I am also anxious that the history of New World be taken into account for another reason: given the scale and magnitude of the last two events celebrating the importance of the New World Group, it may be that some innocent, ordinary participants in this event are beguiled into thinking that New World is still extant. If that is so, but even if it is not so, we are faced here with some very interesting dynamics.[3]

For example, it used to be, and probably it still is, relevant in some of the world's great archives that something known as the 30-year rule helped to protect the reputations of actors on the historical stage by making it virtually impossible for their deeds to be reviewed within their own lifetime. Certainly, that made sense in an age when most important actors, but for a few, did their most influential work and departed this world at a relatively early stage. Life expectancies, however, have been expanding. We all live so long. The New World Group in particular must hold some kind of world record in respect to the survival of its members. As I look around at all the gray heads and gray beards in the room I am mightily impressed by the number of us who have already achieved – or are within striking distance of – the notional three score and ten, and who are arguably now living on borrowed time. However, borrowed time offers us a unique opportunity to share and reflect on events which have been gradually clarified by the passage of time, by long held memories and by the emergence of new evidence, written or oral, published or unpublished, which help to throw a revealing spotlight on events, motives, causes, consequences and outcomes.

That we should review the history of the New World Group is also extremely important for another reason. The New World Group was not only an organisation, an occurrence, a phase, or a moment in the development of the regional intelligentsia; it was also, it seems to be asserted, the gold standard of Caribbean intellectual development, the source of a uniquely penetrating and perspicacious interpretation of Caribbean intellectual, political, cultural, literary and philosophical development. Again, to read the conflated and often hyperbolic accounts of what New World attempted, influenced and achieved, one would have to conclude that there is hardly any field of Caribbean activity that the New World has not magically touched and transformed.

I want to talk about the Group's history for yet another important reason. As I spend more and more years teaching younger and younger people I can see the growing disconnection between what I take to be inseparable from my intellectual and informational universe, and what they wrestle with as new, and sometimes mistakenly perceive to be, unimportant information. So I want to do this for the benefit of the young scholars among us, for many of whom the New World Group is now ancient history, or maybe even no history at all.

Finally, one needs to be at least aware of the fact that the New World Group existed for only a brief span of time in the nearly half century of the so-called era of New World. One needs also to be aware, as painful as it might be, that the work of the nearly four decades that have slipped by since the end of the Group has been the era of Tapia, and that what is celebrated today as the legacy of the New World Group consists to a large extent of the work of Tapia which is a completely different kettle of fish from the New World Group. Indeed, much of the work of Tapia consists of the repetitious advancement of arguments intended to vindicate the existence of that organisation and its publication, the *Trinidad and Tobago Review*, and to defend the notion that the demolition of the New World Group in 1968 was a master stroke of intellectual and political batsmanship.

So that, for all these reasons, the history of New World badly needs to be written. What follows, therefore, is a contribution to the writing of that history. You young scholars in the audience will have to do the work that people like me can probably only suggest. Yet I hope that after I have said what I am about to say, some of you, or maybe even only one of you, will be moved to give to the history of New World at least a fraction of the attention that has been given to the examination of the epistemological and teleological and cosmological and other arcane dialogues that have surrounded the consideration of the Group's achievements.

By my reckoning, the New World Group is about 42 years old. However, that is to speak of it as a living entity running in unbroken sequence from early 1963 to the present, which it is not. It was imagined in Jamaica in the late 1950s/early 1960s. It was conceived in Guyana in 1963, achieved its puberty in Jamaica, Canada, Trinidad and Tobago and Guyana, and died in its youth in Trinidad and Tobago in 1968, where the locus of the group had by then been established. So that, effectively, the New World Group as such existed for about five to six years. Like the West Indies Federation, which had come to grief a few years earlier, the group then split and gave rise at first to rival newspaper publications, *Moko* and *Tapia*, which then metamorphosed into two separate political organisations, the United National Independence Party and the Tapia House Group. As in the case of the federation, the remnants of the New World Group, what we might call the 'little eight,' struggled on until 1972, especially in Jamaica, to perpetuate what was left of New World until that undertaking was subsumed by larger events. The return of the Peoples National Party to power in Jamaica and the general radicalisation of Caribbean politics which ensued between 1968 and 1983, a date suggested by the collapse and destruction of the Grenada Revolution, effectively brought an end to New World activities.

My own role in these events and, of course, the role of Lloyd Best, one of the founders of, and quite clearly the dominant presence in the New World Group from its formation to its demise, is to some extent recounted in the recently published volume *Independent Thought and Caribbean Freedom: Essays in Honour of Lloyd Best*, edited by Dr Selwyn Ryan, which is a collection of the presentations made on the occasion of a conference held Port of Spain to honour Lloyd Best in 2002, to which reference has already been made. It is a very important source of oral evidence about New World and I shall be referring to it frequently in my address.[4]

It is particularly important in trying to understand the New World Group to understand the circumstances under which it was born. Whatever might have happened in Jamaica in its earlier formative years, it was in Georgetown, British Guiana, that the Group hit the spotlight in the throes of the struggles that were then taking place in that country in the decade or so between the suppression of the Guyanese constitution in 1953 and the constitutional overthrow of the People's Progressive Party (PPP) government in 1964. A little more than two years after the suppression, constitutional government was restored, in April 1956, but by then, the suppression had yielded its most lasting legacy to the country's political life. The PPP, united in 1953 under Jagan and Burnham with the mass support of Indian and African workers, peasants, farmers, trade unionists. Significant sections of the professional middle class, local businessmen and small property owners, had split after a very contentious congress held in February of 1955. The founding of the People's National Congress (PNC) had followed after the general elections of 1957, which had seen two factions of the PPP (PPP, Jagan and PPP, Burnham) confronting each other at the polls. Jagan's faction won and, ultimately, two major parties had emerged one, the PPP, led as it had always been, by Cheddi Jagan and, the other, the newly formed PNC led by Forbes Burnham.

By 1957, it was clear that the circumstances of the suppression of the Waddington constitution in 1953, had thrown British Guiana, arguably at that time the most constitutionally advanced of the British West Indian colonies, into political chaos and confusion which the schism in the PPP had clearly deepened. The next few years were characterised by the ongoing struggles between the two parties and the gradual orientation of some sections of the Caribbean left and progressive elements towards participation in the Guiana political situation, usually by way of some kind of interaction with the PPP administration. There were also those who saw the opportunities for intervening by way of finding a solution to the crisis. It was in this second category of activists that we have to tweak out the role of the New World Group in Georgetown in the early 1960s.

The circumstances surrounding this southward migration to Georgetown also included, significantly, the widening split between the PPP and other regional parties, governments and political leaders over the issue of communism and federation. With respect to communism, that was the issue on which the British government had chosen to denounce the PPP and to rationalise the overthrow of a regime which was clearly distasteful to the major planting and other privileged economic interests in British Guiana. It was also the issue which the Cuban Revolution had thrust into the limelight as a result of the political and economic transformation taking place in Cuba in the period between January 1, 1959 and May 1, 1961. By the early 1960s, the rejection or tolerance of communism had also become the standard of acceptable or unacceptable behavior for West Indian politicians eager to proffer their *bona fides* to the metropolitan powers with whom they were negotiating, or about to negotiate issues of self-government and independence.

With respect to the federation, the PPP had at first seemed open to the idea of participation, but had decided to isolate itself from the events which had set the new West Indian Federation on the road to nationhood. In doing so, the PPP government could instance the lack of support, in some cases the very articulate hostility extended to it by the regional administrations in the aftermath of 1953. It could also instance the lack of personal warmth with which Jagan himself had been treated by his regional colleagues. As he complained in his autobiography, at Piarco airport (in Trinidad): 'I was kept under police surveillance at the airport room; Burnham was given the right to free movement.'[5] The fact that on the occasion of Ghana's independence, which he was on his way to celebrate, he was generally ignored and slighted by other West Indian leaders, did little to improve the affection between himself and his Caribbean counterparts. Finally, there was little doubt that on both racial and ideological grounds Jagan feared for the fortunes of British Guiana in a federation certain to be dominated by his racial and ideological opponents.[6]

This is the situation into which Lloyd Best wandered in 1961, and it is against this background that New World emerged into public view. There is not much that can be understood and explained about the New World Group that is not linked to the story of Lloyd Best, and I will be making frequent references to him. I hope he will understand that the point is not to vilify him but to write and speak meaningfully about the organisation that he founded and with which is inseparably linked. I have no doubt that he will understand. He himself said to me when we were discussing the looming split in NW that he was initiating, and I was trying to avert by proposing a broader conversation with the regional organisation: 'Doctor, you don't understand. Where the captain is, the team is. We don't have to go through that foolishness.' So I know that he will understand, as I will understand, too, when and if he speaks of my role in New World. My hope is that others will as well.

Born in Trinidad and Tobago in 1934, Lloyd Best proceeded to the United Kingdom in the early 1950s, at the age of 18 or 19, on an island scholarship to study economics at Cambridge. Incidentally, he is my junior in years. He was born in February 1934 and I in October 1933. We both went through the high school system at about the same time in Trinidad and Tobago, he in Queen's Royal College and I in St Mary's. We also tried out for the civil service at the same time, in 1952. I went into the civil service after topping the lists in the open, competitive civil service examinations. He went to Cambridge on an island scholarship in Modern Studies to study economics. He returned to the Caribbean in 1958 and took up a position at the Institute of Social Economic Research here at Mona. I came to Mona in 1956 and graduated in 1960. I got to know Lloyd in the latter period of my studentship and others got to know him through me as well. As Norman Girvan recently reminded me, in an e-mail:

> I don't know, [James] if you remember but you were the one who introduced me to Lloyd, when we were both students in Taylor Hall, you as Chairman and [myself] as [a] freshman, and Lloyd a young lecturer on campus.

After graduation I worked in 1960–61 as Extra Mural Tutor in St Vincent and Dominica. One of my assistants happened be a certain Ms Eugenia Charles who came to greater prominence in 1983 for the role she played, as Prime Minister of Dominica, in the US invasion of Grenada. In 1961 I proceeded to London to read for my PhD in history and returned to the region in 1964 to take up a teaching position at the University of the West Indies, St Augustine. Between 1964 and 1968, Lloyd and I worked closely on matters pertaining to New World.

By 1961 Lloyd had already become deeply engaged in the course of regional politics and, in my view, was already imagining a very important political position for himself. That much was made clear to me when, on one of his visits to London in the early 1960s, we spoke, among other things, of his perspectives on the developing political situation in Trinidad and Tobago. To put it briefly, a lot was happening in the region. One of the definitive political developments of the time was the rise of the People's National Movement (PNM) in Trinidad and Tobago and the growing intellectual and political influence of its leader Dr Eric Williams, not only in his own country but in the region as a whole. In addition, C.L.R. James had returned to the region, was ensconced in Trinidad, was wielding a mightily influential editorial stick at the *Nation*, the PNM newspaper, and was in the process of amassing his own intellectual and political following. The politics of the next few years in the country would be dominated by the subliminal and explicit rivalries of these two major political figures. So that for the moment, it seemed, Trinidad and Tobago was not a good field for political exploration.

As for Jamaica, we should probably allow Best speak for himself. In 'Reflections on the Reflections,' the last words in the edited account provided by Selwyn Ryan, he speaks as follows:

...there was a very big quarrel at Mona about what Best had been doing there since he had arrived in January 1958, and it was just about that time that Vidia Naipaul came to the West Indies to write *The Middle Passage*, and since we were at school together, Queen's Royal College, he stayed by me for a while. And he was invited while he was staying by me to a dinner at the House of the Principal, Sir Arthur Lewis. He was not then 'Sir Arthur.' He returned home agitated late in the night about 11:30 or 12:00, and told me, 'I have to tell you something; I really have to tell you something; they spent all the time at this dinner talking about you.' I said, 'what about'? He said, 'They said, you are corrupting the students with subversive activity.'[7]

Lloyd Best, therefore, looking for a berth in which to inaugurate his own intellectual and political trajectory chose Guyana, at that time the colony of British Guiana. How he got there is interesting. I was reading recently the lecture he gave at York University on March 3, 2001, the Third Annual Jagan lecture, entitled 'Race, Class and Ethnicity: A Caribbean Interpretation.' In it he recalls that he first 'met Cheddi in 1961, just after the Black Friday riots in 1961.'[8] From what he has written we can conclude that he met Cheddi Jagan in 1961, though his date is subject to question because the riots to which he referred occurred in 1962, not 1961. We can also conclude that his name was already in play in some international circles. He speaks earlier in the same text of having been one of two individuals suggested for the position of economic adviser to the British Guiana government. Also, he says, 'people' had proposed that he should 'serve as the *Guyana professional*[9] on the team, [proposed by President Kennedy], the Kennedy team and Secretary.' He refused the invitation and went to Paris to study and teach at the Sorbonne.

There are also other sources of information about Best's early activities. In January 1958 he was back in the Caribbean at the University of the West Indies. Sir Alister McIntyre speaks of meeting him for the first time 'in the closing months of 1958, when I was on a short research visit to Jamaica.'[10] Best introduced McIntyre to senior UWI personnel and helped him to acquire accommodation on the campus, where he took a lectureship in Economics in 1960–61. Then Best and McIntyre collaborated in writing two pieces, one of which 'The Political Economy of Federation' was published in the pages of the *Pelican*, in November 1961 and March 1962. In between what was to become the New World Group began to take shape. McIntyre recalls that:

> We met at Lloyd's home in College Common every Thursday evening, ending up in the early hours of the morning at Monty's Restaurant, depending on the time of the month and the disposable income then available, for curried goat, patties, red stripe beer (sic) and more talk. These were the seeds of what was to become New World.[11]

At that time, he says, the group was called 'The Society for the Study of Social Issues.'

By 1961 Best had left the UWI, though he returned later only to leave again permanently after a few years. As McIntyre puts it 'he was with Bettelheim at the Sorbonne and...he went to Guyana as a UN advisor.'[12]

Lloyd's British Guiana period is very interesting. We have already noted his meeting with Cheddi Jagan in 1961 or 1962. He himself speaks of meetings with Forbes Burnham and other Guyanese political personalities, but his main links in Guyana were, and still are I would think, with two Guyanese lawyers, and well connected businessmen, David de Caires and his partner Miles Fitzpatrick. According to de Caires, Lloyd and Miles 'co-authored "Working Notes towards the Unification of Guyana" which was the feature of the first issue of the *New World Quarterly*.' It was published in March 1963 and is a document that rewards the closest inspection. I am not too sure how widely published it was outside of British Guiana. It is now on the web and if you do not have it you should get it. I do not recall seeing much of it in the early New World days. For a long time, many of us wondered if there ever was a Volume 1, Number 1. The first volume of the *New World Quarterly* that I recall seeing in my days of active membership in the NWG was Volume 2, Number 1, containing Lloyd's article 'From Chaguaramas to Slavery.' I also seem to think that there was a bluish covered special edition of the *NWQ*, exclusively or nearly completely devoted to Lloyd's direct riposte to Eric Williams's classic speech 'From Slavery to Chaguaramas,' delivered in 1959. Clearly, Best's article was a full-blown challenge to Williams's political and economic programme and really announced his arrival as a major Williams critic in the early 1960s.

New World Quarterly Volume 1, Number 1, is an astoundingly opportunistic document. Largely written by at least one economic adviser to the British Guiana government, possibly two, it was as unconventional a piece of advice as one could imagine. Whether it was seriously intended to advise the government or to exhibit its shortcomings needs to be further explored. What is sure is that the Jagan government never acted upon it, and Jagan himself was scornful of what was seen to be the New World approach to British Guiana's problems. The volume consists, *inter alia,* of a complete set of constitutional proposals for the creation of a new Guyanese state running into more than 120 articles, to which is attached three appendices and a book review.

With respect to the constitutional provisions of the document we need only one look at two or three central provisions which are selected not so much for their intrinsic value as for the fact that they offer an insight into the Lloyd Best/New World/Tapia continuum. The three most interesting clauses are those that deal with the Senate, in which we can hear rollicking through the otherwise testing prose, the antecedents of what has since become one of the standard aspirations of Tapia's constitutional proposals, namely, the creation of a 'Macco Senate.' Interestingly, the clause dealing with the establishment of 'The Executive,' Clause No. 61, iv, seemed designed to place executive power in as complicated an arrangement as can be imagined, as reflected in the following extract and its succeeding clauses:

THE EXECUTIVE

The Executive will be drawn from the Legislature except for the chairman of the National Court of Policy who will be President of the Senate. It may be organised around a policy making body, the Court of Policy, and two administrative nuclei, a Consulate of Domestic Administration and a Consulate of Foreign Affairs. The crucial figures will be the two Consuls.[13]

Consuls? Now where did that come from? Why Consuls? Was this some fresh, new idea never before pre-figured by the mind of man, stirring in the imagination of the future author of 'Independent Thought and

Caribbean Freedom?' And what were these 'Consuls' to do? One was to preside over the 'Consulate of Domestic Administration,' the other the 'Consulate of Foreign Affairs,' two of whose functions were to be the 'Leader of the Legislature (without portfolio),' and the 'Minister of Defence.'

There was also to be a Head of State (Clause No. 61, [iv d]) described as follows:

HEAD OF STATE

There is to be no Head of State in the autocratic conception of that role. Functionally the Foreign Consul will receive ambassadors; at home the Domestic Consul will function as formal head. Together the two Consuls will be the real heads and everybody will know. Headship is then a question of popular acclaim and political choice and not an ascriptive role based on kinship or some other irrelevancy.

Where a neutral tenant of the role is required as a means of institutionalising non-political Headship then the President of the Senate, who is also Chairman of the Court of Policy, can act.

It is better, in the circumstances, to leave these proposals, for the time being to speak for themselves.[14]

There is also some cultural content in Volume 1, Number 1. Interspersed between sections of the documents are poems by Martin Carter, the most prominent of which was 'I Come from the Nigger Yard.' It is one of the finest anti-colonial poems written in the period but I must say there were times in my New World experience when I thought I had heard too much of it. Syl Lowhar, one of the heroes of the NWG and then later of the Tapia House Group, was no mean poet himself. However, I remember Syl more for his frequent articulation of Martin Carter's classic poem than for any of his own creations. As I look back now, I am also forced to reflect on the fact that 'The Nigger Yard' was probably the most frequent extract from Volume 1, Number 1 that most New World members in Trinidad and Tobago ever heard or were aware of. With respect to the three appendices, the first is entitled 'The Problem in a Nutshell – July 1962.' Appendix 2 is an extract from C.L.R. James's classic defense of his position in his clash with Eric Williams, *Party Politics in the West Indies*, and is entitled 'The White People.' Appendix 3 consists of a piece by David de Caires entitled 'Regional Integration.'

The book review was written by Dr C.Y. Thomas. It was a critique of Raymond T. Smith's book on British Guiana.[15] I have always been curious about Clive Thomas's connection with New World, on which he has been consistently reticent.

Now Clive Thomas has never, to my knowledge, clarified his position on New World, but I can imagine it. Here we are in 1961–63, in the vortex of the fiercest and most complicated anti-colonial struggle in Guyana, in which no one can say that 'tea party' independence – or constitutional decolonisation as Munroe so aptly put it[16] – was achieved. Here is this Trinidadian guy, on the payroll of the United Nations, writing an incredible document (and I do not mean incredibly good) with the assistance of members of the local petty bourgeoisie, proposing the complete marginalisation of the PPP, maybe the PNC and quite possibly the intervention of other forces, unnamed, unidentifiable, and unrepresentative and privileged minorities in the name of social, economic and political reform and national consensus. It was decolonisation turned on its head. It was as if, in Trinidad and Tobago, the late William Demas had proposed in one of his advisories to Eric Williams that the Party of Political Progress Groups (POPPG) be empowered in the place of the PNM to lead Trinidad and Tobago to independence. In British Guiana, in the event, it seemed to be a rousing summons, or at least to create an opening for the forces that had already produced the United Force led by Peter D'Aguiar. This is a most amazing speculation and raises serious questions about what New World was all about at a crucial stage in the struggle for independence in British Guiana. Again, I say to younger historians: 'Here is a field of research that will richly reward your efforts. Go to it.'

Suffice it to say that C.Y. Thomas wrote sparingly in the pages of New World publications, including the *New World Fortnightly*, which was later headquartered in Georgetown, and he always kept his distance from the New World Group. What is more, that distance was extended when a piece that Clive had been working on for some time, which had been referred to in Volume 2, Number 1 of the *Quarterly*, emerged as a full-blown book co-authored by himself and Havelock Brewster, and entitled *The Dynamics of West Indian Economic Integration*. As we now know, thanks to the Ryan volume of proceedings, Brewster and Thomas proposed a completely different approach to integration from that which Lloyd had apparently come to espouse. Again, according to McIntyre:

> ...very few people are aware of the fact that he [Best] played a significant role in the move towards CARIFTA [the Caribbean Free Trade Area]. Both of us co-rapporteured the meeting at the ISER in 1965, when Jamaica, through its representative, the late G. Arthur Brown, indicated its interest in joining a regional free trade area.[17]

I can only say, Holy Moses! Until I read that, I did not know it, and if I was told I would not have believed it. The debate over CARIFTA was one of the central controversies in the region in the 1960s. It did much to animate the New World Group in Trinidad and Tobago, to vitalise the New World Group in Jamaica and to stimulate in that country a very important interface with the barons of the sugar industry. That debate with sugar also invigorated and inspired the public consciousness of the limits of existing economic strategies and, to some extent, helped to foster the radicalisation that was to come in the 1970s. In hindsight I can now also understand the vehement opposition of Lloyd Best to the role that I played in criticising the old colonial elite in Trinidad and Tobago in the 1960s. The CARIFTA debate triggered some of the clearest popular responses to the growing neo-colonialist settlement in the country and was at the same time the main reason advanced by Best for, as he put it, 'mashing up' the New World Group.

Of course the real reasons lay elsewhere. First of all, there were the Rodney riots in Jamaica in 1968. Best was somewhere between lukewarm and ice cold in responding to the crisis. The same person who thought that we should be frightened at what he called the heretical repudiation of his 'subversive' activities on the Mona campus, was himself petrified when faced with the repercussions of the larger social and political discourse that Rodney had triggered. His response then was remarkable in that it was not only astounding at the time but it also set the pattern for all his future responses to episodic upheavals in the region thereafter.

Now there is no doubt that Rodney had put the cat among the pigeons. In a flash, he had moved the post-independence debates from the seminar room and the drawing room to the streets. In the second issue of *Moko*, the newspaper that emerged in Trinidad and Tobago out of the Rodney crisis, we gave voice to Rodney's perceptions of where the struggle was going. In a piece entitled 'Bogle's Reminder,' a personal statement he issued from Montreal following his exclusion from Jamaica, Rodney tells his own story of his personal journey from the ivory tower to the ghettoes of Kingston.

> The first essential was to operate outside of the petty bourgeois University campus and outside of the 'respectable' middle class suburb where I resided. My background in Guyana was working class, but after the alienation produced by the educational system, it was up to me to take the initiative to rediscover my brothers and sisters. I sought them out where they lived, worked, worshipped, and had their recreation. In turn they 'checked' me at work or at home, and together we 'probed' here and there, learning to recognize our common humanity. Naturally, they wanted to know what I stood for, what I 'defended.' I never gave anyone money or bought them drinks; that one must leave to the political gangsters of the two-party system. At some point, I ceased to be 'Dr Rodney' and was addressed as 'Brother Rodney' or (better still) 'Brother Wally.' That simple change meant that I was no longer a tool of the establishment, but was readmitted into the moral and cultural brotherhood of the Black Man.[18]

The developments stimulated by the Rodney crisis led to fierce debates among the members of the New World Group in Trinidad. The overwhelming majority of us supported and organised an active and visible response to the Rodney crisis. Many of our members assisted at, attended and often addressed the many public and private meetings called to decide how to respond to the crisis. Increasingly, participants in these discussions included radicalised students, trade unionists, political activists, and ordinary members of the public moved to outrage by the Jamaica crisis over Rodney.

At one of these meetings, we decided to found a newspaper to publicise our views about the crisis and about other matters associated with it, and with us. In fact, quite clearly, the Rodney affair was stimulating not only a response to the Jamaica crisis but also a response to the emerging neo-colonial settlement that was taking place in Trinidad and Tobago at least since 1965.

This newspaper idea was another cat that Best had to deal with. He and I talked about it. He said he was not warm to the idea, but he would support it if it became a New World paper. I said: 'Fine, let us put it to the group' but he did not want to put it to the group, especially the Trinidad and Tobago group. Like other New World groups, the Trinidad and Tobago group was peopled with academic types, both faculty and students, but it had also already incorporated into its ranks many of the militants who would go on to lead the Black Power uprising and to engage in other radical activity. The Trinidad and Tobago group had already been publishing and widely distributing occasional papers on several topical issues. That activity had stimulated a whole genre of pamphleteering on many social and political issues in many areas of Port of Spain and its suburbs. There were many folk in the New World group, Trinidad, who were not dissimilar to the 'Brothers' with whom Rodney was grounding in Jamaica. Best knew what the group would say 'yes to a newspaper, but no to an organ of bourgeois intellectualism!' So he recoiled from the idea of consulting with the group about it.

What he wanted was an organ submissive to New World control, which would have meant the control of the 'captain,' and an organ devoted to 'reasoned discussion,' 'balanced criticism' and no doubt 'independent thought.' I observed that that was what the *New World Quarterly* was for; we were talking about a newspaper. It was clear also that we were talking about editorial control and journalistic content, and we agreed to disagree.

In that discussion I had the upper hand. The paper was to be funded by public subscription, and the notion was to make a quick and relevant response to the crisis. Best was personally averse to the project, partly because he and Rodney had clashed verbally at the Black Writers' Conference in Montreal and he was still smarting from that encounter. Yet he was personally and ideologically averse to action, to political activism aimed at achieving political results.

In the end Best had to accommodate to the publication of the paper, but he refused the invitation to be one of its publishers. The first issue of the newspaper, *Moko*, appeared on Monday, October 28, 1968. For the first few issues, Adrian Espinet, James Millette, and Gordon Rohlehr were the publishers. Soon, however, Espinet, a committed Lloyd supporter, withdrew and became fully incorporated into the

Tapia House Group which Lloyd was in the process of forming. In the end, three newspapers (not one) came into existence – *Moko*, the prototype of a new kind of paper, *Abeng* in Jamaica,[19] and *Tapia/Trinidad and Tobago Review*.

The second reason for the split was, of course, the CARIFTA debates. For the national bourgeoisie and the national political leadership the CARIFTA debates hit hard. For the first time since 1962, an outspoken attack was made on the settlements and arrangements that had followed on the winning of independence. In Trinidad, the new relationship between the PNM and the international bourgeoisie had been cemented by the passage of the Industrial Stabilisation Act, whose avowed intention was the regulation (read emasculation) of the trade union movement. Also in Jamaica, Rodney's exclusion had been followed by initiatives undertaken by the JLP government to pass legislation that would have the effect of excluding non-Jamaicans, or as they were called, 'Commonwealth citizens,' from the University of the West Indies, contrary to existing agreements and previous customs and practices. In addition, the Jamaican government withdrew the passports of two prominent Jamaican academics at the Mona campus, namely, Dr George Beckford and Dr Leroy Taylor.

Most importantly, however, the CARIFTA debates, at least on our side, assailed the ongoing policies and programs that were strengthening, and not contesting, the renewed dominance of the old colonial elite in the economic sectors of the region. It is also an interesting reflection based on what I have previously said that while we, the subalterns of the New World Group, so to speak, were attacking CARIFTA, Lloyd Best, 'the captain' of the movement, was defending it, but he was not defending it openly. At no time whatsoever did the principal protagonist of open discourse and intellectual freedom openly disclose his support for CARIFTA and utter a public word in its defence. In a certain sense, however, he defended it effectively by 'mashing up' the New World Group, which had emerged at the vanguard of the critical assault being waged against it.[20]

To understand what is going on here we have to turn to some issues of theory. It is always important in discussing New World to understand that its mission was not only one of theory, but also of practice. There were, of course, moments in the life of the organisation when it was pretended that the movement was all about theory and that it was disdainful of practice, that is to say of actual political activity: that thought alone was action, and that action was thoughtless. At the time that this position was advanced, more specifically on the occasion of the break up of the New World Group in 1968, the view then expressed was that the break up had become necessary because the organisation had ventured into the field of political activism and abandoned the field of abstract theorising. It was easy to say that then, when the future was as yet undisclosed; it is not possible to say that now, when the future has become the past. After the break up of the organisation, the Tapia House Group tried at first to perpetuate the leisured intellectual contemplation of national and regional events, and then, in desperation, plunged into political activity and remained engaged in active politics until it was clear that the presumptions and the ambitions of its practitioners were doomed to failure.

In reality the New World Group was always about politics and not only in the inane, arcane, and ambiguous versification of that term to which Lloyd and his fervent supporters have always been committed. When the public was not listening Lloyd spoke his mind freely to some of his closest collaborators. David de Caires, for example, shared a reflection at the conference held in Port of Spain, Trinidad in honour of Lloyd Best.

> One of Lloyd's most endearing sayings in those days[21] was, 'when we take the full power.' Such was his enthusiasm and confidence that you always assumed that that would inevitably happen in due course.[22]

de Caires ruefully informed his audience that such was not to be, and told of the occasion when he and other Lloyd supporters gathered in Georgetown optimistically expecting to hear that Tapia would take 'the full power' in Trinidad and Tobago in the elections. After a period of optimistic expectation, the group finally realised that no such event was going to take place and, as de Caires put it, 'it soon became clear that Tapia had not done well, and the session broke up much sooner than had been anticipated and in some disrepair.'[23]

The truth is that not only the New World Group but the Tapia House Movement that succeeded it were always pointed towards the winning of political power. The problem was with the means of obtaining it. This is where the question of theory came to be important. As you will all agree, the mission is only as good as the plan that inspires it. Also the plan that inspired New World/Tapia's political activity was shot through with the belief that everything had to be new, original, and different, even if some of those differences and innovations were superficial. As we have seen with respect to the crafting of the Guyanese independence constitution, the reconciled leadership of the two factions in Guyana proposed in Volume 1, Number 1 was to preside over a political system in which they shared power as joint 'Consuls.' There is very little recognition in the document about the realities of political and constitutional development in the West Indies at that time and of the Crown Colony system that real politicians, parties and peoples were trying to demolish. Words like 'cabinet' and 'chief minister,' 'premier' and 'prime minister' are remarkable for their absence, but really, what was new about the word 'Consuls?' Napoleon was one, and so were several Roman leaders whose title Napoleon was stealing.

In addition, Tapia saddled itself with another major disability. The disability was related to its refusal to recognise the role played by the broad masses of the people in bringing the Caribbean to where it was in the early 1960s. One is almost moved to mirth when reading what Best has to say about the people. In his 'Reflections on the Reflections,' Lloyd states:

> What is the concept of people? I don't have this concept of the people. Which people? When I talk about the people, I mean everybody in the country. I have no concept of the people and the elites. When I talk about the elites, I mean people who are distinguished from the rest of the population because they have different jobs, they have different incomes, different responsibilities, and therefore what they have to do is different in the normal course of things. But I do not believe that this excludes anybody at all from being able to contribute to the process of change.[24]

This is, in my view, a simplistic understanding of the way in which the world works and I want to point this out with specific reference to the theme of this conference 'The Quest for Decolonization.' Again I need to speak directly to the young people in this audience who are probably wondering what this decolonisation business is all about. Why should we be talking, 40 years after independence, about decolonisation? I think we are decolonised, though I admit that some of our institutions may not be decolonised, and I agree with Lloyd that the University of the West Indies may be one of these, though the evidence of this conference may suggest otherwise.

The real problem, however, is that we are not fully decolonised; and there is the rub. The period of decolonisation, roughly speaking, the period since the Second World War, when the formal colonial systems began to collapse and disappear, is one of the most complex and misunderstood periods in the rise of global society in the twentieth century. Decolonisation was nothing less than a major sea change that shifted political power from the hands of the European imperialists and conferred that power on those who were formerly dominated by those imperial systems. In that transfer lay the germs of a possibility for using the new political power to achieve a fuller and more substantive measure of independence.

Receiving independence was one thing, but using it properly was something else. One could not achieve the fruits of independence by ignoring the historical track that had led to its achievement. In order to use it properly, one had to have a sense of how one had arrived at the moment of decolonisation and how one was to proceed from there to full independence.

To return to Best's notion of the people, it is clear that not all the people had the same expectations of decolonisation. For those who were in the political leadership, the essence of decolonisation was political; for the masses of the people, the essence of decolonisation was social, economic, and spiritual. That is to say that while the nation became independent, the enjoyment of that independence, or lack of it, was experienced differently by different sectors of the population.[25]

That is why, for example, the critique of the Puerto Rican model of development, which was one of the salient positions adopted by the New World, was so valid and so important. The Puerto Rican model of development meant the promotion of the values, the interests, and the fortunes of those who were in a position to profit from what industrialisation by invitation was all about. It was in many important senses a departure from the implicit promises of political independence and a surrender to the seductions of economic dependency. For that reason, I always perceived the New World critique of the Puerto Rican model as a forthright rejection of the neo-colonialist model of economic independence; and I applauded it.

That is also why the elaboration of the plantation model of development was, for me, so important. I thought it a very significant intervention in the analysis of colonial structures of dependence, and I waited, as I am sure that others did, to see where its authors, Lloyd Best and Kari Levitt, would take it. Both Lloyd and Kari need to offer an explanation to the conference about this disengagement from their earlier work.[26] For me, the plantation model threw an important light upon the enduring structures of exploitation and expropriation that were, and continue to be, a part of the daily life of Caribbean people, and hinted at serious options for terminating some aspects of that paradigm. What is amazing is that though the model was conceptualised, it was never elaborated into a statement of what its implications meant for the Caribbean and how, in practical terms, the plantation model was to be replaced. Moreover, if it was attempted, it was not attempted by Lloyd Best. It was attempted by Kari Levitt in a critique of Canadian economic dependence on the US, published in the *Quarterly*, and later elaborated in an influential book published in Canada.[27] It was attempted by George Beckford in *Persistent Poverty*; and it has recently inspired Cesar Ayala's recent book *American Sugar Kingdom*.

Clearly, at least in my view, the critique of the Puerto Rican model of development and of the critique of the plantation model of development marked the apogee of the radical phase in the development of New World ideology. Equally clearly, I would argue that that phase came abruptly to and end between 1968 and 1970 and has been succeeded by what I can only politely refer to as ideological 'clap-trap' ever since.

To understand the collapse of New World radicalism, I invite you to read the circumstances of the split that took place in 1968, which I have briefly retold in my article 'Millette and the Rift in New World.'[28] The mashing up of New World in 1968 marked the utter surrender by Lloyd Best to the class forces that had fostered his emergence and promoted his recognition as a major intellectual force in the Caribbean, and which hoped to confer on him the mantle of political leadership in Trinidad and Tobago, in the confident expectation that, notwithstanding his public utterances, he would be a leader they could do business with.

Now we have another problem. I have used the phrase 'class forces.' Best would probably not know what I mean and there are probably many devotees of New World ideology who would not know what I mean either. Lloyd Best essentially denies the existence of classes. For Best, class is a four-letter word. Best abhors class so fervently that he would not recognise it whatever the guise in which it appears. I had great fun recently reading his speech, 'Race Class and Ethnicity: A Caribbean Interpretation,' delivered at York University to which I have earlier referred. If you want to understand where Lloyd best stands on the issues of race, class and ethnicity, I recommend that you put it on your short list of prescribed readings. He speaks as follows:

> The most important thing about the actors in the Caribbean is that they are of two types. One is that you have the proletarians – the multitude of the people, and you have the proprietors. I have argued for 40 years (and the Marxists are going to kill me – those of you who are still here) that the important thing about Caribbean society is that it is *classless* [his italics]. People don't want to hear that at all, but I will show them right now. It is classless in the important sense. I am not talking about stratification; I am not talking about rank; I am not talking about hierarchy or status – you have that. You have differences in occupation in wealth and so on. But class requires a concept of responsibility. You have to have different responsibilities in the place. The thing about the Caribbean is that everybody has the same responsibility, which is no responsibility at all! [Laughter and Applause].[29]

The adoring audience at York University found this funny, I do not, and I hope you do not either. That notion of class is exclusively subjective and has no practical value at all. In fact I very much hope that there are not people on this campus who are teaching students that class does not exist, that if it exists it is what each of us subjectively imagines it to be, or that class is an irrelevant concept in the understanding of Caribbean history, or for that matter in the history of the peoples of the black Diaspora or of the underdeveloped countries of the Third World.

This reminds me that Best, surprisingly, does not seem to understand the meaning of underdevelopment either, and objects to the use of the term 'developing countries' on the ground that First World countries are developing too. I mention it only because it provides an important insight into the ancestral dimensions of Bestian philosophy, which are rooted in a 'punnish' exploitation of words and phrases intended to confer on such use the distinction of ideological originality.

I do not, however, want to be sidetracked, I want to talk about class. Lloyd Best would be happy to reduce class to a conversation about Marxists and anti-Marxists. In fact, in making his statement about classlessness, he presumed that Marxists were going to 'kill him' for talking in that way. Frankly, he overestimates his importance. More importantly, he misrepresents Marx. He says, again in the same lecture, 'Class is race in Marx. That's what he and Engels saw. He saw that when you are from one class you are really a completely different genre of being. A different category of human animal.'[30] Had he been possessed of a mind unfettered by bias against Marxism he might have moved on from this observation, which is not without significance, to an understanding of what class is really about. Yet he did not, and in fact he could not; and it is too late now for him to understand, still less to admit, the error of his ways.

What is class? There are, of course, many definitions of class, and all of us have our own favourite definition, though some of us have no definition at all. My favourite definition of class comes not from Marx, you will be happy to hear, but it does come from Lenin. Are you still happy? Marxism, or if you wish Marxism-Leninism, in the period 1848–1920, wrestled with the problem of formalising a rational interpretation of class. Marx attempted a definition in the third volume of *Capital*, but as we know, the volume was incomplete at the time of his death. When the Marxist definition of class emerged, it emerged not as an extended codification on the question, but as a few phrases buried within the bowels of an article written by Lenin in 1920. In writing his piece 'A Great Beginning,' in which he was much more intent on addressing other matters than on offering a definition of class, Lenin defined classes as follows:

> Classes are large groups of people differing from each other by the place they occupy in a historically determined system of social production, by their relation (in most cases fixed and formulated in law) to the means of production, by their role in the social organization of labour, and, consequently, by the dimensions of the share of social wealth of which they dispose and the mode of acquiring it. Classes are groups of people one of which can

appropriate the labour of another owing to the different places they occupy in a definite system of social economy.[31]

Now you do not have to be Marxist to understand that definition any more than you have to be Christian to understand the significance of the phrase 'Blessed be the poor' or a Muslim to understand the phrase 'God willing.' The definition of class is simple and clear: 'Classes are groups of people one of which can appropriate the labour of another owing to the different places they occupy in a definite system of social economy.' Today we can update the definition: for labour we need to understand not only labour power, for which the definition is still valid, but we need to add, in this more modern age, 'assets,' 'resources,' 'culture,' 'intellectual property' and even lives. It would take us a long time to elaborate on these extensions, but I invite you to think about them. As for the phrase 'a definite system of social economy,' substitute today the 'national and global economies.' Think also about the fact that the period of independence seemed to promise that oppressed national majorities would at last come into the realisation of what capitalist democracy was supposed to provide – agency in their own affairs, autonomy and genuine self-determination. Think further of the fact that these oppressed national majorities have been marginalised by the creation of a new global majority, linked by class, and to some extent linked by race and ethnicity, by 'kith and kin,' firmly located in an Anglo-American, and sometimes broader European and international alliance, which has had the effect of diminishing the significance of national autonomy and independence in individual countries.

Today, we have to confront the emergence of the 'hyperglobalizers' whose stated mission it is to eliminate national boundaries, to establish a 'borderless world,' diminish the significance of national sovereignties and to impose on all countries an effective subordination regulated by a few of the most powerful states.[32]

This is the process that decolonisation might have terminated, or slowed down; instead this is the process that decolonisation has done much to accelerate. The moment for radical change has been almost completely lost. The promise of independence has been subverted by the rise to greater prominence of groups and classes in our societies who have seized the opportunities provided by the search for economic growth and development to reconstruct a new form of oppression of the Caribbean people. Note also that this is not happening in the Caribbean alone; it is the history of the Third World in the neo-colonialist period. The big question is: How did we get there?

We got there via class collaboration between neo-colonialist politicians and the imperialists. We got there via privatisation and globalisation and we are continuing to go there by marching on the road to global capitalism and global imperialism. Perhaps South Africa provides the best example of what I am talking about. In a country in which for more than 300 years black people were exploited and robbed and degraded and brutalised by Europeans, racial apartheid has now been succeeded by class apartheid. The masses of the people, whose struggles made it possible to overthrow and overcome the apartheid state system, are being victimised by a new partnership between the white economic establishment and the black political leadership. As a recent writer has stated: 'The reality is that South Africa has witnessed the replacement of racial apartheid with what is increasingly referred to as class apartheid – systemic underdevelopment and segregation of the oppressed majority through structured economic, political, legal, and cultural practices.'[33]

This is an observation not only relevant to what has taken place in South Africa, but also to what has taken place in the Caribbean. Slavery was our period of racial apartheid. It ended for us in 1838, though the system persisted in many parts of the hemisphere, and in parts of the Caribbean itself, almost until the end of the nineteenth century. That period of racial apartheid was succeeded by indentureship, the creation of mass unemployment, the depression of wages, the exploitation of the working classes, and generally the imposition of a dual stigmatisation marked by race and class. Among intelligent people, Best probably belongs to a handful of individuals who do not understand this process.[34]

Best's main mistake, of course, is to regard class and Marxism as inseparable. It is almost a Pavlovian response, a kind of dog whistle thing, but the association is false. As Marx himself reminded us, classes always existed. He did not invent them, and never claimed to have done that. What Marx did was to unravel the cocoon in which class had always been wrapped, and to expose it for the world to see. It is like neo-colonialism. Neo-colonialism is not new. One could see neo-colonialism in the relationship between Great Britain and the United States after the American Revolution, as well as in the relationship between Great Britain and the white dominions between the mid-nineteenth century and most of the twentieth century. As late as the 1980s, Canada was still wrestling with vestiges of British constitutional domination over Canadian political life. Australia is still, in a constitutional sense, a British colony, as are several Caribbean states. One could see neo-colonialism in the relationship between France and Haiti between 1825 and the present. One could see a neo-colonial relationship between the United States and Cuba, the Dominican Republic, and most of Central America. One could also see a neo-colonial relationship between Italy and Libya.

For most of the twentieth century, however, it was not fashionable to speak of neo-colonialism as an historical reality. The idea of neo-colonialism came into its own after the decolonisation of the post-Second World War period, and after the word came into voguish use particularly as a result of Kwame Nkrumah's publication of his book on the subject in the 1960s.[35] In fact Nkrumah's definition of neo-colonialism set the standard by which the neo-colonialist idea came to be understood.

Similarly, underdevelopment, a word to which Best might assign little meaning, was a live and vicious process sucking the lifeblood of the continent of Africa during the period of slavery and colonisation. However, in the period when Europeans wrote the histories of Africa and the Caribbean and other colonised countries, the word 'underdevelopment' could not be found. It came into its own in the twentieth century when progressive economists, historians and other social scientists began openly to speak of the fact that European development had taken place at the expense of colonial underdevelopment. As we memorialise today the twenty-fifth anniversary of the assassination of Walter Rodney, it is fitting to recall that his book, *How Europe Underdeveloped Africa*, became the classic formulation of the relationship of development and underdevelopment between imperial and colonised countries.[36]

So it is with class. To understand it, we have to historicise it. Strangely enough, natural scientists are often much better than social scientists at understanding this. When Darwin wrote the *Origin of Species*, he was not claiming to invent evolution any more than Marx claimed to invent class, but he was unmasking a reality in human civilisation which only mad people and the creationists are trying these days to refute.

Now I will not say that everybody who tries to debunk class is mad, but I would say that their position is untenable. In fact, Lloyd himself provides a very interesting insight into the impact of class on his own thinking. Born on a sugar plantation, as he often reminds us, Best was able to achieve a position in life by which he could not only 'think independently' but act 'independently.' I do not know of many individuals who have had the capacity to ignore the blandishments and the entreatments of as many national leaders as Best has claimed to have had. To begin with he coined the phrase 'doctor politics' and consigned all the West Indian leaders to the rubbish heap of history in consequence. He argued that 'doctor politics' was equal to maximum leadership and that could not be tolerated. You are probably not surprised to hear that I have a different explanation of 'doctor politics' and if you ask me I will tell you about it. Not only did he theorise the nationalist leaders into oblivion, but he also, by his own words, poured scorn on their efforts to make use of his rather considerable intellectual talents. As he himself put it in 'Reflections on the Reflections,'

> …Norman Manley…wanted me to become his personal economic advisor – or would I? I turned it down, because I can't work in anybody's stable. I would help him if he wanted, but I don't work for people. The University of the West Indies was paying me, but I don't work for them either.

> In a University, you have to decide what work you are going to do and put it before your colleagues, and when I had to leave, I left on those grounds. And Manley, just before he died, called a press interview to see me. I was not even living in Jamaica; I was living in Canada, and Wilton Hill, Housing Minister, and Clem Tavares whom I had helped with Edward Seaga to write the paper on 'haves and have-nots' that made him this wizard that they said he was, or is – they sent me a clipping in Montreal; and Sealy asked Manley who were the people he thought were making sense in the Region, and had a real stake in the future, and he named two people, one was a Jamaican which I feel he had to name. I would not tell you his name, it is too embarrassing. But the evidence has confirmed that. And then he named me. I was not even in Jamaica at the time, so he did not have to do it. I had left there, and I had rebuffed him by

not taking the job, and Michael was there and Michael 'cussed me so much bad word' that night not for taking the job; and Norman was a big man, he could rise above that and say, 'Best.'[37]

With respect to Eric Williams, leader of the nationalist movement in Trinidad and Tobago, he was even more irreverent:

> Williams invited me to be in his Cabinet, and I told him to 'kiss my arse.' I don't take any job from any Prime Minister. Manley could tell you what he told him about me, because he told him. And Mannigat [sic], Dumont, Vera Rubin could tell you, and all these people that Williams begged me to come into the Cabinet. I told him no, there is no chance of that. I know you? I am in politics, I am a free man. And if I get into power, it has to be on these terms – for the things that I stand for, everybody must believe in them, choose them, and so on; and if we get office, we get office. And as David de Caires said here the other morning, I said, 'whether we get power or not' when I was in Guyana where I had absolutely no chance. So I wasn't talking about getting into any Government; I was talking about something else. I said it in Jamaica where I had no chance – but that is not true because Seaga wanted to make me a Senator to pay me back for what I did for them; and I told them no. So I am in politics. And that is a private occupation that has its own rewards, and I say to myself, the constitution reform that we want is to create politics and to create reformation. And therefore the concrete proposals that I am making are very simple and very clear.[38]

On their own, these statements would be reprehensible enough, but when taken in the context of other considerations, they are more reprehensible still. One does not have to search very hard in the writings of Lloyd Best to find fulsome denunciations of the nationalist politicians of the 1960s and 1970s, a denunciation in which many other radical intellectuals of the period, including myself, also share. What is remarkable about Best's writings, however, is that the nationalist politicians and other political activists are the only ones who attract his ire.

I cannot find anywhere, in anything that Best has written, a single denunciation of the colonial elite or its representative figures. In Guyana he has much to say of the weaknesses of Cheddi Jagan and to some extent of Forbes Burnham, but he utters not a word of criticism about Bookers or Jock Campbell, or of Peter D'Aguiar, leader of the United Force. In Trinidad, as we have seen, he is abusive to Williams, abusive to those who opposed Williams, myself included, but makes no criticism of the Chambers of Commerce, Neal & Massy and other regional congLomérates, Sidney Knox, Ken Gordon, Tommy Gatcliffe, or other deans of the old colonial regime. The same is true of Barbados and Jamaica. The New World Group in Jamaica's critique of the Jamaican sugar industry, of Robert Kirkwood, of Tate and Lyle, proceeded without any contribution whatsoever by Lloyd Best. Criticisms of the Private Sector Organisation of Jamaica (PSOJ) and the six families of which Rodney wrote in one of his early papers have never been heard of from Mr Best. All of which is curious, to say the least, and points decisively to his class and perhaps also his racial biases in his discourse on Caribbean political economy. In fact I think that there are more criticisms to be found in New World and Tapia literature of New World colleagues for criticising the upper echelons of Caribbean society than there are statements by Best criticising those upper echelons himself.

In fact, the class forces on which Best has relied for political support throughout his career are precisely those to which the masses of the people have been opposed. There is a funny little reference by Best in 'Reflections on the Reflections' in explication of what Best describes as his immersion in 'real politics.'

> Ken Gordon and Craig Reynald of the *Express* were here the other morning; they could tell you that I used to produce my paper in the *Express*, getting them to help me with the plates and so on, and for certain years they had to prevent me from coming there. They had put a sign on the door, 'Don't let Lloyd Best come in here at all,' because when I go into the *Express* Production, everybody dropped the *Express* work and working on my team, because I am in politics. I am wooing them and persuading them – come on my side. So we need politics, and it is not an ignoble vocation. It is the noblest of vocations. You have to give up plenty jobs, you have to give up plenty big money; you have to give up offers.[39]

As they say in Trinidad, there is more in the mortar here than the pestle! It is true that Best has unusual access to the *Express*. In fact the *Express* is Tapia's party group Number One. It is the only and most reliable base of support for Tapia in Trinidad and Tobago and has consistently and fervently facilitated the dissemination of Lloyd's political views over the years. It is not, as Best puts it, that 'I used to produce my paper in the *Express*,' it is that the *Trinidad and Tobago Review* has been consistently printed at the *Express*. How much of this relationship is commercial and how much of it is political needs to be researched. In part the relationship is explained by the fact that some of the most committed Tapia members or supporters work at the *Express*; but in greater part the relationship is explained by the fact that the owners of the *Express*, and the interests they represent, are precisely the same that ordered Best to 'mash up' the New World in 1968.

Who are these interests? They are mainly centred in the regional newspaper industry, and they represent and speak for important sectors of the national and regional bourgeoisie especially in Trinidad and Tobago, Guyana, Jamaica, Barbados and some of the smaller islands. The principal entity is the Trinidad and Tobago *Express*, and its publisher and chief executive officer is Ken Gordon, lately elected chairman of the West Indian Cricket Board. Then there is *Stabroek News*, whose publisher and chief executive officer is David de Caires, long time friend and associate of Lloyd's. Other papers in the stable are the *Nation* in Barbados, the *Observer* in Jamaica, *Tobago News*, the Grenada *Barnacle* and the Virgin Islands *Daily News*. Some of these papers are wholly or partly owned by the *Express*. All of them are elements in the regional media industry including newspaper, radio and television stations, with strong links to other media interests, and integrated through organisations like the Caribbean Broadcasting Union and the Caribbean Communications Network, whose present chairman and chief executive officer is Craig Reynald, and whose recent chairman was Ken Gordon.

Now Best may not recognise these interests as constituting a class. Yet they are a class, and it speaks volumes about his political commitments that this is the class from which he has derived and continues to derive his most important political support.

So much for class.

One more observation on theory. When one compares the plethora of ideas emanating from Best over the years, and compares them with the paucity of real political impact of these ideas, one has to ask oneself some serious questions. Where do good ideas come from? Anybody can dream up any version of the world that he or she imagines. Whether that imagined world is realisable is another question. History is littered with the corpses of unrealised utopias. Such dreams are often based on an incorrect or fanciful reading of history. In the New World/Tapia paradigm the proof of the pudding is to be found in an endlessly protracted process which will one day inevitably mature. When that day will be is subject to serious mental prestidigitation. The latest estimate offered by Lloyd in 'Reflections on the Reflections' is '...200 years, it might take 100 years, it might take 100 days, I don't know. *I am prepared to engage the process*, because I have faith that people can learn. My experience over 50 years has told me that.'[40]

This was written, or rather spoken in 2002. One hundred days have passed. So we are now in the 100 to 200 year period which none of us, even allowing for our legendary longevities, will be around to witness.

Also, the 50 year history to which Lloyd refers produced an experience that could be distilled into a number of practical political proposals which have been around for a very long time. In brief, they are the constituent assembly, a Macco senate, and, in place of a maximum leader, something that falls somewhere between 'a House of Executives or an Executive House of Members of the Administration with a Chief Executive.'[41] These are essentially the ideas that emerged in Volume 1, Number 1 of the *New World Quarterly* and they have not changed much over the years. None of them have come close to realisation because the aims of politics cannot generally be achieved without winning political power, and political power cannot be achieved without winning political struggles. The problem with Tapia, and the problem with Best, is that political struggles are not part of their agenda; or if they are, such struggles are to be fought without the engagement of the masses. Since 1968, when the Rodney crisis announced the arrival of a more radical politicisation of the Caribbean people, Lloyd Best and Tapia have been running in the rear of the mass movement in Trinidad and Tobago and in the Caribbean. Whether it was the Rodney Riots or the Black Power Movement or the Grenada Revolution, or any other form of mass political engagement, the Tapia House Group was never ready and the movements which were challenging the status quo in the region were all the butt of the severest critical appraisal by Lloyd Best and the Tapia House Movement.

Speaking of Trinidad and Tobago, in particular, whenever an opposition to the status quo emerged it had to reckon with fighting at least two battles: one against the status quo and the other against Lloyd Best and the Tapia House Movement, who could be relied upon to attack the attackers of the status quo.

The problem was that there has never been a mass movement in Trinidad and Tobago or in the Caribbean which Lloyd Best's version of the New World Group, the Tapia House Movement, has been able to create or control. In politics these are the things you have to do if you are going to advance. You either have to be capable of creating a mass movement, or of controlling one when it is created, better yet of doing both. Tapia has never been able to do that or even come close to doing it. That, too, I think might have to do with a misreading of history.

Once again, with respect to 'Reflections on the Reflections,' Best misinterpreted the importance of the labour movements of the late nineteenth and early twentieth centuries. He consigns them all to the nineteenth century. He regards the events of the 1930s as drawing a line between the nineteenth century and the twentieth century and distinguishes the leadership of the twentieth century as elitist and drawn from a substratum of 'new leaders in the boardrooms, in the offices, and in the Parliament.'[42] Unfortunately for these new leaders, however, Best does not think much of them either and having dismissed what he calls the nineteenth century leadership of the labour movements, he also dismisses the twentieth century leadership of the new educated elites. He concludes 'that by the time these people came to office, they were already all obsolete. All of them. And by that, I mean Arthur Lewis, Eric Williams, Norman Manley, all of them.'[43]

These profound observations are based on a theory that the nineteenth century was 'long.' I have always been suspect about the theory of the long nineteenth century because, in my simple-mindedness, I have always understood a century to be exactly what it is. It is 100 years. The fact is that events do not solely march to the drum of the conventional calendar; so that trends and processes can straddle centuries and link one age to another. However, this does not mean that one can dismissively write off what is happening at the end of one century and the beginning of another on the presumption that the preceding century was 'long' and that as a result events of significance can be ignored or minimised.

Even if one were to use this theory, another way of looking at it might be to say that the nineteenth century was short; that the twentieth century began in 1884 with the modification of the Crown Colony system in Jamaica, or in 1887 when Marcus Garvey was born, or in 1897 when the Norman Commission arrived and stimulated the emergence of new organisations and new leaderships that spoke on behalf of the common people, or maybe even one can say that it started right on time with the founding of the Pan-African movement by Henry Sylvester Williams in 1900. In fact if one does that, one cannot go very wrong about what the twentieth century achieved, or what it meant.

Both Eric Williams and Lloyd Best avoided any overt political recognition of the working people or of their organisations. For Williams that was tactical in an age perhaps when one had to be tactical. For Best, however, the marginalisation of the masses is a fundamental commitment that is suggested by several of the issues and observations to which we have already referred. It is doubtful if one can construct a reliable future from emphasising marginal fragments of the region's history while exaggerating the neglect of the most important parts of it.

It is in this context that I find it difficult to imagine that 100 years from now or 200 years from now – to take the long view that Best himself takes – future scholars would find the theorising of the New World Group, except in its halcyon years, or the musings of the Tapia House Movement as reflected in the *Trinidad and Tobago Review,* as a sure guide to the creation of the new world which we are all talking about on this very auspicious occasion.

In Lloyd's recent utterances there is a frequent reference to the 50 years of work that he has undertaken in the service of the Caribbean people. Unfortunately, there may be another interpretation of the work done in those 50 years. It might be said, for example, and this is my own view, that for most of those 50 years, Lloyd Best was like a Trojan horse within the bowels of the nationalist movement, seriously destabilising it at several important junctures. Bright, articulate, fertile in imagination, and always well-funded, glib in thinking and speaking, utterly disdainful of critical process, and contemptuous in the extreme of all the leaders of the regional nationalist and revolutionary movements, Lloyd Best was like a wrecking ball within the processes for political, social and economic transformation in the Caribbean within the last half century. To borrow his metaphor, it has indeed been a long half century, particularly for the masses of the Caribbean people. Yet I remain confident of one thing. The masses will not be denied.

In that spirit, I want to dedicate this lecture to the memory of Walter Rodney. For me this remembrance of Walter Rodney has been a 37 year anniversary, not only a 25 year memorialisation. I have the feeling that the process inaugurated in Jamaica in 1968 could have proceeded differently but for the split in the New World Group and some of the consequences that flowed from it. In particular, I remain convinced that the split had the effect of providing the reaction, in the post-independence period, with its most articulate champion in the person of Lloyd Best, and with providing the conservative cause with the rhetorical support that it needed to foster its putative ideology of change but no change.

Finally, I want to close by invoking a poem used by Walter Rodney in the statement I have already referred to, namely 'Bogle's Reminder.' It is authored by Bongo Jerry and has a much wider application in the scheme of things than it probably did in 1968. In the context of our conversation, or 'reasonings,' in the context of our quest for decolonisation, I find it a very apt remembrance:

Sooner or later,
But Mus'
The Dam going to bus' and every
Man will break out
And who will stop them?
What force can stop this river of Man
Who already know their course?
The water that was used to mix the mortar for the dam
Is the blood of PAUL BOGLE, the lamb who made them need the force
Was used to mix the mortar for the dam that stops our course
The cement was his own black brethren who were the first policemen
And when we reclaim water and cement we will run free again.
But sure.[44]

Notes

1. See Trevor Munroe, 'Bourgeois Idealism and Commonwealth Caribbean Intellectuals,' (Mona: University of the West Indies, 1971); republished in *Jamaican Politics: A Marxist Perspective in Transition*, (Kingston: Heinemann Publishers, 1990), chapter 5.
2. Rupert Lewis, 'Lloyd Best and Epistemic Challenges,' and Anthony Bogues, 'Lloyd Best and the Politics of Epistemic Decolonization,' In *Independent Thought and Caribbean Freedom: Essays in Honour of Lloyd Best*, ed. Selwyn Ryan (St Augustine, Trinidad: Sir Arthur Lewis Institute of Social and Economic Studies, UWI, 2003), 89– 101 and 145–61 respectively. See also, Kirk Meighoo, 'Best and the Radical Caribbean Tradition: Challenges to Race, Episteme and the Vanguard,' *op.cit*, 103–14.
3. In fact, in his closing address to the Conference, Lloyd Best claimed that the Group still exists and is fully engaged in work in Trinidad and Tobago. This raises even more sharply what I referred to above as 'very interesting dynamics.' First, where does the New World Group end and the Tapia House Group begin? Secondly, and, at least equally important, what is the legacy of the New World Group and who owns it?
4. See note 2 above.
5. Cheddi Jagan, *The West on Trial*, (London: Michael Joseph, 1966), 183.
6. Ibid.,184.
7. Ryan, 424.
8. Lloyd Best, Centre for Research on Latin America and the Caribbean, CERLAC Colloquia Paper, April 2004.
9. Ibid. My emphasis – Lloyd was not Guyanese.
10. Alister McIntyre 'Lloyd Best: Reminiscences of the Early Days,' In Ryan, op.cit., 389.
11. Ibid., 392.
12. Ibid., 394.
13. *New World Quarterly* 1 no 1, 22.
14. Ibid., 24.
15. See Raymond T. Smith, *British Guiana*, (Oxford University Press, Royal Institute of International Affairs, 1962).
16. Trevor Munroe, *The Politics of Constitutional Decolonization*, (Mona: Institute of Social and Economic Studies, UWI, 1972).
17. 'Reminiscences,' Ryan, *op.cit.*, 395–6.
18. Walter Rodney, *Moko*, November 15, 1968.
19. George Beckford, to whom copies of *Moko* were sent, immediately decided to bring a similar paper into existence in Jamaica. See, also, David Scott, 'Rupert Lewis: the Dialectic of Defeat,' *Small Axe* 10, (September 2001).
20. It was hilarious, therefore, to sit through Lloyd's closing remarks at the New World conference, Mona, and hear him belabour the regional integration movement for achieving absolutely nothing in the last 50 years.
21. That is, in 1963.
22. See Ryan, op. cit., 406.
23. Ibid.
24. Op. cit., 429.
25. See James Millette, 'Doctrines of Imperial Responsibility,' *New World Quarterly* 2, no. 3, Guyana Independence Issue, (1966): 79–85.
26. Kari Levitt did. In a very important intervention she provided an account of the events that preceded the destruction of the New World Group, and presumably delivered the kabosh to the plantation model. According to

her Best came to the New World group in Montreal and, without warning, declared that he had decided to 'mash up' the New World Group. The audio of the conference proceedings will provide the exact text. The audio should also be consulted for Best's response in his closing remarks to the conference.

27. *Silent Surrender: The Multinational Corporation in Canada*, (Toronto: Macmillan, 1970).
28. See James Millette in Ryan, op.cit., 175–84.
29. Lloyd Best, CERLAC Colloquia paper, (April 2004): 11.
30. Ibid., 8.
31. V.I. Lenin, *A Great Beginning, Selected Works*, vol. 3, (Moscow: Progress Publishers, 1977), 172.
32. See, for example, Lowell Bryan and Diana Farrell, *Market Unbound*, (John Wiley and Sons, 1996); and Richard Falk, *Predatory Globalization*, (Polity Press, 1999).
33. Patrick Bond, 'From Racial to Class Apartheid: South Africa's Frustrating Decade of Freedom' in *Monthly Review Press*, (March 2004): 47.
34. C.L.R. James, whom Best dismisses on occasion and embraces on occasion (see CERLAC paper, 13, 21–2), reminded us in the *Black Jacobins* that race and class questions are ineluctably intertwined. For him, 'The race question is subsidiary to the class question in politics and to think of imperialism in terms of race [or, with Best in mind in terms of "tribes"] is disastrous. But to neglect the racial factor as merely incidental is an error only less grave than to make it fundamental.'
35. Kwame Nkrumah, *Neo-Colonialism, the Last Stage of Imperialism*, (London: Thomas and Nelson, 1965).
36. See Walter Rodney, *How Europe Underdeveloped Africa* (Washington DC: Howard University Press, 1982).
37. Ryan, op.cit., 432–33.
38. Ibid., 438.
39. Ibid., 437–38.
40. Ibid., 432.
41. Ibid., 439.
42. Ibid., 425.
43. Ibid., 424–25.
44. Bongo Jerry, 'Sooner or Later', *Savacou 3/4: New Writing*, (Mona, Kingston 1971).

3 | *Reflections on Intellectuals, the New World Group and Walter Rodney*

David de Caires

I start by offering some thoughts on the role of the intellectual. I will then talk briefly about the New World Group and finally about Walter Rodney.

Intellectuals

First, I suggest that intellectuals must be prepared to accept responsibility for ideas they advance. If, for example, one puts forward the concept that a government is marginalising a section of the population and this leads to hatred, hostility and even bloodshed, one cannot wash one's hands of the matter. The intellectual is not a dilettante, he or she must take his or her job seriously and must not flirt frivolously with ideas as they can and often do have serious consequences in the real world. In a famous lecture delivered at Oxford in 1958 entitled 'Two Concepts of "Liberty"' the scholar Isaiah Berlin noted that the German poet Heine had warned the French not to underestimate the power of ideas and that philosophical concepts nurtured in a professor's study could destroy a civilisation. He said that Heine had described

> ...the works of Rousseau as the blood-stained weapon which in the hands of Robespierre had destroyed the old regime and prophesied that the romantic faith of Fichte and Schelling would one day be turned, with terrible effect, against the liberal culture of the West.[1]

We can think of other intellectuals whose ideas have had devastating consequences. Sooner or later ideas lead to action. There is no more upsetting an experience than to put an idea into currency that one later conceives to be both erroneous and damaging. Intellectuals should be capable of passing judgement on themselves if they have sinned grievously.

Sometimes, too, silence is not an option. When the Ayatollahs pronounced a fatwa against Salman Rushdie for blasphemy, basic principles of free speech were at issue. Regrettably, there was far from universal condemnation among academics and writers for a variety of spurious reasons. There have been assaults on academic freedom in the Caribbean affecting several of our most distinguished scholars like Walter Rodney, Clive Thomas, George Beckford and Norman Girvan. To say nothing on such occasions is unacceptable. Intellectuals should speak out against oppression and injustice anywhere.

Intellectuals sometimes make choices. In the 1930s in Europe, fascism was on the rise in Germany, Italy and Spain. Liberal democracy was under severe threat. The full atrocities of Stalin in the Soviet Union were not yet revealed. Intellectuals made choices. Some fought in the Spanish Civil war on the side of the beleaguered left wing government. The Cambridge spies (Blunt, Burgess and others) betrayed their country to work secretly for the Soviet Union. In extreme situations, agonising choices were made. Even in less desperate times, thinking men and women make commitments, and join movements or political parties.

By contrast, it has been argued that intellectuals have a vocation that should transcend politics and political commitment. In *La Trahison des Clercs* (*The Treason of the Intellectuals*), published in 1927[2] the French essayist Julien Benda criticised what he saw as the betrayal by intellectuals of their vocation. In an article in the *New Criterion*[3] Roger Kimball discussed the issues raised in that book: 'From the time of the pre-Socratics, intellectuals, considered in their role as intellectuals, had been a breed apart.' In Benda's terms, they were understood to be 'all those whose activity essentially is not the pursuit of practical aims, all those who seek their joy in the practice of an art or a science or a metaphysical speculation, in short in the possession of non-material advantages.' Thanks to such men, Benda wrote, 'humanity did evil for two thousand years, but honored good. This contradiction was an honor to the human species, and formed the rift whereby civilization slipped into the world.'

According to Benda, however, this situation was changing. More and more, intellectuals were abandoning their attachment to the traditional panoply of philosophical and scholarly ideals. One clear sign of the change was the attack on the Enlightenment ideal of universal humanity and the concomitant glorification of various particularisms. The attack on the universal went forward in social and political life as well as in the refined precincts of epistemology and metaphysics:

> Those who for centuries had exhorted men, at least theoretically, to deaden the feeling of their differences...have now come to praise them, according to where the sermon is given, for their 'fidelity to the French soul,' 'the immutability of their German consciousness,' for the 'fervor of their Italian hearts.'

In short, intellectuals began to immerse themselves in the unsettlingly practical and material world of political passions; precisely those passions, Benda observed, 'owing to which men rise up against other men, the chief of which are racial passions, class passions and national passions.' The 'rift' into which civilisation had been wont to slip narrowed and threatened to close altogether.

Writing at a moment when ethnic and nationalistic hatreds were again threatening to tear Europe asunder, Benda's diagnosis assumed the lineaments of a prophecy – one that continues to have deep resonance today. 'Our age is indeed the age of the intellectual organization of political hatreds,' he wrote. 'It will be one of its chief claims to notice in the moral history of humanity.' There was no need to add that its place in moral history would be as a cautionary tale. In little more than a decade, Benda's prediction that, because of the 'great betrayal' of the intellectuals, humanity was 'heading for the greatest and most perfect war ever seen in the world,' would achieve a terrifying corroboration.

There is a conflict between the idea of the committed intellectual and the dispassionate seeker after truth. Yet, stated so baldly, it is unrealistic. Intellectuals have never been free of political commitment in some shape or form. The danger must surely be that in their pursuit of political commitment they will abandon ideals of disinterested judgement and faith in the universality of truth, that they will debase traditional principles of intellectual life in the service of politics. It is a problem with which we are familiar in Guyana. Indeed the fault lines of the society have shown ominous cracks and we must at all costs avoid the treacherous paths that have led elsewhere to worst case scenarios including civil war and genocide. Intellectuals surely have a vital role to play in explaining and defusing these conflicts, which are by no means incapable of solution.

The Enlightenment proclaimed a universal, humanising reason, a commitment to the idea that men and women are united by a common humanity that transcends race, ethnicity and gender. I believe we are all, to some extent, children of the Enlightenment though increasingly, one feels, the field of open, untrammelled debate is narrowed by political passions. In this divided world, one must seek some broader, transforming vision. In Guyana, we must aim for an open society of free men and women, a multi-ethnic democratic welfare state based on the rule of law and social justice.

New World Group

The New World Group flourished in the 1960s. It was clearly in some ways a reaction to the challenges posed by political independence. It ceased to exist over 30 years ago. In its time, it published a fortnightly magazine in Guyana and a quarterly magazine in Jamaica. The ideologue of the group, if such a word is appropriate, was Lloyd Best, a Trinidadian economist who did fundamental work with Kari Levitt on a model of the plantation economy. Best rejected metropolitan intellectual and political hegemony. He argued that one must start from one's own realities in constructing models and he resisted the importation of systems constructed in more developed and industrialised countries. Though such systems may contain valuable insights and may in some ways have become part of the common intellectual heritage of mankind, they cannot answer or deal with local problems.

The group sought to reinterpret the region's history, which had been taught all along from the standpoint of the imperial power. All the leading members were committed West Indian integrationists. West Indian unity is, of course, far from being achieved, though there is a slow but gradual progress towards a single market. The fundamental idea of the group, I suggest, was that we should see and interpret the world from our own standpoint rather than see someone else's – we should decolonise our minds.

I have read through the 50 issues of the *New World Fortnightly* magazine, with which I was intimately connected, to prepare for this conference. After a gap of nearly 40 years, I was pleasantly surprised at the independent, irreverent tone of the publication. The format was an editorial, news analysis, a feature, and an arts and culture section. Features included 'Socialism in Guyana' (there were a variety of contributions); the press; the trade union situation; the role of universities in the Caribbean.

New World Quarterly was more academic and its base was the University of the West Indies, Mona Campus. The contributors included some of the brightest members of the first generation of West Indian faculty and graduates of the University of the West Indies including Best, Alister Mcintyre and Clive Thomas. It was edited by George Beckford and Norman Girvan was the Chairman of the Mona group. To quote the introduction of the organisers of the Conference on the Thought of New World, the group 'had a significant role in shaping the Department of Economics at Mona as well as the Institute of Social and Economic Research.' Work by Girvan, Thomas, Havelock Brewster and others gave birth to regional economic integration studies and provided a rationale for the Caribbean Community.

There were special issues to celebrate the independence of Guyana and of Barbados, the first edited by George Lamming and Martin Carter and the second by George Lamming, both of which were very well received.

Walter Rodney

I knew Walter quite well, though not closely. He always struck me as flexible and open-minded. I recall discussing with him, for example, whether it was desirable to keep in the constitution of the Working People's Alliance a statement that it was Marxist-Leninist. I suggested that was not in keeping with a commitment to an open society. Walter had two outstanding qualities that equipped him to make a major contribution to Guyana if he had lived. First, though a radical black intellectual with a deep knowledge of and commitment to Africa and its problems he was above all a Guyanese nationalist, committed to all its people and to a multi-ethnic democracy. There was not an ounce of prejudice or condescension in him. Indeed he was the prototype of that free, intelligent man liberated from the chains of ethnicity that Guyana so badly needs. Secondly, he had a capacity to learn and develop from experience. In the time I knew him, I sensed he was increasingly distilling in his mind the complex realities of Guyana and had achieved a transforming vision. I believe that this is what made him a genuinely popular – even charismatic – political figure, with a wide appeal. He satisfied, I think, many of the criteria for the intellectual that I sought to sketch above.

Notes

1. Isaiah Berlin, 'Two Concepts of Liberty' (lecture, University of Oxford, October 31, 1958).
2. Julien Benda, *The Treason of the Intellectuals* (*La Trahison des Clercs*) translated by Richard Aldington, (W. Morrow & Company, 1928).
3. R. Kimball, 'The Treason of the Intellectuals and the Undoing of Thought' *The New Criterion* 11, no. (?) 1992.

4 | *The Montreal New World Group*

Kari Levitt

The West Indies has a long and historic relationship with Canada. Although the West Indian diaspora in Toronto is now very much larger – and perhaps this was already the case in the 1960s – the roots in Montreal are older and deeper. Generations of West Indians came to McGill University to train as doctors, dentists, nurses, teachers, and many other professions – including Brian Meeks's parents, Corina and Charles Meeks, and Brian was born in Montreal. There was a well-established West Indian community of working class families located downtown, employed as porters, mechanics and in other trades and occupations related to the Canadian railway system, at a time when Montreal was the industrial and commercial capital of Canada. Older generations of this diaspora had links to Garveyite movements. We are reminded of the special attraction of Montreal for Jazz musicians who came to breathe the freer air of Canada in the 1950s; Oliver Jones came and stayed, Oscar Peterson was born and raised there. The Montreal Jazz festival, now in its twentieth year, is the largest in the world. Montreal was and remains the headquarters of the Aluminum Company of Canada, although recently purchased by the British resource and mining giant corporation Rio Tinto. Major Canadian banks, previously located in Montreal, have migrated to Toronto. The study on Canada-West Indies relations authored by Alister McIntyre and myself, with assistance of graduate students, was commissioned by an influential Montreal-based business association.[1]

The Montreal NWG was composed of Caribbean graduate students, mostly studying economics, at McGill University. The story begins in Toronto in December 1960. I was then a graduate student at the University of Toronto, married to a Canadian. I had two children, aged six and eight. One day, shortly before Christmas, Dudley Huggins appeared and asked if he could see me to relay a message from Professor Burton Keirstead who was then spending a sabbatical on the Mona campus at the invitation of his friend Arthur Lewis. I was asked if I could come to assist Professor Keirstead to complete a study he had undertaken for the Federation of the West Indies, about an inter-territorial shipping service. After 13 years in Canada, I was excited at the prospect of a new experience. I got permission from my husband, prepared things for Christmas and off I went. That was my first encounter with the West Indies, first in Jamaica and then in Trinidad.

A few days after I arrived, Arthur Lewis, then Principal of the University, sent for me. He remembered me as Miss Polanyi from my student days at the London School of Economics where he taught the introductory course in Economics. 'We are sending you on a mission to Trinidad,' he said, 'by a West Indian airline, BWIA, flying from one West Indian territory to another, but you have to pass through Puerto Rico.' At that time, that required a full immigration procedure to the US because there were no transit facilities. Bearing in mind my well-known left-wing views from the days of the LSE, he said 'If you have any problems, you may call me.' I thought that was very generous. As it happens, I did have problems. After consulting a fat black book, the immigration officer informed me that I could appear in court on the following day to explain why I wished to immigrate to the United States. I told him I had no desire or intention to enter the United States. I was in transit to Trinidad. He was uncooperative and wished to detain me. I protested and requested a telephone to call the principal of the (then) University College of the West Indies. They thought I was too much trouble and put me back on the plane.

In Trinidad, I was met by Dr Carleen O'Laughlin, Senior Research Fellow of the Institute of Social and Economic Research (ISER). She introduced me to Roy Jones, Eric Armstrong and Frank Dowdy, economists then working for the Federal Government of the West Indies, and to her British yachting buddies at the Pelican Inn. She is remembered for the construction of National Accounts for many of the Leeward and Windward Islands. She surely used colonial statistical records, but it was believed that her preoccupation with making statistical estimates complemented her passion for sailing in the Islands. Dr O'Laughlin complained about a difficult and independent-minded young man who was Chief Economist advising Dr Eric Williams. This triggered my curiosity. I set off to meet William Demas, who became a valued lifetime colleague and friend. My days were spent in the dusty archives of the Furness Withy Shipping Company, and my nights reading West Indian novels under the mosquito net. Many things come to mind. Sugar is back on the agenda. I remember the visual images of the vast areas of cane fields of Caroni, then owned by the Tate and Lyle company, with their staff houses and the Texaco refinery at Point-a-Pierre with the same kind of staff houses and compounds. All of that fed into my later collaboration with Lloyd Best on the sugar plantation as the original economic institution of the West Indies.

When I returned to Canada I shared my newfound interest in the West Indies with fellow graduate students at the University of Toronto – Eugenia Moore, Roy and Ina Thomas, Carl Hall, Victor and Doral Callendar and Leroy Taylor. At the time, I did not imagine that they and so many others would become colleagues and friends in future years.

In the Easter vacation of 1961 I returned to Jamaica to read the proofs of our study on inter-territorial shipping. It was then that I was taken to Lloyd Best's veranda for one of the discussion groups described by Norman Girvan in his excellent opening address here yesterday. I met Lloyd Best, Alister McIntyre, Roy Augier, and a number of other personalities who are dimmer in my memory. Professor Kierstead told me that these were bright young West Indian scholars looking for their place in the sun on a campus still largely staffed by British expatriates.

In September 1961, I was appointed to a position at the Economics Department of McGill University. I was required to teach a variety of courses, but my real interest at that time was in techniques of development planning. I was looking for someone to share my newfound interest in the West Indies and the person I found was Alvin Johnson. I am certain very few of you have heard that name but it is a name that I wish to put on the record. He was a remarkable young man, active and respected in the West Indian community I described earlier in my remarks, a Jamaican who had come to Montreal in the 1950s and worked as a journalist with the then premier English language daily newspaper the *Montreal Star*. Alvin would have had, I am sure, an important career in Jamaican politics, in the PNP I would imagine. He was a mentor and close friend of D.K. Duncan. Together we formed a discussion group, which soon thereafter became the Montreal New World Group.

In 1963, McGill established the Centre for Developing Areas Studies. The three areas selected for study were South Asia, Africa and the Caribbean. Among the first visiting Research Fellows to be invited to the CDAS was William Demas. Four public lectures delivered in 1964 formed the basis of his well-known work, *Economic Development of Small Countries with Special Reference to the Caribbean*. Mr Demas returned to Montreal in 1967 as Visiting Professor at the Economics Department of McGill University.

Among the first recipients of CDAS fellowships were Alvin Johnson, Edwin Carrington (from Tobago) and Hugh O'Neil (from Grenada). Together with Adlith Brown (from Jamaica), Ainsworth Harewood (from Trinidad), Karl Bennett (a Canadian originally from Jamaica), all students of mine at McGill, they formed the heart of the Montreal New World Group (NWG). Other regular members of the NWG included Wilma Augustin and Emelda Rennie (from Trinidad) and Noel Boissiere (from Guyana), who became my principal assistant in the construction of Input-Output tables of the Atlantic provinces at statistics Canada. NWG meetings were open to all. On some occasions there were as many as 25 or 30 people present. We discussed West Indian issues of the day; we read and sold the *New World Quarterly* produced in Jamaica and the pamphlets referred to by Owen Jefferson. We invited interesting personalities to speak to the group, including Cheddi Jagan, C.L.R. James, Osvaldo Sunkel from Chile and Andre Gunder Frank, then teaching at Sir George Williams College (now Concordia University). After Cheddi's visit to our group, which was held at my home, the telephones were monitored. This began in about 1965 and became totally insane by 1969, when virtually all West Indian students in Montreal were under surveillance related to the Sir George Williams affair. We mounted a campaign for the return of George Beckford's passport, including a delegation to the Jamaican High Commission in Ottawa. The purpose was to embarrass the Jamaican government. Canada got to know Jamaica as a place that takes people's passports when they go to Cuba.

In 1964 I obtained a small grant that brought me back to Trinidad for two remarkable days and nights of brainstorming with Lloyd Best and Alister McIntyre. The challenge was to understand how Caribbean economies really worked. The objective was to build a model based on the socio-economic realities of power structures in the region, in order to inform economic planning for transformation. The genesis of it all was the sugar plantation. We recorded our conclusions on a small cassette tape. Regrettably, the tape was lost in a fire in Port of Spain, which destroyed much of Lloyd's library, including documentation and correspondence of the early New World Groups.

In 1966 Lloyd Best and I obtained a two-year grant from the CDAS, with financial assistance from the United Nations Industrial Development Organisation (UNIDO), to undertake a study of 'Externally Propelled Growth and Industrialization in the Caribbean.' Lloyd and his family came to Montreal, I obtained partial release time from teaching and an enormous amount of work was done. I was at that time also engaged in a study of the effect of Foreign Direct Investment on host countries and in directing the work at Statistics Canada. The project was ambitious, with participation by several of my graduate students and a specially commissioned study of the mineral export sector by Norman Girvan, who spent several weeks in Montreal in the summer of 1967. Lloyd was in continuous communication with the Caribbean. We would find ourselves going in Lloyd's Volkswagen down to the central post office at 3:00 am to mail something urgently. It was a most exciting and creative period of intellectual collaboration.

The basic ideas of our work on Plantation Economy were derived from Lloyd's brilliance and insights drawn from his profound reading of West Indian history. My role was to assist in formalising the insights. In 1967 Lloyd presented 'An Outline of a Model of Pure Plantation Economy' to a conference of Caribbean agricultural economists here at Mona, and Lloyd and I jointly presented the accompanying Accounting Framework to a conference of Commonwealth Caribbean Statisticians in Guyana. In the same year, Lloyd accepted a teaching appointment in Puerto Rico and invited Terry Gigantes of Statistics Canada, Adlith Brown and myself to meet with the Puerto Rico Planning Agency in a seminar on economic planning models. In the second year of our rather ambitious McGill project Lloyd was more absent than present, and the full responsibility for direction of the work, including the compilation of work accomplished in four black binders, fell to me.

The NWG was somewhat marginal to the radical currents in the larger community of West Indian student associations at McGill and Sir George Williams College. Its leading personalities were graduate students preparing for professional careers in the Caribbean as public servants, lecturers and researchers at the UWI. The influence of Lloyd Best and his frequent presence in Montreal, connections with New World Groups in Jamaica and Trinidad and the participation of many leading New World people in our research project, gave the NWG an intellectual rather than activist character. While two of our New World members, Alvin Johnson and Hugh O'Neil, assisted in the preparation of the Montreal West Indian Conference of 1966, the conference was initiated by a more radical group of West Indians. The mentor of the Conference Committee, established in 1965, was C.L.R. James. Leading members of the Conference Committee included Alfie Roberts, Robert Hill, Tim Hector, Franklin Harvey, Raymond Watts and Alan Brown. The keynote speakers at the Conference were C.L.R. James and George Lamming. It was here that Lloyd Best delivered his well-known lecture on 'Independent Thought and Caribbean Freedom,' reprinted in the *New World Quarterly* in 1967. When the conference was over, Alvin and Hugh returned some art objects to Toronto. On the way back, a high wind overturned the Volkswagen they were driving. Both were killed in that tragic accident.

The Conference Committee was active in the later organisation of the Black Writer's Conference in 1968. The venue was the McGill student union, and Rosie Douglas, President of the McGill West Indian Students Association, played an important role in its organisation. It was not an accident that this important event, which brought together leading intellectual and political figures of the West Indies from England, the US and the Caribbean, was held in Montreal. Montreal in the 1960s was a very special place and 1968 was a very special year the world over – Paris, Prague, Mexico, and Montreal. As you all know, Walter Rodney was barred from re-entry to Jamaica. The Rodney riots radicalised the political scene on the Mona Campus. New World was marginalised and within four years the quarterly ceased publication.

Less well known was the role of the Black Writers' Conference in inspiring a radical group at Sir George Williams College. They escalated charges of racial discrimination in marking into a major confrontation with the administration. The subsequent occupation of a computer centre resulted in showers of computer cards floating from the top floor of the Hall building and, eventually, a fire and the arrest of hundreds of students, West Indian and Canadian, including Rosie Douglas and a score or more of Trinidadian students. There was a fear that West Indian students would be harshly dealt with by Canadian authorities. The government of Trinidad provided its citizens with legal support. Many of us were involved in raising bail money and I led a delegation of parents and black faculty to Ottawa to warn that if justice was not done and seen to be done, there could be consequences for Canadian investments and property in the region. Students barred a Canadian dignitary from entering the Campus in Trinidad and there were demonstrations in Port of Spain outside the Royal Bank. I was in Trinidad in 1970 when the returning students were celebrated by the Black Power demonstrators.

In 1968 the NWG produced an important issue of the *New World Quarterly*. At Lloyd's insistence, it included my 'Economic Dependence and Political Disintegration: The Case of Canada,' later significantly expanded and published as *Silent Surrender: The Multi-National Corporation in Canada* in 1970. In the context of the nationalisation of ALCAN's facilities in Guyana, Prime Minister Forbes Burnham ordered copies for his entire cabinet. The government of Canada was not pleased.

It was in 1968 at a formal meeting of the NWG of Montreal, that Lloyd announced his intentions to terminate the New World Group of Trinidad, which had become a significant political force under the leadership of James Millette. For all of us who were present – Edwin Carrington, Ainsworth Harewood, Noel Boissiere, Adlith Brown, Wilma Augustin, among others – it was an unforgettable moment. Lloyd came with a large briefcase and a strange look on his face. He had a prepared statement. He explained why he had concluded that New World had become an obstacle to the purpose for which it was founded and all I can tell you is that all of us were in a state of total and complete shock. We were speechless and totally surprised. He announced that he would start all over again by founding economic and educational institutions, including a newspaper, and a political movement, which became Tapia. All of this he did indeed achieve.

I must tell you that after that I did not join Tapia, I decided that I would maintain my independence and continue my work. I appreciate Lloyd's achievements, particularly the *Trinidad and Tobago Review*, which is an excellent and valuable publication, but I repeat that I have stood by my decision of intellectual independence. By 1969 the Montreal NWG was no more. A number of students returned to the Caribbean in that year and I myself left Montreal to serve as technical advisor to the Government of Trinidad and Tobago in the construction of a system of national accounts for use in planning.

Lloyd believes that I have never forgiven him for terminating New World. Not so. In historical perspective, it is my considered opinion that political events simply overcame New World. What happened in Jamaica had little to do with Lloyd's decision. Black Power in Trinidad and Marxism in Jamaica had seized the imagination and commitment of a generation of younger people.

Looking back on those days in Montreal, which were very wonderful days, and full of hope, commitment and friendships, I believe that the most important legacy of the Montreal New World Group was the work which Lloyd and I began, but failed to complete until 2006. In 1969, Lloyd announced, and repeated over the next 30 years, that the completion and publication of the work was not a priority. His priority was in the building of Tapia and other institutions in Trinidad and Tobago. My priority was otherwise. I believed, and continue to believe, that the insights of the Best-Levitt work on Plantation Economy are profound and important to an understanding of Caribbean economy and society. I am an academic and an educator, and I wanted to complete the work and make it available to young West Indian students. My intention was to continue the work through a Canadian International Development Agency (CIDA) funded position at ISER in Trinidad from 1969 to 1971. When my proposed appointment disappeared by intervention from Ottawa, I accepted the invitation of William Demas to work on a statistical database for a national plan for Trinidad and Tobago. The next opportunity to continue the work came in 1974, when I was Visiting Professor at the Institute of International Relations, Trinidad. For the next 25 years, no further progress was made.

In the year 2000, Lloyd obtained funds from the Caribbean Development Bank and I spent five winters at the Trinidad and Tobago Institute, in working on the unfinished manuscript.[2] I believe that this is an intellectual legacy of importance. I believe in intellectual legacies. When I was in Jamaica as George Beckford Professor I spent a full year in collecting George Beckford's works, published as *The George Beckford Papers* by the UWI press. That has been my goal, and it has been a rewarding one, and it has only been possible because of the sort of support, the moral support and the friendship I have received all these years, in Jamaica, in Trinidad, from the West Indian community, for which I thank you.

A last word: the New World movement was seized by the belief that political decolonisation had to be followed by economic transformation to achieve economic decolonisation on our own terms, free from influence of metropolitan theories or mimicry of metropolitan values. Looking back on those times, peopled by the extraordinary number of remarkable individuals that Norman listed in his introductory remarks, including Arthur Lewis, who became the principal target of our critique, the discourse on economic development was more free and open than it is today. The World Bank and IMF had not yet assumed the institutional monopoly they now exercise over development theory and policy. In the 1980s, independent thought went into deep retreat. The structuralist tradition of West Indian economists was marginalised by a younger generation of academics returning from North American universities as converts to neo-classical economics. In the 1990s, globalisation became accepted as an irreversible phenomenon closing options on independent paths of development. In many ways there has been a profound regression; the culture of intellectual mimicry and the embrace of metropolitan values are more profound than 30 years ago. History, however, is replete with surprises. In the years to come, I have no doubt that future generations will rise to the opportunities and challenges presented by the natural and cultural wealth of the entire Caribbean region. I am reminded of the words of George Beckford:

> ...for the full realisation of this great potential, we need to come together as one Caribbean nation. Then, and only then, will we be in a position to be fully independent, sovereign and free to transform what is physically the most beautiful place on earth into a human paradise![3]

Notes

1. Kari Levitt and Alister McIntyre, *Canada-West Indies Economic Relations*, (Montreal: Canada Trade Committee, Private Planning Association and Centre for Developing Areas Studies, McGill University, 1967), 174.
2. The work was finally published in 2009 as *Essays on the Theory of Plantation Economy: An Institutional and Historical Approach to Caribbean Economic Development*.

3.   George Beckford. 'Sovereignty and Self-Reliance' reproduced in Kari Levitt ed. *The George Beckford Papers: Selected and Introduced by Kari Levitt*. (Mona: UWI Press, 2000).

5 | *The Long Transition:*
Thinking Ourselves through Change of Our Circumstances

Vaughan A. Lewis[1]

On returning to the Caribbean in 1968, to teach at the Mona, Jamaica campus of the University of the West Indies after an absence in the United Kingdom of nearly ten years, I found myself at the cross-section of three initiatives. These were largely emanating from the English-speaking Caribbean but they sought to encompass the wider Caribbean area, for which I prefer to use the nomenclature of the Antilles. These initiatives were the establishment of the New World Group led by Lloyd Best, a classical, multilingual Antillean man; the Caribbean Studies Association, in practice initiated from an academic grouping from the wider area; and the Association of Caribbean Universities, led from our Anglophone side by the doyen and UWI Vice-Chancellor Phillip Sherlock.

In those days – the late 1960s – the Trinidad and Tobago airline, BWIA, criss-crossed the Anglophone Caribbean, taking in Puerto Rico as well. Connections could also be made with relative ease through ALM, the Netherlands Antilles airline, into the Dutch-speaking islands and down to Suriname. Air Jamaica subsequently started plying the route to Haiti; and LIAT connected the Eastern Caribbean islands to the French dependencies and Puerto Rico, permitting, in turn through BWIA, a connection between Jamaica and the French Antilles.

All this meant that conferences on Caribbean issues, and occasional and sundry academic encounters could be arranged with minimal difficulty. Many of us, including persons like myself with an active interest in the New World Group and the CSA, took full advantage of such matching transportation facilities, the like of which hardly exist today. We got to know our counterparts in the French, Spanish, and Dutch 'parishes' well, and to communicate frequently. I speak of a bygone age.

On the other hand, in the pre-independence period, formal communication between the Anglophone Caribbean territories and the states of South America was largely through an intermediary, the United Kingdom.

So while there has long been a tradition of 'people communication' through migration, to Central America and Venezuela in particular, there was no substantial tradition of government-to-government communication, even as we proceeded through the graduated 'stages of self-government' prescribed by the British as their pre-requisite to our independence,[2] nor had there been much elite-political to elite-political communication. To go ahead of myself a little, I might observe that the consequence of this deficiency is evident, for example, in the present issue surrounding Brazil's appeal to the WTO on the European Union's sugar subsidies and Europe's general preference system – as the Caribbean has waited virtually till the decision on the case has been handed down to initiate diplomatic action with that country.

Much the same, it might also be said, has been the case with Venezuela's signing of maritime agreements with the major North Atlantic powers with jurisdiction in the Caribbean Sea in the 1970s, using Aves Island in the north-east Caribbean as a departure point. Even when Dominica had to face this issue in the 1980s, as she sought to sign a fisheries delimitation agreement with France, hardly anything was done by CARICOM governments. Our Heads of Government have been left to make tardy protestations in the 1990s.

This tradition of non-communication, or minimal formal communication, has tended to remain, unless specific countries (Trinidad and Tobago, Guyana, Belize) have had to urgently deal with problems borne of close physical proximity to the South-Central American mainland.

The New World Group, the Caribbean Studies Association and the Association of Caribbean Universities can all be seen, from one angle, as efforts to remedy this deficiency, and the false confidence that it bred as to the superiority of the political culture models that we had inherited from our particular metropole. After all, in the 1960s, Venezuela had recently emerged from a long period of dictatorship. France, the metropole of the dependencies in our area, was only beginning to stabilise itself from the perpetual governmental changes of the Fourth Republic and the near civil war emanating from her attempts to come to terms with the Algerian insurgency. Furthermore, for those who knew about it, the system of proportional representation which the

Dutch Antilles had inherited from the 'culturally pluralist' Holland, was deemed to be definitely inferior to what we had, particularly after its application in Guyana.

In that context, the confidence of the Anglophone intelligentsia, which had begun to inherit power, was unparalleled. At the governmental level, they had proven themselves fully capable of mastering the various stages of self-government: accepting the significance of the rule of law and the subjection of governance institutions to law, and the importance of the independence of the legal system from political influence under the conditions of universal suffrage. That many had been trained as barristers or solicitors reinforced this appearance of both practical and psychological adherence to metropolitan canons of government. Who remembers now that, in taking the route of federation, we accepted something called Dominion Status as a last, lingering stage on the way to independence. Yet who, on the other hand, at that time, could meaningfully explain its significance and necessity to the populations, except to inform us that the admirable Canada was a Dominion?

On the other hand, the British Trades Union Congress, through its practical assistance to the emerging post-war Caribbean trade union movements, had again set particular parameters for the operation of these systems. These blended British approaches to conciliation with the emerging worker radicalism, creating an effective linkage between working class leaders and the political intelligentsia,[3] take the form of social democracy rather than Marxism-Leninism.

The sole area of lack of self-confidence for full self-government lay in a concern about the relationship between size of country and effective self-government. However, this was qualified by a countervailing sentiment of nationalism that had been emerging in Jamaica since the early 1930s, one which for a short time, however, was to subordinate itself to the more dominant concern about size.

Later we came to understand more clearly that the commitment of the emerging political class to federalism as an antidote to the size problem, was not simply our own specific concern; but the metropolitan powers' way of ensuring a modicum of international order and security in the Cold War environment, in areas which came under their jurisdiction but which they were committed to releasing. This concern for regional order and security as a basis for international order was uppermost in the minds of the new Great Power, the United States, and both the British and the French, in fact, applied it irrespective of size of territory. In that regard we can look at the desperate efforts of France to knit its huge territories in West and Central Africa into federal systems, matching similar efforts by the United Kingdom in the rest of the continent and elsewhere, most successfully in India.

With respect to this issue of the relationship between size and economic development, the early post-war creation of the Caribbean Commission provided what seemed to be an avenue towards a solution, through the socialisation of the emerging Caribbean leadership into the history of the apparently successful economic development process in Puerto Rico. This had been legitimised, for the Anglophone Caribbean, by the powerful advocacy of Arthur Lewis. Also, the acceptance of the strategy seemed widespread over the multi-lingual Caribbean indicated as it was in the close relationships that had developed between the intellectual Lewis, the then intellectual Eric Williams, the emerging politicians like Norman Manley and the philosopher and practitioner of the 'Puerto Rican Model,' Teodoro Moscoso and his Governor, Muñoz Marín.

At the time, few understood the critical significance of what today we would describe as the integration of Puerto Rico into the wider economic space of the United States of America – a kind of free trade area of those two different Americas – large and small – with instruments for facilitating that integration through a recognition of what we would today call the need for 'special and differential treatment.' The model was attractive because it sought to lead the territories into the needed path of industrialisation (for which larger size/population had been deemed a necessary prerequisite), and not to protect old agriculture. The Puerto Rican system (the price of which was, of course, a limited political autonomy) was well chronicled in the early 1960s by Professor Gordon Lewis, a Welshman then teaching at the University of Puerto Rico, and a frequent traveller and lecturer throughout the West Indies.[3]

Few at that time too, noticed the caveat that Arthur Lewis had put into his 'Industrialisation of the British West Indies:'[4] that the establishment of a customs union (not simply a free trade area), was an absolute pre-requisite to the practical functioning of the model that he was recommending. He well knew that a customs union required what a free trade arrangement did not – the establishment of instruments that would ensure a degree of policy coordination among the territories – and that this would require an institutional commitment to some blending of the decision-making structures of the separate islands – what some in CARICOM pejoratively interpret today as the diminution of sovereignty issue.

The intermediate political-cum-intellectual generation that established the Caribbean Free Trade Area (CARIFTA), in effect, fudged this issue of the policy and institutional implications of an acceptance of customs union. Perhaps the fact that we had become psychologically attuned to the philosophy of 'stages' at the political level induced its easy acceptance at the economic level. Indeed if they had noticed, they had not attributed any importance to the British attempt, in the late 1950s, to convert the strategy of Monnet and the European integrationists from customs union/common market into one of the creation of an initial free trade area so that the British could, in particular, maintain 'sovereignty.' For the British, the supremacy of Parliament could not be compromised; nor could Britain's control over external economic policy – that is to say, the country's leverage over their particular system of twentieth century mercantilism even as their colonies became independent states. However, few in the Caribbean noticed, or bothered to notice also, that even before we started on the path to a free trade area in 1965, the British had decided to abandon the substitute European Free Trade Area (EFTA), which they had established, and sued for peace to join the European Common Market.

In the Caribbean, as we know, what emerged in response to the prevailing opinion that a free trade area was the way to go, was a counter-intelligentsia in and around the University of the West Indies (later more familiar as the New World Group) that developed a new thesis. This proposed a direct move to what was called 'production integration' as against 'free trade integration,' and stressed the significance of institutional arrangements appropriate to the cohesive policy planning that this alternative form of integration would require. The thesis implied a change of political institutions appropriate to this new regionalism. For allied to this was a holistic view of the region, assumed to be necessary to achieve the size and scale implied in their approach to industrialisation. Regional production integration was seen, in other words, as the sine qua non of Caribbean integration.[5]

Indeed there had already begun to emerge a critique of the 'Puerto Rican model' and consequentially a critique of Lewis's 'industrialization by invitation;' and in the socio-political sphere the early policy work and political writing of Best and others on Guyana had begun to open eyes to the political and institutional significance of pluralism – a significance whose understanding our Dutch-speaking Caribbean colleagues could have facilitated, were it not for the absence of linkages between the various higher education institutions in the multi-lingual Caribbean. (The seminal article by Miles Fitzpatrick and David de Caires – 'Twenty Years of Politics in our Land' – published in the Special Issue of the New World Group's journal to commemorate Guyana's independence clearly signalled – at least for me – the potential difficulties ahead for that country deriving from this pluralism).

To my mind, it is the emergence of difference between the post-Lewis/Williams intellectual/policy advising generation (let us call them the Demas generation) and the younger scholars now inhabiting mainly the University of the West Indies over the issue of regional integration, that came to consolidate the basis for fundamental critique of both the economic and political models adopted by the Caribbean political leadership and wider intelligentsia towards and after independence.

For the discussion in the second half of the 1960s over the nature of the economic integration process that we should implement brought together the following issues: (a) the type of economic integration to be pursued; (b) the extent of mutual concessions of sovereignty required to pursue this economic integration; (c) the relationship between the political institutions of the national community and the policy-making and implementation ('political') institutions of the integration system; (d) the nature of the channels of influence, surveillance and control of the populace over the integration institutions; (e) the accountability of political institutions to the people; and (f) the relative responsibilities and accountabilities of the national community political systems and the regional quasi-political institutions – all these classical questions of political science were now brought to the fore, sometimes explicitly, sometimes implicitly.

By the rejection of the concept of federation, and later in the 1990s, the somewhat contradictory simultaneous acceptance of 'single market and economy' on the one hand, and 'community of sovereign states' on the other (imitating the literal words but not the functional meaning given to them by the European Union), the political/intellectual leadership sought to avoid the resolution of the issues I have just outlined. The post-1960s new intelligentsia – largely economics oriented (I say this while noting Best's full comprehension of the significance of 'politics'), tended to elide these issues somewhat also, and to stress, in Beckford's words (verbal, to me) the pre-eminence of 'function over form' (reminiscent of course of the poet's lines: 'For forms of government let fools contest, Whate'er is best administered is best').

However, as the latest political imbroglio involving the (non)approval of the Union Constitution in Europe indicates, these issues/questions concerning form of human political interaction do not go away, as the motive forces inducing economic integration on a regional basis emerge and re-emerge from different structural conditions, over time.

For the post-war generation, the nature of their understanding of the wider international structures existing at the time of the countries' independence at the beginning of the 1960s, indicates the strength of their metropolitan intellectual inheritance. First, no one seemed to challenge 'Dominion Status' as a necessary last colonial stop before the grant of independence to the new Federation obstructing in particular, a rising Jamaican nationalism ready to proceed to some form of independence.

Secondly, the influence that the movement towards European regional integration would have on Britain's role as an apparent independent arbiter in world affairs, and consequentially as guarantor of, and intermediary for, the Anglophone Caribbean's international economic location and objectives, went largely unnoticed. This was not entirely odd, to the extent that the British, though prodded by Macmillan, were refusing to notice it as well). Jamaican Minister of Trade Robert Lightbourne's admonition to Macmillan's government that Britain should provide the West Indies with 'bankable assurances' as to the security of the protection of our agricultural exports after entry into the Common Market, well illustrates the point. (Though it is fair to observe that by 1967 Eric Williams, was warning that the sun was indeed setting on that system, and that what the subsequent French rejection of Britain's application to the European Community simply meant was that a little more breathing space for adjustment and change had been fortuitously provided to the Caribbean).

Thirdly, the Cold War and the American insistence that there were only two geopolitical and ideological columns in the world, and that the Caribbean, given their location, should line up appropriately, provided, for most of the leadership in both political and intellectual life in our region, definitive parameters for acting and thinking as to the future orientation of the area. This was of course not peculiar to our region. As the emerging records show, however, the extent of American insistence in 1962–63 to the British, at a time of Cuban defection from one column to the other, that there was to be no leeway for radical government in Guyana – elected or not – would have been well felt by the Caribbean leadership.

The debate induced by the New World Group, with its hints of new forms of politics and government to match alternative notions of economics, partially broke open the discussion on options for a Caribbean inhibited by the dominating geopolitical-ideological structures in the hemisphere. The debate was not an isolated one in the sense that it did have a certain reference in the New Left discussions that had gained a prominence in British socialist intellectual circles and in the wider European continent. In Latin America too, the evolution of a fundamental critique associated with the UN Economic Commission for Latin America was, as Girvan has observed, a running parallel current to what was occurring in the Caribbean.[6]

We might, however, cover a lot of ground briefly if we say that by the time that the New World intellectuals had reached the political kingdom (particularly in Jamaica, but also with Burnham's use of state-led development and management), recession not only in the Caribbean but in Latin America, put paid to any ability on their part to implement some of the writing that had been undertaken in the 1960s and early 1970s. Prepared as they thought they might have been by Best's invocation of the necessity for prior and proper intellectual preparation – 'thought is the action for us'[7] – domestic economic disorganisation and negative external conditions (gyrations in commodity prices and increasing hostility from the United States) closed the political space for effective policy action.

So the alternative thought of the New World Group and allied actors had failed, where its representatives had had a partial political presence, to effect an alternative economic schema to the prevailing school of thought/practice of the 1960s – the partial implantation of the 'industrialisation by invitation' orientation. (True, by this time, the New World tendency had already split into somewhat different island streams – the Best/Millette controversy – diminishing in some measure the regional resonance of the school – as the issue of the priorities to be attached to thought versus practice began to take precedence in the discussions of the Group, particularly in reference to the issue of intervention in party politics in a then socially agitated Trinidad).

In addition, by the mid-1970s a newer generation of university thinkers reinforced the strain in the group (particularly in Jamaica) that emphasised that the time for practice had indeed come, by attaching to their revisionist thinking – if not putting at the centre of it – a populist/ Marxist orientation strengthened by the increasing salience of Cuba in Caribbean and Third World relations. That particular struggle had its denouement first in the New Jewel Movement's victory in Grenada, and then in the demise of the People's Revolutionary Government there, drawing the United States into active interventionism in the Anglophone Caribbean for the first time (active as against its indirect intervention in Guyana in the early 1960s).

We might therefore note in this era too, the results of the attempt to offer in the Caribbean (i) alternative formulations for political structures in the region; and (ii) alternative external relations orientations to those deriving from the modernisation of plantation economy ('the new mercantilism'), or its wider Latin American variant of dependency.

New World, while criticising the political and constitutional arrangements deriving from Crown Colony domination and its variants, had not proposed a definitive alternative, though discussions on constitutional reform in Trinidad and Tobago after the 1970 revolt there had induced proposals for more populist or 'bottom up' systems. In Jamaica, the Marxist tendency brought about more orthodox Leninist structures of organisation, largely anathema to the original New Worldists, though that tendency came to be emphasised in the writing of the Moko group in Trinidad, then seen as a New World deviation.

It was, however, the New Jewel Movement of Grenada which put a distinctive alternative on the agenda – the concept of 'Assemblies of the People.' The argument of the Movement was that through this political form, it would be possible to properly emphasise the necessity for continuing accountability of people to government, an emphasis deemed to be a distinct deficiency of the inherited Westminster model. However, as in Jamaica, the continuing tussle between a populist emphasis in political management, and the more centralist, Leninist strain, led to unbearable tensions leading to self-destruction.[8]

We say 'as in Jamaica,' because we should note that with the arrival of the Manley government in Jamaica, an opportunity arose for those with different notions of accountability in government from the orthodox Westminster type, to resurrect strains of social democratic thinking prevalent in the British Labourism on which the Peoples National Party (PNP) had historically leaned. The attempt to introduce forms of, what was in effect, Guild Socialism and cooperative movement thinking, while maintaining the outward forms of British parliamentarism, took the ideological form of a distinction between 'social democracy' and 'democratic socialism.' This emphasised the bringing into active participation in the workings of the economy – in addition to their trade union presence – the Jamaican working class.

Suffice it to say that, though running successfully on a platform of democratic socialism in the 1976 elections, the PNP cannot be said to have had practical success in embedding its philosophy into any institutional rearrangement of the state. This became particularly evident as concern with economic recession began to take precedence over ideological questions, and the Government was forced to lean on alliances with the socialist bloc which, as we have seen, caused disorganisation both in the state's domestic and external arrangements, and the government's management of them.

It is, today, probably in Trinidad and Tobago that discussion of 'thought as action' and preparation for action most prominently goes on concerning issues of political and constitutional reform. Here the inspiration is what is taken by some to be the increasing rigidity of race relations and its effect on participation of the various ethnic groups in the management of the state's affairs (though cynics might say participation in the division of the oil and gas spoils). The problem of political stasis, evident in Guyana over many decades now, would appear to be raising its head in Trinidad, a country more narrowly ethnically divided than Guyana, and one in which the availability of wealth at the national level does not appear to ease the wheels of political management.

Suffice it to say that, in my view, what appears on the surface as an emerging struggle among ethnicities in fact reflects the inability of the state to cope with a large degree of social deprivation that does itself not, at the mass level, distinguish between ethnicities; and a failure to cope with the consequences of the disintegration of plantation economy most evident now in the demise of the sugar industry and the popular insecurity deriving therefrom. Indeed the political instabilities arising in the period around the 1970 revolt to the 1990 coup d'état in that country cannot be said to have reflected ethnic/racial tensions among the predominant groups.

The dual recessions in the Caribbean and Latin America also diminished an effort on the part of the central political actors in the region to rethink the issue of the best institutional-cum-political channels through which external relations options might be exercised. At the beginning of the 1970s, the new Jamaican government of Manley had attempted to redefine the boundaries of a wider Caribbean in which the Anglophone Caribbean should be a leading participant and shaper. A certain commonality of view among the two main political parties indeed placed Jamaica at the centre of a Circum-Caribbean that would seek to be an effective actor in the hemisphere. Wider instruments and objectives, like the pursuit of a New International Economic Order (NIEO) advocated by Jamaica under Manley, sought the cooperation of the Latin American countries bordering the Caribbean Sea (Venezuela, Mexico), and through them, the cooperation of other similarly oriented countries like Peru and Argentina.

At that time, the 1970s, the commodity price explosion had given these countries, and particularly Peru, for example, a certain autonomy and flexibility to experiment with new ideas for domestic political organisation and for redefinition of the structures of international economic relations in which they were involved.

Paradoxically, while these orientations also matched a road being taken by Guyana, for perhaps more specific geopolitical and viability reasons, they came to evoke a negative reaction from Trinidad and Tobago, the other leading actor of the CARICOM Region. Briefly we might say that they seemed to Eric Williams to distort the Caribbean search for a specific identity for the Antilles and the Guyanas located in their particular histories as types of plantation economy, the specific implantation of their peoples giving them a particular character and cultural mission distinct from that of other New World peoples in the hemisphere, and in turn emphasising this sub-region as capable of a certain diplomatic autonomy and identity within the wider hemisphere.

Williams's views can be particularly observed in his fulminations against Venezuela in the second half of the 1970s, in response to Jamaica and Guyana's attempt to match a CARICOM production integration scheme with one linking those two countries with Mexico and Venezuela.[9]

In the short run, however, this difference of view, made loudly public, led, for the better part of the late 1970s into the mid-1980s, to a paralysis of CARICOM diplomatic relations, reinforced by the creeping economic stagnation induced by recession in the hemisphere as a whole.

The Latin American response to its 'lost decade' of recession coincided with a developing hegemony in ideas about economic reform defined and sustained in the first half of the 1980s and after by the leading metropolitan countries, the United Kingdom and the United States. The complex of ideas summed up in the phrase 'Washington Consensus' came to dominate the ideas of the original counter-revolution of the NIEO. The concept of 'economic integration into the global economy' came to prevail over the notion of the need to reverse the reality of 'dependency integration into the world economy' or world system.

The effective subordination of Latin American countries to the Washington Consensus was marked by Mexico's decision to move towards the opening of its economy, acceptance of the rules of the GATT trading regime, and then integration into the world economy through integration with its most prominent participant, the United States, in the North American Free Trade Area (NAFTA). Mexico now came to be defined not simply as a Latin American country, but as a North American country, as its geography had actually dictated.

Mexico carried out this policy of external economic reorientation and domestic economic reform on the basis of a highly centralised political and administrative system (a de facto one-party state). Control over popular reaction was capable of being maintained as the policies were being pursued, though the PRI ruling regime knew that a certain democratic reform of the state (a change of mode of governance in the new language of the Washington Consensus) was a de facto conditionality of the economic reform.

In the early to mid-1980s and onwards in Jamaica and Guyana, and then in Trinidad and Tobago in the late 1980s to 1990s, this Washington orientation to economic organisation and governance became similarly dominant, overwhelming and subordinating local theorising about economic growth and political order.

However, as most countries in the hemisphere and the Caribbean felt themselves required to follow suit, while operating within more open and democratic political systems, this course of action proved more difficult. The experience that well indicates this was that of Venezuela, led by the end of the 1980s decade once again by Carlos Andres Perez, an advocate in the 1970s of the NIEO and state-led economic reform. Coming into office during recession on a promise of better times, Andres Perez undertook what appeared to his constituents to be a somersault in accepting the Washington Consensus programme. He consequently found himself the subject of an attempted military coup – the first since Venezuela's return to representative democracy in 1958. (Venezuela had been, since that time, a significant hemispheric member of the Socialist International that stressed representative democracy as an inescapable aspect of good governance, and had been the leader of efforts to create an effective SI movement, including Jamaica, in the wider Caribbean area).

The political/social disruption resulting from that period of commitment to structural adjustment economic reform within an open democratic regime, reverberates into the present period with continuing debate in Venezuela about appropriate political and constitutional forms – in effect reviving our debates of the 1970s.

A similar occurrence affected Trinidad and Tobago, operating relatively similar institutions (the parliamentary regime) to Venezuela. The notion that 'national unity' – defined as unity of the races through the instrument of the newly created National Alliance for Reconstruction – could provide a political basis for substantive economic reform, proved to be false. Here an effort was made towards ending the traditional role of the Trinidad state through the extensive use of financial resources for major improvements in education, access to health and the creation of state-financed economic institutions. Instead the new thrust was a structural adjustment of the economy towards, as we have earlier indicated, international competitiveness. Also, implicit in this was the ending of the role of the state as the guarantor of the British-type trade union regime as a protector of the rights of the working class.

This strategy did not count on the social effects of such substantial changes. For the result in Trinidad and Tobago in 1990, as in Venezuela, was revolt; not by the military but by the only class feeling itself unencumbered enough to revolt – the underclass or proletariat – this time (unlike in 1970) appearing in the religious guise of the Jamat al Muslimeen.

It has been argued that the economic agonies imposed in this period on Trinidad and Tobago were justified in the result – a certain competitiveness of its economy vis-à-vis other Caribbean economies. Yet it cannot now, in my view, be said that the relative national prosperity of the country is a function of the structural adjustment programmes, so much as it is a function of a new upswing, in the traditional way, of plantation economy's exploitation of a natural resource. A substantial portion of the state's financial reward is used to reward the underclass for its present quietism – in exchange for their daily grant of bread. This phenomenon is replicated all over our region, today whether from financial resources fortuitously derived from within, or from the new manna from without – the World Bank's Poverty Reduction and similar funds.

So in summary, with the failure of the counter-revolution of ideas in the late 1970s and early 1980s, no effective response as to the path to combined economic and social development has really been forthcoming. We tend to hold the rapidity of economic growth of countries in other parts of the world to be a function of different cultural conditions and attitudes. The pace of growth of small countries like our own, with original economic and social indices not dissimilar to our own, but growing without the 'special and differential treatment' that we claim, is, as in the case of Singapore for example, waved away on the grounds that autocratic rule is a critical variable in such success – as if our own Guyana did not have its share of prolonged autocratic rule.

So a 'passive incorporation' of the prevailing ideas of the Washington Consensus has come to reign. Few draw the conclusion that the relative success of a country like Barbados, in terms of the educational character of its population pushing it towards human resources' use as a beneficial substitute for a deficiency of natural resources, is in part due to decisions taken long ago. A significant one for example, was the insistence in the 1950s/1960s on the importance of family planning, against the grain of a hostile prevailing orthodoxy in most of our region. The point we make here is that a large part of that country's relative success in economic terms has been a function of decisions taken from within, and not under external constraint.

So we might say, by way of summary of this discussion so far, that a certain insularity of ideas prevails in our region today. Discussions of reforms appear in terms specific to a particular country, except where the international institutions advise that they have universal application. In large measure, policy discussion on the forward movement of the integration process is stagnant, in the sense that even the initiatives towards a Single Market and Economy have little holistic timetabled, programmatic content.

In the meantime, with the exception of one or two countries, external conditions turn against us with a vengeance. External influences inducing rearrangement of our immediate regional environment abound; and we are left to ask, like Robert Lightbourne in the 1960s, for the modern-day equivalents of bankable assurances, and more time, to play for time, to adjust.

Recentring the CARICOM Caribbean

Those of us who had the opportunity, as political technocrats or politicians, of putting thought into action at varying times in this period of review since independence, saw – in my case from my particular vantage point at the Organisation of Eastern Caribbean States from the early 1980s into the mid-1990s and then a brief period as prime minister – how a certain geopolitical isolation was being forced on us by dramatic, unanticipated changes in the private and public multilateral arrangements to which we had become accustomed.

In the case of the OECS countries, the combined challenge of the United States-Chiquita-Dole-Latin American states to the new banana regime proposed as counterpart to the new Single Market and Economy regime of the European Community, indicated clearly that the prolonged mercantilist rule of the United Kingdom – independently or through the EC – as guarantor of our economic place in the world, was coming to an end. As I have written elsewhere, we, who had had ingrained in us the importance of observing the number one rule of Western international relations, *pacta sunt servanda*, (agreements made are expected to be kept) came to understand that it meant nothing if the place of the strong was threatened by new forces for global economic regime change.

I recall indicating to some colleagues at the time that the days of the sugar regime were similarly numbered. However, they felt that the breaking of *pacta sunt servanda* applied only to the European obligations in respect of the banana regime, and not to the sugar regime which was not part of the Lomé Convention.

In the course of dealing with the banana issue, we at the OECS got a taste of the complexities of dealing with our neighbouring hemispheric countries as we sought to persuade the banana producing states of South-Central America to accept the changes wrought by the European Union on behalf of our small entities with small volumes of production. We temporarily split the coalition between the Latin American states and the multinationals – only to find out about the complexity of a relationship involving them – and the American Congress as a locus of multinational lobbying, and therefore involving the powerful government of the United States.

This experience gave us a strong sense of the extent of our isolation from our neighbours and our lack of understanding of the depth and complexity of the relationships of their governments and their domestic political systems with the American political process. This lack of understanding and familiarity existed even though we had been, together with them since 1981, participants in the Caribbean Basin Initiative process; and even though we knew mentally of the historically deep involvement of the United States in the non-Anglophone Greater Antilles. The depth of that relationship is indicated today in the relative ease with which the United States has negotiated a free trade arrangement with Central America and the Dominican Republic, the latter a part of our CARIFORUM system, and at the same time the extent of American interest group influence in the successful promotion of that FTA.

Today, the imbroglio that the banana producing states have found themselves in over the last 20 years (since Europe gave notice in 1985 of its decision to implement the single market and economy) – a long transition indeed – now engulfs the sugar regime.

What all this means, when coupled with the European attempt at reorganisation of the Lomé/Cotonou regime, and Europe's insistence on an institutional penetration of the hemisphere, with her relationship with us being projected in the future as a minor part of such involvement, is a progressive geopolitical and diplomatic isolation of our CARICOM/Caribbean area as we have defined it up to now.

The signing of a new Economic Partnership Agreement with Europe, focusing on the rearrangement of our protected trade relations, will not suffice to inhibit that isolation. What is required is new thinking about our place in this hemisphere itself, whose fate is today a function, in external relations terms, first of the struggle between Europe and North America for dominance of the North Atlantic economy. Secondly it is a function of the relentless search by the rising China (and indeed Asia) for economic and policy-making flexibility, as it integrates itself into that North Atlantic economy through a mutually dependent relationship with the United States, and by extension also with other states of the hemisphere. We, as original creations of the process of Europe's projection into the North Atlantic, feel the pressures directly once our historical intermediaries withdraw from their traditional function as our interlocutor.

So even while we settle accounts with a Europe changing in response to the new WTO regulatory system, we need to be focusing on the issue of the basis on which we can function within the parameters of the hemispheric system, and who that 'we' might be in the future.

In large measure we have sought to avoid engagement with our South-Central American neighbours on the basis that they really are not part of, nor have a substantial interest in, our Caribbean space. We can see that this attitude reflected in a cultural/diplomatic divide sustained by our 'Anglo-Saxon heritage,' which has hardly been diminished by our now decades-old membership of the Organisation of American States, then our later membership of SELA (the Economic System of Latin America) and the Association of Caribbean States whose establishment we ourselves initiated.

As recent events in Haiti have shown, present circumstances no longer permit this. They have rapidly brought Brazil, Argentina and Chile into play as direct actors in the CARICOM arena, and as de facto allies of the United States, in an attempt to resolve the latest political impasse there resulting from social disturbance and the exile of President Aristide. Also, whether we like it or not, their diplomatic and practical intervention in the resolution of the Haitian problem is not inspired by allegiance to the norms of official Inter-Americanism, but constitutes a working out of new role-playing to match evolving self-defined interests in the hemisphere and the wider world.

That role-playing, we need to note, is partly conditioned by the gyrations of social forces in these countries, as they react to the contemporary opening of their economies, and the ability of governments to cope with their effects in a manner that simultaneously satisfies domestic popular social ambitions and the requirements of the new rules of international production and trade. In their diplomacy therefore, as in domestic economic policy heavily influenced by international policy criteria and with its implications for domestic social welfare systems, this is an era of experimentation.

For example, in the space of two decades we have seen Argentina overthrow the principles of Peronism – which focused on close harmonisation of international diplomatic policy and financial policy with the United States of America – both in domestic policy and in its international relations actions. Then we have subsequently seen that country reverse economic course, seeking in its post-Menem phase to contest (in some measure as Malaysia did in 1997/98) the orientation of virtually globally accepted financial and macro-economic policy in the matter of dealing with her accumulated debt.

The fact of the matter is that no sooner had we recognised the implications for our viability as socio-economic systems of our changing international relations environment, than the experimentation to which I have referred began to make itself felt. Cuba, for example, quickly came to fully understand the diplomatic consequences for herself in relation to the new Mexican orientation towards North America. For Mexico had functioned as an effective barrier, until then, to complete Cuban isolation in the hemisphere. It must also be the case that that Mexican position in relation to Cuba would have been an important precedent and platform from which the four independent Anglophone countries could feel comfortable in establishing diplomatic relations with Cuba in 1972. Yet we need to recognise and fully understand the extent to which the traditional Mexican principles of non-intervention and rights of small countries will still influence her policies, even in a situation where her integration into the North American system would increase the variables with which she has to deal, with consequent effects on the effective continuity of that orientation.

Similarly, as I have argued elsewhere, in the context of the emerging stance of Brazil in international economic relations, the geopolitical relationship between Brazil and our countries on the southern flank of CARICOM is increasingly close, and is so likely to grow in intensity in both diplomatic policy and economic terms. So it seems to me that it would be wise to encourage that country to be almost a full participant in the discussion and conduct of the evolution of Caribbean international affairs.

We have belatedly begun to realise that Brazil's actions are having, and must continue to have, a substantial influence on our own situation and conduct. Her ready willingness to participate in the stabilisation of Haiti after the removal of Aristide may have surprised some of us. However, this would only be because we may have forgotten that after the demise of the Peoples Revolutionary Government, she immediately demanded, and obtained, the removal of the Cuban technical and diplomatic presence from Surinam. Furthermore, that (though under a military government) she actively participated in the 'stabilization' of the Dominican Republic after the American intervention there in 1965. Also we cannot gainsay her interest in the boundary security arrangements of the Guyanas and Suriname as being a critically practical one. In this, given France's territorial presence in the area, we can be sure that she will share common security concerns with that country.

In addition, given her integration initiatives towards the Guyanas over the last few years, we must recognise that the course of attaining economic viability in the Guyanas will constitute a part of Brazil's own economic planning and economic diplomacy. We must surely place the implications of her sugar policy initiatives at the WTO, and her concerns about agriculture in any emerging international regulatory regime, within that wider, long term context as we pursue the issue of the future of sugar as an essential element in the economic growth of our Guyana. In the designing of our diplomatic policies, we must see the wider, changing picture into which, like it or not, our discussions about our own economic future are today being framed.

Even within the more limited frame of relations among the Antilles, it is necessary to recognise that it is the European Union itself which, in the early 1990s, broke the log-jam of Caribbean Community institutional self-segregation, by insisting on the establishment of the Caribbean Forum and its inclusion of Haiti and the Dominican Republic. At that time too, the EU began to insist, as is now clear through the Guadalajara Declaration, that its institutionalised trade/aid relations would henceforth cover the whole of the South Central American space through the extension of its new concept of Regional Economic Partnership Agreements (which it had in mind for the Caribbean Community), and free trade areas, to that space. The days, we might almost say that of the delaying tactics of long discussions about 'deepening vs. widening' are, when looked at in the Antillean context, over.

Finally, we need to recognise too, that by the fact of the presences of large Antillean diasporas in various places in the hemisphere, but particularly in a country like Canada, we cannot appear to rule out in our diplomacy the increasingly integral concern of such states in the evolution of Caribbean affairs. Canada's support for a rapid denouement of the Haitian problem (by whatever urgent means?) and then her eager participation in the stabilisation phase should therefore not have surprised us. As with the United States, domestic considerations will have played an almost equally significant part as any general ongoing diplomatic concern with peace, stability and security in the hemisphere.

That is where we are today. This circumstance of an emerging rearrangement of country options and actions across the board of geopolitics and geo-economics in the hemisphere, with the active presence of the European powers as part of the play, must now induce us to hasten to consider the institutional framework from which we shall determine policy in this future.[10]

For if the context has changed, how can the structure of relations remain the same? How can we expect an Economic Partnership Agreement to be just some modernised version of Lomé, plus reciprocity? If the EU/UK has to find itself a way out of Brazil's (and Thailand's and Australia's) victory over its sugar regime, why should we expect its first concern to be Caribbean sugar, in the context of active WTO discussions on the future of agriculture, and as it desperately seeks to sign an FTA with the Mercosur group? Why would we have pride of place in the determination of its policy? Nothing in recent British diplomacy relating to the Caribbean or ACP banana industry would suggest that we should.

The lesson is, that in this we must rearrange our diplomacy to consistently seek to engage the larger powers in spheres of regional and international diplomacy that are of interest to us (including the Caribbean sphere) and attempt to match what to them are our narrower interests, with their wider interests.

To take one example, the European Union's wider interest in assisting our development today is said by them to be to support us in pursuing our own adjustment to the global economic liberalisation process, and therefore our integration into the emerging global economy, through a process of regional economic integration of the Antillean area as a whole, and by inference, through support for the infrastructural apparatus that would make this meaningful. This certainly goes beyond a mere modernisation of Lomé/Cotonou. Can we find the key to this, in a manner, and within a time frame, that satisfies our populations? To work out the principles and mechanics of this should be the current broader task of our Caribbean Community, the Regional Negotiating Machinery assuming some responsibility for it, paralleling its specific tasks of technical negotiation.

So in conclusion, I have been concerned also to indicate three other things in relation to this: first that the task outlined above requires the participation of the wider (beyond CARICOM) Antillean area, and neighbouring hemispheric countries with immediate self-interest in its evolution. Secondly, that consequentially, the activity of arranging a new diplomacy to match developments in the wider Caribbean and the hemisphere, so as to be able to negotiate our specific requirements and objectives (for example the maneuvering of the Haitian issue) in that arena as they arise – a diplomacy continually engaging hemispheric and other countries beyond our immediate Community – is a new and separate task (beyond the immediately practical tasks of the RNM). It requires an institutional system whose objectives, structure and particular mandates must reflect the objectives and mandates of the wider Antilles and neighbouring states, as against those simply of the CARICOM arena. For that is the Caribbean's immediate New World today and thinking that through becomes one of the provinces for New World thinkers of today.

Thirdly, given the openness of countries and communities in this era of globalisation, the international concerns of governments and their diplomats cannot be seen as, or held by them to be, an arena that can be conducted in the traditional way as 'secret diplomacy.' Today there is no distinction between inside and outside, and therefore there are no external initiatives that do not require the legitimacy of the populations or constituencies whom they are meant to benefit or whom they affect. This is particularly so in the realm of socio-economic change that is almost a direct result of international institutional influence, or of processes emanating from international economic regimes.

If we did not know this, even with our own historically open systems, current experience in Europe forcefully reminds us of it. The issues of legitimacy, accountability, transparency – traditional issues of domestic political theory and practice – therefore remain major issues, even as they are extended to apply to behaviour beyond the traditional boundaries of any individual state. Our Caribbean thinkers about the evolving New Caribbean World must have this on their agenda also.

So indeed, there is the necessity now for the urgent participation of today's intellectuals in a cooperative intellectual task across the Antilles, involving persistent academic crisscrossing of the Antilles, in much the same way as our predecessors, Sherlock, Best and others felt that need, and acted upon it a full two intellectual generations ago. Then, as now, as we proceed along the long transition to viability, thought remains 'the action for us.'

Notes

1. This chapter was originally prepared as the Opening Address at the 'Thought of New World' Conference.
2. Except that in the last pre-independence phase of Associated Statehood, the government of Venezuela established a presence in some of the Eastern Caribbean countries, particularly St Lucia, with which it also established air communications.
3. See Gordon Lewis, *Puerto Rico: Freedom and Power in the Caribbean*, (repr.; Kingston: Ian Randle Publishers, Jamaica, 2004).
4. See W. Arthur Lewis, 'Industrialization of the British West Indies,' *Caribbean Economic Review* 2, (1950).
5. The work of the UWI in this regard is indicated in Havelock Brewster and Clive Thomas, *The Dynamics of West Indian Economic Integration* (Mona: Institute of Social and Economic Research, UWI, 1967). There was emerging

also at this time a discussion of differences of view on the relevance of size to economic development, as indicated in Best's 'Size and Survival,' published in the *New World Quarterly* as a critique of William Demas's *The Economics of Development in Small Countries with Special Reference to the Caribbean* (Montreal: McGill University, 1965).

6. Norman Girvan, 'The Development of Dependency Economics in the Caribbean and Latin America,' *Social and Economic Studies* 22, no.1, (1973).

7. Lloyd Best, 'Independent Thought and Caribbean Freedom,' initially published in the *New World Quarterly*, and republished in *Readings in the Political Economy of the Caribbean* eds. Norman Girvan and Owen Jefferson, (Kingston: New World Group, 1977), 7–28.

8. For some discussion, from the left as it were, of these discourses, see Brian Meeks, *Radical Caribbean: From Black Power to Abu Bakr* (Mona: The Press University of the West Indies, 1996); and Perry Mars, *Ideology and Change: The Transformation of the Caribbean Left*, (Mona: The Press University of the West Indies, 1998). See also my 'Political Change and Crisis in the English-Speaking Caribbean,' in Alan Adelman and Reid Reading eds. *Confrontation in the Caribbean Basin* (University of Pittsburgh, 1984) and 'Comment' by Anthony Maingot, 116–24.

9. For indications of these varying orientations see my, 'The Commonwealth Caribbean' in Christopher Clapham ed. *Foreign Policy-Making in Developing States* (London: Saxon House, 1977) and 'Issues and Trends in Jamaican Foreign Policy 1972–1977' in Carl Stone and Aggrey Brown eds., *Perspectives on Jamaica in the Seventies* (Kingston: Jamaica Publishing House, 1981).

10. I have explored some of these issues in two recent essays: 'Inheritances of Plantation Economy: International Relations in the Caribbean' in Selwyn Ryan ed. *Independent Thought and Caribbean Freedom: Essays in Honour of Lloyd Best* (Trinidad and Tobago: UWI, 2003); and 'Configurations of Caribbean Regionalism in the Hemispheric and International Settings: Towards an Antillean Subsystem,' in *Journal of Caribbean International Relations*, no.1 (April 2005).

PART TWO
Imagining

6 | *The Caribbean Rentier Economy, State and Society*

Dennis A. Pantin

Introduction

This paper seeks to provide what it argues is the missing link in the explanations of how Caribbean economies work. It begins by noting that the Plantation Economy Model (PEM)[1] and the Mechanism of the Open Petroleum Economy Model (MOPE)[2] are two seminal contributions to Caribbean Economic Thought.[3] However, they both suffer from one common limitation, which is the reification of a 'legacy' or a 'mechanism' that masks the human agency behind the reproduction of these types of economies. The paper then goes on to suggest that the human agency which undergirds the 'legacy' and/or 'mechanism' is that of the Rentier economy, state and society. The paper defines economic rents and the Rentier economy, state and society. It articulates the technical economic solutions required to transform such Rentier economies but concludes that such policy choices have a very slim chance of being implemented without a parallel shift in the nature of the Rentier state and society. The paper concludes by providing some empirical evidence from Trinidad and Tobago which is identified as a quintessential example of a Rentier economy, state and society. However, these concepts are also considered to be applicable to other economies in the Caribbean and elsewhere that are significantly dependent on natural resources, including renewable, as in the case of tourism-based economies.

Plantation Economy Model Hypothesis

Best hypothesises that:

> The legacy of institutions, structures and behaviour patterns of the plantation system are so deeply entrenched that adjustment tends to take place as an adaptation within the bounds of the established framework. By and large, the economies do not experience any

considerable or sustained relief from their dependence on the traditional export staple.[4]

The Open Petroleum Economy Hypothesis

Seers, on the other hand, postulates that the mechanism of the OPE results in a booming petroleum sector crowding out productive investment in the rest of the economy; growing inequality; and 'disguised' balance of payments problems, which quickly reveal themselves in the bust period. Seers concludes that, 'The Mechanism of the Open Petroleum Economy resembles that of a time bomb.'[5]

The Rentier Economy, State and Society

The main proposition of this paper is that the human agency reified in these two seminal contributions as attributable to either a 'legacy' or a 'mechanism' is revealed in the concept of the 'Rentier Economy, State and Society.'

Definition of Economic Rents

Economic rents can be defined most generally as forms of unearned income. Ricardo noted for example that, 'Rent is that portion of the produce of the earth which is paid to the landlord for the use of the original and indestructible powers of the soil.'[6]

Marshall reserved the concept 'rent' to refer to 'income derived from the gift of nature.'[7]

Definition of Rentier Economy

A Rentier economy can be defined generally as one which has a significant dependence on economic rents, derivative from natural resource-based production. Beblawi defines a Rentier economy as, '...one substantially supported by expenditure from the State, while the State itself is supported from rent accruing from abroad; or more generally an economy in which rent plays a major role.'[8]

Key Characteristics of Rentier Economy

Four main economic characteristics can be identified as associated with such 'Rentier' economies. First, conventional macro-economic indicators utilised for evaluating economic performance can be extremely misleading in such economies. As Seers pointed out in the 1960s, in the case of oil exporting economies such as Trinidad and Tobago and Venezuela, there can be the paradox of persistent and significant growth in real GDP and per capita GDP alongside growing unemployment and poverty (Seers 1964). The reason is that natural resource exports can be extremely lucrative – at least in periods of boom – and hence mask the fundamental structural weaknesses of such Rentier economies. Kaplinsky points out that Botswana, for example:

> ...was one of the most rapidly growing economies in the world over the 1970s and 1980s, despite having virtually no industry and very poor agricultural land. This was almost entirely due to its deposits of low-cost, high-quality diamonds and the workings of the diamond cartel.[9]

Second, resource exports tend to distort and 'crowd out' productive economic activities in the other sectors of the economy. One of the peculiar features of such Rentier economies, therefore, is what Beblawi terms the break in the 'work-reward' relationship, since economic rents finance consumption in the rest of the economy. As a result, as Chatelus observes: '...most economic activities (in Rentier economies) are...a means of ensuring income circulation, rather than production-oriented behaviour.'[10]

In periods of economic boom, in particular, balance of payments constraints tend to be relaxed, and lead to overvalued exchange rates, which facilitate consumption of imports. As a result, other productive sectors-particularly agriculture – tend to be 'crowded out.'[11]

Third, Rentier economies tend to have 'disguised' economic – and hence social – problems that only manifest themselves when there is a downturn in the flow and/or value of economic rents. Seers observes, on this score, in the case of open petroleum economies, that:

> Factors that elsewhere would express themselves in balance of payments crises, such as wage increases or inadequate initiative in

developing local industry, will here cause growing unemployment. An economy of this type has what might be called disguised, rather than overt, balance of payments tensions.[12]

Fourth, there is the reversal of the 'normal' state-business roles in Rentier economies.

In a 'normal' economy, business generates income which the state levies on. However, in the Rentier economy, business 'levies' on the state in terms of whether rents are captured at all; and, if so, how such rents are distributed among competing sectors in the economy.

Katouzian notes that:

> ...the domestic economic sectors, including the private sector,... are dependent upon the state for direct and indirect welfare gains through the latter's disbursement of the oil revenues...it is the common relations with the State – the chief supplier of the means of consumption – which determines the relative welfare position and status of different socio-economic groups.[13]

It is not the fact of having natural resources which determines that a country would be classified 'Rentier' in nature, but whether value is added to the natural resources by owners of capital – whether state and/or private – in such resource-based economies. It is this absence of value added which permits categorisation of such economies as Rentier in nature. Other countries that add such value cannot be so classified. Kaplinsky points out that:

> ...many other countries gain from the exploitation of scarce natural resources, including 'industrialised' economies such as the USA, Canada and Australia. Where the industrialized countries differ is that they have been able to extend their operations along the value chain to undertake downstream processing activities...while the Gulf States extract oil, high-productivity extracting economies such as the USA and the UK have more developed hydrocarbon-based processing activities....Brazil and South Africa produce pulp, but Finland and Sweden also manufacture paper-making machinery....[14]

There is, of course, no complete Rentier economy, in a similar sense as Marshall suggested that there are few examples of 'pure economic rents.' An economy would qualify to be classified as 'Rentier' in nature, however, if natural resource rents play a dominant role in the macro-economy and/or the fiscal operations of the State. Mineral-based economies and, more particularly, petroleum-based economies represent the 'purest' type of Rentier economy.

Transformation from Rentier to Productive-Oriented Economy: 'Technical' or 'Purely' Economic Interventions to Dismantle the Rentier Economy

One can identify a number of 'purely technical' economic policy interventions to redress the negative impacts of the economic characteristics of resource-based economies, which would lead to their transformation into productive-oriented economies.

Modification of the National Income Accounts

In the context of natural resource dependent countries, modification of the accounts is of specific significance, since it reveals both the natural resource dependence and future economic prospects. Repetto makes a similar point:

> ...countries which are typically most dependent on natural resources for employment, revenues and foreign exchange earnings are instructed to use a system for national accounting and macro-economics which almost completely ignores their principal assets.[15]

Resource-based national income accounting systems should take explicit account of the distorted macro-economic image – if not mirage – of resource-based Rentier economies – particularly in their boom periods. The intervention recommended here is to modify the national accounts to measure 'genuine savings.' The 'genuine savings' measurement therefore essentially seeks to separate economic rents generated through the depletion of natural capital from the conventional national income derived from reproducible man-made and human capital.[16]

More recently, the mainstream economic literature has embraced the 'Hartwick Rule' for realising Sustainable Development, which, in essence, breaks Total Capital(Kt) into four distinct types:

Natural Capital (Kn); Manmade Capital (Km); Human Capital (Kh) and Social Capital (Ks) such that:

$$\Sigma\ Kt = Kn + Kh + Km + Ks$$

To maintain a fixed level of Kt or to increase Kt one must increase investments in Manmade, Human and/or Social Capital to compensate for the 'depreciation' of Kn (particularly from non-renewable or exhaustible resources).

In itself, modification of the national income accounts to reflect resource depletion does no more than alert the society to the fact that it may not only be living off its savings, but off of those derived not from its human endeavours and ingenuity, but from the gifts of the Gods, or nature, depending on one's religious predilection. In addition, therefore, there is need for an appropriate economic strategy.

EMMCI Principles

Five economic principles ought to inform such an economic strategy in Rentier economies. These are the principles of Equity and Maximisation of value added together with Measurement, Capture and Investment of Economic Rents.

Equity Principle

Two related concepts of Equity arise in natural resource-based economies. Both follow from the fact that, by definition, natural resources are owned in common by all members of such societies and therefore, in accordance with well enshrined principles of property rights, such owners ought to obtain an equitable share of the benefits from the utilisation of such natural resources.

The first concept is that of intra-generational equity in terms of the benefits accruing to the present generation. The second relates to inter-generational equity which, of course, addresses the concern of benefits accruing to future generations. The operationalisation of these two equity principles are given effect in terms of the four which follow below.

Maximisation of Value Added Principle

The owners of any asset ought to naturally maximise the benefits that derive from its use. In the case of natural resource assets, the obvious objective for natural resource-based economies is to have the highest feasible ownership rights, along the entire value chain, from raw material to final product. Historically, however, natural resource countries have tended to benefit largely from shares of royalty or taxation of profit income at the natural resource extraction end rather than across the entire value chain. To maximise value added also implies creating knowledge systems for human resources to be deployed along the value chain.

Measurement (of Economic Rents) Principle

To give effect to the Equity principle therefore requires that there be a measurement of the value of economic rents generated from natural resource exploitation. There is an obvious linkage between the maximisation of value added principle and the measurement principle.

The Capture (of Economic Rents) Principle

Given the equity and measurement principles, the logical corollary is the need for those who own the natural resources to be able to 'capture' economic rents. Again, this relates both to renewables and non-renewables.

The Investment (of Captured Economic Rents) Principle

Given the capture of economic rents, the equity principle – particularly that of inter-generational equity – implies that such economic rents should be invested. In the specific case of oil exporting economies Al Janabi proposed, in 1979, that, 'the only rationally acceptable depletion rate is one where the wasting resource is compensated simultaneously and concurrently by an investment process that will yield the highest rate of economic development.'[17]

In the case of a natural resource-based economy, the challenge is larger than simply maximising the return on capital. It also involves reducing the future dependence on the very natural resources that generate the captured rents in the first place, and the implementation of strategies and policies that contribute toward the sustainable development of the NR based economy. One key element here is that of natural resource risk minimisation via diversification.

Risk Minimisation via Diversification within the Natural Resource Sector

Diversification of the natural resource risks has two dimensions. On the one hand, there can be diversification within the natural resource itself. This is linked to the maximisation of value added principle and would take a NR based economy, for example, from investment only in the national geographic location for natural resource exploitation, to the development of knowledge as to how to find, extract, transport, process and ultimately market such natural resources. In this way, the knowledge could be transferred to other countries or geographic spaces even if, or when, the particular country's own natural resources are either exhausted or no longer economically viable to extract. Or, if renewable, to internalise capabilities in other geographic spaces.

In other words, natural resource-based countries should establish firms that can operate across national boundaries in the same way as transnational corporations do as a matter of course. The competitive advantage of such transnational corporations is not in owning natural resources, but in their knowledge of how to exploit market opportunities and to generate the necessary capital to give effect to this.

There is some evidence of such transborder diversification within the natural resources. Both Kuwait and Venezuela, for example, have invested in refining and retail vehicular fuel markets in the US and Western Europe. In the case of tourism, two Jamaican-owned hotel chains have invested elsewhere in the Caribbean.

Diversification Outside of the Natural Resource Sector

The second more obvious form of diversification is in terms of investment in other natural resources or, more particularly, in non-natural resource-based industries including the now much vaunted knowledge industries.

In fact, economists in oil-exporting economies also have long pointed to the need to achieve inter-generational equity through productive use of the income flows from the depleting natural resource. Motamen advocated, in 1979, for example, that the non-oil export sector should be developed in the early stages of resource extraction: 'The non-oil sector should be promoted towards the beginning of the resource's life, which will enable it to develop before the oil resource is terminated.'[18]

The 'Impure' Economics (and hence Political Economy) of Hydrocarbon-based Rentier States

Hydrocarbon-based economies illustrate the realities of natural resource-based Rentier economies at the 'purest' or most extreme levels since the rise to dominance of oil in the twentieth century. The paradox of hydrocarbon-based economies has been addressed for many decades in the economic literature. As noted earlier, Seers (1964) sought to explain two related paradoxes in oil exporting economies: growing real GDP alongside growing unemployment and, as well, growing real per capita GDP alongside growing poverty. Later, the concept of the 'Dutch' disease was advanced to explain the distortions in the economy of Holland resulting from the onset of booming oil and gas production. More recently there has been discussion in the literature of the 'resource curse.' In a summary of much of this literature, Mikesell (1997) points to several technical solutions including, in particular, preventing windfalls from suddenly increasing domestic demand through a range of interventions including sterilisation of such inflows.

Essentially, what all of this tells us is that oil or natural gas policy requires conversion of non-renewable wealth into renewable wealth or the 'sowing of oil or gas' to reap development.

Political Transformation of the Rentier State to Provide for Real Transparency, Accountability and Participation

Beblawi defines a Rentier state as '…any state that derives a substantial part of its revenue from foreign sources and under the form of rent.'[19] Transforming the natural resource Rentier state to one which is transparent, accountable and focused on economic production and efficiency is therefore an economic objective that is a prerequisite for the technical economic policies to be implemented. In other words, the above proposed policy interventions to redress the negative impacts of the 'pure' characteristics of Rentier economies are naïve, first best solutions, that stand little chance of implementation without recognising the fact that Rentier economies tend to beget Rentier states.

The reality of a Rentier economy is such that s/he who controls the state, controls rents. The more opaque, non-transparent and non-accountable is the State, then the greater is the capacity for a small group (including foreign investors) to control the economic rents.

This process begins with the political parties that contest for state power, and their financing. In a paper on Trinidad and Tobago, Enrensaft (1970) spoke prophetically, for example, of 'entrepreneurial politics' in which those who invest in political parties can earn handsome returns in office.

Transforming the Sociology and Psychology of the Rentier Society

The most powerful force, subversive of the Rentier economy and state, is an informed, educated and socially conscious population that recognises the need to maximise value added, to measure and capture economic rents and to invest them in order to achieve intra and inter-generational equity.

The recognition of the economic, political and socio-psychological transformation requirements would propel such a society to take responsibility for the redesign of the apparatus of state.

Some Trinidad and Tobago Evidence

Trinidad and Tobago most closely fits the bill of a Rentier economy, state and society in the Caribbean, given its long and increasing dependence on hydrocarbon production and exports.

While oil production began very early in the twentieth century there were then other traditional agricultural commodity exports such as sugar, cocoa, coffee and citrus. However, by the onset of political independence in 1962, oil began to assume primacy in terms of foreign exchange earnings and government tax revenue. Since the turn of the 1990s, the natural gas sector has also begun to loom large in terms of total hydrocarbon production and exports, although its fiscal contribution has lagged. A major reason for the latter is that major fiscal concessions have been granted to predominantly foreign investors in the natural gas sector. For example, the first Liquified Natural Gas (LNG) plant began operation in 1999, with a ten-year tax holiday. The second, third, and fourth LNG plants operate with undisclosed tax rate. All other natural gas plants producing methanol and ammonia, which were established over the decade of the 1990s have also received tax holidays of between five and seven years.

Empirical Details on the Role of Oil and Gas in Trinidad and Tobago from 1908–2040[20]

Figures 1–4 provide empirical details on both the increasing role that oil and gas have played in the Trinidad and Tobago Economy since the start of the twentieth century and the prospects for a peaking of production given growing demand by the end of this first decade of the twenty-first century.

Figure 1: Oil and Gas Production, Trinidad and Tobago: 1908–2001

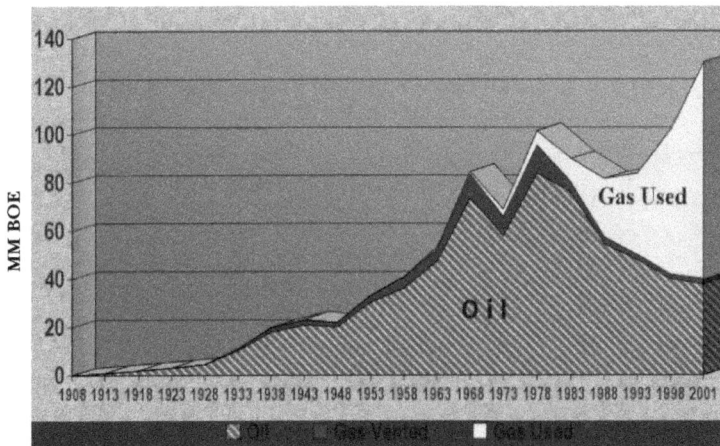

MM BOE (Millions of Barrels of Oil Equivalence)

Figure 1 shows, for example, that oil production began very early in the twentieth century, and that by the Second World War the first peak of oil production was realised. The Figure also shows that natural gas was largely vented until the late 1960s, when it began to be used commercially.

Figure 2: Oil and Gas Production: 1980–2001

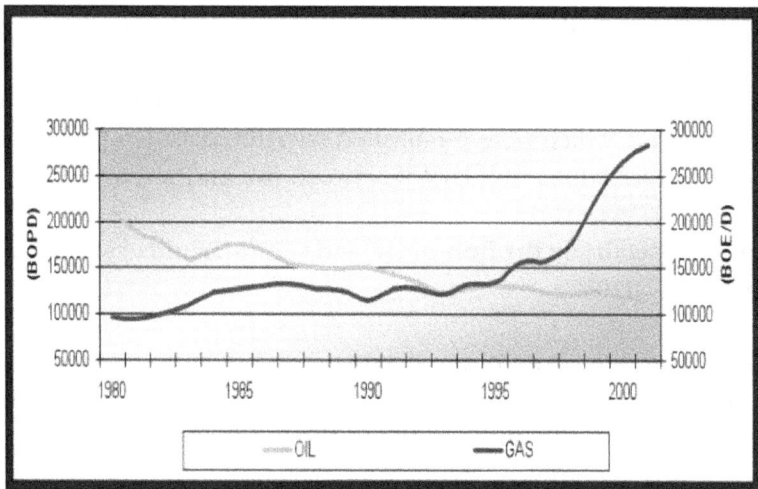

Figure 2 takes up the story in the period from 1980–2000 to illustrate how natural gas has eclipsed oil in terms of barrels of oil equivalence per day by the early 1990s.

Figure 3: Oil and Gas Projected Production to 2015

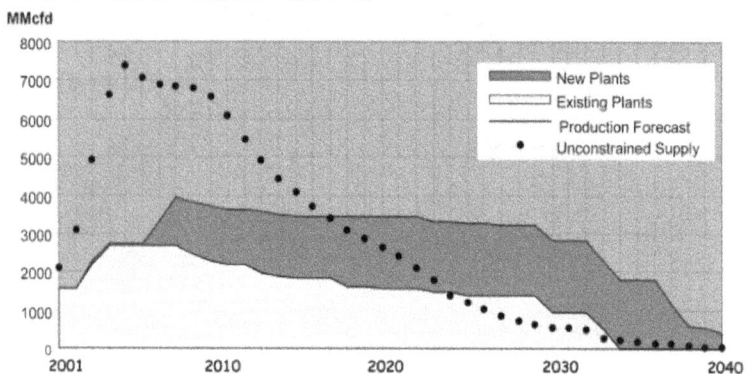

Figure 3 reviews oil and gas production from 1970 to a 2015 projection illustrating, again, the increasing role of natural gas.

Figure 4: Projected Uses of Natural Gas to 2040 by Type of Product[21]

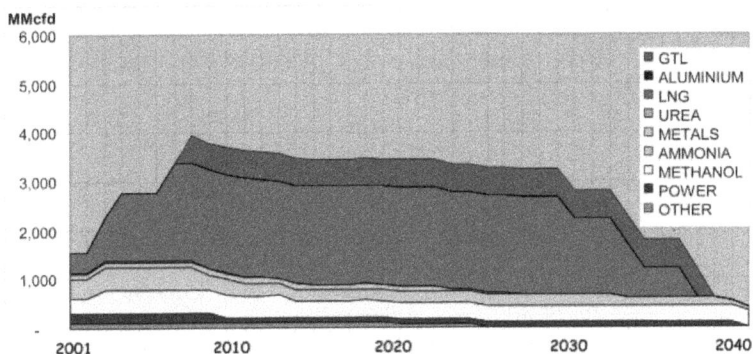

Figure 4 reveals that Liquified Natural Gas dominates projected use of natural gas, dwarfing all other sources in the projection to 2040. Such LNG represents the quintessential example of failure to add value to natural resources. Moreover, the majority of other uses of natural gas – with the exception of power – represent bulk commodity products with limited value added.

Conclusion: Generalising the Rentier Economy, State and Society Hypothesis to Small Island Developing States

While hydrocarbon-based economies are almost textbook examples of Rentier economies, states and societies, these concepts are more generally applicable to all economies that are highly dependent on primary natural resource production. More particularly, it is suggested, these concepts are applicable to Small Island Developing States (SIDS).

Four sub-categories of natural resource-based dependent SIDS countries can be identified. First are those countries dependent on their agricultural soils for export of primary agricultural commodities. Second, those whose economies are based on the amenity values of their natural resources for tourism or natural products including, increasingly, pharmaceuticals. Third would be those whose incomes are derived primarily from non-hydrocarbon minerals such as bauxite and copper. Finally, we can identify those who draw their economic sustenance from the export of oil or natural gas. The first two sub-categories are therefore dependent on renewable resources and the third and fourth sub-categories on non-renewable resources. What all of these economies have in common is a dependence on natural resource-based commodity[22] exports to finance national consumer and producer demand.

Notes

1. See Lloyd Best, 'Outlines of a Model of Pure Plantation Economy' *Social and Economic Studies* 17, no. 3, (1968); also in Dennis Pantin ed. *The Caribbean Economy: A Reader* (Kingston, Jamaica: Ian Randle Publishers, 2005); see also George Beckford. *Persistent Poverty: Underdevelopment in the Plantation Economies of the Third World*, (Oxford University Press, 1972).
2. See Dudley Seers, 'The Mechanism of the Open Petroleum Economy' *Social and Economic Studies* 13, no. 2 (1964); also in Pantin ed. (2005).
3. See Pantin ed. (2005) for a collection of papers on Caribbean economic thought from 1950 to the present.
4. See Best 1968, 294.
5. See Seers 1964, 236.
6. See David Ricardo, *On the Principles of Political Economy and Taxation*, (London: John Murray, 1817), 33.
7. See Alfred Marshall, *Principles of Economics* (London: Macmillan and Co. Ltd, 1920).
8. See Hazem Beblawi and Giacomo Luciani eds. *The Rentier State* (New York: Croom Helm, 1987), 11.
9. See Raphaelie Kaplinsky, *Globalisation, Industrialisation and Sustainable Growth: The Pursuit of the Nth Rent*, IDS Discussion Paper 365, (1998): 16.
10. Michel Chatelus and Yves Schemeil, 'Towards a New Political Economy of State Industrialization in the Arab Middle East' in *International Journal of Middle East Studies* vol 16, no 2 (1984): 255–56. As cited by Beblawi, in Hazem Beblawi and Giacomo Luciani eds *The Rentier State* (New York: Croom Helm, 1987), 13.
11. See Ait-Amara, in Beblawi (1987) for an analysis of the impact of oil on agriculture in the Middle East.
12. Seers 1964, 235.
13. M. Katouzian, *The Political Economy of Development in Oil Exporting Countries: An Analytical Framework*, (Kent, UK: University of Kent, 1975). mimeo. 20
14. Kaplinsky1998, 17.
15. Robert Repetto, 'Environmental Resources in National Income Accounting' in Girvan, Norman and David Simmons eds. *Caribbean Ecology and Economics*, (Caribbean Conservation Association, 1991).
16. See Kirk Hamilton and Michael Clemens 'Genuine Savings Rates in Developing Countries' *The World Bank Economic Review* 13, no. 2 (May 1999) and other references therein for further elaboration on the concept and technique for measuring 'genuine savings.'
17. See A. Al-Janabi, 'Production and Depletion Policies in OPEC' *OPEC Review* 111, no. 1 (1979): 33–4.
18. H. Motamen, *Expenditure of Oil Revenue: An Optimal Control Approach with Application to the Iranian Economy* (New York: St Martin's Press, 1979; London: Frances Pinter, 1979), 69.

19. See Beblawi 1987, 11.
20. These figures were sourced from presentations by officials of the Ministry of Energy, Trinidad and Tobago.
21. GTL is gas to liquids.
22. Where amenity values for tourism are seen as a commodity.

7 | Organic Theorising in Inorganic Societies, or the Need for Epistemic Sovereignty beyond Radicalism and Rebellion

Kirk Meighoo

This paper argues that though Lloyd Best's thought is fundamental to the New World Group's distinction, it is atypical in the Caribbean and poorly understood in general. This seems clear from the contributions to this conference on New World, for example. This paper attempts to bridge the gap in perspective by trying to explain some key aspects of Best's thought in general, and then, in particular, providing Best's analysis of Jamaica's political challenges of the 1970s as a key example of his unique mode of interpretation.

New World not Dead

As a first key to understanding, it must be clearly emphasised that New World is not dead. New World, it appears, had two main tendencies. One was the revolutionary tendency, which eventually adopted various brands of Marxism. The other was what one can retrospectively call the Tapia tendency, which is perhaps the most important single descendent of New World. Tapia's claims are very strong, in that Tapia has continued very faithfully to adhere to the procedures and measures espoused by New World. One only has to read any edition of *New World Quarterly*, *Tapia*, and the *Trinidad and Tobago Review*, to observe the continuity and consistency in thought. This is not to say that there was no intellectual life or organisation in the region other than Tapia's which emerged from that stream of New World. In Guyana in particular there was a vigorous stream of thinking which made the *New World Fortnightly* possible, and then the *Stabroek News*.

Since leaving New World in 1968, Best began publishing *Tapia* and building a related institution which has attempted to secure for the paper a permanent and more varied life in the national community. Today, the Tapia stream is expressed in the Trinidad and Tobago Institute of the West Indies, which is the product of those efforts, and of which I am an Honorary Fellow, Executive Member, and a Board Director. Since 1977, the Institute has continuously published the *Trinidad and Tobago Review*. That stream of New World continues its mission in other ways as well: by holding an Annual Allan Harris Permanent Conference on Education, by holding its regular Seminars for Professionals series in Port of Spain, and by engaging in various collaborations with government, parastatals, the private sector, citizens' organisations, major multilateral institutions, Universities and Colleges in Trinidad and Tobago, the Region, and North America. On principle, it lives primarily by independent earnings from its intellectual work, rather than international, university, or government grants.

Responsibility and Epistemic Sovereignty

Best's body of ideas – which form the heart of the distinctive Tapia stream – is perhaps most notable because it is an unorthodoxy that is not a variant of radicalism or rebellion. By this I mean that Best's unorthodoxy has not been motivated by a sense of dispossession and the desire to right historical wrongs.

Rather, it is based on the notion that the West Indies is a distinctive province of human endeavour, over which we, its citizens, have full responsibility. That is the starting point of the interpretation: responsibility not victimhood. Ours is a special situation, however, for although we are our province's responsible inheritors and governors, the bulk of us have emerged from former serfdom, having to create a native ruling class for the first time since the conquest of the autochthon. Emerging at the cusp of independence, it is a body of thought that has been prepared to inherit and work with the entire culture-zone, its chequered history and social groups, without demanding further reparations or amends.

It calls attention to the need for responsibility and selfhood, to fulfil the human challenge of becoming higher men and creators of our own orders. It might be more accurately described, however, as a sort of classically conservative anti-Imperialism. If Best were Japanese, he might have been a Yukio Mishima, for example, calling us to our most civilised selves.

The first of our responsibilities as inheritors of these pieces of earth is to understand our province on its own terms. This is the goal of epistemological sovereignty. With this goal in mind, not only has Best rejected whole theories, but he has discarded so many of the current and borrowed concepts upon which these theories have been built, and which are shared by both the so-called right and left (a distinction itself which Best repudiates). He does not speak about 'the People,' masses, free market, middle class, developing countries, poverty eradication, sustainable development, grassroots, neo-liberalism, globalisation, or the capitalist world-system. He declines the usually uncritically accepted distinctions between the public sector and private sector, right and left, radical and conservative, North and South. These simply do not serve our purpose.

Rather, Best has created his own lexicon for dealing with specifically West Indian issues. These concepts, in fact, have found their way into common usage in Trinidad and Tobago, and beyond: plantation economy, maximum leadership, doctor politics, industrialisation by invitation, Afro-Saxon, 'Afros' and 'Indos,' unresponsibility, East-West corridor, ethnicity as 'automatic solidarity,' the 'party of parties,' national reconstruction, 'Macco Senate,' onshore and offshore economic sectors, and on and on.

Organicism

Despite the iconoclasm, the imperative requirement of epistemic sovereignty does not require unorthodoxy for its own sake. Although Best is nonconformist in his conclusions, he has a quite orthodox and almost classical respect for science (in its largest sense) and truth (as opposed to ideological worldviews which sees knowledge as serving primarily political ends). This understanding, of course, has philosophic roots. Best is by no means unique, though he is exemplary. Philosophically, his thought may be described as 'organicism,' and it appears to be essential to achieving his aim of epistemic sovereignty for the West Indies.

Best insists on seeing the whole, the long-view and wide-view, in both space and time, centred in our own specific, distinctive human province. Best is concerned with thick description, heavy on observation. He has a classical understanding of human society, almost Aristotelian, which cannot extricate things from their contexts, nor separate economics, history, politics, language, and geography except for temporary reasons of practicality.

He approaches intellectual endeavour like an artist of the highest order. Best does not seek to create an alternative orthodoxy. He is anti-formulaic. Observation is key and it must always be sensitive to the ironic, the complex, and even the tragic. Best has a novelist's eye, which explains his similarity to V.S. Naipaul, George Orwell, and C.L.R. James at his best. His conclusions are always provisional, though always seeking for our own, universal, enduring truths. At this stage, he is concerned with creators and conceptualisers, not followers and reifiers. Indeed, his language is far more like that of the artist rather than the critic. Like true artists, Best is a law unto himself, and not for others. He does not call for people to agree or disagree with him, but rather to engage.

A Culture-Zone which is not a Civilisation: The Inorganic West Indies

There is, however, a challenge with seeing the whole here. That is, the West Indies is fundamentally incomplete and inorganic, being a thoroughly colonial creation. Our pre-Columbian past has virtually no presence here, unlike in Latin America, the 'settlements of conquest,' where the legacies of the first peoples are still alive, or within reach.

At most, any of us – except the autochthon – has been here only 500 years. Though the West Indies does form a distinctive culture-zone, in the perspective of humanity's 10,000 years of civilisation, 500 years is barely enough time to have rooted any enduring civilisation from scratch, particularly under colonial conditions of almost pure exploitation, without any sizeable numbers of autochthons (as in Africa, Asia, and Latin America) or colonial settlers as in the temperate zones of North and South America, South Africa, or Australia. Slaves, indentured labourers, traders, pirates, employees, and agents of overseas investors were poorly equipped to found a civilisation. Indeed, opposite to every other human social formation, the West Indian economy existed *before* it was settled by permanent inhabitants.

Perhaps some time is needed to explore the matter. To my knowledge, the first time the idea of a Caribbean civilisation was publicly stated was by Barbadian Prime Minister Errol Barrow in a speech at the

Miami Conference on the Caribbean in November 1986 titled, 'Our Caribbean Civilisation.'

More recently, Prime Minister of St Vincent and the Grenadines, Ralph Gonsalves had put together a collection titled, *The Politics of our Caribbean Civilisation: Essays and Speeches.*[1] The late Tim Hector commented extensively in March 2001 on it. Gonsalves further forwarded the idea at the Inaugural Lecture in the Distinguished Lecture Series Sponsored by CARICOM on February 12, 2003 titled, 'Our Caribbean Civilisation and its Political Prospects.' In addition, O. Nigel Bolland, Professor of Sociology at Colgate University, New York, has recently edited and compiled a collection of readings titled, *The Birth of Caribbean Civilisation: A Century of Ideas about Culture and Identity, Nation and Society.*[2] For a few years now, the University of the West Indies at St Augustine has been offering an introductory course for all undergraduates – in every faculty, including Science and Agriculture and Engineering – titled, 'Caribbean Civilisation.' The Trinidad and Tobago Institute of the West Indies also offers a course to overseas students titled, 'Caribbean Civilisation in the Americas.'

So the idea of a Caribbean civilisation seems to be accepted in important circles, but on what basis are these claims made? A civilisation is difficult to define. Specialists generally disagree on the criteria used to judge a civilisation and, by extension, the number of civilisations in world history. However, it is vital that we state here at least a working definition.

The existence of Caribbean civilisation cannot be derived simply from the indignant sentiment that if others have one, we must have one, too. Barrow's claim seems to be based on the existence of a distinctive identity, culture, and history; the viability of the region's societies; the intellectual and institutional resources to understand and grapple with our problems; resource potential for continued development; and a heritage of exquisite natural beauty entrusted to it.

In his own analysis, Gonsalves identifies eight core characteristics which mark out the civilisation: the geography of the Caribbean archipelago; a shared history of European conquest and empire; a population mix of indigenous peoples, British, Portuguese, Africans, Asians, Jews, and Arabs; political values from Western Europe, transformed by Caribbean experience; a distinct cultural matrix fashioned by pre-Columbian Caribbean, Africa, Europe, and Asia, with in-grown developments; European languages distinctively modified; a productive and technological apparatus that sustains the region's viability; and a permanence of being in the Caribbean landscape and seascape.

I am unaware of any systematic statement on the matter from the UWI or the TTIWI. The Principal of UWI St Augustine, however, has referred to the fact that Samuel Huntington (1993) in his famous article, 'The Clash of Civilizations?' (briefly, in one passing reference) identified the (Anglophone) Caribbean as a civilisation. On the other hand, Marxists and other radical (Western) critics have dismissed the idea of civilisation as is commonly understood, seeing it as a mask for economic relations of dominance. Tim Hector[3] takes this position in his sympathetic, but critical, discussion of Gonsalves's book.

However, none of the above seems satisfactory. The definitions by Barrow and Gonsalves seem to be based on peculiarities, distinctions, and differences. This is not sufficient. Mere difference from other civilisations does not make that cultural formation a civilisation. A Caribbean culture-zone may exist, but this should not be confused with a Caribbean civilisation.

Illuminating as the radical critique of the idea of civilisation can be, I am unaware that anyone who has studied the phenomenon and travelled widely can realistically accept that national cultures and distinct civilisations do not exist, are not significant, or are ideological superstructures of capitalist substructures.

I venture my own working definition. Rather than a checklist of features – like the classical metallurgy, writing, class stratification, economic and natural resources, a complex of political, religious, and social institutions, military capability, and so on – I prefer a more intuitive definition. This is crucial to our endeavour here, because the Caribbean does possess many, if not all, the attributes of a civilisation; but I think we miss the essence, the main feature.

That feature is that a civilisation must provide a centre for its people – political, economic, philosophical, linguistic, cultural, military, moral, judicial, aesthetic, and so on. A civilisation is often composed of many societies, nations, and peoples. However, there usually is an identifiable cultural – and often geographic – centre, around which others revolve, feed off of, rebel against, or feed into. A civilisation must generate, own, and distribute – according to its own rules – economic surplus which can sustain its relative autonomy. The details are less important than the effect or purpose. A civilisation provides for its peoples a primary point of reference and orientation, its people are sure of the standards it sets, while constantly questioning and challenging them, if the civilisation is dynamic.

The Caribbean does not fit this definition. It remains a collection of satellites. Its states and peoples revolve around centres of authority outside of the Caribbean: the US, England, France, Spain, the Netherlands, even Latin America. The frequency of external reference in Gonsalves's definition, for example, should give one caution. Indeed, Gonsalves expresses many fears for the survival of the Caribbean, even of its identity. He argues that if we do not recognise ourselves as an independent, authentic civilisation, the Caribbean could be working out an associate status with the US or EU within 50 years. Surely the civilisation of which he speaks is extremely tenuous.

This is not unusual, however. The Caribbean is perhaps like Australia, South Africa, Canada, or Singapore. They have the potential to be autonomous, but for complex reasons, remain extensions or satellites of other, great mother cultures (England, China, Germany, France, etc). C.L.R. James[4] has argued that the Caribbean is an outgrowth, tropical extension, or branch of Western civilisation. There is much truth to this. In the (Anglophone) West Indies we speak English and our ideas and institutions are largely derived from or make primary reference to the UK or US. Indeed, what French or Spanish – let alone African-language – books do we read in the West Indies? Our intellectual world is overwhelmingly American and British.

Yet this does not encompass all of our cultural life, of course. Many cultural strands – native and ancestral, genuinely West Indian, and also African, European, and Asian – survive, even thrive here. Yet they only do so at the informal level. This is what makes our societies half-made: the profound disconnection between the formal and the informal, between our lived experience and our official institutions. I do not think that in the history of the world more inorganic societies than ours ever existed. The 500-year-old Enterprise of the Indies is a unique human episode.

What we need to do is to understand what we are, and where we are in terms of our historical development (which should not be assumed to follow a simple linear progression). In this respect, C.L.R. James's

1962 Appendix to *The Black Jacobins*, 'From Toussaint L'Ouverture to Fidel Castro' is crucial. James describes the forging of a nation, of a people, as an historical unfolding, with surprising twists and turns. Going through the nineteenth century, between the wars, and after the Second World War, James draws from politics, society, economy, and the arts to show us a people in the curious and unpredictable process of recognising themselves and their capabilities.

Obviously meaning to inspire, James was nevertheless careful to honestly acknowledge limitations. In his 1960 lecture, 'West Indian Personality' James takes the example of the Americans and Australians.[5] Like West Indians, they are a new people who have developed characteristics of their own that separate them from the Europeans, to whom they are so closely related racially, and in the foundations of their civilisation (like us, he argues). Importantly, the West Indian type, James notes, is not a finished type, though it has certain characteristics that distinguish it, and its outlines are clear. It is in many ways an attractive type, he affirms. It is 'very graceful in manner and style, quick of wit, extremely intelligent, with more than average intelligence,' producing an astonishing number of men and women – in proportion to our small numbers – of remarkable ability, in various fields. James acknowledges rapid development in the West Indian personality, in particular the confidence with which West Indians have developed in their relationships with whites, and their ability go abroad and compete successfully with representatives of far richer, larger, and more advanced countries.

However, James notes that despite all of this, 'we miss something:'

> I know, I have noticed it in Trinidad where I have lived for the most part these days, and I wonder if you in Jamaica will have noticed it among yourselves, or among your neighbours. It is this. We lack what I will call a back to the seat on which are sitting.... When you speak to a body of English students about literature, you can almost feel the confidence from which they start...Chaucer, Milton, Shakespeare, the Victorians, Dryden and the rest of them, they know that they have taken a splendid place in the history of the literature of the world, and they can discuss with great ease from this background. You speak to French students and you will find their consciousness that France has the reputation of being the Mother of Laws and of civilisation. Americans by the

way and Australians too are very self conscious when they are in Europe before the sophistication and the reserve of the European and his consciousness of his background. But the Americans are increasingly conscious of the fact that they occupy a great position in the world and that they are a nation of great wealth and power.... [We West Indians do] not have that background that the others have instinctively. We will have to work for it. I believe it will complete the West Indian type when we have that consciousness. [6]

In relation to my definition of a civilisation, West Indians are unsure of their autonomy and independence in matters they consider serious. In economic organisation, justice, military matters, constitutional systems, and other institutional arrangements, our native sense is marginalised in favour of the 'international.' If the English-speaking West Indian feels this about his own society, how much more does he reject the lived experience of his Spanish, Dutch, and French Caribbean kin? Indeed, this is a central aspect of the West Indian character, or indeed the culture area. Lloyd Best has remarked on this in his 1964 'Letter to C.L.R.' Best observes,

Perhaps the most important among these is the basic ambivalence of the West Indian people and particularly of the West Indian leadership. To me this is the most important single structural fact in the situation. This peculiar Afro-Saxon 'way of seeing' is so much part of us that we are unable to formulate any strategy to deal with Prospero. Indeed, among our leaders there is a covert acceptance of the Caliban role....

The emergence of the African presence and 'way of seeing' (and by extension, of the Afro-Asian) is an essential condition for West Indian emancipation. Our basic ambivalence springs from the fact that we have this dual consciousness. But the African (or Afro-Asian) half is a Freudian consciousness, inarticulate and involuntary. This has two effects. One is that the more articulate half always triumphs in times of conflict since it has the supporting elements of a known language and history and all the points of reference that come with those. The second is that we are incapable of bringing about any integration of the two halves and distilling what is our new Afro-Saxon heritage; the two halves have not yet been brought on the same level and that is an essential prerequisite for bringing them together and sorting them out.[7]

Indeed, the hallmark of our independence movements in the Caribbean has been ambivalence. This has a history. From the ending of slavery up to the mid-twentieth century, Afro-Saxon strategy was largely one of intensive self-upliftment and self-fashioning. Intellectual and social achievement won respectability, public dignity, and independence in a time of readily expressed racism and actual colonialism. The establishment of villages and communities, the pursuit of education and the professions, and the achievement of political office were crucial. These 'Afro-Saxons' often out-Britished the British, excelling in European institutions.

At the same time, they were deeply resentful of the openly expressed opinions that they did not have the required intellectual ability to fully participate in civilised life, and they resented the prejudicial policies that excluded them from these pursuits. Yet they could conceive of nothing more admirable that British civilisation (they should not be overly criticised for holding this opinion, for indeed, British civilisation contained much to be admired, while much of African civilisation remains difficult for us to accept). Afro-Saxon protest was accordingly peculiar. John Jacob Thomas[8] in *Froudacity* (originally published in 1889) and C.L.R. James (1967) in *The Case for West Indian Self-Government* (originally published in 1933) persuasively argued that Negroes were not only 'fit to rule,' but even 'far more advanced in Western culture than many a European community.' Indeed, as some sought independence from Britain, it was largely an administrative affair, with little more ambition. We were, and are, far from being the centre of our world to ourselves.

This is not a pessimistic argument. The Caribbean is blessed with much talent, its experience is of great value to the world (and to itself), and it has much to offer that is genuinely new. Yet this is not merely a matter of will. Public relations must not substitute for honest self-examination. We do not need yet more self-delusion. The truth of our past and present – as best as we can understand it – will not, and should not, be wished away. This is all we have to work with.

Perhaps most importantly, living in a culture-zone that is not yet a civilisation provides peculiar intellectual challenges. Whereas 'organicism' in the other provinces of humanity has provided a foundation for Nationalism or Functionalism, an 'organic' view cannot support such theory here. We neither have a sense of an ancient nation, nor are we particularly functional as a unit. This gives rise to peculiar West Indian challenges (intellectual, political, economic, aesthetic, moral, and otherwise), and objectively provides the opportunity for truly original thought. We are obliged to distil and to create, against tremendous odds.

Beyond Radicalism and Rebellion

In my paper for the Conference held in honour of Lloyd Best at St Augustine Campus of the UWI,[9] I argued that it was misconceived to put Lloyd Best in the Caribbean Radical Tradition. This is true not only philosophically, for Best sees the distinction between Radical and Conservative as unnecessary, irrelevant, and intellectually harmful. Best's approach shares much with V.S. Naipaul and C.L.R. James, and also with Edmund Burke, George Orwell, and Walter Bagehot. The only other person who could conceivably be called 'New World' and who shares such sensibilities, it appears to me, is Orlando Patterson.

Best's aloofness from Caribbean Radicalism is perhaps even greater in practice, as it has in his view missed the challenge of the long, slow process of building a viable civilisation, from the earth, in preference for too-quick solutions and easy populism. Furthermore, Best refuses to see us as victim. Throughout his career, Best found himself in opposition to such Caribbean icons as Michael Manley, Walter Rodney, and Maurice Bishop, because they did not face the real challenges of building authentic and enduring West Indian institutions. For example, in his 1983 Wilberforce Lecture at the University of Hull, England, Best develops an insight as follows:

> I want to suggest that just as Trinidad is a highly fragmented social order where the cultural insurgency produces a large number of ethnicities, needing to make coalitions [that is, Afro-Saxons, Garveyites, Butlerites, Tobagonians, Hindus, Muslims, Christians, French Creoles, in-betweens], Jamaica is at the other end of the spectrum....

In Jamaica, being an older colony – Trinidad was started in the 19th century, Jamaica was started in the 17th century – has settled many of the questions. Over time the minor ethnic groups have lost their identity and therefore you can collapse the social order into two main groups.

One of which is distinguished not by its European ideology of being social democrats or being the capitalist class or anything like that. What distinguishes it is that it's the class which is more driven than the other by the possibilities of becoming incorporated into the world scheme, by education and churching and all those institutional arrangements that make people 'fitter to rule' and better equipped to work the world system, and live in London and go to Cambridge, and play cricket, and so on.

...The Jamaica Labour Party led by Mr Bustamante in the initial period, and later on by Seaga, was the party of the maroons and the peasants. Everybody knows that Mr Bustamante was the leader of the poor, peasant blacks in Jamaica. And Mr Manley (Senior) was the leader of the public school, and grammar school, and the artisan class in the city, leading a modern European existence.

...Michael Manley, coming on the scene in the 1970s appreciated that [the old Afro-Saxon culture] had come to an end. He was a politician, plenty of political wit and so on, he understood all of that. And because he understood that he was caught in a contradiction. Because the basis of his legitimacy in Jamaica was that he was the fittest man to rule in the West Indies, ever....

Even Mr Michael Manley's opponents thought that he was the man to rule Jamaica. When you hear him with the command of the Queen's English, when he stands up and talks, and you see him on television, you realise that he is the darling of the West Indies.... The basis of his legitimacy was that he was the prince of Afro-Saxon culture. Of the right breeding, he went to the right school. His father was the right person, and he had the right history for it....

...He was legitimated by the old order, but the policies he intended to pursue and the rhetoric he had adopted was taken from the new. He went to Ethiopia and he came back with the rod of Joshua, Rod of Correction, and he began dealing in the reggae and the weed and all the imagery of the new legitimation of the maroons and Rasta and the black culture appropriate to a new age when Independence had been won....

What was put on trial in Jamaica in the 1970s was not his social democracy, as all these outsiders are saying – they don't understand anything that's going on there – what was put on trial was the capacity of the brown man class in Jamaica that acceded to office on a legitimate basis, to make the transition to the demands of the post-Independence period. And they couldn't make the transition. They ran. They all ran....

The Manley Cabinet broke up repeatedly. Bell went to work for the IMF, Core went, Fletcher went, all these bright men left. They could not take the pressure....

And Manley ran in a different way in that he adopted a rhetoric that was quite irrelevant. He could not face the decisions, and he began to talk about the New International Order, all this business with Castro and so on, the Americans and destabilisation. It's pure substitute activity. There were very hard decisions to make in Jamaica, about the economy, tough decisions to make, decisions to make about the party and the leader. And they couldn't do it....

That explanation of the Jamaican situation is much more legitimate than all this foolishness in the newspapers about how Manley was introducing communism in Jamaica, and there was a big clash between socialists, there were no socialists there. And the lesson from that is that we have to have our own algebra.[10]

Understanding West Indian civilisation on its own terms is crucial. Only from this base can we proceed to build humane, free, and independent societies. We do not need to get consumed, yet again, in other people's defined battles, of 'right' versus 'left,' or of 'radical' versus 'conservative.' We have a responsibility to ensure our own independent viability and prosperity, as well as to enlighten the world about this province of human endeavour over which we have full responsibility.

Notes

1. See Ralph Gonsalves, *The Politics of our Caribbean Civilisation: Essays and Speeches* (Kingstown, Saint Vincent and the Grenadines: Great Works Depot, 2001).
2. See Nigel Bolland, *The Birth of Caribbean Civilisation: A Century of Ideas about Culture and Identity, Nation and Society* (Kingston: Ian Randle Publishers, 2004).
3. See Tim Hector, 'Ralph Gonsalves and the New Idea of a Caribbean Civilisation,' 'Fan the Flame,' *The Outlet*, 2001; and Tim Hector 'Is the Caribbean Really a New Civilisation?' 'Fan the Flame,' *The Outlet*, 2001.
4. See C.L.R. James, 'West Indian Personality' *Caribbean Quarterly* 35, no. 4 (December 1989):11–5.
5. Ibid.
6. Ibid.
7. Lloyd Best, 'Letter to C.L.R.' *Tapia*, no. 13 (Tunapuna: The Tapia House, 1964).
8. See John Thomas, 'Froudacity: West Indian Fables' by James Anthony Froude explained by J.J. Thomas, author of *The Creole Grammar* (London: New Beacon Books; original publication, London: T. Fisher Unwin, 1969).
9. Kirk Meighoo, 'Best and the Radical Caribbean Tradition: Challenges to Race, Episteme, and the Vanguard' In Selwyn Ryan ed *Independent Thought and Caribbean Freedom: Essays in Honour of Lloyd Best*, (St Augustine, Trinidad and Tobago: Sir Arthur Lewis Institute of Social and Economic Studies, 2003).
10. Lloyd Best, 'A Worldview for a City-State.' Wilberforce Lecture, University of Hull (1983).

8 | Size, Survival and Beyond: A Critical Underlabouring for 'Fleeing the Plantation' [1]

Patricia Northover and Michaeline Critchlow

Introduction

Under contemporary pressures of globalisation the Caribbean Community (CARICOM)[2] appears threatened by increasing global and regional insecurity, vulnerability and marginalisation as it is seemingly once again carried across another 'middle passage rite' in the turbulent waves of a neo-liberal globalisation.[3] How can the region's working peoples find safe passage in this contemporary crossroads marking yet another chapter in their struggle for 'survival and beyond?' What are the imperatives for successfully navigating globalisation, or negotiating a space – if there is little to none – in order to cross over? Do contemporary analyses and policies for regional development provide an improved or even relevant basis for small and vulnerable states to achieve competitiveness? What exactly are the preconditions for CARICOM's success? In this paper, we explore these questions and point towards elements of an answer, which prioritises analyses about ontology, through a critical engagement of some of the existing approaches to these issues.

We argue in the paper, along the lines of Lloyd Best's critique of Caribbean epistemology,[4] that securing the region's survival and beyond still requires an escape from functionalist, formalistic or aprioristic and deterministic analytical methodologies, in order to properly explore the paths for regional empowerment or competitive ascent. At a minimum, we argue that a reliance on methodologies that can accommodate process, as well as analyses of complex open systems, will be required in order to examine the nature of the relationship between society, economy and the state, and to pursue the needed research into the particularities of the social and political processes shaping Caribbean development.

In the absence of such approaches, we contend that there will be a failure to substantively explore the complex ontological structuring of social power or the 'state of the state system' in Caribbean societies. This, in turn, underpins a failure to provide analyses capable of providing a better grasp of the forces shaping/challenging the dynamic of development in the Caribbean's 'Creole societies,'[5] as well as the nature of their adaptive capacities as expressed in *creolisation.*'[6] Furthermore, without this research and analysis of the ontology and dynamic of the Caribbean's particular social powers there is a limited ability to *cogently* explain the nature of the region's *possibilities* to sustain contemporary local or global success in a modern 'world system' of neo-liberal capitalist sway.

This chapter thus attempts to develop by way of three sections a more adequate model of social power. This model, we suggest, can not only enable a fuller exploration of the nature of the possibilities for, and limits of, progressive social change in the context of the Caribbean, but also, facilitates a better understanding of these small states' attempts to negotiate spaces of freedom through discourses on 'competitive ascent' in the global capitalist system. In the first section, we identify the methodological and analytical guideposts that have helped to shape and frame our foray into these debates on Caribbean development. In the second section, we engage in the critical overview of prevailing approaches to the problem of development or progressive social change in the Caribbean. Two strands of analysis are identified. The first conceives of development as a process of modernisation which prioritises the state, (or rather the 'developmental state'), as the main macro-institutional agent in directing and managing social change. The second approach, described as 'pragmatic,' is centred in a bottom-up orientation that tends to stress the micro-actor and their culturally embedded rationality in approaching the issue of national development or regional progress.

Both approaches are argued to be relatively deficient in the analysis of the state-society-economy relationship, or more generally the problem of the relationship between modern 'power and its subjects,' in processes of social change. We argue therefore that an alternative approach is required, which rests on more adequate methodological, theoretical and empirical analyses of the ontology and dynamics of social power – the relationship between 'power and its subjects.' This model is theorised in Section 3 of this chapter.

Section 1: A Critical Underlabouring (and Labouring) for Fleeing the Plantation

We wish to continue in the New World tradition of progressive politics for, so to speak, 'fleeing the plantation' by a process of underlabouring. That is, we seek to clear the way for a better analysis of the problems of regional development, by critically engaging with old and new ideas on growth and regional success to reveal their limits, as well as, to point towards an alternative methodological foundation, which prioritises analyses about ontology and politics, and that, we believe, facilitates explanatory power. This idea of underlabouring has been popularised by the adherents of a new philosophical framework, generally known as Critical Realism, which has been developed through the path-breaking writings of Roy Bhaskar.[7] This philosophical perspective stretches across many disciplines and is famous for its critical stance towards both positivism and varieties of postmodernism.[8] Tony Lawson, a leading proponent of this philosophical approach in the discipline of economics, explains the work of critical realism as acting in the role of 'underlabourer for a more fruitful approach to scientific explanation.'[9] Our approach here is informed by this philosophical positioning. However, rather than elaborating on its metatheoretical arguments for an adequate explanatory approach in the social sciences,[10] the chapter proceeds by drawing on the insights of these arguments as we critically engage the existing approaches.

We offer, furthermore, to go beyond simply identifying critical deficiencies in existing explanatory accounts. In particular, we advance a theoretical discussion on development in the Caribbean by re-examining and rethinking the nature of the relation between 'state,' 'society,' 'economy' and 'history.'[11] In this regard, we seek to overcome the recurrent inadequacies of both theory and method by paying closer attention to the *complex ontological structuring of power* or the *'state of the state system'* and its shaping of *social powers and capacities* in Caribbean societies. This substantive theoretical effort is part of a larger project to rethink power relations and social hi/stories (human identity stories) in Atlantic space, through a renewed analysis of *'creolisation'* processes; a work that has been developed in the recent text, *Globalization and the Post Creole Imagination*. In that text we have argued for rethinking 'creolisation,' (referred to by Michel Rolf Trouillot as *historicised processes* of *'selective creation and cultural struggle'* to realise the repeated *'miracle of survival,')*[12] as not just *practices and processes* of cultural innovation or transformation, but also *as projects* of 'spatial history.' Such projects, as Elden notes, relate to practices that attempt to 'historicize space and spatialize history.'[13] *'Creolisation'* then, as process and project, captures the main idea of Marx's oft-quoted phrase that '[m]en make their own history, but they do not make it as they please; they do not make it under self-selected circumstances, but under circumstances existing already, given and transmitted from the past.'[14]

Our interventions are thus guided by a desire to more fully grasp the nature of the complex processes in which Caribbean small states are embedded, and to which they are contributing. For this end, the analysis and investigation of power relations and their roots and routes in Caribbean social history are considered paramount. Moreover, this work is also central to moving the debate on the mechanisms for realising greater spaces of development for the Caribbean. Indeed, we suggest that a first step in understanding Caribbean people's continued efforts for enhancing their degrees of freedom in the global political economy is to come more fully to terms with the nature of the region's entangled spaces of power.

Entangled Spaces of Power and Place: Creolisation, Freedom and Possibility

While 'competitiveness' appears to be the buzz word for small states engaged in a process of navigating and negotiating contemporary globalisation, the region's search for success, as reflected in the debates on processes of transformation in the Caribbean, seems also inescapably tied to a process and politics of *'creolisation.'*[15] This may be seen in the longstanding preoccupation with notions of endogenous, or 'home grown,' development, freedom and sovereignty.[16] Indeed, the efforts of small states to secure space for themselves beyond the margins allotted to them by contemporary neo-liberal pressures, resonates with memories of previous struggles for survival in the context of enforced 'middle passage rites' in the turbulent waves of an emergent globalisation, as articulated through a complex modernity. Accordingly, while contexts have changed, the efforts of CARICOM small states still seem embedded in a general 'process of selective creation and cultural struggle,' as manifested in their contemporary struggles for economic space, or their struggle to creatively adapt and create space, where there is little or none being given. The process of development, thus impels a politics of realising 'freedoms' which is arguably reflective of a more general politics of 'making place' – the capacity to be present – the issue at stake in the strategy of *'creolisation.'* Yet how do Caribbean peoples' powers of freedom translate into their shaping of their *conditions* of freedom?

We take 'freedom' to mean the following senses as Bhaskar outlines them. First, being 'free' implies '...knowing, possessing the power and the disposition to act in or towards one's real interests;' and second being 'liberated' consists of 'the transformation of unneeded, unwanted and oppressive [sources of determination] to needed, wanted and empowering *sources* of determination,' which 'depends on the transformation of structures and not just the amelioration of states of affairs.'[17] The praxis of freedom is thus mediated not only by, so to speak, an ethical disposition to make 'right choices,' (or, as Foucault would say, to express an ethic of care for the self, *and* others), but also by our knowledge of the *'sources* of determination' for empowerment or for realising an authentic state of freedom. These moments of freedom are, as Bhaskar argues 'necessarily informed by explanatory social theory,'[18] (but we should caution here that one's lines of escape cannot be wholly derived from such rationalistic epistemologies). This in turn, we suggest, calls for, *at a minimum*, something like the critical realist's philosophical commitments[19] as a mode of removing unwarranted restrictions in the pursuit of explanatory power, and relatedly, emancipatory praxis.[20]

This position, namely, that one needs to be equipped with *tenable* epistemological and philosophical grounds for sustaining emancipatory practices, underlies the basic insight that Lloyd Best sought to instill in his ongoing wrestling with the prevailing paradigms for growth and development. It was his enduring belief that the existing paradigms, ignored the complexity of Caribbean ontology – emergent from unique yet systemic 'global' and 'local,' 'structural' and 'institutional' 'plantation' and 'postcolonial,' processes and forces. Hence his trenchant critiques of the epistemology emanating from Caribbean scholars and politicians and their failure to sufficiently grasp the nuanced textures of Caribbean's ontology, (and relatedly, the nature of its politics and process) as reflected in his seminal 1967 essay, *Independent Thought and Caribbean Freedom*.[21]

Like Best then, we argue that in the absence of more adequate and ongoing research and analysis on the 'ontology and dynamics of social power' driving processes of Caribbean development, positions staked concerning the region's transformational *possibilities,* or '*emancipatory necessities,*' for contemporary local or global success, will fall short in *cogency*.

Our efforts in this regard reflect an attempt to be highly sensitive to these issues of ontology, by breaking out of epistemological frameworks or orientations which threaten to delimit and derail one's grasp of the complex forces shaping/challenging the dynamically and complexly constituted, but in many ways still plantation embedded 'states' and 'Creole' societies. Such an approach we believe should foster a better a deeper understanding of how Caribbean people's powers of freedom are connected to the processes of, and possibilities for, small states repositioning for space and place, in contexts of neo-liberal globalisation. We now turn to the critical examination of the arguments used to support the process of 'regional ascent,' or the enhancement of the region's capacities for competitiveness, development, empowerment, or freedom.

Section 2: Conditions of Possibility for 'Achieving Ascent' in the Caribbean?

The countries of CARICOM have experienced complex and diversified social histories that have been shaped by divergent geographies and geopolitics. These histories and geographies have led to variegated processes of socio-economic change, reflected in the patterns of economic structure and performance, with some states regarded as 'out performing' others, but all today remain, by and large, vulnerable small states, (see Table 1).[22] Furthermore, as small or small island developing states[23] they face increasing *insecurity* at the national, regional and global levels given the complex socio-economic, environmental and political effects of globalisation processes,[24] as well as, deepening *vulnerability* and threatened *marginalisation* in the competitive circuits of global capital.[25]

Table 1: Vulnerability of Caribbean States and Per Capita GDP

	Low vulnerability	Medium vulnerability	High vulnerability	Total
Low per capita income	Guatemala	Honduras Haiti* Nicaragua Cuba *(estimated)*	Guyana	6
Medium per capita income	Venezuela Colombia	Costa Rica Panama Jamaica Dominican Republic El Salvador	St Kitts and Nevis St Lucia St Vincent & Grenadines Grenada Dominica Belize Suriname	14
High per capita income	Mexico	Barbados Trinidad and Tobago	Bahamas Antigua and Barbuda	5
TOTAL	**4**	**11**	**10**	**25**

Source: Association of Caribbean States (ACS) – Small Economies of the Greater Caribbean, July 2001, 45, http://www.acs-aec.org/small_econ_eng.htm

a. High, medium and low vulnerability are as estimated by the Commonwealth Vulnerability Index scores.
b. High per capita income is >US$5,000
c. Medium per capita income is US$2,000–5000
d. Low per capita income is <US$2,000
  * Haiti is the only Least Developed Country amongst all the ACS countries

The Caribbean Regional Negotiation Machinery (CRNM), set up by CARICOM has been given the complex task of negotiating 'reciprocity' in the 'cross currents of globalization and regionalization,' in order to facilitate 'strategic global repositioning' for the competitive viability of its members.[26] What, however, are the regional and/or national socio-political constraints and conditions of possibility for 'achieving ascent in the next century'?

Roughly, two broad types of arguments on the 'conditions of possibility' or 'necessary' social and institutional forms and processes for achieving ascent can be detected in the Caribbean development literature. They are either prescriptive, top down and single exit explanatory perspectives on modernisation. These typically call for national and/or 'supra-national' 'state autonomy,' (the latter premised on political union within the Caribbean Single Market and Economy [CSME] as *the* necessary institutional form for enabling ascent as 'modernized' capitalism. On the other hand, one finds instead pragmatic perspectives on modernisation that have evolved and revolve around the need for more fine-grained actor perspectives on the nature of Caribbean 'identity,' ideology and cultural forms, and thus call attention to the need to seek out the distinctive political, socio-economic and moral institutions that will sustain local endogenous transformation processes.

The first perspective generally embraces a vision of an essentially top-down national and/or regional type of '*Developmental State,*' that is strategically engaged in the political engineering of the conditions for modern economic change,[27] *viz* modern industrialisation – whether based in manufacturing, agriculture, or both.[28] In this approach, however, there is a failure to go beyond a generally broad-brush and essentialising method in the analysis of complex processes. Thus, despite the introduction of historical categories, such as 'class' or 'culture,' into the discussion of Caribbean state-society relationships, a systematic empirical interrogation of these analytical constructs is absent, reflecting the avoidance of, or limited foray into a deeper engagement with the nature of the social processes and practices underpinning this aforementioned relationship and Caribbean experiences. Accordingly, the conclusions *ultimately* remain rooted in, or dependent upon, a form of *aprioristic* reasoning that offers to deductively generalise possibilities given theoretical premises of *institutional or political development* 'laws' that have been abstracted as the conditions for national or regional success. In this case, we have the implied 'law' of development – that strong states idealised as those with (somehow generated) embedded autonomy,[29] will (somehow) effect the right mixture of repression and incentives, and thereby produce the trajectory of developmental 'ascent' and enhanced well-being or freedom(s).

The second perspective points to the need for more fine-grained actor perspectives on the nature of Caribbean 'identity,' ideology and cultural forms and on the distinctive political, socio-economic and moral institutions that will sustain local endogenous transformation processes.[30][31] In other words, this approach is more pragmatic,' or less driven by 'formulaic' social laws and institutional prescriptions, and more centred in a bottom-up, or micro-actor orientated and culture embedded rationality approach to modernisation. This type of analysis, albeit typically nation-centric, is in turn expected to more adequately inform and shape the building of a Caribbean regional ideology and development. The tendency in this approach is thus to try to focus on social, socio-economic and cultural conditions and the related empowerment issues required for achieving regional ascent in the form of an embedded, indigenous, or Creole,[32] modernisation process. The second perspective lends support to *a more a posteriori* approach and thus tends to call attention to the issues of particular social and/or cultural histories, or particular constructions and readings of these, that are seen as shaping distinctive paths to national and regional development. However, what is the relationship between the society, economy and the state, that is implied in this more pragmatic envisioning of creatively achieving 'ascent' under contemporary globalisation? Indeed, if a key recognition within the pragmatic approach is that the viability of the Caribbean state and society in a global capitalist system depends on its Creole subversion of the process of modernisation through flexible creative engagement, then, the ineluctable political questions to be addressed for this approach are these. Can such desirable outcomes be achieved without, as Migdal would say, a 'state-in-society,' acting strategically, and not merely functionally, to enhance domestic capabilities through *specific* political processes?[33] Plus, more pointedly, what exactly is *the nature of the concrete political processes* or dynamics shaping this unfolding potential for the emergence of an emancipatory 'Creole' social power?

Silence on these questions would tend to support a position of functionalist political agnosticism on the strategic role of the state-society relationship, which operates by bracketing, or setting aside state-society relationships and the complex issues of their formation as well as transformation. We argue that the presence of silence, omission, functionalist agnosticism, or even a too limited attention on this issue would hinder the expression of the transformational interests of Caribbean peoples. Especially, those groups that have been at the root of the creative subversions of, and cultural struggles with, the experienced paradoxes of modernity – paradoxes such as growth without equity, or modernisation without higher or better social capabilities or rising productivity. The imperative here in order to support the theme of the Caribbean's social empowerment in the pragmatic approach is thus to rigorously problematise the nature of the ongoing political processes shaping the 'state of the state system' in Caribbean social life worlds and hence the potentials and probabilities for specific *social capabilities, powers and state capacities* emerging. In turn, we suggest that this requires a deeper theoretical and empirical understanding of the *'creolisation' processes* which underpin Caribbean state, society and economy relationships in order to better understand (analytically and empirically) the nature and basis for transformational relationships to be forged between the state and society in the making of history. This would also help one to better judge the tendencies and possibilities for a state strategically acting, for example, to link and build 'social capital'[34] or indeed acting or engaging *with* 'social movements'[35] for Caribbean regional development.

While issues of 'power' seem more transparent in the first perspective given the ostensive linking of state and society in attempting to grasp the basis for transformational processes, it relies on an *ultimately* deterministic and 'aprioristic' reasoning reflecting an inadequate attention to the nature of the (socio-cultural and political) *'creolisation' processes* entailed in them. These processes are undoubtedly germane to institutional development trajectories yet they are assumed not to (causally) matter much for extrapolating an institutional policy formula mix for success. Alternatively, the 'desirable' blend of repression and freedom associated with 'embedded state autonomy,' is apparently to be determined through blanket class categories, or worse, is left as a relatively unexamined socio-political process, that is somehow expected to produce the right outcomes. More generally, despite the fact that modern capitalist states are clearly 'doubly embedded' in global and local, as well as, cultural and structural processes, this approach glosses over the ways in which generic 'real interests' acting on the state are *translated* into particular *'imagined necessities.'* In so doing, the complexity and open-endedness of the social spaces and dynamic path conditions embedding states, (even where they must meet structural demands of economic viability within the circuits of global competitive capitalism) are, quite simply, analytically brushed aside.

In other words, the issue, as highlighted by Migdal (2001), of *how* states are embedded in societies, and how, as Bhabha (1994) emphasises, social spaces of structural relations or interests *are to be interpreted, translated or re-imagined*, given the fact that social forms of political expression *are constantly being negotiated* with *diverse* peoples and social groups, is left (relatively) unattended.[36] Yet these complex constraints, (underpinned by the boundedness of state capacities as well as the fact that the state must attract a level of legitimacy and public trust, within and without its shifting borders of 'sovereignty'), will act to *shape* the state of the 'state system,' or the nature of power exercised in the society. This power thus concerns not just the state, but more broadly, the state of the social powers and subject capabilities exercised in the society, upon which, arguably, rests the technological dynamism of the society. Despite the relative success of developmental states in certain social and historical contexts then, the outcomes of these political processes of state and society relationships, simply cannot be read either deterministically, or by recourse to institutional or structural formulas for development.

Overall, the presence of a preponderant tendency to overplay aprioristic reasoning has led to two major weaknesses in this approach to development policy. The first, of these is an insufficient depth of empirical analysis, as seen for example in the absence of an adequate study of *the processes and forms of* Caribbean empowerments. This means that the arguments to substantiate and guide the *'how'* of politically acting for the claimed law-like transformational 'necessities' to sustain local or regional success possess limited cogency. Second, there is a tendency to oscillate between a *deterministic* pessimism on the weakness of existing states and an *unjustifiable* optimism that such weak states could execute the changes for the 'developmental state' project prescribed, given the penchant for 'aprioristic' reasoning again reflecting an inadequate attention to the nature of processes of social development.[37] On the whole then, both perspectives are insufficient for guiding an approach to regional ascent because of inadequate methodological, empirical and theoretical bases for the analysis of processes of social development. These inadequacies in turn engender a failure to sufficiently, or more concretely, examine the institutional and socio-political *'how possible' process and agency conditions* producing and shaping the probabilities and dynamics for ascent.

The above brief discussion reinforces Lloyd Best's critique of Caribbean epistemology, as it is clear that securing the region's survival and beyond, requires an escape from functionalist, aprioristic and deterministic analytical methodologies, in order to properly explore the paths for regional ascent, and the nature of the relationship between society, economy and the state, as articulated through specific *'creolisation'* processes. *At a minimum*, we argue that a reliance on critical realist methodologies, or something like this, that can accommodate process *and* complex open systems analysis, will be required. In other words, we believe that elements of such an approach enables one to pursue the needed research into the particularities of the social and political processes shaping the 'state of the state system' in social life worlds, and the complexity of 'real interests,' or imagined necessities, influencing the state in its unfolding role in relating to the society, and influencing the economy to enable a Caribbean development.[38]

In the next section, we seek to overcome the aforementioned analytical deficiencies by suggesting a model for grasping the ontology and dynamics of power in our 'modern' societies. We develop the arguments for this model by moving through a brief critical review of recent discussions examining the nature of the relationship between the state, society and history.

Section 3: 'Imagining State Systems:' Critical Reflections and Elements for New Directions

Recent approaches seeking to understand the processes and politics of development and change, reflect divergent views on the state's significance to history making and have varied conceptualisations of its mode of articulation with society. The strengths and limits of these efforts however seem correlated with the extent to which they have effectively redressed the weaknesses in the perspectives on the state that have been developed out of the modernisation paradigm. One approach in particular that represents an effort to pull together the most important contributions on thinking about the state-society relationship is Migdal's (2001) 'State in Society' approach. We believe our approach represents an advance on this and also escapes the modernisation paradigm. We begin the discussion with a brief look at this dominant paradigm's treatment of the issue of the state-society-history relationship, drawing on the discussion in Migdal (2001), and then introduce our model of the relation between 'Power and its Subjects.'

In Migdal's (2001) discussion of the dominant modernisation perspective informing the study of development and change, he notes that the accomplishment of modernisation has been constantly associated with the presence of a Modern Nation State (MNS). In introducing the state as actor, these modernisation orientated development discourses tended to rely on the Weberian tradition of defining the state as a bureaucratic organisation with a monopoly over legitimate violence, and with a *modus operandi* of bureaucratised *scientific* rationality. The effect of this characterisation is to focus social power as embedded within the institutionalised bounds of the MNS, and thus restrict an analysis of political power in societies to this organisation's ontology and its managerial dynamics for executing power. With the ontology and dynamics of social power neatly packed into the MNS as 'representational political power,' the state becomes *the 'representative' locus of authority and power in the modern society and world*. The MNS is constructed as *the centre* for the acting of the modern subject, *the representative author* of modern change.

Unsurprisingly, given this scripted entrance onto the modern world stage, the MNS quickly assumes, at least on stage, its 'representative' authorship over the process of modern history-making. This is accomplished by submerging all history into its history of '[T]he acting subject or [T]he critical prime mover in society and mover of society,' with the latter, that is, society, to be 'represented,' acted upon, and transformed by the representative holder of Modern Subjectivity-Sovereignty, the MNS. In abstracting power in this way, and in this 'imagining' of the modern state, the path was thus prepared for both the crafting of sterile dichotomies along old analytical axes of centre/periphery and subjects/objects, and the engendering of critical dissent, in theory and practice. For example, from the equation core=subject=state and periphery=other=passive object='society' we engender the state/society dichotomy and the image of *verticality* which is interpreted as the state being 'outside' and 'above' society. [39]

Criticisms abound of such analytical dichotomies with their implied separations between the state, society or culture, and its associated analytical premise of a state acting with *autonomous* history-making powers, in virtue of its claimed '*autonomy*.' For example, one may question the direction of the power relation in society, or the nature of the power relation between the state and society/culture, as Geertz (1980) does by highlighting situations of causal inversion, for example 'Power *serving* Pomp'[40] and not vice versa. One may also question the ordering powers ascribed to the state, with the attribution of state autonomy then becoming 'state effects' according to Mitchell (1991) – an appearance or spontaneous illusion produced because of the pervasive extension of Foucauldian disciplinary technologies or governmentalities of which the state is *but a part*, rather than *apart from*, standing above like some reified structure.[41] Migdal also argues that, the ordering powers desired by the state become concretely complicated by powerful societies which produce weak states.[42] Alternatively, as Gramsci emphasises political and social order is achieved by complex class struggles in wars of position to establish *hegemony*, which is irreducible to state force but rather points more to the subtle condition of, and inequalities in, an active cultural production of consent.[43]

Migdal's objective in his 2001 text is to critically weave these critiques against the state's image of verticality into his 'State in Society' approach in order to argue that the practices and *experiences* of the state – as organisations with certain powers and capabilities, whether 'weak' or 'strong' – are embedded and meaningfully constituted in society/groups/civil society, and are negotiated through culture/representations. Through this critical synthesis, Migdal attempts to break new ground on, or critically develop, the analytics of the ontology and dynamics of power in society. Indeed, Migdal's critical shifts have wide appeal in the contemporary literature on the state, which as Hansen and Stepputat argue, is now more concerned to 'explore the local and historically embedded ideas of normality, order, intelligible authority and other languages of stateness.'[44] Accordingly, as Ferguson and Gupta comment:

...states are not simply functional bureaucratic apparatuses, but powerful sites of symbolic and cultural production that are themselves always culturally represented and understood in particular ways. It is here that it becomes possible to speak of states, and not only...nations as 'imagined'– that is, as constructed entities that are conceptualized and made socially effective through particular imaginative and symbolic devices that require study.[45]

Indeed, they do require study, but what sorts of questions should we be asking in these more culturally and conflict sensitive investigations of the state-in-society/culture?

Despite the breakthroughs being made here, we submit that much of what is going on in these contemporary discussions may still be reflecting a *prioritisation of the way in which the problem of order has been previously framed and solved* in the study of the practice of domination and change in society.

Towards Imagining 'State Systems in Social Life Worlds'

Our main concern here is to try to go beyond Migdal's study in his tendency to focus on *securing order, in his State-in-society framework*. As Migdal argues,

...the challenge for political leaders has been how to remain apart from society – the state as the ultimate authority – while somehow still benefiting from people's 'collective self-consciousness,' their sense of belonging to something bigger than themselves of which they are an integral part.[46]

Thus, we note Migdal's appeal to Shil's notion of the 'image' of the state as a powerful *normative social centre*, imagined to produce the social whole, and broker the peace between its individual elements in the world. Ultimately then, Migdal's study is characterised by the tendency to define the problem of order, not only in organisational terms as guided by the MNS construct, but primarily in terms of a problem of adhesiveness and its lack.

Thus, Migdal appears to frame the problem of social power, or the state-society relationship, in terms of the Hobbesian problem of order which premises atomistic human beings in extrinsic relations with others.[47] This reinforces a focus on interactional conflict and uncertainty as the heart of the problem of social order. With this methodological/ontological frame, the relations between power and the subject are fundamentally contingent and external, a relation of force and domination. Given the above, a platform is established for oscillating between two models of social order, namely the under-socialised man (rational economic modern man living solely through contracts or markets, Homo Economicus) and the over-socialised man (traditional man lively by rule following, Homo Sociologicus). In both, the problem conceptualisation remains the same, that is, deviation or conflict is to be addressed by finding a super-structural adhesive, for example, state or culture as superglue, and thus legitimacy of order problems are addressed through rituals and negotiations for producing this glue.

To go beyond this level of analysis it is necessary to break with the framework for discussing order that is shaping discourse on the state, and power in society. To do this, three ontological departures will be made based on alternative analysis of 'human subject being' in the world, which paves the way for establishing a different view of the ontological structure of 'social being in the world.' This enables us to then offer a new conceptualisation of 'social power in social life worlds' or 'state systems in social life worlds,' which is the model that we wish to set out in contrast to the approach briefly analysed above.

We wish to begin our discussion by arguing that the question guiding the existing approaches to the study of power and change in society, that is, 'how is order possible?' implicates an oscillation between rationalistic and functionalistic accounts of social order and impoverishes our understanding of dynamics. We should instead begin by asking *how does disorder, or processes of separation or even alienation, emerge?* This feeds in to the related problem, *how does that experience of disordering productions shape the dynamics of process?*

This problem refocusing requires empirical support by examining the nature of human beings' social life in the world. Tim Ingold provides a very detailed examination of this very issue in his text, *Evolution and Social Life*. In that text, he argues for a model of the human being as 'a conscious subject, whose life is a trajectory as entwined with those of others around him as the lives of the latter are with his [and] whose conscious life...is a movement that adopts

SIZE, SURVIVAL AND BEYOND

culture as its vehicle.'[48] Social life thus 'exists in the intertwining...it is the process by which we constitute one another as persons.' Indeed, he argues that our social relations are produced in the *'movement'* of this intertwining process of social life.[49] Drawing on Mauss's analysis of the exchange of gifts, he goes on to argue that the production of the social relationship is achieved through the mutual giving of oneselves, thus creating an inter-subjective bond between persons, a mutual subjectivity production. Accordingly, social order reflects processes of interpenetrative and constitutive dependence, and the experience of social order is constituted in and from these social relationships that reflect 'the temporal unfolding of consciousness through the *instrumentality* of cultural forms.'[50] Implied in this theory of the social, and as Archer (1995) succinctly states, is the proposition that 'social identity is an emergent from personal identity.'[51]

From this perspective of the human being in the world the problem facing persons in the mutual constitution of their social lives and selves is *not how to glue together* separated beings, but rather *how to transform* the inescapable internal relations of 'being together' and 'becoming together.' This process is threaded through the personal and social levels, in a way that seems to offer the enhancement of personal and subject being in the world. Since this subjectivity is formed through the inter-subjective experiences of social life, the search for a better expression of person being is simultaneously a self-interested and altruistic choice for the sustaining of social life. Taking this human subjectivity and its internally related constitution of person being, as the vital agents in history, the question thus becomes, how do these agents engender change? On the other hand, as Archer (1985) would say, how do they engender the *morphogenesis* of their social worlds and consequently the state of social and subject powers?

In order to explore the analytics of this morphogenetics of power, we thus wish to turn briefly to Archer's (1985), *Realist Social Theory*. In that text, she has argued, drawing on the philosophical orientation of critical realism, that in order to address the question of articulation between *the people* (the subjects) and *the parts* (the given conditions of social power for agents' social formation) it is necessary to maintain the notion of emergent properties at the level of agency and structure. This position requires that one adopts a model of complex ontological stratification of the social life world. To this end, she elaborates on models that explain the morphogenetics of structure, culture and agency, by taking 'Time' to link, structure and agency and unpack the critical realist's Transformational Model of Social Activity (TMSA), elaborated by Bhaskar (1989).

In brief, the social ontology model holds that structure and agency are ontologically separate yet mutually constitutive or determining of each other. Not, however, in a mode of 'instantiation' as argued in Gidden's structuration theory, but rather, by a process of morphogenetics. This model allows for the complex time-structure mediated, *ontological interplay* between the parts (which she analytically separates into the structural emergent powers [SEPs][52] of cultural and structural systems), and the people. This, in turn, enables a study of their dynamics of transformation and avoids collapsing into models of individualism or holism for explaining social process. As she explains, 'the morphogenetic task is to supply an account of how the powers of the "parts" condition the projects of the "people" – involuntaristically but also non-deterministically, yet none the less with directionality.'[53] While one may still wish to engage Archer on her substantive arguments about the theories of the world and the nodes and modes of articulation taking place between persons, agents, collectivities and structurally emergent properties that she has developed, we believe her contributions are critical for thinking through the dynamic of the relations between power and the subject. In particular, Archer's social models, along with Ingold's arguments on social life, allow us *to begin to pose vital questions* as to the *how* our vital agents, human subjects personally, relationally and collectively *co-produce and change* their complex world drawing on structural resources, or as constrained/enabled by structurally emergent powers (SEPs).

Thus far, by beginning with Ingold's 'constitutive' model of social life and personal identity, we arrived at a view of the ontological stratification of human beings in an ontologically stratified world. That is, the human being is (at least) a doubly emergent person. In other words, our person being is ontologically dependent on our relations with nature and with social conditions that date person being in the world, but this person being is irreducible to neither.[54] There is thus an ontological articulation between social and personal being in 'space,' via the positions that we encounter in life, and as mediated by the conscious subject.[55] The possibility for disorder now emerges given the inter-generational, time-dated, co-evolution of our complex social life in the world. That is, this disorder emerges if, and in so far as the structural emergent socio-cultural conditions shaping social being and action *negatively* shape/constrain the subject's experiences of inter-subjectivity and their interactive exploration of themselves in the mutual shaping processes of social life production.

The sketch above outlines the ontology of power from a very generic set of theoretical perspectives. In order to reconnect to the specific points of finding an adequate model of the state-society relationship that could help one better account for the nature of history, and the process for achieving states of relative empowerment or development, we wish to focus upon next, the shaping of power relations in modern spaces and time. In what follows, we lay the basis then for describing *contemporary* power relations and its mode of expression as a 'modern state system in social life worlds.'

Modern Governmentality as a 'Modern State System in Social Life Worlds'

In his general analysis of power, Foucault described the way in which power relations have generally been complicit in sustaining processes of disordering social life through 'modes of objectification which transform human beings into subjects.'[56] The first two modes of this objectification, or subjectification, process are given as follows. First, one has the production of 'subjects of *scientific* study' through the formation of discourse systems or fields, such as 'political economy,' which are 'the set of rules which at a given period and for a given society define the limits and forms of the sayable...conservation...memory... reactivation [and]...appropriation.'[57] Second, there are 'dividing practices' where 'the subject is divided inside himself or divided from others,' as exemplified in sane/mad, modern/traditional, good/bad or sacred and profane dividing practices.[58] These twinned processes are *implemented with* disciplinary technologies, highlighting the embedding of body politics in all knowledge-power discursive regime formations.[59] However, as Foucault was to later emphasise,[60] *these disciplinary technologies governing the body, while implicated in governmental technologies of dominance, have also become routed through technologies of the self, and as such are being exercised through* complex processes of modern *governmentality* – described by Foucault (1983, 1991) as 'the conduct of conduct.' These emergent forms of contemporary power relations that Foucault observed and described as modern governmentality, based on his analysis, were argued to entail a structural shift in the mode of *thinkable* power relations for organising social life. In this emergent form, social power became structurally divorced from the sovereign and was displaced into the social body, and the individual. [61] Modern power becomes recast as a field of space held together by multiple 'forces, attractions and co-existences.'[62]

Accordingly, a critical feature of modern governmentality is that these two processes of 'objectification' or 'othering' identified before are necessarily articulated with a third form of 'objectification,' which is 'the way in which a person turns him – or herself – into a subject.'[63] This last process is internally but not determinately linked to the other forms of objectification through *governmentality – which is Foucault's structure-agency point of articulation* – and it is more concerned with the work of a self, or subject expression, or how we form ourselves into meaning giving subjects. Accordingly, the first two modes of objectification are mediated by a person's sense or consciousness of themselves in the world and so *experiences* of disorder will be subject, or person sensitive. *If* there *is an experience (in the subjective sense indicating awareness) of disorder* this implies the engendering of a disturbance in relations of reciprocity sustaining social relationships, that is, a disturbance in the process of *inter-subjective bonding between persons in their mutual subjectivity production.* This disorder or disturbance will then form the basis for person's inter-subjective and ontological insecurity in social relationships, and lay the ground for the presence of fundamental uncertainty and conflict in negotiating interests and managing uncertainty in social life. Finally, this disorder or disturbance, given its (ontological and epistemological) impacts on person or subject being via social being, will also form the conditions for the subject driven social processes of the politics of identity (or meaning) in the world, as can be seen, for example, in the complex dynamics in post colonial and gender identity politics.

Modern governmentality, we suggest however, is *not just* about inter-subjective power relations and its new rationalities in shaping the conduct of conduct, as well as modes of subjectification/objectification. Nor is it only about the *management* of an emergent political neo-liberalism, its varieties,[64] and its tensions in macro-political relationships that engage governments and their political subjects in the struggle for rights, cultural expression, or the reshaping of identity relations in modern 'world systems.' Rather, we believe that Foucault also meant for it to indicate the presence of structural conditions and tendencies operative within a social process, determining a field of social space, and delimiting the ontological possibilities of *social* life. In particular, if one further examines Foucault's (1983) analysis of power one sees more clearly that Foucault's treatment of power is consistent with a treatment of power as a structural emergent property (SEP). That is, as a condition for the actions of the *subject* – which Foucault also treats as a *person*, that is 'someone...tied to his own identity by a conscience or self.'[65] In particular, Foucault in speaking to power, states that:

> In itself, the exercise of power is not violence: nor is it consent which, implicitly is renewable. It is *a total structure of actions* brought to bear upon possible actions: it incites, it induces, it makes easier or more difficult; in its extreme it constrains or forbids absolutely; it is nevertheless *a way of acting upon an acting subject or acting subjects* by virtue of their acting or being capable of action. A set of actions upon other actions[66] (our emphasis).

After which Foucault is quick to make the deliberate link back to conduct, when he argues that:

> ...perhaps the equivocal nature of the term *conduct* is one of the best aids for coming to terms with the specificity of power relations. For to 'conduct' is at the same time to 'lead' others (according to mechanisms of coercion that are to varying degrees, strict) and a way of behaving within a more or less open field of possibilities. The exercise of power consists in guiding the possibility of conduct and putting in order the possible outcome.[67]

The point we wish to suggest here is that Foucault is seeking, through the concept of governmentality, to elaborate on what may be termed a *state system*, defined very broadly, in the first instance, as an *irreducible social power, shaping (that is, constraining or enabling) the social life worlds of persons*. We argue that this view of governmentality as expressive of a 'state system in social life worlds' is consistent with Foucault's emphases in explaining how in 'modern governmentality' 'one governs things... government is the right disposition of things, arranged so as to lead to a convenient end.'[68] Here 'things' have to do 'not with territory but rather a sort of complex composed of men and things. The things... are in fact men, *but men in their relations, links, and imbrication with those other things....*'[69] Finally, in Foucault's contention that governmentality, 'is at once internal and external to the state.'[70]

Foucault's comments above, we believe, are thus clearly signaling modern governmentality as the concrete expression of *modern social power*, a move which then enables him to shift the focus in the analysis of modern social power from the institutional-organisational level to the structural-institutional level. Having outlined the general ontological character of power, through the revisiting of modern governmentality in Foucault's work, we now wish to elaborate a bit on the definition of a 'state system,' by treating the nature of a state system as exhibiting the characteristics of a type of *elementary form of religion.*[71] This step represents a creative analogical extension of Durkheim's ideas of *the politics of 'social order'* to contemporary state systems. Thus we wish to refine the definition of modern governmentality as not just a 'state system,' or complexly constituted form of social power emergent in society, but also wish to examine it as a peculiar social mechanism of re/presentation. In particular, our interpretation of a Foucauldian govern/mentality stresses its work as a representational system for the collective expression of positional political identities or cosmologies of social being in the world that turn on sacred and profane identity relations. We argue then that the state system of modern governmentality articulates the sacred and the profane generally along the contemporary cultural axis of *modern power rationalities.* However, the nature of the specific sacred/profane positional identities associated with this concrete state system, or state of social power, will be dependent on the concrete nature of the specific adaptive and governmentality engineering tactics shaping the expression of modern governmental ensembles.[72] This engenders not just complexly structured identity struggles, but also complex entanglements of spaces and times. In our larger work interrogating globalisation processes as rooted and routed in Caribbean 'worldings,' we have pointed precisely to these sets of forces as being differentially expressed within *'creolisation'* processes. Creolisation processes are arguably therefore the basis for the making and morphing of the representation of both modern power (the state of social power) and *its subjects,* and relatedly the social spaces constituted by disordering processes of objectification in this modern state system. Of course, it is important to note here that in general, and as Foucault emphasised, the historical emergence of this new culture of power is a contingent story of history and geography, or rather time, place and space. It cannot be operative over all time-space regions, and where its presence is dominant, such as in Atlantic Space, it may co-exist and be entangled with (or even be displaced by) other forms of social power and temporalities, that are, or have been, present in definite hi/stories and geographies.[73]

To recap our discussion of power so far, our approach has been to insist on tracing the ontology of power through the inter-subjective realm. However, we pointed to the difficulties in sustaining inter-subjective power relations by identifying the potential of disordering processes that may derive from emergent socio-cultural forms which disturb the flow of mutual inter-subjective productions. Governmentality, which generically describes the 'conduct of conduct' was then shown to *also* represent a specific species of *emergent* social power, *viz.* modern governmentality, which has been addressed by Foucault, and others, in the study of modern forms of power. We then sought to make the ontological links between the inter-subjective and emergent structural levels in the relations of power, by noting that for Foucault, modern governmentality described not just techniques of modern government rationality but rather pointed to a 'state system.' That is, a state of social power encompasses power relations that are not just inter-subjective, or institutional, but more broadly, it also articulates emergent structural properties which are 'guiding the possibility of conduct and putting in order the possible outcome.' Thus, only by engaging in an analysis that addresses *all the ontological layers of the state system* (structural, institutional and inter-subjective social powers) will one be able to identify the set of political conditions important to strategically guiding the transformation of conditions needed for deepening the experiences of subjects' empowerment in the Caribbean or elsewhere. We suggest that the following model of 'state systems in social life worlds' provides such a framework for the analysis of the relationship of state-society relationships in the region. Also for grasping the peculiar openness of forms of social power despite state (qua institution) models of articulating cultural styles of relationship between *Power* (as desired vertical autonomy) and *its subjects* (qua citizen).

It is important to recognise here then that the state-qua institution plays a significant mediating role in constraining or reproducing disordering power relations between the inter-subjective and the structural levels of power relations embedded in the modern state system. In particular, in virtue of experiencing social power *within,* (that is, as a representative and governor of 'biopolitics' in a city-citizen game), *and without,* (that is, as represented subject and agent of modern social power in a shepherd-flock game), the modern state-qua institution holds a highly pivotal role.[74] This role extends *not just* to the *mediation* of the state-society relationship given these two games, it *also* includes a strategic role in *the transformation* of that relationship and hence the very nature of these two games. Thus, as Deborah Thomas has recently commented, 'the state is a contradictory ensemble of practices and processes of governance that manage both the subjugation of populations and the elaboration of subjectivities by naturalizing the arbitrary.'[75] The *experiences* of the state in terms of these practices and processes, or in terms of 'its survival and its limits on the basis of the general tactics of governmentality,'[76] will moreover set in train changes in states of consciousness, or states of subject experiences, which will disturb the nature of the 'governmentalization of the state.' Also, consequently, engender tendencies for the reconfiguration of social power formations *in conjunction with* reforms emanating from the state's governmentality tactics. The processes of governance and modern governmentality are thus open-ended, and generally *not exclusive* of the nation-state, even where such nation states have been bypassed strategically, at various moments, and their powers reconfigured by this bypassing.

To conclude this section we offer a brief recap of how we see this model of the modern state system being usefully summarised, by pointing to a 'politics of the cross' reflected in the general nature of the politics sustaining the *morphogenetics of cultures of power,*[77] or the transformation of the relations and conditions of power and freedom. Thus, from our model above, we have the 'vertical demands' on a person's active existence in the world that are produced through 'cultures of power,' which are *representations of social power for* the expression of social reality at various levels, that is for the expression of 'conduct of conduct' and for the determination of structural positionalities and possibilities. While these vertical demands in the state system seek to reinstate the verticality effect of social power, and 'the state,' being above, separate, autonomous and yet apart of the body politic, these demands are contingent on mediation in social relationships. However, since social relations reflect a 'process by which we constitute one another as persons' then vertical demands will stimulate the 'horizontal necessity' of a *'struggle for meaning;'*[78] a *'cultural politics' that is exercised through* modern processes of *governmentality* – 'the conduct of conduct.'[79] The *'cultural politics'* emanating from the intersecting vertical demands (in the social spaces of the state system determining 'cultures of power') and horizontal necessities (the struggle for meaning by articulating cultures of power through strategic conduct and subject practice), may thus be thought of as producing a *politics of the cross*; a politics that is moreover routinely implicated in the production of social life and social history.

The process described above, while resonant with interpretations of the exercise of power as hegemony, by Gramsci and others, in so far as a dominant power is recognised as mediated through cultural politics, however speaks not just to the involvement of cultural forms in the negotiation of the exercise of social power in a society. Indeed, our model of the state system in social life worlds does not presuppose a separation of 'civil society' as distinct from 'political society.' Rather, the cultural politics of the cross speaks to a general struggle over the very 'culture of power' itself, that is, a struggle over the modes of discursively determining 'what is 'power' and/or 'the political.' Our model highlights then a struggle with forces shaping the exercising of one's existence *through a strategic mediation* of vertical demands and its horizontal disordering processes of othering/subjectifications; a struggle over the framing of 'the political games' to be played for the expression of 'self,' 'subjectivity,' and 'citizenship;' and a struggle over the assumptions in representational spaces and politics, for grasping the possibilities (or limits) of power. In brief, our model centres on the struggles over the assumptions for locating *the powers to realise history, transformation, or freedom.*[80]

All in all then, we consider the idea of the 'politics of the cross' as an open plea for recognising process and ontology, for recognising the open-endedness of the horizontal articulations of vertical demands, and for recognising the 'state system in social life worlds,' as a lived open system. In keeping faith with this 'politics of the cross' then, one must perforce sustain a recognition that the multiple 'forces, attractions and co-existences' that it ontologically stitches together 'is a realized complex of experiences, relationships, and activities, with specific and changing pressures and limits.'[81]

Conclusion

As we have sought to argue then, in the absence of adequate analysis of the ontology and dynamics of power in the Caribbean, the existing analysis on the possibilities and processes for development in the region will unavoidably perpetuate an insidious bias against endogenous social transformation, by the handicaps they place on explanatory power. In so doing they continue to ignore the lessons from Lloyd Best's observations on the complexity of Caribbean ontology – emergent from unique yet systemic 'global' and 'local,' 'structural' and 'institutional,' 'plantation' and 'postcolonial,' processes and forces – and his related critiques of Caribbean epistemology.

Our model for reconceptualising the power relations in the Caribbean's Atlantic space, and the links between state, society and economy will hopefully act to help deepen one's grasp of these processes shaping the nature of the development dynamic in the region, and to provide at least one more plank in support of a progressive politics for the region.

Notes

1.   The title of this paper draws its inspiration from the work of Lloyd Best. In particular, his reflections on the development possibilities for small states, first presented in his article, 'Size and Survival,' published in 1966, in *New World* (Guyana Independence Issue), 58–63, and republished in *Readings in the Political Economy of the Caribbean*, eds. N. Girvan and O. Jefferson, (New World Group, 1971). A part of the title, also borrows from the forthcoming book, *Globalization and the Post Creole Imagination: Notes on Fleeing the Plantation* M. Critchlow with P. Northover, (Durham: Duke University Press, 2009). The first chapter of that text has been dedicated to the memory of Lloyd Best. This chapter also draws upon an earlier version of a paper presented at the 2004 Conference of the International Association for Critical Realism, University of Cambridge, UK. A substantially revised version of that conference paper has been published as 'Freedom, Possibility and Ontology: Rethinking the problem of Caribbean Ascent' in *Developments*

in Social Ontology eds. C. Lawson, J. Latsis, and N. Martins (London: Routledge, 2006), 205–30. Also part of that conference paper informed the recent publication, 'Beyond Survival: Rethinking Strategies for Sustainable Economic Growth in the Caribbean' in *Social and Economic Studies* 54, no. 3 (2005): 247–74. This chapter rehearses some of the arguments made in these published works, but with several major modifications introduced in light of the productive critical comments made by the editors of this text. We wish to thank these editors and the many others who have commented on this work through the various presentations that we have made.

2. The CARICOM member states are Jamaica, Trinidad and Tobago, Barbados, Dominica, St Lucia, St Vincent, Grenada, Bahamas, Haiti, Guyana, St Kitts/Nevis, Antigua and Barbuda, Suriname, Belize and Montserrat. It represents 15 million people and has an aggregate GDP of approximately US$36 billion (2003).

3. The modern Caribbean, or those group of countries linked by the Caribbean Sea, (which includes more states than just those within the CARICOM group), was shaped as a socio-economic and cultural political space through the geo-historical structure of 'the Atlantic.' The space of the Atlantic is defined by Tomich (2004) as a 'historical region of the capitalist world economy' which is distinguished by its particular complexes of production and exchange rooted on the infamous Atlantic triangular trade, see Dale Tomich (2004) 'Atlantic History and World Economy: Concepts and Constructions' in *ProtoSociology*, 20, 102–21. This trade entailed taking peoples from Africa to the 'New World,' transforming them from freedom to slavery in their middle passage journey to the plantation colonies of 'the Americas,' and thereby financing the growth of industry and empire across the Atlantic.

4. See, for example in this regard the essay by Lloyd Best 'Independent Thought and Caribbean Freedom' *New World Quarterly* 3, no. 4 (1967).

5. There is, of course, a large literature debating the utility, politics and meaning of the term 'creole' and its derivatives, such as creolisation, créolité etc. See, for example, the essays by O. Nigel Bolland 'Creolization and Creole Societies: A Cultural Nationalist View of Caribbean Social History' and Percy Hintzen 'Race and Creole Ethnicity in the Caribbean,' both in *Questioning Creole: Creolizing Discourses in Caribbean Culture*, eds. V. Shepherd and G. Richards (Kingston: Ian Randle Publishers, 2002; Oxford: James Currey, 2002). See also, Rex Nettleford's reflections on Caribbean culture stated in 'Caribbean Culture: Paradoxes of the 1990s' in *Caribbean Public Policy: Regional Cultural and Socio-economic Issues for the 21st Century*, eds. J. Braveboy-Wagner and D. Gayle (Boulder, Colorado: West View Press, 1997).

6. Whilst steeped in controversy, as most social science concepts tend to be, we believe there is still much analytical value in the concept of *creolisation*, as a referent to the dynamic processes of socio-historical creativity, mimesis and alterity associated with the emergence of that other highly contested process and concept, *viz.* 'Modernity.' We follow Munasinghe here and thus use italics for *creolisation* because we wish it to refer to a theory of processes of cultural change and identify formation, which go beyond particular models of Creole identities associated with the plantation areas of the New World. See Viranjini Munasinghe, 'Theorizing World Culture through the New World,' *American Ethnologist* 33, no. 4 (2006): 549–62. She adopts this practice in order to reinforce her recent arguments that one may treat with the notion of *Creolisation* as offering rich analytical insights on the 'dynamics of cultural change and synthesis in deeply hierarchical

and heterogeneous social polities' even in spite of its political baggage of an exclusionary identity politics (see ibid., 557). However, we place the concept in scare quotes as well, to highlight that also at stake, is a different interpretation of the nature of *'creolisation'* processes. In so doing we seek to highlight the fact that *'creolisation,'* is not just about patterns of cultural change, or possessions of cultural products. Rather, it also refers to, and is entangled in, mappings of 'cultures of power,' or of imagined modern spaces and times, see, *Globalization and the Post Creole Imagination: Notes on Fleeing the Plantation.* M. Critchlow and P. Northover (Durham: Duke University Press, 2009).

7.   Roy Bhaskar, *A Realist Theory of Science*, 2nd ed. (Sussex: Harvester Press 1978; New Jersey: Humanities Press, 1978) and Bhaskar *The Possibility of Naturalism: A Philosophical Critique of the Contemporary Human Sciences* 2nd ed. (New York, London: Harvester Wheatsheaf, 1989).

8.   Critical realism is a wide ranging philosophical paradigm that stretches over several disciplines, and that sets itself up against the philosophical traditions of Positivist Philosophy, inclusive of the so called Popperian post-positivist tradition based on falsification principles of rational belief, as well as against the contemporary waves of radical constructivism, or strong relativism, as well as varieties of post-modernism. The hallmark of Critical realism is its insistence on the need for principles of ontological realism and truth, albeit reformulated to acknowledge the varieties of realist and truth theories, and its advocacy of methodological principles consistent with effective social scientific explanation in open systems; that is, systems outside of experimental control, and that are constituted through intentional human agency. For elaborations of the critical realist perspective, see Andrew Collier, *An Introduction to Roy Bhaskar's Philosophy*, (London and New York: Verso Press, 1994); I. Cruickshank *Realism and Sociology: Anti-Foundationalism, Ontology and Social Research.* (London and New York: Routledge, 2007), and the collected readings edited by M. Archer, R. Bhaskar, A. Collier, T. Lawson, A. Norrie, *Critical Realism: Essential Readings*, (London: Routledge, 1998).

9.   Tony Lawson 'Developments in Economics as Realist Social Theory,' in. *Critical Realism in Economics; Development and Debate*, ed. Steve Fleetwood (London: Routledge, 1999), 3–20. See also C. Lawson, M. Peacock and S. Pratten, 'Realism, Underlabouring and Institutions,' *Cambridge Journal of Economics* 30, no.1, (1996): 137–51.

10.   It is beyond the scope of this paper to elaborate on the nature of the critical realist theories of social ontology and explanation, but for an introduction to these issues the reader is encouraged to see A. Collier, 1994 above or A. Sayer, *Method in Social Sciences: A Realist Approach*, 2nd ed., (London: Routledge, 1992). Suffice it to say here that the main planks of the critical realist position are as follows: first, it posits a realist ontology, where reality is structured into the real, actual and empirical, with the real being a part of whatever exists but irreducible to the actual (what happened) and the empirical (what is experienced or represented through experience). Second, it rejects both inductivism and deductivism as theories of knowledge in favour of retroduction; that is causal inference to underlying generative mechanisms that are real but irreducible to events of experience, such as regularity laws. They also hold that social systems are open (i.e. non-deterministic systems) in virtue of agency. Finally, their model of social being is described by the Transformational Model of Social Activity (TMSA), where

social structure is reproduced and transformed through agential praxis, and is irreducible to human activity.

11. Indeed, we see the work that we are offering here as addressing some of the concerns expressed about the critical realist underlabouring project. For example, Davidsen (2005) has argued that not enough is being done by critical realists to advance the analysis of substantive phenomena using critical realist arguments on the nature of social reality and of viable explanations for open social systems. See Bjørn-Ivar Davidsen, 'Critical Realism in Economics – A Different View,' *Post-Autistic Economics Review* 4, no. 33 (September 2005), http://www.paecon.net/PAEReview/issue33/Davidsen33.htm. Our work can thus be seen as precisely such an attempt to enrich the nature of theorising on substantive issues by expressing a closer sensitivity to the issues raised under the critical realist project.

12. Michel-Rolph Trouillot, 'Culture on the Edges: Caribbean *Creolization* in Historical Context,' in *From the Margins: Historical Anthropology and Its Futures* ed. Brian Keith Axel (Durham: Duke University Press, 2002), 199.

13. Elden discusses this project of spatial history as a critical thread linking Heidegger's, and Foucault's work. See Stuart Elden *Mapping the Present. Heidegger, Foucault and the Project of Spatial History* (London and New York: Continuum, 2001), 3. It is a thread however, that also connects diverse modern thinkers on the relation between time and space, most notably present in Lefebvre, Deleuze, Derrida and Homi Bhabha. It is indeed a multiple and rich vein of thought that underpins Postcolonial and Poststructuralist inflected Marxist studies. Within Atlantic Space, this question of the relation between time and space is evident in the works of C.L.R. James, Franz Fanon, Wilson Harris, Kamau Braithwaite, Derek Walcott, Stuart Hall, Sylvia Wynter, Dale Tomich, Edouard Glissant, Michel- Rolf Trouillot, Sydney Mintz, Richard and Sally Price, Paul Gilroy, to highlight a prominent few. For a rich discussion of the notion of space in contemporary literature of the French Caribbean, see N. Coates (2001) 'Gardens in the Sands: The Notion of Space in Recent Critical Theory and Contemporary Writing from the French Antilles' http://web.mac.com/nick.coates/iWeb/Cabinet%20of%20Curiosities/Places_files/Thesis-masterB.pdf, accessed February 27, 2007.

14. Karl Marx (1852) 'The Eighteenth Brumaire of Louis Napoleon' in *The Marx-Engels Reader* ed Robert Tucker 2nd ed. (New York: Norton & Company, 1978), 595.

15. See for example Deborah Thomas, *Modern Blackness: Nationalism, Globalization and the Politics of Culture in Jamaica*, (Kingston: UWI Press, 2004; Duke University Press, 2004).

16. See, for example, Lloyd Best 'Independent Thought and Caribbean Freedom' *New World Quarterly* 3, no. 4 (1967); Anthony Bogues 'Investigating the Radical Caribbean Intellectual Tradition' *in Small Axe* 4 (September 1998): 29–45; George Lamming *The Sovereignty of the Imagination* (Kingston: Arawak Publications, 2004); and David Scott 'The Government of Freedom' in *New Caribbean Thought: A Reader* eds. Brian Meeks and Folke Lindahl, (Mona: University of the West Indies Press, 2001). See also, the recent text in honour of Sylvia Wynter, the Caribbean philosopher and ardent expositor for Caribbean freedom, *After Man, Towards the Human: Critical Essays on Sylvia Wynter* ed. Anthony Bogues (Kingston: Ian Randle Publishers, 2006).

17. Roy Bhaskar 'Rorty, Realism and the Idea of Freedom' in Bhaskar *Reclaiming Reality: A Critical Introduction to Contemporary Philosophy* (London: Verso, 1989), 146–79.

18. Ibid., 198.

19. We wish at this point to emphasise that the philosophical position of critical realism should not be understood here as representing an all encompassing methodological prescriptive, or descriptive for that matter, of the nature of social scientific practice, if only for the fact that multiple rationales exist for the practice of science. In particular, not everyone agrees that the primary goal of science is 'explanatory.' However, where there is an ostensive aim to enhance explanatory power, it provides a systematic, focused and – at this moment in human history – critical intervention on foundational issues facing the practice of (explanatory) social science. The most salient issues at stake here are the nature of explanation, the status of truth functional statements, the ontological presuppositions of any practice engaged in the pursuit of causal knowledge, the debates over structure, agency, freedom and the nature of social processes. It should also be noted here that critical realism is not beyond critique regarding its own approach, aims and specific claims made regarding the substantive nature of specific social scientific practices, as the growing debate about critical realism in economics attests to, see in this regard the special issue on Critical realism by the *Cambridge Journal of Economics* 26, no. 6 (November 2002) as well as *Critical Rrealism in Economics: Development and Debate*, ed. S. Fleetwood (London: Routledge, 1999). Not surprisingly, critical realism is undergoing dynamic transformation, in response to these debates. See, for example, the several texts published by Routledge that bear witness to this constructive engagement taking place across philosophical traditions. Note here as an example, *Realism, Discourse and Deconstruction*, Jonathan Joseph and John Roberts (London: Routledge, 2004). This process can also be seen in the continuous development of critical realism by Roy Bhaskar's prolific writings, see for example, the Wikipedia's on line Encyclopedia entry on Bhaskar, http://en.wikipedia.org/wiki/Roy_Bhaskar.

20. It may be noted here that Bhaskar has discussed the issue of the relation between critical realist philosophy, explanatory social science and human emancipation in his text *Scientific Realism and Human Emancipation*, (London and New York: Verso, 1986). A discussion of Bhaskar's views as articulated in that text is also presented by Andrew Collier in 'Explanation and Emancipation,' in *Critical Realism: Essential Readings* ed. Margaret Archer et al. (London: Routledge, 1998), 444–72. For a post'ist view on the gaps in critical realism in promoting a process of human emancipation, see Nitisha Kaul 'A Critical Post to Critical Realism' *Cambridge Journal of Economics* 26, no. 6 (2002): 709–26. In our own engagement with the issues of the relation between explanation and emancipation, as presented in this chapter, we have found it necessary to draw upon the insights of both critical realism and post-structuralism. This provoked one referee reader to draw a cautious comment on the possible 'inconsistencies' at the level of method between the ontologically bold and epistemologically cautious stance of 'critical realists' and the ontologically cautious and epistemologically radical deconstructive stance of post'ists, (post-structuralists, post-modernists, etc). In partial response to these readers' comment, we wish only to note that at the level of specific methodological differences, in the work of at least one key post'ist figure, Foucault, from whom we draw heavily in this essay, we find no necessary inconsistency between post-structuralist perspectives at the level of method and that of critical realism. This has also been argued in a recent reading of Foucault by Ismael Al Amoudi, (2006) 'Redrawing Foucault's Social Ontology: Towards a Critical Realist Reading

of Michel Foucault' http://www.criticalmanagement. org/publications/
AlamoudiFoucault.pdfhttp://www.criticalmanagement.org/publications/
AlamoudiFoucault.pdf.

21. This essay has been reprinted in a recent text entitled *Independent Thought
and Caribbean Freedom*, in honour of Best's ongoing struggles to promote
a process of 'Fleeing the Plantations' in the Caribbean region. This text,
edited by Selwyn Ryan, was published by the Sir Arthur Lewis Institute of
Social and Economic Studies in 2003.

22. For an overview of the economic performance trends of the CARICOM
Caribbean countries under globalisation, see ECLAC (2002) 'Globalization
and Development,' Chapter 11.

23. See Jose Ocampo (2002) 'Small Economies in the Face of Globalization'
http://www.revistainterforum.com/english/articles/052702arteco_en.html;
UWICED (2001) 'Vulnerability and Small Island States' in *Development
Policy Journal* 1, www.undp.org/wssd/docs/BDP_Policy_Journal_Vol_1.pdf;
and *Caribbean Survival and the Global Challenge* ed. R. Ramsaran (Kingston:
Ian Randle Publishers, 2002).

24. See Ivelaw Griffith *Drugs and Security in the Caribbean: Sovereignty Under
Siege* (University Park: Pennsylvania State University Press, 1997); *Caribbean
Security in the Age of Terror: Challenge and Change* ed. Ivelaw Griffith
(Kingston: Ian Randle Publishers, 2004).

25. See ECLAC, *Foreign Investment in Latin America and the Caribbean. 2003
Report* http://www.eclac.cl/

26. Richard Bernal, 'The Caribbean's Future is Not What it Was' *Social and
Economic Studies* 52, no. 1 (March 2003): 185–217.

27. This perspective is akin to that expressed in the classic 1985 text *Bringing the
State Back* edited by P. Evans, D. Rueschemeyer and T. Skocpol, which set off
a storm of criticism on the seeming 'apartness' required between the state
and society in explaining the successful state. For a review of these issues
see Joel Migdal, *State in Society: Studying How States and Societies Transform
and Constitute One Another* (Cambridge: Cambridge University Press, 2001).

28. See C. Y.Thomas, *Dependence and Transformation*, (New York and London:
Monthly Review Press, 1974); C.Y. Thomas, *The Poor and the Powerless:
Economic Policy and Change in the Caribbean*, (London: Latin American
Bureau, 1988); Don Marshall, *Caribbean Political Economy at the Crossroads:
NAFTA and Regional Developmentalism.* (Basingstoke and London: Macmillan,
1998); N. Karagiannis, *A New Economic Strategy for the Bahamas: With Special
Consideration of International Competition and the FTAA.* (Kingston: UWI Press,
2002); N. Karagiannis and D. Alleyne, *A New Economic Strategy for Jamaica:
With Special Consideration of International Competition and the FTAA.* (Kingston:
Arawak Publications, 2003).

29. Peter Evans introduced the concept of 'embedded autonomy' in his classic
text, *Embedded Autonomy: States and Industrial Transformation* (New Jersey:
Princeton University Press, 1995). This idea was used to help elucidate the
form of the state in promoting industrial transformation, and the success
of the East Asian Newly industrial countries (NICS), by examining the ways
in which states are organised and related to society.

30. C.Y. Thomas explains the shift in his approach for a suitable political
economy, as an attempt to 'elaborate on the meaning and content of political
democracy, the state...as well as state-civil society relations [in order to
allow for]...relaxing the [earlier] assumptions in regard to political and
social conditions,' in *New Caribbean Thought: A Reader* eds. B. Meeks and
F. Lindahl (Jamaica, Barbados and Trinidad and Tobago: University of

the West Indies Press, 2001), 507. See also Clive Thomas, 'Designing and Implementing Development Policy' in *Governance in an Age of Globalization: Caribbean Perspectives* eds. K. Hall and D. Benn (Kingston: Ian Randle Publishers, 2003).

31. See W. Arthur Lewis, *Theory of Economic Growth*, (London: George Allen and Unwin, 1955); Ian Boxill, *Ideology and Caribbean Integration*, (Mona: Consortium Graduate School of Social Sciences, University of the West Indies, 1997); Stuart Hall, 'Negotiating Caribbean Identities,' in *New Caribbean Thought: A Reader*, eds. Brian Meeks and Folke Lindahl (Mona: University of the West Indies Press, 2001), 24–39; Rex Nettleford, 'Caribbean Culture: Paradoxes of the 1990s' in *Caribbean Public Policy: Regional Cultural and Socio-economic Issues for the 21st Century* eds. J. Braveboy-Wagner and D. Gayle (Boulder Colorado: West View Press, 1997).

32. 'Creole' as deployed here has several layers of meaning. It highlights the presence of racialised subjectification processes as well as racialised cultural identity projects and also the emergent 'syncretic' creative outcomes from processes of social relationships among persons in the 'new world,' see Charles Stewart, 'Syncretism and its Synonyms: Reflections on Cultural Mixture,' in *Diacritics* 29, no. 3, (1999):40–62. We thus use the term 'Creole' here to highlight these contradictions and ambiguities of 'Caribbean – being in the world.'

33. Joel Migdal, *State in Society: Studying how States and Societies Transform and Constitute one Another*, (Cambridge: Cambridge University Press, 2001).

34. Social capital – defined as norms, networks and trust, has become an important variable in explaining comparative economic performance based on its effects on reducing conflict and supporting cooperation in firms, among firms or between the state and the civil society. This view on the role of social capital is analytically linked with discussions that focus on the relationship between the economy, civil society and the state, stimulated by Robert Putman's (with Robert Leonardi and Raffaella Y. Nanetti) book *Making Democracy Work: Civic Traditions in Modern Italy*, (Princeton: Princeton University Press, 1993). For a discussion of the role of social capital in the relationship between the state and society, see Peter Evans, 'Government Action, Social Capital and development: Reviewing the Evidence on Synergy,' *World Development* 24, no. 6, (1996): 1119–32. The social capital literature though blooming, reflects various treatments of this concept, causing some to question the theoretical value of the concept, and instead flag its political and rhetorical use value, see Baron et al *Social Capital: Critical Perspectives*, (Oxford: Oxford University Press, 2000).

35. The literature on social movements is also blooming, and is also defined or methodologically treated in various ways as emphasised in Arturo Escobar and Sonia Alvarez *The Making of Social Movements in Latin America*, (Boulder: Westview Press, 1992). The notion seeks to capture the phenomena of the overlapping and contesting interests articulated in diverse social responses and practices that continue to negotiate political and cultural space in social life/society. Given the focus on agents and their 'coming together' relationships, this idea is conceptually linked to the concept of social capital but the literatures on these two phenomenon are not linked, and tend to express divergent political concerns. The former concept, social movements, is mainly concerned with correctives to the existing status quo of rights and recognitions; while the latter is more functionalist in pre-occupation and thus tends to oscillate around a concern for social integration or social order and the attainment of common social goals. The two concepts in their own

way seek to grapple with the problem of 'making history,' or constructing processes, but they are nonetheless mired in difficult methodological issues regarding the nature of the relationship between society, culture, economy, state and the subject.

36. See Homi Bhabba, *The Location of Culture* (London: Routledge [1994], 2004).

37. For a similar critique on aprioristic reasoning related to the behaviour of states in Africa, see Thandika Mkandawire 'Thinking about Development States in Africa' http://www.unu.edu/africa/00sps-global.html (1998), and published in *Cambridge Journal of Economics* 25 (2001): 289–314.

38. It should be noted here that those held to adhere to critical realism, whether explicitly, or implicitly by virtue of historical reconstructive analysis, are from diverse political, ideological and theoretical backgrounds. Thus, there are many who define themselves as Marxist critical realists and others who eschew Marxism, who are also defined as critical realists. In particular, through the underlabouring role of critical realists in economics, thinkers as diverse as Hayek and Commons have been labelled as adhering to seminal tenets of critical realist method, such as non-idealism or open systems, or a view of the social world as stratified, with emergent social properties, or shaped through a Transformational model of social activity. See, for example, T. Lawson, 'Realism and Hayek: A Case of Continuing Transformation' in *Capitalism, Socialism and Knowledge: The Economics of F. A. Hayek* 2, ed. Maria Colono, H.Hagemann and O. Hamouda (Cheltenham: Edward Elgar, 1994) and Clive Lawson, 'The Transformational Model of Social Activity and Economic Analysis: A Reinterpretation of the Work of J. R. Commons' in *Review of Political Economy* 4, no. 1, (1994): 37–78. The need for critical realism as espoused in this paper *therefore does not solve* substantive problems of theory and analysis. In fact, what critical realism does is to open up the space for a richer debate on the substantive problems of social theory.

39. This concept of 'verticality' was adopted in James Ferguson and Akhil Gupta, 'Spatializing States: Toward an Ethnography of Neoliberal Governmentality,' *American Ethnologist* 29, no. 4, (November 2002): 981–1002.

40. Clifford Geertz, *Negara: The Theatre State in 19th Century Bali* (Princeton: Princeton University Press, 1980).

41. Mitchell, Timothy 'The Limits of the State: Beyond Statist Approaches and Their Critics,' *American Political Science Review* 85, no. 1, (1991): 77–96.

42. Joel Migdal *Strong Societies and Weak States: State-Society Relationships and State Capabilities in the Third World*. (Princeton: Princeton University Press, 1988).

43. See Antonio Gramsci, *Selections from Prison Notebooks*, edited and translated by Quinton Hoare and Geoffrey Smith, (New York: International Publishers, 1971).

44. Thomas Hansen and Finn Stepputat eds., *States of Imagination: Ethnographic Explorations of the Post Colonial State* (Durham and London: Duke University Press), 9.

45. Ferguson and Gupta (2002) 'Spatializing States' 981 *op cit.*

46. See Migdal (2001, 257).

47. This schema of methodological individualism is also in keeping with a Cartesian dualism that treats 'subject being' as standing independently of relations with being and becoming through the natural and social world.

48. Tim Ingold *Evolution and Social Life*, (Cambridge: Cambridge University Press, 1986), 222, 293.

49. Ibid., 222.
50. Ibid., 293.
51. Margaret Archer, *Realist Social Theory: A Morphogenetic Approach* (Cambridge: Cambridge University Press, 1995), 284.
52. Archer defines SEPs as being 'irreducible to people and relatively enduring...and are specifically defined as those internal and necessary relationships which entail material resources, whether physical or human, and which generate causal powers proper to the relation itself' (1995, 177). In other words then, a structural power is a social power that is exercised through social being and acts with a certain intensity in a certain direction in constraining or enabling the action/experiences of the subject in their social relationships.
53. Archer 1995, 201.
54. One could also argue, in line with Archer (1995), that this person being is a triple emergent, if one locates the creative properties of a/the person being as emergent from some non-natural, non-social creative source.
55. Of course, this social process itself is a co-emergent from human being's evolution of practical and discursive consciousness in the world, see Ingold (1986).
56. See Foucault 'The Subject and Power' in *Michel Foucault: Beyond Structuralism and Hermeneutics*, Hubert Dreyfus and Paul Rabinow 2nd ed., (Chicago: University of Chicago Press, 1983), 208.
57. See Foucault, 'Politics and the Study of Discourse,' in *The Foucault Effect: Studies in Governmentality*, eds. G. Burchell, C. Gordon, and P. Miller (Chicago: University of Chicago Press, 1991), 59–60.
58. Foucault (1983, 208) in Dreyfus and Rabinow (ibid.).
59. These two objectification processes have received intensive examination in post-structuralist approaches. This perspective, in general, has reconceptualised the problem of objectification in terms of the politics of 'othering' and 'difference,' see for example, Homi Bhabha, 'The Other Question: Stereotype, Discrimination and the Discourse of Colonialism' in *The Location of Culture*, 94–120; Jonathan Rutherford, (1990) 'A Place called Home: Identity and the Cultural Politics of Difference,' in *Identity: Community, Culture, Difference*, ed. Jonathan Rutherford, (London: Lawrence and Wishart, 1994) and John Beverly, *Subalternity and Representation: Arguments in Cultural Theory* (Durham: Duke University Press, 1999).
60. Thomas Lemke. 'Foucault, Governmentality and Critique,' paper presented at Rethinking Marxism Conference, University of Amherst, MA (September 21–24, 2000): 2–3, accessed July 2004 http://www.thomaslemkeweb.de/publikationen/Foucault,%20Governmentality, %20and%20Critique%20 IV-2.pdf.
61. Modern governmentality has since come to studied as a new political force that is defining the rationality of power in modernity and its associated technologies of power, see Nikolas Rose *Powers of Freedom: Reframing Political Thought* (Cambridge: Cambridge University Press, 1999) and Mitchell Dean, *Governmentality: Power and Rule in Modern Society* (London: Sage Publications, 1999).
62. Nikolas Rose, *Powers of Freedom*, (1999, 33).
63. Foucault 1983, 208.
64. See in this regard, Thomas Lemke, '"The Birth of Bio-Politics;" Michel Foucault's Lecture at the College de France on Neo-Liberal Governmentality' *Economy and Society* 30, no. 2 (2001): 190–207.
65. Foucault 1983, 212.

66. Ibid., 220.
67. Ibid., 220–21.
68. Foucault, 'Governmentality,' in *The Foucault Effect: Studies in Governmentality*, ed. Graham Burchell, Colin Gordon and Peter Miller, (Chicago: University of Chicago Press, 1991), 93.
69. Ibid.
70. Ibid., 103.
71. Durkheim in his introduction to his text, described religion as '…something eminently social. Religious representations are collective representations which *express* collective realities: the rites are a manner of acting which take rise in the midst of the assembled groups and which are destined to maintain, or recreate certain mental states in these groups.' Quoted in Kenneth Thompson, *Key Sociologists: Emile Durkheim*, (London: Routledge [1982]1990) (our emphasis). Of course, in light of the fact that our conception of social life as guided by Ingold, an appeal to Durkheim's insights in no way therefore implies that we are treating human as mere actors on the social stage driven by the social script.
72. For some recent interpretations of how modern governmentality shapes Caribbean power relations see David Scott *Refashioning Futures: Criticism after Postcoloniality*, (Princeton: Princeton University Press, 1999) and Nalini Persram 'Guerrillas, Games and Governmentality' in *Small Axe* 10, (September 2001): 21–40.
73. See for example, Donald Moore, *Suffering for Territory: Race, Place and Power in Zimbabwe* (Durham and London: Duke University Press, 2005). Also in this regard, see Chapters 1 and 2 in Critchlow and Northover, *Globalization and the Post Creole Imagination* (2009) and Chapter 6 in Ato Quayson's, *Calibrations: Reading for the Social*, (Minneapolis, London: University of Minnesota Press, 2003).
74. Mitchell Dean (2001, 45) argues for an interpretation of Foucault's comment on the demonic coupling of these two games as the attempt to combine 'sovereignty and biopolitics,' where 'biopolitics refers to the relationship between the government and the population,' (47), see Mitchell Dean, '"Demonic Societies:" Liberalism, Biopolitics and Sovereignty' In Thomas Hansen and Finn Stepputat eds. (2001) *op cit*. We wish to suggest that the games also imply that the state is seeking to serve, so to speak, two masters, one the citizen-subject-population and the second the 'Subject' or 'Sacred being' identified in the modern cosmology of social life. These games are used by Foucault to illustrate the tension in modern systems of trying to manage power relationships through the coupling of individualisation and totalitarian strategies, see Colin Gordon 'Governmental Rationality: An Introduction, in The Foucault Effect' in *The Foucault Effect: Studies in Governmentality*, eds. Graham Burchell, Colin Gordon and Peter Miller (Chicago: University of Chicago Press, 1991).
75. See Deborah Thomas 'Development, "Culture" and the Promise of Modern Progress' in *Social and Economic Studies* 54, no. 3 (September 2005): 98. See also in this regard the study by Michaeline Critchlow on the processes of agrarian and modern change in Jamaica, M. Critchlow *Negotiating Caribbean Freedom: Peasants and the State in Development* (Lanham: Lexington Books, 2005).
76. Foucault (1991), 'Governmentality' in *The Foucault Effect: Studies in Governmentality*, 103.
77. We follow Archer (1985, 5) here in adopting the term 'morphogenetics' to allude to two points in change processes. First that social power has no

preset – form or inherent natural state of equilibrium – the morph element of the term, and also that changes are like a morphing, a transformation of one image into another. Second that social power takes its shape from and is formed by, agents qua persons, and thus originate from their activities, relationships and all the intended and unintended consequences flowing from those – this is the second part of the term the genetics. The whole term together implies a focus on the processes of change and transformation of social power, state systems, in social life worlds, societies.

78. We were inspired to use this phrase by Paulin J. Hountondji's text, *The Struggle for Meaning: Reflections on Philosophy, Culture and Democracy in Africa* (Ohio University Center for International Studies, 2002).

79. We adopt the definition of cultural politics put forward for Alvarez et al as follows: '...cultural politics as the process enacted when sets of social actors shaped by, and embodying, different cultural meanings and practices come into conflict with each other' in Alvarez et al, *Cultures of Politics, Politics of Cultures: Re-visioning Latin American Social Movements* (Colorado and Oxford: Westview Press, 1998), 7.

80. For a recent and highly interesting intervention on this last point regarding the assumptions about the possibilities of power in relation to making history see Catherine Malibu, 'History and the Process of Mourning in Hegel and Freud' in *Radical Philosophy* 106, (March/April 2001): 15–20.

81. Raymond Williams, *Marxism and Literature*, (Oxford and New York: Oxford University Press, 1977), 112. We have deliberately drawn on Williams comments here in his analysis of the concept of hegemony not because we wish to reintroduce a case for hegemony, but rather to emphasise that one's models of social power, should be ones that are consistent with an ontological perspective that consistently stresses the open ended and dynamic nature of social systems. That is, if we care enough about the explanatory power of our models. However, as emphasised before, the need for critical realism as argued for in this paper *does not solve* substantive problems of theory and analysis. In fact, what critical realism does is to open up the space for a richer debate on the substantive problems of social theory. For example, the question of interpretation as to what open systems really means when addressing human social systems, seems to be at the heart of the conflict between Marxist and post-structuralist positions, including post-structuralist Marxists, such as Ernesto Laclau or Ato Quayson. This latter problem reflects the difficulty of hoping to resolve agency-structure debates simply by recourse to critical realism. This difficulty, I believe, is present in a recent critical realist interpretation of hegemony pursued by Jonathan Joseph. In particular, Joseph, in defending the value of critical realism, engages in what appears to me to be a simplistic reading of the articulation between 'structural determination' and the causal power of agency. This is most clearly seen in his insistence on the deeper hegemonic power of structures such as capitalism in shaping agency, despite the moments of agency in its 'surface hegemonic articulation' see Jonathan Joseph, *Hegemony: a Realist Analysis* (London: Routledge, 2002). Joseph's reading of hegemony seeks to distance itself from, not only the work of the 'post-structuralist' Derrida, but also the efforts of other Marxists such as Raymond Williams, Laclau and Althusser, writers who I believe, certainly could be argued as providing for a more agency sensitive and complex conceptualisation of the processes of producing social life.

9 | Caribbean Dependence in the Phase of Informatic Capitalism

Paget Henry[1]

The plantation model of Caribbean economies, as formulated by Lloyd Best and Kari Polanyi Levitt,[2] took as one of its central concerns the persistent problem of Caribbean economic dependence. The model made this problem more explicit and hence more visible than earlier approaches to Caribbean economies. With the neo-liberal turn in Western economic theory, the plantation model, along with similar dependency approaches in Latin America and Africa, entered a period of eclipse. The paradox of this eclipse is that as the plantation model has receded, the problem of dependency has only become more stark, urgent and visible. This paper is an attempt to explore this paradox. In the course of its exploration, the paper will establish four basic claims: 1) that the rise of Asian capitalism has forced the advanced capitalist countries into a new or informatic phase; 2) the continuing relevance of plantation theory in this new phase of advanced capitalism; 3) that in this informatic phase Caribbean plantation economy has gone through a fourth 'ratooning' – a reference to the practice of reusing already cut stalks of cane rather than uprooting them and replanting new slips for the next crop; and 4) that in addition to structural factors, this fourth repeating of the plantation pattern may also be linked to persistent effects of the colonial capture of the auto-poetic processes by which Caribbean economic and entrepreneurial identities were established. By 'auto-poetic,' I am referring to the creative processes of symbolic self-representation, affirmation and negation by which we establish identities and differentiate them from other identities. The paper concludes with the notion of a mobilised entrepreneurial sector that cuts across classes, as a possible structure that could break this repeating pattern and prevent a fifth ratooning.

Caribbean Dependence before the Plantation Model

Although Best and Levitt were the first to put the problem of economic dependence at the centre of the theoretical stage, the problem was well recognised by many, such as C.L.R. James, Arthur Lewis, and Eric Williams, who were involved in the reforms that followed the uprisings of the 1930s. The problem of dependence was recognised by all three as a dark shadow that Western imperialism had cast over regional economies. However, it was never systematised and made explicit as the plantation theorists would later do. All three saw imperialism as the hostile cocoon out of which Caribbean colonial economies emerged. The restrictive aspects of this imperial cocoon led to features such as overspecialisation, domination by foreign capital, and foreign technological expertise. However, they differed among themselves about how to overcome the legacies of this restrictive colonial birth.

In the case of James, the imperial roots of Caribbean economies and the dependence it produced on plantation agriculture was well established in his classic text, *The Black Jacobins*. In this work, James is critical of Toussaint L'Ouverture's decision to re-establish the plantation system in spite of the resistance of the ex-slaves that he had freed by defeating the French and the British. James writes:

> The ultimate guarantee of freedom was the prosperity of agriculture. This was Toussaint's slogan. The danger was that the blacks might slip into the practice of cultivating a small patch of land, producing just sufficient for their needs....He confined the blacks to the plantations under rigid penalties....[3]

That produced what James called the new despotism. In contrast to the plantation theorist, James's objections focused not so much on the negative developmental consequences for the Haitian economy, but the policy's suppression of the economic impulses and self-organising activities of the labourers.

This inability to make the badly needed move beyond the plantation system and trust the economic creativity of the masses is a theme that recurs through James's writings on Caribbean economies. It is most clearly seen in the two models that James developed for transforming Caribbean economies.[4] The first was an industry-led strategy of transformation, while the second was a peasant-led strategy. In the course of outlining the latter, James asserted that 'no economic regime has had so demoralizing an effect on the population as the sugar estates.'[5] Here too, his economics was shaped by his search for a modern form of political organisation that could accommodate the self-organisation of workers and peasants as classes. Thus the key feature of both alternative models was the participatory form of economic organisation, rather than the strategy of development, that would institutionalise principles of worker control of production. This was James's socialist answer to the imperial origins of Caribbean economies.

In the case of Williams, *Capitalism and Slavery* was the text that established his view of the imperial origins of Caribbean economies and the colonial legacies of over-specialisation and dominance by foreign capital. In an earlier (1943) essay on Caribbean development, Williams wrote: 'Colonialism, there is the enemy of Caribbean diversifications.'[6] The diversifications that Williams had in mind were local food production and industrialisation within a federated Caribbean. Thus, he made the following special note of peasant crops such as limes in Dominica or bananas in Jamaica: 'these democratic crops stand out in striking contrast to the dictatorship of foreign capital and foreign management which characterizes the sugar industry.'[7] The dictatorship of foreign capital was not only responsible for the lack of agricultural diversification but also the lack of industrialisation. Williams wrote:

> ...the most natural industry of the Caribbean, sugar refining, was and is deliberately prohibited by foreign competitors. The prohibition began in England in 1671, and was a part of the general colonial policy in the eighteenth century which banned iron and textiles industries in colonial America.[8]

Here we can recognise some of the themes that the plantation school will develop in a much more systematic fashion.

Before turning to the case of Arthur Lewis, whose work bore more directly on the emergence of the plantation school, it is important to note that the theme of Caribbean dependence can also be seen operating implicitly in the work of scholars from outside of the region who were also involved in the discussions that followed the uprisings of the 1930s. This was true even of some British and American scholars who were involved in these discussions. A good example of the latter is Annette Baker Fox's 1949 text, *Freedom and Welfare in the Caribbean: A Colonial Dilemma*. This work has as its main theme the tensions and contradictions inherent in a still colonised Caribbean demanding autonomy and economic development at the same time. In her view, the nature of colonial societies was such that the 'satisfaction of one demand was very likely to prejudice the fulfillment of the other.'[9] In other words, given the colonial history of economic exclusion in the region, autonomy might bring on economic collapse, while continued economic aid from the West would extend and possibly increase existing patterns of dependence. She insisted that as long as 'social and economic development takes place mainly through outside aid, there can be no real independence.'[10] Not surprisingly, she saw the region as being caught in a vicious circle from which there would be no easy exit.

In response to this dilemma, Fox discussed in detail the shifts in both British and American colonial policies that occurred after the uprisings of the 1930s. The shift in the American position she described as a 'new deal' and in the case of the British 'development and welfare.' Both were marked by a Keynesian shift from *laissez faire* to state intervention in a number of economic fields including direct production, land reform, subsidies, and increased educational opportunities. The result was a containing of the violence of the uprisings and significant moves toward political independence. Although a strong supporter of these initiatives and the policies of planned economic development put forward by the Caribbean Commission, Fox was only guardedly optimistic that these would solve the problems of economic dependence, even though the region might succeed in gaining political independence. Needless to say, Fox was correct in this assessment.

Arthur Lewis and Caribbean Dependence

The restrictive shadow that Western imperialism had cast over Caribbean economies was established in Lewis's early works such as *Labour in the West Indies*. However, as in the cases of James and Williams, the external dependence it produced, was not explicitly thematised. Lewis's response to the problems of Caribbean dependence remained implicit in his Fabian or democratic socialist response to his own question regarding 'what can be done' to realise the transformative goals of 'the new labor movement' of the 1930s.[11] For Lewis that realisation required two basic changes in Caribbean economies: first, total income 'must be considerably increased and in the second place, it must be more equitably distributed.'[12] This redistributive but also growth-oriented view of democratic socialism remained with Lewis most of his life. Thus in 1971, he wrote that the aim of democratic socialism is 'to combine political democracy with...economic equality.'[13] He then proceeded to defend the view that there were no irreconcilable conflicts between democratic socialism and economic development, although there were real tensions.

However, in spite of the permanence of these two poles of income growth and redistribution, Lewis's thought went through several stages of development. Norman Girvan has suggested a division of Lewis's thought into three basic phases: the first was that of Caribbean industrialisation; second, was the phase of the dual economy; and third, that of trade and development.[14] Further, Girvan convincingly shows that over time Lewis moved closer to some of the positions of the dependency approach – particularly those of Raul Prebisch.[15] However, Lewis's Ricardian views of trade remained a basic source of difference with the dependency view of the relationship between trade and imperialism. In the following short review of Lewis's work before the rise of dependency theory and the plantation school, my remarks will cover only the first two of the three phases suggested by Girvan.

In both of these phases, to increase total income, Lewis insisted on both the industrialisation of Caribbean economies and the expansion of agriculture. However, given commodity prices of the 1930s and the emergent nature of the Caribbean bourgeoisie, Lewis saw two crucial areas in which his two part strategy for transformation would be in need of immediate but hopefully short term assistance. As in the case of Fox, the first was for increased preferential treatment, grants and loans from the West; unlike Fox, the second was a carefully worked out strategy of industrialisation that would include the problematic requirement of importing a foreign capitalist class to lead the associated process of capital accumulation. The rare skill possessed by members of this class was 'the technique of managing large undertakings.' This skill was rare because it cannot be learned in colleges or universities but 'only in the practice of managing businesses.'[16] The role of this imported capitalist class in the expansion of national income, Lewis would develop with great care and brilliance in classic essays such as 'Economic Development with Unlimited Supplies of Labour' (1954), and 'The Industrialization of the British West Indies' (1950). Only with assistance in these two areas did Lewis see total income increasing, which could then be more equitably redistributed.

However, without naming them as such, assistance with both price and entrepreneurial support pointed to two crucial areas in which the success of this Caribbean workers movement would be dependent on the cooperation of the very capitalist and imperialist forces that it had been fighting. This contradictory but necessary bringing together of opposites such as capitalism and socialism was one of the defining features of Lewis's thought. For him, there were no absolute economic laws, only partial principles and empirical generalisations whose limits he always kept in mind when applying them to concrete situations. In this case, capitalism and socialism were not treated as absolute principles, and neither were market and plan or peasant and bourgeois entrepreneurship. For Lewis, all of these partial principles of economic thought conditioned each other, at the same time that their general scope was being constantly challenged by new concrete cases. This unusual approach is particularly evident in his book, *Principles of Economic Planning*. Thus to understand Lewis's concept of democratic socialism is to grasp the manner in which it was changed by the capitalist imperatives of the economic growth needed to increase total income. In more poetic terms, we have here the proletarian tradition of Caliban risking deeper entrapment in the capitalist imperatives of Prospero to achieve a desired expansion and redistribution of national income.

In the course of making the imported capitalist the primary agent in the process of increasing total income, Lewis was forced to confront two important factors bearing on Caribbean dependence: 1) 'the sociological problem of the emergence of a capitalist class;'[17] and 2) 'the relative efficiency of peasant and plantation production.'[18] The strategy of importing a capitalist class necessarily raised questions about existing levels of entrepreneurial capability in Caribbean societies. These inadequate levels Lewis assumed to be fairly common for newly developing countries. However, in *The Theory of Economic*

Growth, Lewis assumed that this form of entrepreneurial dependency would end fairly soon with the rise of a local capitalist class.[19]

With regard to the expansion of agriculture, Lewis strongly supported programmes of land redistribution to increase the size of peasant farms and peasant output. With the appropriate institutional support, Lewis saw 'no reason why the West Indian peasant should not learn to utilize the land as capably as the planter.'[20] In short, Caribbean peasants also had an important role to play, along with the imported capitalist class, in the project of increasing and redistributing national income. The coordinating of these strategies of industrialisation and expanding peasant output would be the job of the state, as it had to provide the combination of incentives and protection to foster the growth of both an industrial bourgeoisie and a more viable peasantry.

Lewis's democratic socialist ideas on industrialisation, increased peasant output, and income redistribution became the foundations of economic policy in much of the region. Programmes of industrialisation and peasant land settlement were undertaken in territories such as Jamaica, Trinidad, Barbados and Antigua. In these more concrete forms, because of the difference in the power values of its opposing socialist and capitalist dimensions, Lewis's proposals pushed the political economy of the region in the direction of state coordinated capitalism. Only in the cases of Trinidad, Guyana and Jamaica did the latter go beyond mere coordination and approach real forms of state capitalism. This new direction made this third phase distinct from the second – or post-slavery – phase of the plantation model, but also not the democratic socialist order that Lewis envisaged.

For this third phase in the history of Caribbean dependence, four important outcomes emerged from this state capitalist turn in Caribbean political economy. First, Caribbean state coordinated capitalism did significantly increase national income;[21] second, it did not succeed in redistributing it according to the ethics of Lewis's democratic socialism; third, it did not succeed in developing an independent peasantry; and fourth, while it did succeed in stimulating the growth of a local bourgeoisie, this class has not achieve the assumed capability of being able to replace the imported capitalist class. This local bourgeoisie sprang from the merchant classes at a time when the planters were breathing their last. This rising bourgeois class was primarily English, Middle Eastern and Indian in ethnicity. The names that we associate with this further evolution of the Caribbean bourgeoisie are firms such as Kirpalini, Neal & Massy in Trinidad, and in Jamaica, the Matalons, the Ashenheims, and Desnoes & Geddes. The aspirations and outlook of this class were those of Ariel rather than Caliban. The former identified with Prospero and worked to further his imperial project, while the latter resisted it. Thus in Jamaica after the upheavals of the 1930s, this emerging bourgeois class formed a party with the declining planter class in an effort to block the workers from gaining control of the state. Such were the ambiguous outcomes of the attempts of local political parties to implement Lewis's democratic socialist response to the problems of Caribbean dependence.

Plantation Theory and Caribbean Dependence

As these ambiguous outcomes of the attempts to implement the Lewis model of transformation left the problem of dependence very much unresolved, they determined to a large degree the issues that the plantation theory of Best and Levitt would have to address. At a minimum, the new theory would have to account for the failure of the peasantry and the local bourgeoisie to perform in the manner suggested by Lewis. It would also have to account for the more obvious continuities in the overall structure between the earlier plantation capitalism and the newer state coordinated capitalism.

To understand these and other crisis tendencies of Caribbean state coordinated capitalism, Best and Levitt shifted their gaze from the industrialisation of regional economies and their local classes, and focused more directly on the anti-developmental consequences of the behaviour of imported capitalist classes. Consequently, they would attempt to show that there were aspects of their behaviour that were inhibiting the growth of local classes and making investment decisions that not only reinforced dependence, but also transferred excessive portions of the region's surplus to the metropole. We can sum up these aspects of the behaviour of imported capitalists under the thesis of the imperialism of trade. As we will see, this thesis linked the imperial aspects of trade to the simultaneous production of development in the centre countries, and underdevelopment in the peripheral countries.

As in the case of Lewis, the plantation theory of Best and Levitt was grounded in a historical/institutional approach that divided the history of Caribbean economies into three broad phases: 1) the phase of pure plantation economy; 2) plantation economy modified or the plantation in the post-slavery period; and 3) plantation economy further modified or the plantation in the period of state capitalism. This historical approach was a backward glance in historical time in order to see more clearly the paradoxes of the third and then present phase.

Within the framework of this historical perspective, Best and Levitt recognised four variations in the ways in which Caribbean economies made the transition from phase 2 to phase 3. First, there was the variant in which imperial ties were cut, but the old export sector was retained, as in the case of Cuba. Second, was the one in which, again, imperial ties were cut, but the old export sector collapsed, as in the case of Haiti. Third, was the variant in which old metropolitan ties were broken but new ones established through quasi-staples such as tourism. Good examples of this case are Barbados and Antigua. Fourth and finally, we have the variant in which a new staple such as oil or bauxite was added without breaking older ties as in the cases of Trinidad, Guyana and Jamaica. Yet in spite of these variations in the transition to the state coordinated capitalism of the third phase, there were really no successful cases of industrialisation to report. None of these economies moved from 'subsistence production to small scale, wage employing business serving a national market, and from there to large-scale corporate enterprise.'[22]

For Best and Levitt, the primary cause of this failure to industrialise was to be found in the assumption of the Lewis-based policy makers that the developmental consequences of using imported capitalists would outweigh the anti-developmental ones. Plantation theory was an attempt to show the major problems that were now associated with that assumption. It attempted to show the manner in which this cornerstone of Caribbean state coordinated capitalism was a carryover from earlier phases that was still inhibiting the growth of local entrepreneurship, local capital markets, and thus more autonomous links between local savings and investment decisions. By inhibiting or weakening these links, the use of imported capital and capitalists reinforced rather than undermined Caribbean dependence.

At the most general level, plantation theory pointed to the existence of fundamental continuities between the three basic phases of Caribbean economies with regard to both structure and their less than viable functioning. These continuities were in five crucial areas. First was the continuing subordinate role of the manager or resident capitalist in the larger net of metropolitan capitalists, merchants and financiers who made the crucial surplus distribution and investment decisions affecting the developmental outcomes of this new staple or quasi-staple. Second, was the reappearance of the old staple cycle – a foundation period, a golden age, and a period of maturity and decline – in the new staples of the state capitalist period. Third, was the continuing dependence of Caribbean economies on metropolitan demand, capital, and entrepreneurship for its growth dynamic. Fourth was the persistence of incalculability in the transactions of these newer plantations and their parent companies. Fifth and finally, we had the continuing dominance of the further modified plantation sectors of the state capitalist period over the 'residentiary sector' or what Best and Levitt sometimes referred to as the 'national economy.'[23] Indeed, it was the negative effects of this dominance of the further modified plantation sectors on the national economies that constituted the heart of the Best/Levitt critique of the Lewis approach.

For Best and Levitt, the overall effect of these newer plantation sectors on national economies has been that 'the national propertied class is born in circumstances which restrict its capacity for innovation and self-assertion and stunt its growth. The national economy emerges with a bias towards production of output requiring traditional plantation skills and serving traditional markets.'[25] Because of this, 'when a new national resource is discovered or an old one is revived, the national economy has neither the capital nor the entrepreneurship nor the international marketing experience to organize production.'[26] The financial sector is also inhibited in a similar way:

> The fractured and partial nature of the capital market of the hinterland countries is not due to low levels of income, or a low rate of saving from domestic product. It is the result of mercantilist relations of production with metropolitan corporations, and a system of financial intermediaries which is similarly characterized by the free flow of funds between branches of metropolitan commercial banks and their head offices.[27]

In short, Best and Levitt argued that when the imperialist trade relations of the state capitalist period are superimposed on those of the previous periods, 'the barriers to the emergence of indigenous enterprise are reinforced.'[28] Further, the classes of this circumscribed national economy cannot really mature. These underdeveloped classes – 'the quasi-proletariat, the quasi-peasantry, and the quasi-bourgeoisie – are creatures of the plantation export sector.'[29] Confined in this manner, these classes are unable to give the national economy the internal dynamic that it would need to replace the dynamic supplied by imported capitalists. Thus in spite of the Haitian case, Best and Levitt recommended a breaking with this model that based industrialisation on the developmental consequences inherent in mercantile relations of production and trade: 'a severance of the metropolitan ties is a precondition of structural transformation.'[30] This was the sharp break that Best and Levitt made with the Ricardian views of international trade that informed Lewis's model. Hence we get the statement by Best that the real differences between plantation theorists and Lewis are to be found 'in the causes we adduce to explain mal-distribution of gains from trade which had so agonized him along with Myrdal and Singer.'[31]

The Model and Its Critics

As well-known as the model itself are the criticisms that have been made of it. These criticisms have been of two types: negative and positive. The negative criticisms have come from two groups of scholars: first, the positivist economists who are uncomfortable with the historicism of Best and Levitt, and would like a more scientific theory with greater predictive power and more testable hypotheses. Second, were the more orthodox Marxists who insisted on a clearer specifying of a proletarian change agent and more definite strategies of transformation. The constructive criticisms came from neo-Marxists scholars, such as George Beckford, Norman Girvan, Clive Thomas and I, who attempted to extend the theory in various ways. Thus, in my case, the attempt was to develop in detail the suggestion that the transition to state coordinated capitalism in Antigua was of the third or quasi-staple variant (1985), and also the cultural dimensions of the problem of dependence – in particular philosophical dependence (2000).

George Beckford

Beckford's contribution to plantation theory was a detailed comparative analysis of Caribbean agriculture in the third phase of plantation further modified, or what we have been calling state capitalism. What was new about agriculture in this phase was its thorough integration into the organisational structures of transnational firms that were processing and transporting plantation outputs. Consequently, Beckford was concerned about the developmental impact of this corporate reorganisation on both Caribbean agriculture and the larger economy.

For Beckford, the corporate consolidation of plantation agriculture was twinned with the growth of the Caribbean peasantry that followed the ending of slavery. This was the sector of the 'national economy' that he focused on, describing in detail its determined struggles to develop in spite of constraints and competition coming from the now corporate plantation sector. Particularly in the case of Jamaica, Beckford showed that these constraints included plantation control of the best lands and local financial institutions, strong dominance over local labour markets, and also the new national government. Like Best and Levitt, Beckford argued that these continuities with earlier phases outweighed the discontinuities:

> ...the emergence of the vertically integrated corporate plantation enterprise has really served to preserve the character of the slave plantation system. Three characteristics of that earlier institutional environment – appendage in overseas economy, total economic institution, and incalculability – have been preserved and strengthened since Emancipation.[32]

In spite of these inhibiting effects of corporate consolidation, however, the Caribbean peasantry was able to grow. Beckford argued that they diversified production by introducing new crops, and created an internal marketing system, and rudimentary banking and credit systems. This growth in peasant production in spite of plantation constraints led Beckford to the following important claim: 'it is this expansion which has been the chief source of economic development of the West Indian economies since emancipation.'[33] In other words, even with the corporate reorganising of the plantation sector, Beckford argued that the really dynamic sector of Caribbean economies was the peasantry, and that national resources and government policies should be steered much more strongly in their direction.

For Beckford, the peasantry was therefore the crucial agent of change and development that could supply the missing entrepreneurial dynamic and end the excessive dependence on imported capitalists. On the point of which of these two sectors is more dynamic, Beckford is most explicit in his disagreements with Lewis, and comes much closer to the Best/Levitt position on the 'national economy.' In his view, the corporate plantation sector, like its predecessors, continues to release its developmental dynamics in the centre and its anti-developmental dynamics in peripheral areas like the Caribbean.

Norman Girvan

Girvan's contribution to plantation theory was an intense focus on the fourth variant of the transition to Caribbean state capitalism in which the new staples of oil and bauxite were added to the old in the economies of Trinidad, Guyana and Jamaica. Consequently, there is a definite shift from the strong focus on agriculture to the transnational, corporate organisation of mineral exports. Yet, in spite of this shift, it is the continuities between the imperialism of trade between all three phases that is the centre of Girvan's argument. This argument rests on the claim that while anti-colonial movements of the 1950s severely weakened political imperialism, the new relations between postcolonial states transnational corporations have in fact strengthened the practice of economic imperialism. This new form of the imperialism of trade, Girvan referred to as 'corporate imperialism,' and the response of the region to it as 'economic nationalism.'[34]

For Girvan, as for Best and Levitt, the primary channel through which imperial strategies work is the subordinate position of the manager of the local subsidiary in the overall hierarchy of corporate decision making. In addition to this weak position of the manager, Girvan analysed problems of incalculability in inter-company transactions and other channels through which the transfer of surplus to the centre from the Caribbean took place. He summed up his analysis as follows:

...it is the imperialism of the parent over the subsidiary, as embodied in the power relationships and economic transactions characteristic of the transnational firm, which, when reproduced on a world scale and transposed onto the center-periphery pattern of the international capitalist economy, gives rise to the phenomenon that we have called corporate imperialism.[35]

The economic nationalism of Caribbean state capitalism is, in Girvan's view, an attempt to assert sovereignty over the resources of the region. However, he also suggested that this push for sovereignty was not necessarily an attempt to overthrow the corporate imperialist order, but to improve the positions of Caribbean states within it. This stance was linked to the declining quantitative importance of Third World minerals in corporate processes of accumulation, as distinct from their qualitative importance. In spite of this declining strategic position, Girvan insisted on a more radical subverting of corporate imperialism that would require a 'genuinely revolutionary socialist change.'[36]

Clive Thomas

In Thomas's *Dependence and Transformation*, we find the most comprehensive attempt to outline a socialist alternative to the plantation system. As with Beckford, the peasantry is a very important change agent in Thomas's extension of the Best/Levitt plantation model. However, in this case it was not just the peasantry, but workers and peasants in alliance with a socialist state that was the suggested agent to replace the imported capitalist and to supply the missing internal dynamic.

Thomas's insistence on a socialist state points to a significant difference with Beckford on the role and capability of the peasants in this process of transformation. Thomas's estimate of the ability of the peasants to fill the entrepreneurial gap left by the displacing of the imported capitalists was different from Beckford's. To fill this gap, Thomas saw a very definite need for his socialist state to engage in the practice of 'class creation.' All of the major classes of Caribbean societies were underdeveloped in relation to the challenges of economic transformation. Thus, Thomas's socialist state was in the paradoxical position of having to create the functional equivalent of a capitalist class, a state bourgeoisie. Here Thomas is confronting the same problem of an entrepreneurial deficit that Lewis attempted to solve by importation. In other words, it is a state bourgeoisie leading a worker/peasant alliance in a centrally planned process of transformation that would end the ratooning of the plantation and establish the autonomy of the national economy in relation to the appropriating and reinvesting of the Caribbean surplus.

These ideas about transformation came closest to being implemented with the writing of *The People's Plan* by George Beckford, Norman Girvan, Louis Lindsay, and Michael Witter (1985). This plan was submitted in 1977 to the Michael Manley regime that had been re-elected in 1976 on a democratic socialist platform. However, on grounds of feasibility, the regime did not implement the plan.

The Best/Levitt Response

In spite of building in very creative ways on the foundations of plantation theory, these transformative extensions of the theory were never really embraced by Best and Levitt. Thus, it is on the issue of the practical policy implications of the thesis of the imperialism of trade that the theory has really floundered. Levitt has noted the incompleteness of the theory because of their failure to b elaborate a model in which the national economy was either dominant or independent.[37] In response to this particular challenge, four responses can be observed on the part of Best: first, a distancing from the failures to implement some of the delinking policies of plantation theory in the contexts of the Bishop regime in Grenada and the Michael Manley regime in Jamaica. Second, is to shift from economics to the need for a genuinely participatory politics that would be educative for the masses in the Jamesian sense. Third is a shift to the level of culture and the problem of Caliban's and Ariel's continuing entrapment in the economic discourses of Prospero. Fourth and finally, is a shift to an improvisational stance that sees calls for plans, strategies, and more scientific theories as dogmatic.

A good example of Best employing all of these strategies can be seen in the indirect and elusive manner in which he presents his position in the paper he wrote for the Fourth Sir Arthur Lewis Memorial Lecture (1999). In particular, we can see the shifts to the political and cultural levels in his attempt to explain the failures of the Lewis model. With regard to the cultural shift, Best links Lewis's failure to adequately grasp the specific realities of the region to his long absence from the Caribbean, and his intellectual entrapment in the categories of the British economic tradition. Drawing on Wilson Harris, Best portrays Lewis as a creolised Afro-Saxon, a poignant case of Caliban's entrapment in the economic discourses of Prospero. It is this entrapment that leads Best to the startling assertion that Lewis was 'not a West Indian economist at all.'[38] This cultural and epistemic alienation in turn not only forced Lewis into theorising the British situation, but also prevented him from seeing clearly the political dimensions of Caribbean economies.[39] For Best, the core of this political dimension remains the contradiction between the plantation and residentiary sectors. However, in this paper, we do not get a direct stating of the combination of political, epistemic and economic strategies that will remove or resolve it.

However, in spite of this less than enthusiastic response on the part of Best and Levitt, the visionary significance of these above extensions is undeniable. If the imperialism of trade has been and still is our reality, then we have nowhere to go but in the direction pointed out by the extensions that have been made by Beckford, Girvan, Thomas and others. The way forward can only be extensions of combinations of these extensions. However, before taking these up more directly, we now have a new theoretical problem to confront: whether or not we have entered a fourth plantation phase as a result of the emergence of yet another phase in the history of metropolitan capitalism – a phase that I have called informatic capitalism. This new phase shows all the signs of once again adding new staples and shifting the location of overseas production but incorporating these changed peripheral sites in very dependent ways.

Informatic Capitalism

To understand the shift in our current economic gaze, to grasp why our eyes are now on economic survival rather than economic nationalism or radical transformation, we must come to terms with the peripheral implications of the major restructuring of Western capitalism that has been taking place over the past 25 years. The rise of the informatic phase has been the result of the coming together of two major forces: 1) a severe crisis of accumulation in the Western economies in the 1970s; and the rise of Asian capitalism fed by an expanding revolution in information and communications technology. The informatic phase has been emerging from the responses of Western capitalism to these two major challenges.

The crisis that gripped the American and Western European economies in the 1970s is well recognised by economists of widely differing persuasions. On the left, it has been well documented by economists such as Paul Sweezy (1978), Gerard Dumenil and Dominique Levy (2004). On the right, it has been analysed by scholars like Roger Alcaly (2003), economist and also the manager of a Hedge fund. This crisis, which continued into the early 1980s, was evident in rising rates of inflation and unemployment, declining profit rates and rates of labour productivity.[40] In addition to the phenomena of stagflation and growing international competition, what was also unusual about the crisis of the 1970s was its resistance to established doses of Keynesian stimulation.

The basic response of Western elites to this crisis of accumulation was led by finance capital as they were being hurt by rising inflation. Consequently, they pushed for higher interest rates and reform of corporate governance that would make it more sensitive to stockholder interests. In short, the initial response to the crisis took the form of a revolt by angry investors who were dissatisfied with the ways in which corporate managers were responding to inflation and foreign (particularly Asian) competition.

The ideology of this revolt was shareholder value. In the US, the leaders were the takeover entrepreneurs such as Irwin Jacobs, Carl Icahn, Michael Milkin, and Ivan Boesky. Their primary weapon was the hostile takeover, which had the effect of putting corporate managers on the defensive. It also forced them to deal more effectively with foreign competition through mergers, and enlarge rewards to stockholders by increasing the price of company stock. Closely related to these changes was the making of managers also into shareholders. As owner/managers, CEOs would now share the views of stockholders.

The American state, which after 1980 had turned sharply to the right, supported these initiatives of finance capital in two important ways: 1) by deregulating banking and broadening the range of activities deposit banks could engage in by repealing the 1933 Glass-Steagill Act in 1988; and 2) by supporting finance capital's drive to globalise and liberalise financial markets. It was in this new policy context that finance was able to stimulate the US economy in the second half of the 1980s. However, this ballooning of the financial sector also created a speculative bubble in the economy that would cause problems later. This bubble was evident in the 'dot com' phenomenon, rapidly rising stock values, and skyrocketing increases in corporate remuneration. In 1970, the average American CEO made 69 times the wage of the average worker. In 2000, that figure had risen to 300 (msn.com).

Although the shift to finance eased the crisis somewhat, the pressure of foreign competition only increased. Thus the decade of the 1990s was marked by a turn to the information sector as a strategy for coping with foreign competition. This competition was coming primarily from Japan and the larger Pacific Rim. Drawing on the new information technologies, Japanese capitalists, particularly those at Toyota, pioneered what today has come to be known as high-volume flexible production and just in time production.[41] The former was a mode of production whose internal structure was significantly different from that of the Fordist mass production assembly line that still dominated American and European auto companies. This post-Fordist or Toyotaist mode of production had an assembly line that was capable of making many more stops for quick changes and so was better able to make small batches of customised products. In other words, to mass production this new mode of production added mass customisation. To deal with the pressure of foreign competition, it was this shift from the Fordist to the Toyotaist assembly line that would have to be successfully executed in the West.

Making this transition has not been easy for the major Western firms of the monopoly era. They have responded in six basic ways: 1) making themselves bigger through mergers and acquisitions; 2) partnering with Japanese firms; 3) developing new informatic technologies of their own; 4) breaking the post-war pact with American labour in order to lower labour costs and in some cases reneging on pension commitments. This has destroyed the classic Galbraithian firm (1972) which was the centrepiece of the monopoly phase: 5) the globalising of commodity markets, particularly in peripheral areas; and 6) the reorganising of their peripheral operations, relations and locations.

These still ongoing changes, together with the initial response of financialisation have been sufficiently profound for us to speak of a new era in the history of Western capitalism – the informatic phase. Because it is still developing inside of the financial bubble of the 1980s it is the combination of these two sets of forces that have been behind this transition to a new phase.[42] In this new economy, it is companies like Wal-mart, Microsoft, and Dell Computers rather than General Motors, Ford or IBM that have emerged as the new model companies. Indeed the troubles of the latter, particularly Ford and General Motors – classic Galbraithian firms, have been extensively reported in the press. Particularly in the cases of Wal-mart and Dell it is the new informatic technology along with the new labour and peripheral regimes that have given them their competitive advantage over the dominant firms of the monopoly phase. This transformation is an ongoing one, the outcome of which is still not certain. However, my argument for a new and distinct informatic phase of Western capitalism rests on the assumption that informatic production will at some point in the future gain control over or significantly lessen the current dominance of finance capital.

The Caribbean Periphery in the Informatic Phase

When we look at the globalising of financial and commodity markets and the reprioritising of peripheral areas in the informatic phase of Western capitalism, we find a lot that should be of interest to plantation theorists. In particular, Best and Levitt focused quite intensively on the adjustment strategies of metropolitan capital in the declining phases of the growth paths of peripheral plantation economies. They suggested that these metropolitan responses included divesting from old staples and old peripheral sites, while shifting investments to new staples or to new terrains which offered virgin soils, cheaper labour, and better technological possibilities. Keith Nurse has developed very insightfully this aspect of the original model (1998). The Best/Levitt strategies of adjustment certainly help us to understand the shifts in location and patterns of divestment and investment that have emerged in the peripheral areas of informatic capitalism. With regards to the Caribbean, we can note five important changes in its peripheral relations with Western capitalism.

First, there has been a decline in overall peripheral importance with the emergence of China as the most attractive peripheral site and India a rising second. Indeed the model firms of the informatic phase such as Wal-mart and Dell would be inconceivable without access to these Asian peripheries but very conceivable without access to the Caribbean periphery. This decline in Caribbean peripheral importance has resulted in major contractions in Lewis-style programs of industrialisation which have added to the difficulties of Caribbean state coordinated capitalism, particularly in countries like Barbados, Antigua and St Lucia which had attempted to build industrial sectors on the Lewis model. However, the interest of metropolitan finance and real estate capital in the regions beach front areas remains very strong. In many islands these have indeed become the new plantations. Hence we get the persistence of external interests in Caribbean tourism. However, this interest has not been strong enough to avoid an overall decline in peripheral importance. The semi-peripheralisation of China, which officially is still a communist state, has important implications for both socialist theory and plantation theory. It raises anew the old question of the necessity for a capitalist phase in the formation of modern societies. However, we cannot deal with that issue here.

A second important change in the Caribbean mode of peripheralisation has been the decision of metropolitan capital to divest from plantation agriculture in the region, impacting very significantly territories like Dominica, St Lucia, St Vincent, and Jamaica, where there were significant investments in bananas. From the perspective of plantation theory, this withdrawal of metropolitan capital should have been a welcomed opportunity. Instead, however, we had the mounting of a major effort to preserve this classic plantation sector and the system of preferences upon which it would have to depend. From the point of view of informatic capital, it was a doomed attempt to keep alive a practice from the second phase of Caribbean plantation economy in this new and fourth phase that has been brought into being by the changes in the organisation of metropolitan capital.

The third important Caribbean peripheral change of the informatic phase has been the addition of the new staple of natural gas in Trinidad and the new informatic quasi-staples of electronic data processing, internet gaming, call centres, and hospitality centres. Thus Trinidad, which has continued its pattern of adding new staples without divesting from old ones, has been the site of the most dynamic changes, and thus has moved more deeply into this fourth phase. At the other extreme, is Haiti, whose situation has only deteriorated, along with Dominica and St Vincent that did not really develop strong state coordinated capitalist regimes based on new staples or quasi-staples. The latter two countries are now standing between the collapse of plantation agriculture and an alternative that is yet to emerge. In economies like those of Antigua, Barbados and St Lucia, the persistence of metropolitan investment interest in tourism along with the new informatic quasi-staples has been the basis of this fourth restructuring of their plantation sectors.

The fourth important change has been the preference of finance controlled informatic capital for open financial and commodity markets, and for private sector leadership in the Caribbean periphery. This has meant pressure on Caribbean states to downsize, to weaken their already weak developmental roles, and to support the role of the market in determining economic outcomes. The consequences of these pressures were seen very clearly in the Seaga, the second Michael Manley, and Patterson regimes in Jamaica. Thus for Caribbean economies that made strong state coordinated capitalist turns, they are now wavering rather undecidedly between private and state led capitalism. On the whole, however, these attempts to reverse the roles of the state and private sector have been strikingly unsuccessful.

Fifth and finally, informatic capitalism's return to market fundamentalism has brought with it a direct theoretical and ideological challenge to plantation economy's thesis of the imperialism of trade. The major effect of this neoliberal/informatic view of markets has been a relegitimising of the position that trade between centre and periphery is not only free and fair, but is the primary route to development. As such it sanctions as good for the Caribbean the investment, pricing, and relocation policies of metropolitan capital that plantation theory has so severely criticised. Because of the failures that have accompanied the attempts to implement the policy recommendations of both Lewis and the plantation theorists, a theoretical and policy vacuum opened up and was filled by these neoliberal theories and policies. Consequently, the region has experienced a significant loss of autonomy in economic thought, as it has been forced to affirm ideas and policies that are alien to its own economic imagination and tradition of thought.

These in brief are the major changes that the informatic phase has made in the status and organisation of its Caribbean periphery. These changes are significant enough to constitute a fourth phase, a fourth ratooning of the plantation sector of Caribbean economies. If this is indeed the case, then it really puts the pressure on plantation theory to come up with a model of transformation that could really interrupt this repeating pattern that it has systematically thematised and thus eventually eliminate it. To do this it must build on the attempts of Girvan, Beckford, Thomas and others to develop this transformative dimension of the theory.

Transforming Phase 4 of Caribbean Plantation Economy

The fourth ratooning of the Caribbean plantation in the informatic phase raises a number of questions about the persistence of this pattern and how it is reproduced. I want to suggest that our poets and novelists, whose focus has been Caribbean identities, may be of great help here. In *Caliban's Reason*, I argued that the philosophical foundation of plantation theory was historicism. However, one of the major limitations of Caribbean historicism has been its reluctance to fully embrace it philosophical twin – Caribbean poeticism. The latter has produced a vast literature on the formation of colonised identities and self-consciousness that can usefully supplement the more insurrectionary views of the Caribbean economic subject held by plantation theorists. We have not thematised as systematically as the poeticists the structures of individual and class consciousness that the plantation has produced. Kamau Brathwaite has described this distinct colonial field of consciousness as an 'inner plantation.'[42] The value of integrating these poeticist accounts is that they focus much more directly on the forces that limit the growth, horizons and capabilities of colonised subjects, including entrepreneurial subjects. There are hints of such a synthesis in Best's many references to the works of V.S. Naipaul and Wilson Harris.

From our earlier analyses of the failed attempts at transformation, we can conclude that Caribbean economies have equilibrated around a crisis-ridden state coordinated capitalism beyond which it has been difficult to move them either to the left or the right. Further, we can also conclude that there is no single class in its present form that is really up to the task of replacing the foreign bourgeoisie. Most recently, the persistence of this external dependence has been dramatically exposed by the figure of Allen Stanford in Antigua, and who was threatening to extend his influence regionally.[44] This vacuum points to an inescapable entrepreneurial problem that has to be addressed more directly if the entrepreneurial dynamic of these economies is to be localised. Such a transfer would require the creating of a designated entrepreneurial sector that would cut across the major classes and also include the state. The mobilising of this sector would have to include both its technical training and consciousness-raising in an effort to bring its capabilities up to the task of shifting and controlling the entrepreneurial dynamic. It is in the areas of changing entrepreneurial identities and raising self-consciousness that poeticist accounts of Caribbean subjects can be helpful.

Poeticists such as George Lamming and Sylvia Wynter have argued that transformation in the region has been hindered by retrogressive responses to postcolonial challenges that are linked to the reproductive logics of colonial identities. As W.E.B. DuBois noted, colonised and racialised identities are divided formations, marked by what he called 'double consciousness.'[45] Colonised subjects see themselves through their own eyes but also through the eyes of their colonisers. The latter view is very often what Wynter has called a liminal gaze, such as 'the negro' or 'the coolie' that stereotypes and limits the capabilities of the colonised.[46] This stereotypical identity constitutes the colonised as 'the other' of the colonised and establishes hierarchical and non-interchangeable roles between these two. In spite of their negativity, once they are internalised these liminal values and roles become integral parts of the reproductive routines of these identities – thus ratooning these externally imposed limitations. These self-limiting dynamics of colonial identities need to be more carefully included into our analyses of the subjective formation of Caribbean classes and their puzzling entrepreneurial performances. Thus what follows is a socio-philosophical contribution to this problem of entrepreneurial under-performance and how it contributes to the ratooning of the plantation sector. The socio-philosophical nature of this contribution builds on some of the themes of cultural and epistemic entrapment raised earlier by Best in his comments on Lewis. Thus, no attempt is made here to deal with the specifically economic aspects of the proposed entrepreneurial sector.

Entrepreneurial Ability and the Colonial Subject

The formation of the Caribbean entrepreneurial subject cannot be separated from the broader socio-discursive processes that have produced the more general conceptions of the Caribbean subject. As a culturally plural society, the economic self-consciousness of the classes of Caribbean society has been shaped by quite different cultural, racial and political experiences. More precisely, these differences also represented different ways of framing what Lewis called 'the will to economize.'[47] Further, these culturally different ways of structuring and expressing this will were subjected to very different patterns of identity-based exclusion from engaging in specific business practices. In short it was the combination of these culturally distinct expressions of the will to economise and the colonial/racial negations or affirmations they encountered in the market place that determined the entrepreneurial identities of individuals in these different groups.

Drawing on Lewis, I will define entrepreneurial self-consciousness as the size and nature of the undertaking that one will attempt to manage. As noted earlier, entrepreneurial identities and capabilities, unlike many others, are not learned in colleges and universities. Rather, they are developed within families or apprentice-style relationships. Thus entrepreneurial outlooks and capabilities are uniquely dependent on how these identities are constructed and reproduced over the generations. The 'I' or self-consciousness of the entrepreneurs who continue to control the commanding heights of Caribbean economies were shaped by the cultural traditions, the racist practices and the self-organising strategies of the Western bourgeoisie. Further, they encountered strong legal and political affirmation as they entered various market places. On the other hand, the framing of the will to economise among the smaller middle tier capitalists was shaped by Middle Eastern traditions of trading along with their exposure to both the entrepreneurial and racist practices of the dominant Western capitalists. Third and finally, the economic self-consciousness and will to economise among the professionals and workers who occupied the lower middle and working class positions were framed by African and Indian traditions of farming, trading and manufacturing, along with the intense legal and political negation they encountered in the Caribbean marketplace. In spite of this culturally plural background, however, our focus here will be primarily on the formation and deformation of entrepreneurial consciousness among the Afro-Caribbean and Middle Eastern groups.

Entrepreneurial Self-Consciousness among Afro-Caribbeans

The roots of the Afro-Caribbean 'I' and hence its will to economise are of pre-colonial West African origin. From Africa, future Afro-Caribbeans brought with them cooperative traditions of farming that were rooted in communal/lineage and tribute paying modes of production. In these modes of production, land was owned either in common or by the state.[48] Further, economic production was embedded in social norms of reciprocity and redistribution in the interest of reducing inequality. Markets were specific places where goods were sold and not abstract deterritorialised invisible hands coordinating economic signals and decisions. They were socially regulated spaces in which activities were coordinated by principles of social interaction, reciprocity and state sponsored redistribution.[49] Consequently, in the pre-colonial African context the will to economise and to accumulate was not framed primarily by the calculus of markets abstracted from all notions of social space, but by an economic calculus that was encoded within and subordinated to other systems of meaning.

Enslavement on the plantations of the Caribbean radically disrupted these African economic and entrepreneurial traditions. By the latter, I am referring to the individuals who take responsibility for initiating things and regimes such as the pre-colonial kingdoms of Dahomey and Buganda (the latter now a part of Uganda) that took responsibility for long term planning to avoid famines or shortages in dry seasons. As plantation workers, they acquired new economic identities that conflicted with the older ones. African women became primarily domestic workers but also field slaves. African men became house slaves, field slaves and urban slaves for hire. Thus began the plantation redefinition of Africans as agro-proletarians, urban workers and domestics. These restricted economic identities constituted the contours of Brathwaite's inner plantation that relations with Prospero had established in the entrepreneurial self-consciousness of Caliban. As such economic subjects, they were being created for a surplus extracting relationship with Western capital. These identities as various forms of labour power were economic definitions of self that were created and imposed by the needs of the plantation sector. It was the coloniser's view of the African economic subject and not the latter's view of him/herself. As a worker and a black, the African by definition would not be socially recognised as being capable of performing the roles of the white capitalist. This is what it meant in this case to be defined and 'othered' by the liminal gaze of the planter. However, once internalised, this restricted conception became a part of the economic self-understanding of Africans that would now be reproduced along with other aspects of their economic identities.

However, in spite of the imposition of this predominantly agro-proletarian identity, some of the old ones survived. These could be seen in the small plots that slaves were allowed to cultivate and in marketing practices such as higglering. Thus I am suggesting the emergence of a double economic identity – one based on African traditions of farming and entrepreneurship, and the other on plantation constructions of agro-proletarians. The former has been the basis for the strong drive among rural Afro-Caribbeans to reconstitute themselves as an independent peasantry, as the cases of Jamaica[50] and Haiti[51] have made particularly clear. The agro-proletarian identity has been the basis upon which others have sought to insert themselves more satisfactorily into local labour markets. In the oppositional tensions between these two economic identities and the difficulties of realising them, the entrepreneurial traditions of Afro-Caribbeans struggled to assert themselves.

In the decades after the ending of slavery, the Caribbean masses continued to move rather unproductively between these two identities. Positively they were able to reassert some of the old farming traditions and apply them to the production of crops for local consumption and also for export. On the negative side, they were unable to overcome the structural constraints of the plantation on their economic activities or to effectively break the entrepreneurial constraints that came with an agro-proletarian identity. Consequently, they were unable to surge into the entrepreneurial spaces of the middle and big capitalists.

However, important changes came with uprisings of the 1930s. The latter made the insurrectionary consciousness of Caliban visible among the Caribbean masses once again. This consciousness was given organisational form by the trade unions and political parties that were formed in the aftermath of these uprisings, and which eventually gave Afro-Caribbeans access to state power. However, in the decades following this access to state power, classic Michelsian oligarchic patterns[52] began to develop within these mass organisations, which instrumentalised and clientelised relations between leaders and led. The result has been a partyist capturing of this insurrectionary consciousness of workers and a channelling of it into the electoral and other strategic concerns of leaders. The essence of partyism is the absolutising of the creative agency of the party and its election to power. As such an absolute, one's party becomes the precondition for economic success. The will to economise, whether in proletarian or peasantist form, became deeply politicised, but did not produce any great increase in the entrepreneurial dynamism of this class. It did result in the growth of small one or two-person enterprises by members of this class, but no major increase in entrepreneurial capability that would have enabled it to assume major responsibilities in localising the productive dynamic of Caribbean economies.

From the foregoing brief account, it should be clear that the economic and political self-organisation of workers and peasants in the post-insurrectionary period did not sufficiently break down the structural barriers of the outer plantations or the inhibitions of the inner plantations. These have continued to lock workers and peasants into subordinate wage roles in ways that make it particularly difficult for them to move into more entrepreneurial and economically independent roles. It was these weak impulses toward taking control of production in the movements of Caribbean workers that led James, in *Party Politics in the West Indies*, to outline an intermediary program of state capitalism for workers in Trinidad.[53] Consequently, if workers and peasants are to play significant roles in a model of transformation aimed at transferring the entrepreneurial dynamic from the peripheral sector to the national economy, they are going to have to break out of their current partyist entrapment, reorganise themselves more autonomously, and expand the horizons and capability of their will to economise. To the extent that they do not, they will be contributing to the ratooning of the plantation sector and to the entrenchment of the current crisis-ridden forms of state coordinated capitalism.

The Middle Eastern Capitalists

The inability of the bourgeois classes of colonial societies to replace its metropolitan counter part has been given classic formulations by James.[54] In 1961, Fanon argued that the colonial bourgeoisie 'is in no way commensurate with the bourgeoisie of the mother country which it hopes to replace....The psychology of the national bourgeoisie is that of the businessman, not that of the captain of industry.'[55] This difference in psychology has led many on the left to dismiss this class as irrelevant for any process of socialist transformation. However, given the above assessments of the entrepreneurial capabilities of Caribbean developmental states, workers and peasants, strategic necessity requires a rethinking of this position. It suggests the inclusion of nationalist elements of this class into an entrepreneurial sector that can be mobilised around bringing a phased transfer of the productive dynamic of the economy into effect. Thus, rather than dismiss the possible contributions of this class, I will suggest a poeticist reading of its under-performance that could possibly help us to understand it better.

As already noted, the local bourgeoisie in the Caribbean has been for the most part racially/ethnically distinct from both the big capitalists and the masses of Indo and Afro-Caribbean peasants and workers. Their ranks have included businessmen of Jewish, Lebanese, Syrian, European ethnicity, and more recently businessmen and women of Indian and African backgrounds. Many of these individuals rose from positions of itinerant traders to become successful merchants who would occupy and then dominate the intermediate economic positions between the European planters and the Afro and Indo-Caribbean masses. Unlike the case of the latter, the liminal gaze of coloniser confirmed the basic economic view that Middle Easterners had of themselves as traders. However, this gaze also inscribed their identity in a racial hierarchy that established it as intermediary between black and white, workers and plantation capitalists. This was the bounded space in which their will to economise would be recognised. Here, this space outlined the perimeter of the inner plantation that relations with planter Prospero established in the entrepreneurial self-consciousness of this Arielist stratum. The latter's will to economise would not be recognised as capable of transcending this intermediate space and entering the terrain of the planters. Such moves were forbidden by the racial hierarchy into which their identities were now embedded. Once this place in the hierarchy was internalised, it became a part of the reproductive dynamic of their own identities, converting these external prohibitions into internal, self-limiting inhibitions that facilitated their long and static adjustment to their designated place as merchants.

As in the case of workers, the insurrections of the 1930s were also important turning points in the formation of the economic consciousness of these intermediary classes. These uprisings made the Arielist tendencies that resulted from the internalising of their place in the colonial/racial hierarchy more explicit. However, the failure of their attempts at alliance with Prospero forced them into new relations with the African and Indian masses. These new relations produced a politicising of their will to economise that was different from – but comparable to – the cases of workers and peasants, as it made them also integral parts of the then emerging state coordinated capitalist order. Earlier, we noted the rise of their more corporate identity and their limited industrial responses to the state incentives of the Lewis era. As a result of these policies and movements, merchants became merchant-manufacturers, producing commodities like cement, soft drinks, garments, beer and rum. These shifts toward manufacturing also produced the conglomerate structure that has become typical of the major Caribbean corporations. This structure is one of family-based shareholding groups owning controlling interests in these merchant-manufacturing combinations.

The rise of the informatic phase has been the next major turning point in the formation of these bourgeoisie classes, as it introduced policies in support of private sector as opposed to state leadership of the economy. Adapting to the reality of globalisation has not been easy for these classes. There were many casualties, making the corporate terrain of the region quite different from what it was before 1980. As noted before, the attempts to push these classes more deeply into manufacturing was not successful. Indeed, the major expansion of their activities during this period has been in the areas of finance and tourism. Spurred by deregulation, there were rapid expansions in the financial sector. Commercial banks, development banks, insurance companies and building societies increased in number, adding finance to the conglomerate structure of major Caribbean corporations. In Jamaica, this expansion was too rapid, leading to a major collapse of the sector and a rescue by the state. This event foreshadowed in many ways the global collapse of financial sectors in 2008. In Trinidad, the growth of this sector has been steadier, with major forays across the region.

As expected, this brief account of the formation of the Caribbean bourgeoisie has not been the portrait of a dynamic developmental class such as the Taiwanese or the South Korean bourgeoisie. Indeed, in many ways it confirms Fanon's portrait of it. It is important, however, to take note of what movements have taken place and their significance for a project of mobilising the entrepreneurial potential of the region. Further, this class is as much a part of the national economy as the productive activity of workers. Not only do we need to take note of these movements, but we also need to understand as best we can why they have been so slow and cautious. Here I think that we can see evidence of self-inhibiting patterns that block or limit responses to market signals and investment opportunities. It is as though these patterns block out signals coming from the terrain of the planter and let in only those coming from intermediary terrains and that are of intermediary proportions. In other words, market signals and investment opportunities are still being interpreted through the lens of the liminal restrictions placed on the trading activities of this class by the plantation sector. Thus, there is significant inertia coming from the self-reproducing patterns of bourgeois identities that is limiting the entrepreneurial activities of this class. As Fanon noted, this class 'is unable to give free rein to its genius, which formerly it was wont to lament, though rather too glibly, was held in check by colonial domination.'[56] This inability to be creative, to surge into the terrain of planter Prospero, has been both a puzzle and an embarrassment even to these classes themselves. To unravel this puzzle, we need to grasp the extent to which the entrepreneurial identity of this class is still caught in the dynamics of the relationship between Ariel and Prospero. To the extent that these identities have remained Arielist they will continue to reproduce their need for Prosperean complements. The continued reproduction of these needs, together with those of Caliban's inner plantation constitutes an important socio-psychological base that has enabled the outer Caribbean plantation to go through its fourth and current ratooning.

Conclusion

Given that Caribbean economies are now well into the long cycle of their fourth ratooning, the question that we must confront is: can we prevent a fifth? In the last sections of this paper, I emphasised the need to raise the level of entrepreneurial performance by mobilising a sector drawn from all of the major classes, on whose local shoulders the productive dynamic of the economy would rest. From past experience, I have concluded that at present, this sector would not be ready for such a takeover. Training and consciousness-raising for such a mission will therefore be a necessity. The performance of this entrepreneurial sector would be part of a larger model of transformation that targeted specific industries for phased competitive takeovers. The persistent functioning of such a sector could significantly expand the national economy and thus break the pattern of the repeating plantation.

We need to work out the economics of such an entrepreneurial sector carefully. From a sociological standpoint, economics has consistently been the rationalisation of the productive practices and capabilities of a particular class – landlords, merchants, industrial capitalists, financiers, and so on. Thus, a new challenge before Caribbean economics would be the improving and rationalising of the productive activities and capabilities of the combination of classes that constitute such a sector. The economics of such an entrepreneurial formation need to be carefully worked out in a model that reverses the sectoral dynamics of the Lewis model by specifying the first, second, third, and consequesnt sets of industries that will be competitively transferred from the plantation to this sector and thus to the national economy. The ideological framework of such an economic transfer must also be determined by careful readings of current insurrectionary tendencies among the masses if it is to have both legitimacy and efficacy.

We should begin with those economic resources over which we have control or could easily control. Initially the focus should be on low-tech industries like tourism and those in which we have a cultural advantage. Decolonising, and hence raising, levels of entrepreneurial self-consciousness and capability will also be very important. In particular, I have suggested that current readings of investment opportunities and other economic signals by our entrepreneurs tend to be distorted by Prosperean deferrals that put certain undertakings off limits. Changing these patterns will involve focusing on practices and faculties over which we have control. At present, this control is sufficient to enable us to change the cultural constructions that limit or distort entrepreneurial readings of investment opportunities and other economic signals. In his *General Theory of Employment, Interest and Money*, Keynes showed that there is no simple market relationship between savings and investments.[57] Working relations between the two are in part a result of new ways of seeing oneself and the risks in one's environment, as well as the result of actions of the state. Consequently, there must be more that we can do in this fluid region to make the entrepreneurs in our sector take more risks and respond more positively to opportunities in the Caribbean environment. By doing something like this, we just might be able to avoid a fifth ratooning of our plantation heritage.

Notes

1. I would like to thank Norman Girvan for his very helpful comments on an earlier draft of this paper. However, I take full responsibility for the claims made and the positions taken in the paper.
2. See Lloyd Best and Kari Polanyi-Levitt, 'The Character of Caribbean Economy,' in George Beckford ed. *Caribbean Economy* (Kingston: ISER, 1975).
3. See C.L.R. James, *The Black Jacobins* (New York: Vintage Books, 1989), 242.
4. See Paget Henry, *C.L.R. James and the Antiguan Left* (Durham: Duke University Press, 1992), 158–65.
5. Arthur Lewis, 'Socialism and Economic Growth' in Mark Gersovitz ed. *Selected Economic Writings of W. Arthur Lewis*, (New York: New York University Press, 1983).
6. See C.L.R. James, *At the Rendezvous of Victory* (London: Allison & Busby, 1983), 154.
7. See Eric Williams, 'The Economic Development of the Caribbean up to the Present,' in E. Franklin Frazier and Eric Williams eds. *The Economic Future of the Caribbean*, (Dover: Majority Press, 2004).
8. Ibid., 22.
9. Ibid., 23.
10. See Annette Baker, *Freedom and Welfare in the Caribbean: A Colonial Dilemma*, (New York: Harcourt Brace & Co., 1949), 3.
11. Ibid., 220.
12. Arthur Lewis, *Labour in the West Indies* (1977), 44.
13. Ibid., 44.

14. See Arthur Lewis, 'Socialism and Economic Growth' in Mark Gersovitz ed. *Selected Economic Writings of W. Arthur Lewis*, (New York: New York University Press, 1983), 669–70.
15. See Norman Girvan, 'W.A. Lewis, the Plantation School and Dependency: An Interpretation,' *Social and Economic Studies*, (2005):119.
16. Ibid., 204–10.
17. Arthur Lewis, *The Theory of Economic Growth*, (New York: Harper & Row, 1970), 258.
18. Ibid., 301.
19. Arthur Lewis, *Labour in the West Indies* (1977), 49.
20. See Arthur Lewis, *The Theory of Economic Growth*, (New York: Harper & Row, 1970), 280.
21. Arthur Lewis, *Labour in the West Indies* (1977), 49.
22. Norman Girvan, *Foreign Capital and Economic Underdevelopment*, (Kingston: ISER, 1971), 41–3; and *Peripheral Capitalism and Underdevelopment*, (New Brunswick: Transaction Books, 1985), 127–36.
23. See Lloyd Best and Kari Levitt, 'The Character of Caribbean Economy,' in George Beckford ed. *Caribbean Economy*, (Kingston: ISER, 1975), 45.
24. Ibid., 44–5.
25. Ibid., 45.
26. Ibid., 49.
27. Ibid., 53.
28. Ibid., 52.
29. Ibid., 46.
30. Ibid., 47.
31. On this, see Lloyd Best, 'Economic Theory and Economic Policy in the 20th Century West Indies: The Lewis Tradition of Town and Gown,' *The Fourth Sir Arthur Lewis Memorial Lecture*, (Basseterre: Eastern Caribbean Central Bank, 1999), 43.
32. See George Beckford, *Persistent Poverty* (New York: Oxford University Press, 1972), 48.
33. Ibid., 48.
34. See Norman Girvan, *Corporate Imperialism: Conflict and Expropriation*, (New York: Monthly Review Press, 1976), 5.
35. Ibid., 25.
36. Ibid., 9.
37. See Kari Levitt, *Reclaiming Development* (Kingston: Ian Randle Publishers, 2005), 67–8.
38. See Lloyd Best, 'Economic Theory and Economic Policy in the 20th Century West Indies: The Lewis Tradition of Town and Gown,' *The Fourth Sir Arthur Lewis Memorial Lecture*, (Basseterre: Eastern Caribbean Central Bank, 2005), 28.
39. Ibid., 37.
40. See Gerard Dumenil and Dominique Levy (2004, 11–8); and Roger Alcaly, *The New Economy*, (New York: Farrar Strauss and Giroux, 2003), 6–7.
41. Stephen Cohen 'Geo-economics: Lessons from America's Mistakes' in Martin Carnoy et al. eds. *The New Global Economy in the Information Age*, (University Park: Pennsylvania State University Press, 1996), 105–20; and James Womack et. al, *The Machine that Changed the World*, (New York: Rawson Associates, 1990), 12–20.
42. Since my paper was completed, this financial bubble exploded with unprecedented force in the fall of 2008, producing the biggest crisis of global capitalism since the great depression of the 1930s. Ironically, it has

been massive doses of Keynesian medicine that have helped to stabilise and contain the destructive effects of this 'economic tsunami.' Although my paper had grossly underestimated the size and the forces within the bubble, its containment after the collapse of the financial sector, and the information policies of the new Obama administration in the US have only strengthened my argument regarding the informatic future of global capitalism.

43.   See Kamau Brathwaite, 'Caribbean Man in Time and Space,' *Savacou*, 11/12 (1973): 6.

44.   Fortunately or unfortunately, Mr Stanford's financial empire collapsed in early 2009 as part of the larger crisis of the US financial sector. His empire was brought down by the Securities and Exchange Commission on the charges that Mr Stanford was running a Ponzi scheme rather than making genuine investments.

45.   See W.E.B. DuBois, *The Souls of Black Folks*, (New York: Fawcett Publications, 1969), 16.

46.   Sylvia Wynter, 'The Ceremony Must be Found: After Humanism,' *Boundary* vol. 2 no. 2, (1984).

47.   See Arthur Lewis, *The Theory of Economic Growth*, (New York: Harper & Row, 1970), 23.

48.   See Richard Reid, *Political Power in Pre-Colonial Buganda*, (Oxford: James Currey, 2002), 98–108; and Karl Polanyi, *Dahomey and the Slave Trade*, (Seattle: Washington University Press, 1966), 33–59.

49.   Karl Polanyi, *Dahomey and the Slave Trade*, (Seattle: Washington University Press, 1966).

50.   See George Beckford, *Persistent Poverty*, (New York: Oxford University Press, 1972).

51.   See Alex Dupuy, *Haiti in the World Economy*, (Boulder: Westview Press, 1989).

52.   See Robert Michels, *Political Parties*, (New York: Free Press, 1968).

53.   See Paget Henry, *C.L.R. James and the Antiguan Left* (Durham: Duke University Press, 1992), 233–9.

54.   See C.L.R. James, *Party Politics in the West Indies*, (San Juan: Vedic Enterprises, 1962) and Frantz Fanon, *The Wretched of the Earth*, (New York: Grove Press, 1961).

55.   See Frantz Fanon, *The Wretched of the Earth*, (New York: Grove Press, 1961), 149–50.

56.   Ibid., 151.

57.   John Keynes, *The General Theory of Employment, Interest and Money*, (New York: Harcourt, Brace & World, 1964), 125–35.

10 | *On Realising Jamaica's Wealth*

David C. Wong

Introduction

Imagine that Jamaica was sitting on a vast oil field, 'black gold,' that mystically replenishes itself forever. Would it be rich? Yes, if it could *economically extract and export the oil* at a rate that would generate sufficient real income to meet its demand for real income at each point of time into the indefinite future (I assume that this is done without destroying the natural beauty of Jamaica and with due regard to ensuring an adequate distribution of income so as to prevent the breakup of the social order). Is this a fantasy world? No! Jamaica does in fact sit on a vast pool of resources that is capable of replenishing itself forever – its labour force. Did Adam Smith say something like this in the *Wealth of Nations*?

> The annual labour of every nation is the fund which originally supplies it with all the necessaries and conveniences of life which it annually consumes, and which always consist either in the immediate produce of that labour, or in what is purchased with that produce from other nations.[1]

I am not aware of any of Adam Smith's successors who repudiated this statement, which is the very first sentence of *Wealth of Nations*, indeed, page one, 'Introduction and Plan of the Work.' Even those who pretend to read the *Wealth of Nations*, too few people today, would not miss it.

Development and Allocation of Labour

Given this point of view, the real issue of economic development for Jamaica is how to develop and allocate its labour force efficiently so as to generate the real income required to pay for its expanding needs on a sustainable basis at each point of time. This is not an easy question in political economy – otherwise the problem would have been solved long ago.

A big obstacle in the way of solving the problem is that most people in Jamaica do not view the problem from the point of view that I have assumed. Instead, too many people take the unalloyed Malthusian view and are apt to see only the new mouth to feed that God sends with each child and not also the new brain that the child brings, and its potential to be developed into a creative mind. The old saying, 'With every mouth, God sends a pair of hands,' should always be kept in mind because the pair of hands guided by a creative mind is the ultimate source of economic dynamism. The development issue of issues is exactly how best to develop the mind and use the hands of the labour force productively.

This is neither a new nor a particularly idiosyncratic doctrine. So-called 'manpower planning' was actually an integral part of the development planning process envisaged back in the 1960s, designated by the UN as the 'Development Decade.' Nevertheless, the present viewpoint is quite different from the old nostrums of the 1960s and 1970s because I am not here talking about an old-style development plan formulated by the National Planning Agency and the government-sponsored training of so many workers in each of various skill categories as determined by the plan. That sort of national economic planning reflects a command economy view with its top-down planning process and is generally weak on the crucial issue of how to provide the proper incentives and disincentives to make the plan work. Oftentimes, the planners viewed mere ideology and wishful thinking as sufficient motivation to get the plan to work in the desired manner. Moreover, such a planning process usually wastes a lot of time and energy for many government workers and supporting intellectuals and, finally, ends up producing frustration and a feeling of hopelessness. This old-type of development planning approach (I am reminded of the People's Plan for Jamaica's development under Democratic Socialism that Witter and Beckford formulated in the late 1970s), smacking of creeping socialism and all those other red flags that enrage our powerful neighbours unnecessarily, is most definitely not the way to go in thinking about how to develop and employ the Jamaican labour force effectively in the present state of the world political economy.

Towards a New Development Strategy

The way to go is to formulate a politico-economic development strategy. I use the term strategy in the sense of game theory. This is the way that it is used when we speak of a business strategy, such as, a low-price strategy. A strategy in the sense of game theory is a very flexible thing – a complete plan of action – that indicates what to do in every possible contingency that might arise for a participant (player) in a game that may extend over time into the indefinite future. A game is simply a system of strategic interactions in which each player tries to get the most out of the situation for himself or herself using his or her resources and in the full knowledge that all other players are attempting to do the same.

The formulation of a development strategy for Jamaica necessarily begins with the recognition that Jamaica is objectively a small and relatively insignificant player in an international capitalist game of production and distribution of wealth (the term real US dollar income measured at Purchasing Power Parity [PPP] is to be preferred to wealth, which is ambiguous, but I will still use the term wealth from time to time as more colourful and reminiscent of Adam Smith). Jamaica does not participate in this strategic game by choice; it is the only game in town, and there is no other way to make a living outside of it.

The external political and economic constraints decree that Jamaica can only be dependent on the US, the EU, and the world institutions. There is simply no way to maintain a sustainable departure from the overall system of economic and political relations in the world today, that is, the rules of the game, no matter how vile many of us, myself included, may perceive them. For emphasis, I repeat that the present global system of wealth production and distribution, dominated as it is by the US and the EU, is the only material sphere that determines our success or failure in the struggle to realise our potential wealth. In this world capitalist game, one can absolutely not count on the charity or benevolence of any other player; all players make decisions with an eye toward realising some perceived advantage for himself or herself, and this is the only expectation that we can rationally form about the behavior of other players in formulating our optimal strategy. (International loans, aid, trade concessions, and so forth are never given out of mere Christian charity. Cf., John Perkins' recent book, *Confessions of an Economic Hit Man*, for a multitude of verifying examples.)

The next crucial step in the formulation of the development strategy is to ask: what are Jamaica's resources and its real income earning possibilities, given the constraints imposed by its objective position in the global capitalist economy as a small player with no influence over the rules of the game? (For those with neoclassical economics leanings, Jamaica is a small open economy in an oligopolistic global economy with the US as the dominant oligopolist economically and the hegemonic superpower politically and militarily.) Before elaborating the politico-economic strategy that I believe to be the optimal one today, let me lay out a brief diagnostic of the case.

I will use real US dollar accounting values throughout the discussion, that is, US dollar PPP measurements. Jamaica has a real demand for income, Y^*, that is primarily determined by US and world consumption patterns (lifestyle). Its supply of real income, Y, is presently much less than its desired expenditure, Y^*. Not surprisingly, as Dicken's Mr Micawber sagely observed in *David Copperfield*, the result is predictable grief – an ever present and growing balance-of-payments deficit and foreign debt. It is self-evident that one cannot borrow oneself out of debt. Sadly, in desperation, many of us (individuals and countries alike) forget the obvious and fall into the infamous 'debt-trap.' There are two basic approaches to addressing the problem (and, of course, feasible combinations of the basic approaches.) These approaches are as follows: 1) reduce Y^* to Y and ensure that its subsequent rate of growth matches that of Y; and 2) increase Y to Y^* and ensure that its subsequent rate of growth matches Y^*. I discuss these two approaches in turn.

This was the basic approach advocated by the New World Group (NWG) of political economists in the 1960s and 1970s. C.Y. Thomas and G. Beckford were perhaps the clearest exponents of this approach in the West Indies, and the PNP government under M. Manley attempted to adopt it in the 1970s. It failed, as indeed did similar purely 'nationalist' development strategies elsewhere in Asia, Africa, and Latin America, because it is impossible given the logic of the world economic process and the political constraints at home and abroad. In order to work, this approach requires that people be re-educated to change their natural desires to live like others in the developed world and, instead, to desire living contentedly in proud poverty (poverty is always relative). Correlatively, this approach requires that production be geared to satisfying domestic needs (self-sufficiency), but it fails to take sufficient account of the fact that capitalists aim at profit-making, not satisfying the needs of people as defined by a politically-driven and artificial system of demand. (Black markets, smuggling, general crimes against both property and people, and, importantly, corruption in government administration were the predictable consequences. *Vide* the Soviet Union and the rest of the socialist camp did not escape these negative consequences even at the height of their achievement. Note further, the KGB and Stasi were no match for the criminals.)

Naturally, socialisation of the commanding heights of the economy and the formation of worker cooperatives were developed as aspects of the reorientation of the productive structure, but this did not go far enough to address the difficulties inherent in this approach. Only full-scale socialisation and central planning in the manner of Cuba would have stood a chance, and the subsequent difficulties of the Soviet Union, China, and Cuba show that the approach of self-sufficiency (even within a socialist union) is not workable in a bipolar world economy with a very dynamic capitalist sector and the human tendency to be opportunistic.

The result of following this approach anywhere is necessarily subversion from within and without and the development of widespread corruption in the society. In the final analysis, this type of nationalist economic strategy is a pure illusion – the very understandable product of the fantastic imaginings of the early postcolonial intelligentsia and politicians in their burning desire to put distance between themselves and their former colonial masters and therefore to view national independence as implying a degree of national autonomy (self-determination) that simply did not square with the objective world situation. (Note that national independence is ultimately not a legal or abstract political condition of existence, but a concrete and objective social relationship in the interdependent world of nations. It cannot be otherwise.) This approach, however attractive and dear to the hearts of many of us, is a siren song and is certainly not feasible now. It can only serve us ill to spend more time talking about it. *Tempus fugit!* Time is money, and as Shakespeare says so very nicely in *Twelfth Night*, 'in delay, there lies no plenty.'

This approach is more complex and a bit more subtle. First, $Y=Y'+Y''$, where Y' is the part of the supply of real income that is created in Jamaica and stays in Jamaica and Y'' is the part that comes from abroad through remittances, and so on. Y'' is largely beyond Jamaica's control and, in any case, is not a dynamic factor anyway even if it is presently of quantitative significance. The focus of this strategy has to be on raising the home-grown part of the real income supply, Y', and boosting its rate of growth to match that of Y^*, the national demand for real income. How to raise Y' and its growth at the required, exogenously-determined, rate to ensure sustainable growth *ad infinitum* is the heart and soul of the matter before us. It is at this specific point that consideration of Jamaica's political economy, as distinct from mere accounting, enters into the formulation of the development strategy.

Here are the basic stylised facts:

Jamaica has:
a small land area and few exploitable natural resources.
a relatively large resident population.
a primitive capitalist economy.
a corrupt governmental machinery.
a very uneven income distribution.
a large overseas population.

The large resident population of Jamaica is both a (Smithian) blessing and a (Malthusian) curse. It is a pool of potential labour power that is ultimately the foundation of Jamaica's wealth. Properly educated and trained, it can generate the required real income to meet the national needs on the average and thereby ensure sustainable development. However, the potential must be realised now for it is definitely a wasting asset; it is time. Labour not used productively today is real income for society lost forever although the labour power itself endures if the worker is physically and mentally reproduced. The immediate curse of having a large resident population is that it must be reproduced – God did send mouths with the workers after all. No doubt about it. The issue then is precisely that of finding the optimal way of employing Jamaican workers so as to produce more than they need to consume in order to ensure their physical and mental reproduction and to provide for growth at the required rate. This is an issue of productivity, that is, real income per unit of labour-hour. It is productivity and, more so, productivity growth that makes it conceivable and possible for the workers to produce more than is required to reproduce themselves at higher and higher standards of living over time.

Who will educate, train, and direct the workers' efforts so as to generate the required growth in labour productivity? Can the existing primitive capitalist system allied with the corrupt government machinery be counted on to do it? Will the workers submit to having their efforts directed to generate the required income in a system where the inequality in the distribution of national income is so unfavourable to them? What dynamic roles can the large overseas Jamaican population, with all its skills and contacts, be counted on to play in the development process? Will the small land area and limited natural resources be a serious limiting factor in the country's economic development? These are the hard issues that the strategy must address.

Clearly, contrary to any previous prognostication, a viable development strategy must not be either a land or natural resource intensive based one. The classical law of Diminishing Returns rules this possibility out decisively. (The case of parts of Africa and the frequent genocidal and fratricidal struggles for control of scarce natural resources springs to mind. This lamentable case shows that the population dynamics of Malthus and its extension by Darwin still have great force.) I imagine that agriculture and natural resource extraction will continue to be significant contributors to Y' and sectors of employment of labour for years to come, but these sectors cannot provide the engine for economic development. I also imagine that manufacturing, agro-industrial and export-oriented manufacturing, will continue to contribute to Y', but, given the competitive situation in the world today and the vast potential of other better-placed rivals, this is simply not a feasible engine of growth. By elimination, this leaves only a service sector-based development strategy.

Service Sector-based Development

The service sector is a large and varied sector of economic activities, some tradable and others non-tradable. Tourism and related hospitality services such as hosting business conferences are very important components of this sector and no doubt will continue to play a significant role in generating US real income for Jamaica, but I do not see the dynamic for sustained development in this area. Moreover, these types of export services are notoriously unstable and susceptible to recessions abroad, crime, and both local and international political events. The component of the service sector that has the potential to serve as an engine of growth is export business services. This sub-sector of services, which includes accounting, billing, call centres, income tax preparation and processing, and other back office type work for international firms, is where the true dynamic for development resides. This sub-sector of business services has to be diversified and tied to international business as a whole so as to avoid fluctuations in the demand for services from individual branches of business while benefiting from the overall momentum of the world economic engine. In both good and bad times in the global economy, certain essential business paperwork must be done and this should help to reduce instability in the sector as long as it stays competitive. (I note that the large global enterprises that dominate the world economy are in an essentially oligopsonistic relationship to most of their suppliers and competition between suppliers will tend to be fierce.) No one should expect that life under this strategy will be easy or that any competitive position attained will be permanent. This is the very reason why this dynamic sub-sector of services has to be organised by entrepreneurial capitalists. It has to be forward-looking and constantly prepared to change and adapt to meeting the shifting demands of international business and to match or outperform international competitors.

Before I discuss the essential political and economic prerequisites for this strategy, let me note that production of export services is not fundamentally different from producing material commodities for export be it bauxite, yams, bananas, sugar, coffee, or garments. Services produced for the market are commodities too. Service production tends to be relatively labour-intensive even when the use of modern technology is taken into account. Labour services of specified quality are relatively high priced in the advanced countries and relatively low priced in the developing countries. (The overall cost of employing a worker and not just the hourly wage rate in US dollars is what should be considered in this comparison.) Office space in the cities of the advanced countries is generally more expensive than in the developing countries and transportation and communications costs are constantly falling. These several factors give a competitive advantage to developing countries in production and sale of business services. Jamaica's proximity to Canada and the US, its English language skill, and its large immigrant population in those two large economies give it a decided leg up in the competition to supply business services.

Political and Economic Prerequisites for the Strategy

For this service sector-based development strategy to work effectively, it is clear that certain political, legal, and economic conditions must be put in place. An adequate infrastructure of reliable electric supply, transportation, communication, and so forth is absolutely needed. Government will have to take the lead in building or modernising the necessary infrastructure. Also, a rigorous system of elementary and secondary education and practical training of workers is needed. Government will have to take the lead here as well. However, there is much scope for a privately funded and operated education and training sector. The government needs to undertake serious legal reforms that will reduce protection for monopoly industries, create space for the growth of entrepreneurial firms, and promote competition in all spheres of the economy. Legal reforms should also seek to encourage skilled immigrants from the rest of the Caribbean and elsewhere into the country to improve its mix of skills and entrepreneurship. Political changes that aim at empowering local governments and giving them financial independence would allow them to compete as locations for businesses and spread economic development more evenly across the country.

How are the above necessary conditions to be realised? A pool of labour power is not after all the same as a pool of oil. Managing a pool of oil efficiently is a purely technical problem in dynamic mathematical programming while managing a pool of labour power is a very delicate problem in political economy. Workers have minds and wills and, yes, class interests too, and will not necessarily submit to a technically determined pattern for the allocation of their labour to meet the desire of their employers for maximum profit. I really do not know the answer to this question since a lot depends on what's already on the ground and in the pipeline, what the state of the labour force and the class struggle is, what the will and the capacity of the political parties and leaders are to bring about the required changes, and the capacity of the government administration to get the job done. These issues are best addressed by practical men and women of affairs with concrete knowledge of the state of affairs in Jamaica. What is abundantly clear is that considerable political and administrative skills will be required to manage the class struggle so as to reorient the country on the growth path dictated by the service sector-based development strategy. Also, this assumes that the political will is there to get the society moving in this direction to begin with and that the whole basis for a viable and progressive economy exists. I really think that Jamaica is presently at a crossroads and that it is a question of do or die. Walking on two legs is fine as long as the country moves at a suitable rate in producing the required national income and distributes it so as to avoid social revolution or breakdown. This underlines the vital need for the government to provide an adequate safety net to protect the poorest section of the working people and pass adequate laws to protect the interests of the working class.

A Retrospective on Previous Thoughts

I claim no originality for the foregoing analysis of Jamaica's wealth and the prescription of how to realise it. A few commentators on the sketch of the ideas that I presented in an earlier e-mail pointed out that the analysis and prescription were a mere redux of Arthur Lewis's famous surplus labour model of 1954 and his prescription of 'industrialization by invitation.' Since I did not consciously begin the hasty assembly of my thoughts on this subject by thinking of Arthur Lewis's model, I am flattered because Arthur Lewis was a great economist and few of us can hope to rise to his level of accomplishment. No doubt, the main reason for the similarity lies in the fact that both of us began with Adam Smith's thesis on the wealth of a nation being its annual pool of labour services. Lewis spoke of a labour surplus economy to emphasise the inability of the colonial economy that would be inherited at independence to employ the labour force productively and also, no doubt, to warn against the Malthusian dangers inherent in such a state of affairs. I can find no fault with that analysis. After well over two hundred years of political economy, it is not easy to be original in basic analysis. Hence, I don't claim any originality. The development problem of Jamaica remains what it was at independence

– identifying a reliable engine of growth that will employ its large labour force and provide a decent living for its people. While Lewis prescribed a strategy of export-oriented manufacturing under the guidance of foreign capitalists with local partners, I would prescribe a strategy of export-oriented business services under the guidance of entrepreneurial local and foreign capitalists. This is not reinventing the wheel; it is rotating it into a better position so as to realise Jamaica's wealth more effectively.

Given that Lewis's labour surplus analysis and prescription was so decisively rejected and roundly criticised by the New World economists and even denounced as a neo-colonialist strategy by many on the left, I expect that my analysis and prescription will be viewed in much the same light. Indeed, a few commentators have already alluded to the strategy as a version of neo-liberalism and pointed to its similarity to the old Marxist prescription of using capitalism to develop the productive forces in the less developed countries (LDCs) and to prepare the ground for the inevitable proletarian revolution. I have already, and I hope adequately, indicated in the section of this essay which speaks on a new development strategy, why I do not think that the economic development strategy favoured by the New World economists and many others on the left could ever work. In my judgment, the situation in the world today is even less favourable to the success of such a nationalist strategy than was the situation in the 1960s and 1970s. I am cheered, along with others, to see the recent emergence and growth of several global civic society movements and attempts to form coalitions by developing and newly industrialising countries in Latin America to protect their interests vis-à-vis the advanced countries. However I am mindful that, in the not too distant past, developing countries have formed all sorts of global alliances such as the Non-aligned Movement and the New World Order Movement that initially showed very great promise to alter the course of global capitalist development, and that such movements have not been able to extend the sphere for the exercise of national autonomy significantly. Whether or not we label the service sector-based development strategy that I am advocating as neo-liberal or old style Marxist, the fact is that we need a more dynamic alternative to the strategy that has been followed by Jamaica since its independence. Perhaps it is time for the stone that the builder rejected to become the head cornerstone. (Didn't Bob Marley say something about that?)

Conclusion

The ideas expressed in this essay are strictly tentative and I have not written the essay in a dogmatic or doctrinaire spirit. I certainly do not claim to know the details of the political economy of either Jamaica or the Caribbean and Latin America more generally. I am not a development economist as such and my only excuse for venturing into this area is what I perceive to be the urgent need to rethink Jamaica's development strategy. I don't think that we can afford to reject reasonable ideas out of hand and I hope that you will find the arguments expressed clearly and logically. I have tried to avoid repeating old formulas and other divinations that, in my judgment, serve only to inhibit creative thoughts and expressions. I have neither attempted to write a primer on political economy nor have I attempted to answer all questions on global political economy because I am ignorant on many issues.

Note

1.   Adam Smith, *The Wealth of Nations*, (New York: Cosimo, 2007), 5.

PART THREE
Remembering

Lloyd Best

11 | *A Caribbean Life –*
An Interview with Lloyd Best[1]

Anthony Bogues and Brian Meeks
with Norman Girvan

Origins of New World: Jamaica

BM: Lloyd we are happy to be here, and we are going to go straight
       into it. Can you begin by tracing for us the origins of the New
       World movement?

LB: Well that is a very long story as you can imagine, a very long
       story. Perhaps we should begin with the antecedents. What we
       are calling New World now, operated under different names
       before. It was only after we brought the journal out in March
       1963, in Georgetown, that this activity began to be labelled New
       World. I came back from Oxford in January, well sometimes
       we say December, sometimes we say January, sometimes we
       say February, and the reason for that is that I was recruited in
       December, but it took time to get to Jamaica, and I travelled
       by boat in those days, so by time I got to ISER[2] at Mona it was
       already the beginning of February.

AB: What year was that?

LB: That was 1958, and you can imagine the kind of ferment I
       found there, because that was a few weeks after the Federation
       of the West Indies had been founded and I can tell you it was
       a time of great anticipation and hope. All the young people
       were caught up in this idea of West Indian nationhood and
       I was an ignoramus, even more then, than I am now. I came
       back from England where the only exposure I had ever had
       to anything West Indian and I'm going back to QRC,[3] was the
       thesis of William Demas, on which I worked as a junior assistant,
       I helped him on all kinds of things, and I learnt a few things
       about the Caribbean.

AB: What was his thesis?

LB: His thesis was on the post-Emancipation economy in Barbados, Jamaica and Trinidad.[4] I can't remember the exact title, but that's what it was,

LB: And that was the first time I had any exposure whatsoever, to anything West Indian. They never taught us anything, at QRC because the 'A' forms were always taught English history, European history, anything but West Indian. So for me, really, it was going off the deep end, it really threw me into a pond with which I was completely unfamiliar, but the discussion was raging, and it was assisted very greatly by the University of the West Indies, which organised a thing called 'open lectures' in which they brought scholars from all over the world to talk, I think it was every month, or it could have been shorter – the interval. And one of those lectures was given by C.L.R. James, and that was the most magnetic, the most electric of all, because he spoke about the West Indies, and about the West Indies Federation, and about Williams and people we knew about, and issues that we knew about.[5] Anyway, I think the most important thing about these open lectures, was not so much the content of what they delivered in these lectures, though as I say James's was exceptional, it was that the University financed, after the lecture every time, discussion groups, by young faculty members: Elsa Goveia, Roy Augier, there was a young Jewish girl from London, Esther Unger, who was very much involved in these kinds of things and in discussion with young West Indians. This really accelerated the process of consciousness because they paid for the rum and everything. And it really made the campus what it became, which was the eleventh country, what was in fact, an extra country in the Federation and that would become important later when the Federation broke up.

Anyway, the people who were mainly involved in this, apart from the young faculty, were Lawrence Bunnyman from Georgetown who became famous as a member of Burnham's Cabinet and then as ambassador to Washington and later killed himself. He was involved in the big scandal with Jonestown, but that was much later, but in those days, he was one of the seminal figures. There was Duke Pollard, who is now in the

222

CARICOM Secretariat as the chief lawyer; there was Attie Graham, Frank Solomon, a whole lot of other faculty, and for me the important thing about them was that many of them had been in school with me in Trinidad. So when the open lectures were over, my house became the natural retreat for a lot of these fellows, for the simple reason that I had a car, I had a house, and I had rum. That meant they gave me just the same veneration. They came, took off their shoes, they slept there, ate there and this discussion started informally. So that when New World came into existence some time later, it really had these antecedents. Of course, there was a hiatus because that was in the early years 1958, 1959 and then by 1960 the discussion became more formalised. It still was not called New World, but it was more regular, it involved many more students and it evolved into something called The West Indian Society for the Study of Social Issues, of which the main promoters were Orlando Patterson, Walter Rodney; Norman Girvan and Eric Abrahams. There was a whole nuclear centre that began to organise these things in a very systematic way and Walter and Orlando were quite highly structured in their whole proceedings. Now in the middle of all this, I had gone to Trinidad, on the invitation of William Demas and Eric Williams to work on the Third Five Year Plan with Demas and while we were there, C.L.R. James and Williams broke openly.[6] They had been breaking up clearly before James came to Mona and he came twice, once in the formal lectures, and shortly after he came back. Norman, is that so?

NG: Yes. That's when the accident happened.

LB: And I spent the years, not the years, the year, from the middle of 1959 to the early months of 1960 in Trinidad. Braithwaite and I had been invited as a team.

AB: Is this Lloyd Braithwaite?

LB: Yes, Lloyd Braithwaite. We were very close, and I'll come back to that. And while we were there, we held 16 seminars for the civil servants in planning and all the professionals about Port of Spain, because this was a project of course, of great intellectual ferment in every Caribbean country, certainly in Kingston and Port of Spain and these seminars were largely focused on economic policy and social policy and planning for Trinidad and Tobago. But the background to this was the split between James and Williams and of course, when I went there I didn't know about this. The moment I got there James recruited me, I fell on his side, in fact all of the what we may call 'intellectuals' around the PNM and the professional classes split, either with Williams or with James, the great majority going to James. And I actually put up a lot of the money for what became *Party Politics in the West Indies*[7] (James was writing it then) and the first version of it was called *PNM Go Forward* because he was at that point, trying to make a reconciliation with Williams, so he didn't want to appear to be denouncing him, although the text – you know James – was doing just that. Anyway, he soon abandoned that posture, and the book came out later as *Party Politics in the West Indies*, and you know what it's about. So when I was there in these months, holding these seminars, by then I was completely against what Williams was doing, so you can imagine my situation – working for the Prime Minister, from his office, because Demas was in his office and being on James's side. It was extremely awkward, and that was when I invented the phrase 'industrialisation by invitation' in a flight of rhetoric and I even forgot that I said it until Lloyd Braithwaite said 'That's a good line that you have there,' and that has now been translated into many languages. People actually think that the title of Lewis's work was 'industrialisation by invitation' – nothing of the kind, but it was politically a very attractive title, it touched a chord with people.

While I had been in Jamaica, before I came back, V.S. Naipaul visited and you could see how all this is adding to the ferment I'm talking about. Naipaul came to speak and he turned up at the Students Union, which was quite a different place then, from what it is now. It really was a social centre. Every night almost the whole of the student body used to go down there, dancing and playing table tennis, and it was a wonderful place, the 'Mona Moon'[8] was down the road from it and so on. Everybody went down with their wives and their children and there were swimming pools. It was a wonderful place to be in the evening and it is very cool in Mona. Naipaul was billed to speak there one evening, and he turned up two minutes before the time he was due to speak, and there were only about a dozen people there, and he said, 'I'm giving you two minutes, if you're all not ready in two minutes I'm going away,' and that's what he did. He said, 'Why aren't you on time?' You know Naipaul. And he said, 'Lloyd, take me home.' Of course, we had been at school together and he came to my house and held court there, because all those people who had come to the lecture just followed us down to my house and my drawing room on College Common was very big and people were all in the yard. He loves holding court where he's the centrepiece and everybody is just assembled to hear him. I have never forgotten the occasion. He also came to Trinidad when Braithwaite and I were here and the famous thing about that was that one evening I had a dinner in my quarters – government quarters in Petit Valley, which were new then. Braithwaite was in one house, and I was in another. And one evening I had to dinner – James and his wife, Braithwaite and his wife, Naipaul and his wife and me and my wife. It was a real champagne occasion with these three fellows there, and all of them are 'ole talkers' of the first rank. So it really continued to add to my education and I wrote a piece about this, which I think, appeared on the front page of the *Trinidad and Tobago Review* because I had been asked to do it by somebody when Naipaul got the Nobel Prize. I came back from Trinidad in, I think it was February 1960 by boat, the same boat by which I had come from England to Jamaica. It passes through the Caribbean, goes to Haiti first, then comes to Barbados, Trinidad then on to Venezuela, then Curacao and then Jamaica. A wonderful trip, it's like the 'Mona Moon,' to travel on these boats in the moonlight, in the Caribbean – there's nothing more dazzling, more stunning a spectacle as the Caribbean moon in the night with this placid water. A wonderful thing. Anyway, I went back to Jamaica by boat and this is when James came again.

By now he was in open conflict with Williams and he was readily entertained by dissenting people everywhere and they wanted him in Jamaica. One day he went to Hugh Morrison's radio programme to speak about, I think Shakespeare and on his way back, he was in an accident that was near fatal, so that he stayed in hospital for a week or two. After he came out he stayed by me for quite a long time, possibly for two months or more. So I really got to know him and Selma intimately and we were really great friends then. Later on we parted company. I'll have to tell you about that later. But the point I'm making is that this whole period from the Federation right up to the independence of these countries [Jamaica and Trinidad] in 1962 was really a period of enormous expectation. People didn't know which way to go and all the possibilities were open and the discourse was raging everywhere, and so we happened to be lucky to be on campus at that time. I always tell people that accidents are very important in history and that the best thing that has ever happened to me was that I came back from Oxford, left the thesis and came to Mona, because they offered me a job – they wrote me and offered me a job, and that's the best decision I ever made. It has made me what I am now because I was thrown into this thing and I developed all my ideological perspectives, all my theoretical perspectives of the Caribbean, I developed in those years, and everything after that is really a playing out of what I learnt then. I was only 23 years old. I had met Elton Richardson, is it Elton?

BM: Edgerton.

LB: Edgerton Richardson. He was at Oxford and I was at Cambridge at the time. I went over to participate in a conference that they had there, I can't remember what is was about, and after the conference he said to me, 'You really must come to Jamaica to work, we'd like to have you as an administrative cadet in the Prime Minister's office,' and I told him 'No, I don't work for people' that 'I am very pleased, very flattered that you like what I had to say and that you respect me, but I don't take jobs very easily.' When he went back to Jamaica he told Dudley Huggins that you must get this man Best to come to the University and I think William Demas and Ray Smith, who had also been at Cambridge as a graduate student when I first went up there, recommended me to Huggins and that's how I got to Mona. They wrote me and asked me to come there. I didn't apply for a job or anything like that. So that's how I got there and it really is the best thing that ever, well, there are some other things, perhaps on the same level, but that was it.

AB: Could I ask you, what were the young students like? What was Walter [Rodney] like? What was Orlando [Patterson] like?

LB: Norman could tell you more than I could. They were all very bright – that first year of social sciences had some exceptional students, David Dabydeen, David Beckles. I mean, their future tells you already what they were like then. The thing about them then was that, because of the context, they were extremely articulate and not afraid to speak. Don't underestimate the significance of that because there would come a time after the 1970s in the University of the West Indies, when people would in fact be afraid to speak, a completely different climate. Especially in Port of Spain, it became a completely different place. And this was the other end of the spectrum. Students spoke freely about anything and they got up and spoke in meetings with their seniors. Walter was really quite exceptional even then. Orlando Patterson was also a very significant figure as was Bunnyman, Solomon and Pollard, who spent all their lives speaking. I mean they were looking for seminars and looking for discussions all the time. I'll tell you off the record that one (I won't tell you whom) spent so much time in this kind of activity that he didn't read the novels he was supposed to read for his course and one month before the examination he told me, 'Lloyd you better read half the books for me.' So I read half the books, and he read half the books and I told him about that half, and he got through. It was very good for me, because I had to read all kinds of things that I wouldn't ordinarily have read.

AB: What were some of the discussions that you all were having in The West Indian Society for the Study of Social Issues. What kind of issues were you discussing?

LB: Federation was the main thing. Integration and the economics and politics of it. The agenda was set for us by the times, you know. I should mention – Norman would remember this – that those were the days that the *Gleaner* kept talking about subversives on campus who were trying to bring communism into the country. When Naipaul stayed with me for a bit, one night he went out to have dinner at the house of the Principal, who was Arthur Lewis and he never told me exactly who was there, but I'm sure Theodore Sealy[9] and Norman Manley were there. When he came back he told me, 'What have you done? Why are they all talking about you?' He said they spent all night talking about subversives on campus and they said Best was not doing his work, he was only stirring up trouble on campus, so he told me 'You better watch yourself.' Well, I didn't watch myself. After my contract came to an end, the University didn't renew it, and there was a lot of disputation over it. The only person who was not concerned with the disputation was me, because I never tried to stay or to make any attempt to get them to renew my contract. Lloyd Braithwaite who was my very great friend, mentor and supporter in every way, thought it was absurd that they should not be keeping me, as indeed most people did. And he went about collecting all the things that I had written to prove that I had done work. I did nothing of the kind, because I had a feeling that it was a good thing for me to go back to Europe. I never tried, Norman can vouch for this, I never tried to get the students to demonstrate for me. They would have, if I asked them. I had tremendous support. Norman, you remember that night I left?

NG: You mean that night when you gave the talk?

LB: Yes, the night I gave the talk at the Union. The place was full, I mean overflowing with students. I spoke and it was reported by Wenty Bowen, I can't remember the name of the journal at the time, was it the economist, the *Jamaican Economist*?

NG: I think it was *The West Indian Economist*.

LB: I could have, they were eating out of my hands, if I had asked them to demonstrate for me, but I'm not that kind of person. And I really thought that the University was right in the sense that I certainly was not doing what they wanted me to do. Carleen O'Laughlin was supposed to be my boss, or so she thought, and she was doing some very pedestrian work on national accounts for the smaller islands and I didn't think that I should be doing that. I had a completely different agenda. I was working mainly on West Indian history, reading all the things that I could find in Lloyd Braithwaite's library,

which was voluminous. He had not only the books about West
Indian history, of which there weren't so many, but all the
reports, government reports and so on. He was a collector
of everything and that was my education. I didn't feel like I
could write anything, yet. I have a sense that what we're doing
has been and still is in the making, and I don't think it should
be put in a form that is definitive and you'll see later that I
invented the concept of working notes. And when New World
was founded, you'll see that it was, essentially, working notes.
And all my things are working notes because that's where we
are. You don't have the pre-history of research, on which you
could build solid theory. We're now writing a theory of society
and a theory of the economy that is very frail, very fragile
because these things cannot be read in any book, they have
to reveal themselves. The present reveals what the past must
have been like, so you have to keep observing all the time and
you can reconstruct the theory of the past from what you see in
the present – it's the only way. Anyway, that's beside the point.
I left.

A Year in Paris via Georgetown

BM: What year was that?
LB: That was 1961. I came back [from] Trinidad in February and I
       left in October or something like that, just after the beginning
       of the academic year.
AB: When you left these groups, The West Indian Society for Social
       Issues, was it fully formed?
LB: It was fully formed, it was a growing concern, and Norman
       would know more about this than I do. But after, something of a
       gap for me, but not too much, because I was in correspondence
       with Alister McIntyre,[10] I was in correspondence with Archie
       Singham[11] regularly. And I'll tell you what I told Singham when
       I went to France. When I went to France I found that they were
       treating me like a senior scholar, simply because I was from a
       part of the world that they knew nothing about, and I knew
       something. And I wrote to Singham and said, 'I have to come
       home,' because when you're in these countries, they don't

know anything about where you're from. You get a completely inflated idea about what your strengths are and what you really know and that happens to a lot of people. Anyway, I went to France into another kind of ferment, no less important than when I was in Mona, and in the West Indies. It was because two things were happening. One was that Castro was emerging – he had made the revolution in 1959, and the Algerian war was on, between Algeria and France. And both of these things absorbed the French media and the French Left in particular, into which I found myself as a matter of course. When I left Mona, I was recommended to work with Professor François Perroux who was the inventor of the concept of 'Poles of Growth' and was then a very significant figure in French social sciences. But I didn't take a job there. I was recommended by Kari Levitt's professor, Burton Keirstead who knew him and who thought it was scandalous that I should not have been kept at Mona. I did not take the job, because on my way to Paris, I passed through Port of Spain, Georgetown, Paramaribo, Lisbon and London. This was very circuitous, but the main reason for that is that I wanted to see Cheddi Jagan,[12] who, when I was still in Mona, wrote to ask me would I come there and consider being the secretary of a commission that President Kennedy was setting up. Immediately after he won the elections, he went to North America to visit Kennedy on an official visit and Kennedy told him he would send a commission there to see if he could give him assistance and what assistance he could give him. Of course, Cheddi was a hot potato, being an avowed communist and not backing off from it. So I went and we had long talks. I have written about this at length and what Cheddi looked like – he was very handsome – and the clothes that he wore. We both introduced shirt-jacs in those days. Everyone at Mona still wore jacket and tie to teach. Only Lloyd Braithwaite and I did not. We introduced shirt-jacs all over the region, Cheddi and I, and it was something of a statement to the country that the Prime Minister should not be dressed in jacket and tie. Anyway, I remember we went to the Red House, where he lived. There was, of course, the same kind of ferment in Georgetown, because he had won the elections and then you had Black Friday, the riots and so on. The whole place was abuzz with political talk. I think by that time Bunnyman had gone back home, and was a minister in the new government. Anyway Cheddi and I had lunch and I remember exactly what lunch we had – a lunch of what they call 'hassa' in Georgetown, what they call 'cascadou' in Trinidad. Cascadou – plain white rice and salad, lettuce and tomato, cleaned and served with salt and pepper. That was frugal but very tasty, and we discussed at length and he said he wanted me to come there. I told him I didn't think I could take the job, even if it were offered to me – if Kennedy did in fact set up the commission, for the same reason I didn't take Richardson's job – I didn't want to work for a government in that way. I told him I would come to Guiana if I came as an international civil servant for one of the UN agencies. I would help him, but I couldn't come in that capacity because on what basis would he explain that he brought me there other than as his man, and that, right away would ruin my credibility, or if not ruin would certainly raise questions about my credibility. And it did, later on I will tell you about it.

We decided that I couldn't do that and I went off to Paris, but he said that when you go to Paris you must go and see Charles Bettelheim, because Bettelheim was his economic advisor appointed by Moscow, and he was also the economic advisor to Mali and Guinea, all of which had declared for socialism at that time. So I took a job with Bettelheim at the Sorbonne in Paris, for that academic year. I taught a course in economic development in Latin America, which compelled me to learn a lot about Latin America and it was very vital, because Cuba was a big question and nobody knew anything about Cuba and they wanted to know. So much so, that while I was there they had a conference of the Left, of Marxist thought and economic development at the Academy of Sciences in Warsaw. They wanted [Arthur] Lewis to come, of course, as the man from this part of the world and he could not come, so they asked me. And the conference was of course all big names – [Gunnar] Myrdal was there, my teachers Joan Robinson and Maurice Dobb, Ignacy Sachs, Oscar Langer and Michael Kalecki, the great Marxist economist from Poland, who had gone back to work for the revolution. It was really a tremendous intellectual occasion. On the first night of the conference Cuba came up, and many people spoke about it, most of them knowing absolutely nothing about Cuba – couldn't expect them to. Then I spoke and it brought the house down. Not that I had anything special to say, it simply was that I was from that part of the world and I knew where Cuba was, what sugar was about and what the revolution was about. The next morning, Myrdal came up to me and said, 'Are you Lloyd Best?' He said, 'Joan Robinson and Maurice Dobb told me that you are Lloyd Best. I want to get to know you, because I heard you make a major statement last night on Cuba.' It was no major statement, but information…for uninformed people. He said, 'I want us to travel to Krakow together.' The conference was going to Krakow – the old capital of Poland over the weekend, by bus, which is 100 kilometres. So I travelled with him all the way, on this bus to Krakow and we talked about all kinds of things of course about the Caribbean and Cuba and so on. After all that he turned and said, 'You know what I really want to find out from you? Tell me, what is the main problem with education in your country?' I hadn't thought about it really, I waffled and said a few things. He said, 'The reason I asked you is that in Sweden, the main problem is maternity – that by the time the girls are 16 they want to have all their children. Therefore all the secondary schools have to make arrangements now for maternity – for girls to have their children and come back to school and continue their work.'

When I came back to Paris I was so enchanted by the occasion that I missed my stop on the way from Orly to where I lived, which is a famous communist district. So I went to Le Bourget, the other airport and I had to take a bus and come back. I was so excited. It was Easter and April in Paris was really beautiful. The birds were singing and everybody was collecting pacards. That is what they do. Pacard was the word for the yellow flower that comes out at Easter time. And I was so heady with this occasion and the amount I had learnt in a very short period. That is when I first met Ignacy Sachs, incidentally and he is still a very good friend of mine. He was a Pole who worked in Latin America then, and now works in Paris. I had a wonderful time in Paris mainly because, as I said, the ferment I had left in the University of the West Indies in Mona was reproduced in Paris because of the Algerian war, which was a major development in world politics. The French don't give up at all, as you know. Algeria was just across the water. They were fighting to the last man. The reason it became so important to me was that I became involved in reading the French press on this question. *Le Monde* was the main reporter on Cuba and Claude Julien, who was the famous *Le Monde* reporter – he subsequently became the editor – actually brought the news back from Havana that Castro had said, 'I'm a Marxist Leninist.' So when Claude Julien came back from Cuba they had a cocktail party and I was invited. That's where I first met René Dumont. All the French Left were there. The place for discussion of world politics, especially the politics of the Left, is Paris. Everywhere you go, in any bookshop, everybody is completely informed about these things. The country is definitively divided between Left and Right. So you can imagine how this discussion was going on. I was teaching at the Sorbonne, but when I was not teaching I spent all my time at the library, which I went to every day, largely because I could read all the papers there. I later became interested in *L'Express* which still exists now, but [today] it's a milk and water journal; it's taken on the format of *Time* [magazine]. The two people who edited that journal were radicals in the French sense, not to say that they weren't on the Left but they weren't far on the Left and they were arguing the case beautifully. It was a wonderful journal. I used to smell this journal when I bought it; I used to just smell the pages. I got my own inspiration for papers later from that. Anyway, it was beautifully laid out, graphically and it was very pointed, highly informed journalism; very committed. They wanted France to leave Algeria and every time they came out, they hit on the story, every aspect of it; a lot of columnists, editorials on all kinds of things. It had a tremendous influence on me as a journalist later on. I got my first bite of that cherry when I was a graduate student at Oxford, when Stuart Hall was bringing out the *Universities and Left Review*, which later became the *New Left Review*. That journal was founded in Oxford at 11 Richmond Road, where William Demas lived, where Stuart Hall lived and I used to go there for lunch everyday. Of course, you can imagine: Stuart Hall, Demas, these fellows, and a lot of the New Left people came there. The discussion had started there in a way, before I came back to the University of the West Indies, but it wasn't about the West Indies, but the British Left.

Origins of New World: British Guiana

I left Paris at the end of the academic year with my head abuzz with all these things. I had become a completely different person in that year. The vast amount of things that had been impressing upon me, I was interested in and was compelled to come to terms with. Being in Paris was really something. I came home because Jagan recommended me, put my name up, with a whole lot of other economists, as possible economic advisors to the Government of British Guiana and I was appointed. They had grave doubts about me; they thought I was an apparatchik; a Jagan man who would just do what the government wanted. They were very afraid of that. For many hours, they spoke to me about who I was, what my background was, and what I was likely to do. They said that I was the first young, black man they were appointing to a post of this stature – economic advisor to government – that they were taking the chance and, if I did this job well I could rise very far and very fast, because there were hardly any blacks in there – people from what they called the third world. I took the job.

BM: Who were the people raising these questions?

LB: UN people. The head of the committee of the people who interviewed me was called Dunlop, he was an American. He would hardly be alive now, but these things were discussed very frankly. When I came to Port of Spain, which was then the UN office for Suriname and Guiana and some other countries, as well as Trinidad, James Keens from Eaton was very ironical, he said to me, 'Ah, so you're going to do technical work in Georgetown aren't you? You're going to produce good planning materials.' I said 'Yes, that's what you've appointed me for.' But this was all taking the mickey out of me, because he had bought what he had heard from people – that I was likely to go down there and just do what Jagan wanted. I went to Georgetown and when I got there, I gave Jagan a manuscript, which I had partially written in Paris. This manuscript had been written jointly by Bettelheim and me, but he was the senior man and of course, his views prevailed wherever we differed. I told him I didn't think this should be the orientation of the work that he was writing for Guiana in exactly the same way he was writing for Mali and Guinea. He just didn't know anything about Guiana. One of the most absurd things he proposed for Guiana was that all of the sugar estates should be made state farms. No chance! The British were still there for one thing, quite apart from anything else. Anyway, I translated the work from the French and then I wrote an introduction to it that was two-thirds the length of the work, setting out my own position. When I got to Georgetown, I gave Jagan the manuscript and told him this was what we had done in Paris and I think that what we should do is to have a series of meetings with the senior people in the Party, the senior people in the cabinet, the technocrats and so on, so we could talk about it. I never saw that document again and my copy was burnt in the fire at the Tapia House in 1982. I don't know if a copy exists anywhere, if Jagan kept it or it can be found in his papers. I never heard about that document again. Jagan never had a single discussion about any of those questions. He just set us to work. I was the junior of the two advisors – the other one was Piendar from the Delhi School [of Economics], the rector of the Institute of Economic Growth, a very fine man, very able, very Indian – he was from North India really – a Kashmiri Brahmin. He has written a book about Indira Ghandi, which carries a chapter about our time in Guiana. C.Y. Thomas[13] spent that year there, and he's in the book too.

BM: Was he a graduate student at that time?

LB: He was a graduate student doing his third year elementary studies. Again, in Georgetown the discussion was something else. It was really compelling, because Jagan was in a very tight situation, he had no money and he was negotiating with Reynolds – Norman would know this – over a new price for bauxite. They had been robbing Guyana blind before and he brought Tommy Balogh there, who had been my teacher at Oxford. I'm ashamed to say that, any expert from the big industrial countries – I won't say white – who came to Guiana, and they were coming all the time, could persuade Jagan in a morning. Everybody who came [to advise him], the next morning that was what he [Jagan] would be talking. Balogh gave him some ideas about how to handle Reynolds and he went to Reynolds with this but it didn't work. I dissented from it. I told him I don't think you should approach it in this way. We went to the budget of 1963 with no money at all, hardly any revenue, and a lot of expenditures that could not be escaped, so they gave me the job of balancing the budget. I don't know how good it was for Guiana, but it was for me another source of education. I had studied public finance in Cambridge in an abstract kind of way. I know all the theoretical things, but now you're faced with a real situation where you have to find money or you have to cut back expenditure. I went through every item of revenue and every item of expenditure. I examined every one, down to the finest detail, to see what we could cut and where we could increase taxes or raise money. We ultimately came out with a budget that passed but really was a shoestring and you could imagine what the mood was in the country. Having had the riots, Black Friday[14] with Burnham pressing in on him in Georgetown, in Demerara, when I got there everybody said that there are Indians everywhere, in Demerara and I asked them, where are these Indians? I looked at the figures – 16 per cent of the population of Demerara was Indian and most of them were in rural Demerara where you don't see them. But it tells you the nature of the politics there – that people were seeing Indians everywhere. They were complaining and I couldn't see them. So the conflict, the sharpness of the conflict in Georgetown was everywhere to be seen. That is what precipitated us, me in particular, from the public sector, which was completely futile. Jagan was not flexible at all. In anything that you proposed to him, he held on to either something from an expert abroad or some very strict Marxist things that didn't make any sense for Guiana. So I turned my attention away from public sector engagement. Of course, I went to work and I did my job, but that's how we started New World. We started a discussion group there. And it was electric, really. We had the whole of Georgetown, all the young professionals, almost all the young educated people coming back from universities and so on, were part of that. It really was a tremendous intellectual mobiliser.

AB: Who was in this initial discussion group?

LB: David de Caires and Miles Fitzpatrick, were the two key figures, and of course Bunnyman used to come to the thing as well and a lot of others. I can't remember their names. You would have to ask David[15] but these were the two key figures that you have to remember. These were my two closest friends. Of course, I had a lot of discussion with Burnham as well. I used to go to his meetings. On one or two occasions, I travelled with him when he was going to the countryside, to see him operate. Both he and Cheddi, I've never seen anything like it in the way that they could raise money. They would go on a trip in the countryside and when they came back, they would have thousands of dollars all over. Every pocket would be full of money. The reason for that, of course, is that the conflict was very sharp and people were supporting *their* side. Burnham was very skilful, very skilful. After a time, he started coming to my house. Every Friday we would have black pudding and souse. He was very fond of black pudding and souse. I got to like Guyanese black pudding, which is made with rice. In Trinidad, we make it with potato and other things. Burnham and I also had something in common, which was that we both drank the same rum. Most people in Georgetown would drink one of the D'Aguiar rums, but we drank Houston, H-O-U-S-T-O-N, because it was a very light rum. In Jamaica, I also drank Charlie's White because I like light rums. I learnt to drink rum in Jamaica, so wherever I go I look for something like Charlie's. (Laughter)

LB: So one night, I think it was New Year's night, or old year's night, Hugh Cholmondeley's father, who was a kind of factotum for Burnham, had a party for all the people who were in the discussions in Georgetown and Burnham came to that party. I told him we want to promise you something for this coming year. I had in mind the New World journal. I told him that we are doing a lot of work in this group and we want to publish an analysis of the Guianese situation to see whether we could make any difference. That was old year's night, 1963 and the first edition of the journal appeared in March.

AB: Why was it called New World?

BM: Before that…what was your view of Burnham at this time?

LB: Oh no, I didn't trust him at all, and he knew that, and everybody knew that. He used to tell people that, 'I don't agree with Lloyd at all, but his ideas are so important and so many, that I like to talk to him.' I used to tell people that Burnham is a man you can't trust. I said 'Oh no, we can't put you in power.' We were very frank. I said 'We can't put you in power, we can't trust you, we don't know what you stand for – you stand for everything.' Of course, I didn't know at the time that he was literally being backed by the CIA and he was in with the State Department. So we promised him that and we did bring out the journal for that purpose, but we also tried to arrange a reconciliation between Jagan and Burnham. The way we did it was to bring Raymond Smith, who had done his thesis and had written two books about Georgetown, his wife was from there and he was well known. We got Raymond Smith to come to Georgetown, so we arranged for him to meet Burnham and Jagan. Anywhere that we suggested that they should meet, one of them would have an objection. It didn't matter where you suggested, either Burnham would be against it or Jagan would be against it, so you know what we did? We hired a car and a driver and put Burnham and Jagan to sit down in the back seat and talk, trying for reconciliation between them. It didn't work. They talked and they promised a lot of things but nothing ever happened thereafter. Burnham was already tied up completely with the CIA, and Jagan himself was also tied up with Moscow in a way that it was hard to disentangle.

This period in Georgetown was for me another Mona, and another Paris. I keep telling people I have had a seamless existence in that I go from one place to another, by accident. I don't plan these things, I didn't know I was going to any of these places, but for one reason or another, I went to these places in succession. Each of them was an education of a kind that I would never have anticipated because of the context at the time, the moment; you know, the shaping power of moment. So Georgetown of course is known for the New World group because that is where we brought out the first edition of the journal. We had brought out a number of pamphlets in Mona, just sporadic things on particular issues. I'm not even sure we had done this when I went there the first time, it may have been when I went there the second time. But we hadn't done much, by way of publication. People of this generation might not understand that, but in those days, to publish anything at all in the West Indies, by a West Indian was a miracle. To see something by you, in black and white, was unheard of. So the real contribution which *New World Quarterly* was to make to the West Indies, was that it showed all these young scholars that they could see themselves in print and that what they had to say and what they wrote was valid. There was a proliferation of publications from ISER shortly thereafter, under the direction of McIntyre. New World really opened up the way to this by creating the climate, the context in which people could feel free to write.

BM: Let us go over some sequence here. The first journal was published in March, 1963.

LB: Yes.

BM: Did the pamphlets you mention precede the journal?

LB: I'm not sure; maybe one or two.

BM: But they were not considered *New World*.

LB: Yes, they weren't called *New World*, nothing was called *New World* before the journal.

AB: Were there pamphlets put out by the group that existed in Mona?

LB: I think so, because [to Girvan] when did Beckford come back to Mona?

NG: 1964...

LB: Exactly, so I'm not sure when we put out the pamphlet called
        'Dr Beckford's Passport,' but that was after. So I'm not making
        a big thing about it. In fact, my point is stronger, that before
        Georgetown and *New World Quarterly*, publication was hardly
        on the agenda at all. We were just finding our feet, learning
        about one another, and defining the issues. It required money
        and organisation of a kind that we didn't have the skills for,
        then. So the journal in Georgetown really marked a watershed.
        It was the first publication and it really opened the floodgates
        thereafter. That was the real significance of Guiana. The
        discussion was really a continuation of the discussion that we
        were carrying on at Mona, except to the extent that it was
        localised on the Guianese situation – the conflict between
        Jagan and Burnham, and by extension the Cold War conflict.
        But the real difference that Georgetown made was that we
        put out something and I tell you, you can't imagine what the
        impact of that was – we sold 2,000 copies in the first two days.
        I might be exaggerating if I say two days; it might have been
        three days, but the whole print run went immediately, and we
        reprinted right after. The country was hungry for it. That is
        one part of it. The other was that we sent the journal all over
        to friends and colleagues and collaborators in universities,
        including Mona and St Augustine. That really was a lightning
        rod, because people had something they could hold on to. They
        felt now that they knew us. Its not that they knew us any better,
        but that there was something real going on in the region. We
        got a lot of people in different parts of the world, in Puerto
        Rico, North America and Canada mainly, prepared to sell the
        journal and send articles. So you could see thereafter, once
        the first journal had come out, it transported the group from
        being a discussion group into a group that was communicating
        with a whole fraternity of young West Indian scholars and
        students. If you [could] look at the backs of earlier journals
        you'll see the names of people who were selling the journal,
        or receiving the journals in different universities. After I left
        Georgetown, I travelled a lot, because by then the UN had been
        persuaded that I was not a wild revolutionary and although I
        went to Georgetown for two years and gave up the job after

one. It was pointless staying, we weren't doing anything useful in government with Jagan, and we had had an organ, so to speak, with the journal. After that they recruited me for a lot of other jobs. I became their Caribbean Consultant for the FAO World Food Programme and that's how I came to know Suriname. I worked in Suriname. I worked in Guiana. I used to go to Guiana regularly as if I hadn't left. And if you go to David de Caires, his wife will tell you how often I came there twelve o'clock in the night and wake up everybody and say, 'I just come from somewhere, I want to stay by all you.'

I also worked in Jamaica. I got to learn a lot about Jamaica. I knew a lot about Jamaica from the first time I was there because I used to do, for [Philip] Sherlock, every week – every Friday, a lecture somewhere in Jamaica and I discovered how much work Norman Manley had done in building structures all over. Jamaica really had a responsibility in a way that no other Caribbean country had. Wherever you went, there were people who would welcome you, who would organise the lecture and you would have a serious discussion about Jamaica, or whatever you were talking about. I would go down on Friday night and I would come back on Sunday. Saturday morning and Sunday morning I would eat these Jamaican breakfasts of ackee and salt fish and yam and things that I didn't know or do before. I got to know everywhere. The first time I was there and the second time when I was working for the World Food Programme, I had to visit a lot of projects which they were giving food aid to, all up in the Bullhead [mountains], all down in Clarendon…in south Clarendon, Hayes, Cornpiece, Yallahs, one in Christiana. I really became immersed in Jamaican material. I got to know a lot of people on a real level. Anyway that's beside the point; perhaps I should really continue from Guiana properly.

AB: Just how did the name New World come up? And what was the kind of discussions behind the name?

LB: We discussed it at length, it wasn't arbitrary. We had open meetings, more than once as to what this thing should be called, and people made suggestions. And the idea that we had a new civilisation in America, which you will see runs through the work afterwards. Later on, in terms of North America being colonies of settlement; South America being colonies of conquest and the Caribbean being colonies of exploitation. That runs through all our work. We said, why don't we call it New World – a new world in America. And that stuck.

I left Guiana in the middle of 1963; I stayed just over a year there, perhaps, 14 months or so and the reason I overstayed my time was, the last seven weeks that I was there…a time, really, of mortal conflict, in the sense that we couldn't even go to work. All the offices were tear-gassed by the police. The police were on Burnham's side of course. And our office was originally in the Prime Minister's office and then we were moved to a place in Brickdam, much more ample quarters and there too they kept tear-gassing. There was a general strike for seven weeks – my last seven weeks. We had just finished the report and we handed it in and left, in haste. I had to take a small plane from Georgetown to Paramaribo with my wife and three children and then join the national flights there, because you couldn't get out of Georgetown – the airport was under siege. Burnham was really riding roughshod over Jagan. He couldn't do anything, because as they say in the French Revolution, Paris was always more important than the provinces. You could have the whole country on your side, if you don't have the capital you were in trouble. That was proven. Jagan had more support than Burnham, certainly, in the country, but he was completely paralysed in Georgetown. So we left. Dhar[16] left about a week before me. Then I left and came back to Port of Spain.

AB: When did the *New World Fortnightly* begin to come out?

LB: A little later. I went back to Mona, and I asked Georgetown if they would allow me to carry the *Quarterly* with me to Mona, where we had the resources to do it. We were struggling; we only did one in Georgetown, it was very expensive to print. That's when we founded the *New World Fortnightly*, as a different kind of journal – as a fortnightly journal, that would be commenting on current affairs, and therefore could get advertising support – a whole different thing. It couldn't have been possible unless David de Caires had been there. And you can see that has continued; he is now the editor of the *Stabroek News*. So there is a continuity from *New World* right up to the present. *New World* can claim paternity to the daily that we have now in Georgetown. David comes here all the time. We are still very close friends. But that's jumping ahead of the story. The reason that [*New World Fortnightly*] was possible was that I was doing this job from 1964 to 1966 as Caribbean Consultant at the World Food Programme of the FAO and I was travelling a lot in the region. I could go to Georgetown regularly and maintain contact and confidence. I recommended that we should do the *Fortnightly*, but if I had not been able to go back there; anyway, that was another accident that allowed us to do *New World Fortnightly*.

Return to Trinidad

I left Guiana and came home to Trinidad and immediately found myself in a different situation. [James] Millette was there; that's when he came into the picture seriously. I had known him before at school, he was at St Mary's and he had been on campus when I first went there, as a student. He became the lead figure in Port of Spain, but that was not for a while. There was an interim before that when Adrian Espinet who became the first editor of the *Tapia* journal ran a discussion group on campus,

James Millette

under the rubric of New World. That was the first New World grouping in Trinidad.

BM: When exactly was that?

LB: Late 1963.

BM: So he just took the name? Was he in contact with you when he took the name?

LB: I was there. So we were starting a new branch, that's all. So apart from whatever was happening abroad, we could talk about Georgetown, Port of Spain and later on, other branches. Espinet was really the first person to take the baton there and take responsibility. We decided to found a journal in Trinidad as well, of shorter interval than the *Quarterly*. It was called *Antillean Record* and it was close to going to press when we were stopped in our tracks. Dr Williams announced a commission of enquiry into subversive activities, before which I was called to appear, along with all the trade unionists – George Weekes, Joe Young, anybody who was with C.L.R. James and dissenting from Williams, was called up before that Commission. The man who was on the Commission was [Roy] Marshall, who later became Vice Chancellor of UWI. The head of that Commission was a Nigerian judge called Mbanefo.[17] I was completely cleared from it. It was just nonsense for him to have asked me. Williams knew it would have intimidated a lot of people and that the whole thing would collapse. Everybody was afraid. So the group collapsed for a while, until [James] Millette came. Of course, Millette was not afraid; he was a politico, like me. I think that was when we first met [George] Beckford. I met Beckford by chance one day in the Agricultural Economics Department at UWI St Augustine. Kari Levitt reports somewhere that I told her, 'I want you to meet a man. He's one of us.' I got to know Beckford and ever since then, we were soul brothers.

I continued in Trinidad for a while and I was very rich. My salary was in US dollars and was ten times that of a permanent secretary. These international things, especially in those days, everybody in the UN travelled first class. I remember when I was coming to Guiana from Paris, I travelled first class. The UN really made you very rich and I was able to live for a year in Trinidad without working and paying high rents and keeping my family more than alive – to the standard to which they were accustomed. I spent all the time in political activity. I became involved with C.L.R. James's acolyte Walter Anamunthudo, who is the brother of the professor. He is the man who printed *Party Politics in the West Indies*. We became very great friends and we campaigned in Central Trinidad against Bhadase Maraj. All over Trinidad we campaigned almost every day because I was not working anywhere. There is a sequel to that, because he introduced me to a group of cane farmers, one was called Lau-to. He's still a member of our organisation in McQueen Village. One was Ramdas and a whole lot of others. When he died I went to his funeral. Those people remained faithful to me and to my ideas and when we started Tapia that was the only place in Central Trinidad where we had an active group. They maintained a Tapia group in McQueen in a place where it was impossible for anybody who was not for [Basdeo] Panday or the DLP [Democratic Labour Party] to have groups. That was a very fertile period because I learnt a lot about Trinidad. When I left Trinidad I knew a lot about sugar, but only from the perspective of my father's farm, on which I worked and grew up. I got to know the whole industry properly, that is when I really got to know it, every aspect of it, from that campaign. That came to an end and New World started again under Millette and I went back to Jamaica.

Jamaica via Puerto Rico

This was 1964, but on my way to Jamaica – you know I always make these detours – I took an assignment to teach summer school in the University of Puerto Rico, in San Juan. Gordon Lewis was there, Alfred Thorn was there and Sybil, Gordon's wife. I got to know all of them, and recruited them and started a group there. Puerto Rico was in a quiet period, in that there was nothing going on there. The *independentistas* were not making any headway. I think they had just participated in an election, or they did in 1964. And nothing happened except – what's the name of the head of the Puerto Rican *independentistas*? – I got to know Reuben Berrios very well. He was emerging then. Any way, I went back to Jamaica for the new term, academic year 1964–65. We got very busy, very quickly.

BM: What was the nature of your appointment in 1964–1965?

LB: A research fellow at the ISER. I had been a junior research fellow before.

AB: Who was in charge of ISER then?

LB: Dudley Huggins was in charge. I forgot to tell you about that the first time but it is important. When I had gone to the

ISER, I was Junior Fellow in 1958. Part of that ferment I was talking about can only be explained by the faculty that you had at the Institute. There was at that time no teaching and no West Indian was teaching in the Social Sciences. They had a few English men – Peter Newman, a fellow called Davidson teaching in the arts programme. There was one course in economics or maybe two, before they established the Social Sciences faculty. Therefore the centre of daily discussion about West Indian affairs was the ISER under the aegis of M.G. Smith, Raymond Smith, Lloyd Braithwaite and others. Roy Augier used to come over because he had been a fellow there before he was appointed to teach in the History Department. Elsa Goveia came over regularly as did Chandra Jayawardena who was to leave and go to Australia and Dudley Huggins. A lot of people would be coming in, like Charlie [Gladstone] Mills and people from the public sector – [Edgerton] Richardson and others. The thing that went on everyday at coffee at the ISER was this discussion at 10:00 am and sometimes we would be there at lunchtime. People thought we were not doing work. Braithwaite was really the leader of that and he was the wisest man that we had in the faculty – the most educated scholar there. There was no book that you could mention in any discipline that he would not have read or didn't know about. You know his library was something else. We were very close friends. He took me under his wing, really and every day after coffee, if it didn't go on too late, we would go to Sangster's Book Shop which was then Downtown Kingston and subsequently opened a branch by Matilda's Corner. I got to learn about books from Braithwaite, about buying books and knowing about books and checking catalogues. Without Braithwaite there, the intellectual life would not have been half as rich. M.G.[Smith] was very good, very able, but he never really took part in the discussions. He came, he took his coffee and he went back to his office. He was very crisp and curt and didn't like company too much in those days. I think he was making a point about work. He is sold everywhere as the great work man who has really produced a vast of amount of stuff as compared to Lloyd Braithwaite. I think he was emphasising that point in those days in a way that did not really cut ice with most people. They didn't like it. Nevertheless, sometimes he would join in the discussion and it certainly was an active centre of intellectual life in the University then.

I went back there in 1964 on quite different terms, of course. I felt very free to do what I wanted. Much water had flowed under the bridge in terms of intellectual life. The Federation had collapsed. The mood had changed considerably in the country and in the University. New World was looked upon as a kind of outsider institution. [Philip] Sherlock and [Rex] Nettleford[18] have written a book about the University and a lot of people thereafter have embraced New World as something good for the University. No doubt that is true, but I think I have to say that when it was happening, the administration, the establishment was hostile to it. They didn't want it at all. We got a place on campus going to the Union from the SCR. On the left side there was one of these old buildings that we rehabilitated and re-outfitted as the headquarters of New World. After we were there for two or three months, they put us out. They didn't want it on campus.

AB: When you went to Jamaica who was there to begin New World?

LB: Beckford was there for one. [Havelock] Brewster was there. [C.Y.] Thomas came back and there was [Owen] Jefferson. Of course there were younger people who were close to it like the sociologist who died – Derek Gordon and Don Robotham – they were close to Raymond Smith. They had reservations about New World because they belonged to something called the Young Socialists, which was affiliated to the PNP and they thought we were just talkers. This whole debate about thought and action was really with them. It started with them and it was taken on by [Trevor] Munroe afterwards and a lot of other people. But it was an island, or an oasis if you like and in the University that kind of activity was now frowned upon by the establishment and the *Gleaner* was running riot on that whenever it suited them. *New World*, the journal was something concrete and firm. People could see it was something constructive. I must say that Roy Augier was a very important person in establishing that. Augier was central to it. I remember he and I wrote that pamphlet on Dr Beckford's passport[19] and there were some others. I think McIntyre was probably there when we did that one in 1967, the one on the monetary system, on devaluation. You see, there were a whole series of pamphlets, a string of things. And I said a floodgate; you really had the confidence and this is the time when the ISER began publishing everybody. That was the time when the integration studies came up.

BM: So McIntyre was now in charge of ISER?

LB: Was he? He and I were co-chairmen of these studies.

NG: What happened to Mervyn Alleyne?

LB: He [Mervyn] was my close friend from school days in QRC. That is why I keep telling people that we have to distinguish who came to New World now and again, were sympathetic to it, but were not in it. That also involves McIntyre. McIntyre was my very close buddy. I knew him long before anybody else did when he first came and that relationship stands to the present day. McIntyre was aloof from the political definitions of New World. He was an administrator and part of the establishment in UWI. Intellectually he was drawn to it and personally, so he came to many of the things that we had but he never considered himself to be in it. Now Augier did not have that problem. Augier identified and he had no problem with that. But there were a lot of people, even Havelock [Brewster] I am not sure was. I see he is defined as a New World person, but I don't think he was.

AB: How did the New World group function? I mean you were meeting, you had a journal, discussions, and there were occasional pamphlets?

LB: No, nothing like that. It was a University organisation but not welcomed by the University. It was intellectual life. We never had any political intentions, we never became involved in any public meetings or anything like that. We did have meetings on campus – that is the conferences and seminars to which we invited people from off-campus. And there was a rich debate about the sugar industry.

NG: Yes they discussed it in the film *Life and Debt*.[20]

LB: Exactly. And a lot of people came from off-campus because it was a vital issue.

AB: So you intervened in political and social life, intellectually?

LB: Intellectually, yes, as we should. We were just doing our work, but the University didn't think we should be doing that work at that time. They only welcomed it after it happened. For New World, that was its best period, it really flourished. I went back in November 1964. For the Crop Time edition 1965, we put out 'From Chaguaramas to Slavery' and thereafter we published as often as we could.

BM: You mentioned people who were in and people who were out, and earlier you mentioned C.Y. Thomas in Guiana. What was C.Y.'s relationship to New World in Jamaica?

LB: When he was in Guiana he was definitely in it, but I always say this in his favour, he always said that when he was in it that he was not a part of it, that he was a socialist, that he didn't favour the ideological orientation. But he was a very close friend of mine, he was a family friend, my wife and his wife and children. Every day we saw each other and we lived very close to each other. When he came to Jamaica I think he participated too, but there it was really different because in Jamaica there were many more socialists. So he had other company, he was not an active participant in New World and he drifted away from me, in a way that I have never understood.

A Short Break

BM: The question asked in the break was, when you were fired or your contract was not renewed, who was Principal and how do you see what happened at the time?

LB: Well [Arthur] Lewis was right. That's what I felt. Carleen O'Laughlin, who was my boss, told him that I was not doing anything that she asked me to do. My consciousness had grown very quickly and I discovered that I did not subscribe to the economics that they were teaching or to the theoretical system that underlay all the social sciences. I have been on that kick ever since because that is when it started. I started on my own to work up a theory of Caribbean economy and society, the first of which was the economy. I have subsequently moved a great deal to cover a whole lot of other ground. But Lewis said, 'You are not doing the work that you are supposed to do.' I did not quarrel with that. He told me 'And don't you know that as a young scholar you should be writing and publishing in reputable journals abroad?' I said to him 'If we don't make our own journals here and make them reputable, what will happen to our university?' I said 'We have to found our own journals and how will we get reputable if we don't write for them and put our own stuff in them and then get known on that basis?' That is what I had in the back of my head, partly because of what I told you about Stuart Hall.

BM: Yes, Hall and the *Universities and Left Review*.

LB: I had in my mind all the time that we had to publish something, we had to publish a review and up to now I hold that position. People ask me why I don't put out books and I don't. There are many reasons for it, all valid, but the most important single one is that it does not fit our circumstances here, because we don't have the intellectual life. What you need are journals, an assembly of scholars talking to one another. We don't have that in the Caribbean up to now and journals are a way to get that. The discipline of every week or every month of putting a journal out and talking to one another; we have yet to create intellectual life before we can go into a definitive statement about societies like the West Indies. That is my position and I have held it against all comers.

BM: What was Lewis's response to this?

LB: He just dismissed me, really, he thought I was just saying that. I suppose he had every right to, I was twenty-something years old and he was...

BM: Arthur Lewis

LB: Yes, Arthur Lewis, a senior scholar. I think the reason that it happened at all was that Dudley Huggins just did not have the confidence to treat with Lewis and to tell him what kind of work we should be doing at ISER and what I had told him and what Lloyd Braithwaite told him. He just kow-towed to Lewis. Whatever Lewis said he would do it and come with his shoulders bowed. He was a very bad Head of the ISER and they made him head of the University at St Augustine. That is frightening. I don't know how Lewis could have done a thing like that – everybody wondered. And I tell you something, a sequel to that, which was that while I was in Montreal, I haven't come to that yet, I was put up, by Lloyd Braithwaite, for the job of senior lecturer in Caribbean Affairs in St Augustine. The selection board appointed me and Huggins blocked it. He said 'No, you can't bring Best here, he will cause a lot of political trouble' and that is how they brought [Steve] Camacho. He was brought there on a series of one-year contracts. To get a three-year contract you have to go through the process of the selection board and appointments. To get a one-year contract the Head of Department simply had to bring you in, and nobody questioned it. So that is why he was there on one-year contracts – to keep me out. I never told people this – it became a big scandal in Trinidad after Camacho died. There was a big enquiry into it here in Port of Spain of the appointments process and how Camacho had gotten there and it did actually say that somebody else had been appointed. He had been brought in and I was here and it just wasn't my style, I told nobody at all that it was me who was kept out. I am not looking for jobs. I have never applied for a job in my life. When I came back to Mona I came back because Braithwaite told them that it was a lot of nonsense that you got rid of Best in the first place. They brought me back, just as they brought me the first time. I never applied for jobs. If I don't get a job I run my own thing. I am running my own thing here, for how many years now? I left the University, I mean I wasn't fired, I was the most senior man there, and they promoted me. Do you know that they promoted me and I sent it back? I sent it back because I don't want any promotion. I left it and people told me 'What are you doing now that you are unemployed?' They think that if you are not working for somebody, you are unemployed. They have no concept of intellectual work and intellectual life as something you do as a matter of course. You don't have to work for people. I don't go around telling people these things. You fellows who are younger than me have to write these biographies. But it's no skin off my nose.

So I came here in 1968, you know that, that is when you were there, that's an old story.

BM: I came two years later but I know about that.

LB: I don't want to go into that. That is another story. I don't want to go off on things other than New World for the time being. But you are quite right to ask me about Lewis. I think Lewis was right. If I were the Principal, and a young man of 24, 25 or whatever it is, is telling me that he is not doing my work because he has some other thing, what are you going to do?

BM: I might have to dismiss him.

LB: You have to say I am not renewing your contract unless you have some compelling case and there was no compelling case that Lewis could hear. I mean Huggins had the case but he was not capable of putting it himself. Keirstead came there in that period – Kari's professor – and I got to know him very well largely because I challenged him. He gave a lecture about input/output studies and I challenged him on it in front of the whole community. He came over to my side and we became great friends thereafter. I told you that he suggested to Perroux that he should give me a job there. Adler was the head of the economic division in the World Bank – the one that they teach in. He came to Mona and held a seminar for two weeks and at the end of the seminar Adler told Huggins that 'You have a very good man here, you have to get him involved in something.' Huggins was telling people that all over the place. He would not tell Lewis that because he didn't think that he could discuss it with Lewis on that level. But they were quite right. I mean I don't see why the University should support anything that I say. You have to pay the price for what you are....I didn't pay any price in my view. Because the sequel for me could not have been better.

BM: Where was Huggins from?

LB: Huggins was from Nevis. A very nice man, very nice man, but a very bad head of an intellectual institution.

BM: What about the Jamaican political people? You mentioned Manley and others having met and discussed you.

LB: I must tell you about that. It is very, very important. Manley and Lewis and Sealy, being very senior people in the country, couldn't hear anything authentic. That is the danger when you are the head of anything or eminent. People tell you what you want to hear. They had a very simplistic notion as to what New World was about. They really thought I was a stark raving revolutionary who was going to mash up the University. They really thought so because that is what people told them. You know about the *Gleaner*. So that is the view that they had and no doubt Mr Manley had that view at that time. I want to tell you the sequel to that, when I went back to Jamaica in 1964. Shortly after I got back, probably in 1965, after two or three issues of the journal had come out, he [Manley] wrote me a letter in his own handwriting saying, 'Dear Lloyd Best, I've been following you and what you have been writing and what you have been saying and I feel that you are one of the few people in the Caribbean who would make a difference by what you are doing and I would like you to come and see me.' I told him I would come on one condition; I would like to bring George Beckford with me. He had a meeting at his house in Drumblair in the night and we had coffee and pleasantries first and then he got on to the business. Michael was there. He said 'I have read all your stuff and I am following what you are saying and I would like you to be my economic advisor, my personal economic advisor because I think I have a very good chance....' He had lost the elections for independence. He said 'I think I have a very good chance of winning the next elections and I want to get my plans in place well before. Would you come on board?' I told him 'Mr Manley, I respect you very much, and I admire you, but I don't work for people. You are not the first person I have told that, I've told many people...I don't work for people. I am prepared to help you, I am prepared to give you a statement to exchange ideas, write things for you and so on but I can't be seen to be in your stable.' That's the word I used. And he was very disappointed, very crestfallen about it, and he just stayed quiet for a while and Michael burst out, you can't imagine, in the worst way, who you think you are and so on, you know about Michael. That's how he gets on and he cuss me up and said 'Who you think you are, you come from Trinidad and my father offering you a job and you say no.' I am telling you, in the worst way, the worst language. His father had to quiet him down and we left there, Beckford and me, rather inconclusively. We didn't say we won't see you again or anything like that but we never did because I went away to Montreal after a while to work with Kari. And that thing just stayed hanging there until, just before he died, Theodore Sealy interviewed [Norman] in the *Gleaner* about his perspectives on Jamaica and the past, you know sort of summing up his life and when Sealy was finished with that he said 'I want to ask you one more question. Who are the people in the Caribbean who you think are going to make the difference?' He gave two names: Lloyd Best and Trevor Munroe. I was not living in Jamaica when he said that, he was not compelled, I was not a Jamaican. He really believed it. I hadn't been there for some time. I was not in the public and he said that...you know so he must really have believed it. And somebody sent it to me, you know...there was Hill, Seaga, who was the third one?

BM: Lightbourne?

AB: Hart?

LB: No, not Lightbourne but I will tell you about Lightbourne in a minute.

AB: Tavares.

LB: Clem Tavares. We were very close friends. I was very close friends with all three of them. Not on my initiative. I forgot to tell you in all of this that Singham was a very seminal figure. Archie Singham was a figure in the Faculty of Social Sciences. He was a very fine man in many ways, a builder. He got scholarships abroad from Manchester and other places for a lot for the young scholars. I told them at Mona that I cannot understand how it is that Singham died and we could not have a conference in his honour. I said that I am willing to do what I can, I can't do very much but we must do it. We can still do it. In fact, I just sent a cable to his wife Nancy a few days ago, for the New Year. Singham was very much a product of his upbringing and he was very much an authoritarian Hindu-Tamil. He could not resist people in power. He could not resist people in power – I can say this now especially since it is not the whole story about him – this is the negative part.

He was the most ardent devotee of the PNP in the years when he first came to Jamaica. I was the first young black to come back there, then McIntyre came, then Mervyn Alleyne came over on the other side and then Singham came. And he was very close, all of us and he came to all the New World meetings and he was very articulate, very bright. He made an enormous contribution to thought. But for some strange reason when the PNP lost power, he shifted to the JLP without any shame.

NG: I remember that very clearly.

LB: Yes. And the thing on which he built his relationship with Tavares and Hill and Seaga was that Seaga was very close to me before he was in the JLP. People were saying to me that he was going to be in the PNP. They didn't know which party he would go to, because ideologically, the way he spoke, he sounded like a PNP and everybody was surprised when he joined the JLP, purely, I think purely opportunistically, because he saw how he could rise in that party much more quickly.

AB: He was refused membership.

LB: I didn't know that. He went into the JLP and he became very close to the establishment there. Before that, Seaga decided to write a paper on 'haves and have-nots,' a very famous paper on which he got the reputation for being a wizard in economics and finance. Now, the fact of the situation is that that paper was written largely by me in my house at College Common. And Seaga had been trying to pay me back ever since because he knows that debts in politics are a hell of a thing to have. You have to pay off people who have done things for you or else they might tell people. I really didn't make very much of it when I was in Jamaica or anywhere else for that matter. And we have remained good friends. The last time I was in Jamaica I spoke somewhere in Downtown Kingston, I can't remember who invited me and he introduced me. We were great friends and he was a great admirer of mine and he tried to buy me off, not in any obscene way but to give me a job. When I was in Trinidad in 1964, that is before I went back to UWI, he sent G. Arthur Brown to tell me that he wanted me to come back and take a job in the planning division. I thought that was very nice. Anyway, I shunned that offer. One day I got a letter from Lightbourne who was then the Minister of commerce and trade. He was a very powerful figure in Jamaica because the IDC [Industrial Development Corporation] was the most important single institution in the public sector in those days. I got a letter from Lightbourne appointing me to be the head of research in the IDC with a lot of money, a car, and all kinds of things. This was Seaga's work, trying to get them to pay me off. I showed it to Lloyd Braithwaite and he told me 'Boy, you see I know you are not going to agree with me, but I think you should take the job because money is important, you have young children and this kind of money and all these perks you should really take it.' I told him I don't see how I could. I am not one of them. So I wrote them and told them that I would consider the job if they agreed that Beckford should be appointed with me and of course I never heard anything about the job again. Yes. I have had a wonderful life, a wonderful life. All kinds of things happen to me, lovely things you know. I didn't take it of course because, once you take money from people, then it is a problem.

BM: You were discussing Archie Singham.

LB: Yes, I was telling you how Singham came to be important to the JLP. Seaga got a great reputation for this haves and have-nots paper and he has been close to me ever since because of that. I went away to Montreal and lo and behold, while I am away, Archie becomes the great guru of the JLP. Thoroughly on the basis that he was my friend and he drew all the rewards from my connection. He became the head of all kinds of things in the JLP and he had been a big PNP before. McIntyre and Singham...used to hold a Saturday morning... it wasn't curry goat but it was a Jamaican food. Every Saturday morning at about 10 or 11 they would meet at the house of one of them to discuss problems of Jamaica – a kind of mini-New World group. And so Tavares, Hill and Seaga got to know me. Hill and Tavares got to know me because of this, because McIntyre was my very close friend and the other was Ernest Wells. Archie emerged from this thing as a real master, a real master manipulator and organiser of people and a politician who was not in politics. The irony of it was that Singham became a flaming Marxist thereafter. That was his third incarnation. He went away to Washington. First, he was teaching at Howard University. He was very active in the Non-Aligned Movement. He wrote a lot of papers there. I used to see him and we remained very good friends. The last time I saw him I was appalled to see how he had been wizened and dried up by cancer. I didn't recognise him. I saw him and I didn't know who he was. And he died and rather unsung I thought. I have kept in touch with Nancy. I think you all should do something. It's not too late. Find an occasion to do something for Singham. For all his faults which are really cultural things that he inherited, he really was a builder. Archie was something else. But he had his positive sides which should be recognised in an institution like the University. You know, you have to give people their due for their work.

AB: Certainly for those of us who came to UWI to do political science he was a major figure, you know the book on Grenada.[21]

AB: And he got the scholarships for graduate students.

BM: And the placement of them in particular institutions to return.

LB: He definitely was builder. There is no doubt about that.

NG: Like Edwin Jones, Carl Paris and Vaughan Lewis.

BM: There were two streams: Vaughan, Edwin, Neville Duncan and…

LB: Stone came out of that….

BM: There was the Michigan stream…

LB: But Archie came from Michigan, you know that.

AB: He was able to set up Michigan.

BM: And then there was a Chicago stream all of which Archie helped to do. Including Gordon and Robotham who went to Chicago.

NG: I thought that was the Ray Smith connection.

BM: Chicago was Ray but Archie was always working to position people, because the aim was to get out all the expatriates and get these young scholars to come back.

LB: Yes, I have no doubt at all that he was a builder. He was a positive person but he had this thing that he couldn't resist power at all or office.

BM: Lloyd you just gave us a little insight into the cultural thing, the 'Hindu-Tamil authoritarianism.' You want to spend one minute explaining that?

LB: It's not only the Tamil Hindus but all the Hindus. The older and senior figures are taken at their word. You don't question a senior person in the Hindu hierarchy and of course, I think it was excessive in the Tamils who went to Sri Lanka or Ceylon as we knew it. There were two waves of Tamils that went to Sri Lanka. One was the one that Archie belonged to and they became very much integrated and constituted a technocratic and bureaucratic class. All the permanent secretaries that ran the state were Tamil. All the ministers were Sinhalese and all the permanent secretaries were Tamil. I think it was pronounced in that situation because they were very insecure and Archie inherited that. His father was in the same thing that he was; his brothers, they were all civil servants in Ceylon. I think that just growing up in that hierarchical authoritarian situation, you just learned that way of living to get by and he never forgot because he could do it so easily. I mean, after he was so deeply involved and everybody knew it, with the PNP, it's not as if it was a secret.

AB: Let me ask you about one other person. Sylvia Wynter was in Guiana with Jan Carew and I was just trying to find out whether she was there at the time of the excitement, whether or not she was around New World at that time.

LB: No. she was there, we crossed in Georgetown, I can't remember whether it was my first, my second time in Georgetown when I spent a whole year or whether it was later. But not for very long, they left shortly after I arrived. I didn't get to know her very well. I got to know her very well later in Jamaica.

After A Break

AB: New World has begun.

LB: Yes, as New World now and there was a lot of activity, a lot of intensive activity and we were really building a journal, you know, with a long horizon. It was not easy. We couldn't sustain the journal as we would have liked. It was quarterly but that was very hard. We gave it legal foundations. Fletcher's firm did that. What was the name of that?

NG: Myers, Fletcher and Gordon.

LB: [Eric] Bell was in that firm, Fletcher, who else? They were very sympathetic to us and they did all the legal work free. So we founded a company, on a proper legal footing and we began to raise money, advertising and we started getting regular contributions.

AB: What was the plan? How did you all see it?

LB: It was just a vehicle for our thought. We certainly had no political ambitions in Jamaica, at all. There was no entry for a thing like that anyway, even if we wanted, but we didn't want. We just continued on that path and the main thing was trying to establish connections with universities all over. That is the period in which we got Kari in Montreal. Paul Chen-Young was a representative, first of all at Howard, and then he moved to Pittsburgh. And then we had in New York Nathan Richards. Then there was Puerto Rico and in the Caribbean there was St Kitts – Vinetta Ross, she had come on campus and was teaching and she set up a group there. We had Charles in St Lucia.

AB: How did the journal function? How were editorial decisions taken, how were articles solicited, did people just write, was there an editorial team?

LB: Very informal, we had no editorial team and I wrote most of them.

NG: You were the editor at this time?

LB: Well, in effect yes, although I often did not put my name. We changed the names all the time to encourage people. You had a long list of people who really never did anything but we called them this or that and we changed the editor's name. I was effectively the editor. I mean it was my main business whereas for most other people it was just something subsidiary. But we talked and there was no conflict over it. When I wrote something it reflected what we were saying, just that it happened afterwards. We never had any formal editorial structure. Whoever wrote the editorial would have been coming to the meetings regularly and we discussed, every meeting we discussed the party, the programme and the country; three things.

AB: And what do you mean by that, the party, the programme and the country?

LB: In Trinidad?

AB: No, in Jamaica.

LB: No it was in Trinidad where we worked because we had a party here, and we had the paper and we had the country, and the programme. Well in Jamaica it's the same thing except of course we had no party. But we had an organisation and we were talking all the time. We had meetings all the time, every week. Every Thursday night.

AB: Where did you meet if I may ask?

LB: At anybody's home. Francis Mark, we forgot to mention.

BM: Francis was in Jamaica at the time?

LB: He came there. He was a member of the Department of Government. He joined shortly after Archie and we had many meetings at his home. We would have it at Roy Augier, we would have it by me.

NG: When I came we used to have it at Gloria Lannaman's flat at Seacole Hall.

LB: Lannaman and Davis, Ermina. There were two sisters, Ermina and Evie Davis. They were very active and after I left there every time I came to Jamaica they would have a stew peas lunch for me. Gloria had a helper called Miss D and we were very close. She is dead now. She was very old even then. That was really an active centre.

AB: And the agenda would have been the organisation and the journal?

LB: And the situation in the country and the region of course. We talked about the region all the time. But it was all very informal; not many formal structures because there was no need for them.

BM: So Gloria was in the inner circle of New World?

LB: Well I don't know if we…Did we have an inner circle?

BM: I mean regular attendance at meetings.

LB: Oh yes.

BM: Because, of course, Gloria went, like Archie to the JLP.

LB: Yes, I know that. That's much later. She was the head of the JBC [Jamaica Broadcasting Corporation]?

AB: So this continues until 1964?

LB: 1965, 1966. I left in 1966 to go to Montreal.

NG: When you went to Montreal was it not to do the work on Plantation Economy?

LB: Yes of course, three years. Yes, we got a grant.

AB: So you went to Montreal in 1966.

LB: Yes, but you have to know me because I went to Montreal in 1966 but in January of 1967 I left and went to teach in Puerto Rico and while I was there I went to the Dominican Republic and of course I was still carrying on…still finishing off my FAO World Food Programme thing in 1966. I just happened to be located somewhere, but doing all kinds of things all the time. I went back to Puerto Rico. That was a very important period because unlike the first time when I just made contact, when I went back in 1967 we founded a group there which used to meet every week.

AB: What happened when you were away then, how did New World function between say 1965, 1966, and 1967 in Jamaica and other places?

LB: It continued as usual. I was not indispensable to the operation. Beckford certainly emerged as the key figure to whom people looked from abroad. He was an easy man to get on with and he really believed in it, he was not like Archie or McIntyre, he was central. These were things he believed in and wanted to work on. And his work followed out of that. You can see in his book, it comes out of that work.

AB: What relationship did you have to the grouping in your travels? When you went to Puerto Rico, Dominican Republic, you stopped by Jamaica, Trinidad….

LB: I was travelling all over, all the time. I had all kinds of opportunities for travel for one reason or another. At that time very few people travelled. But I had a life of travel, I had so many connections to do things and I got invitations and I used this as an evangelist would, so to speak. I spent all the money I made from *per diem* and so on to establish things. If I got an invitation to Barbados for example, I would go to Barbados and

I would get the *per diem* and I would use that money to travel to Antigua or to St Kitts or so on. We were trying to establish a regional organisation. Without even thinking in those terms, almost implicitly that is what we were doing. I was the lucky one to be able to be in the forefront as the evangelist for all this, for many different reasons of course: personal inclination, seniority in this kind of thing, all kinds of things, made me do it. I never left any stone unturned to try to establish groups because I knew the important thing is the institution and organisation. You can have as many people liking what you are doing as you want but if you don't set up an institution with groups running and meeting regularly then it does not work. In Puerto Rico in fact we had a conflict over that. Mervyn Alleyne was the man in charge of foreign policy so to speak, relations between groups. He was in the Mona group and he was responsible for contacts with other New World Groups. While I was in Puerto Rico, I got the group there to agree to put out an edition of the journal. I wrote to Mervyn and I told him everything that we wanted to do and for him to put it to the group and find out what they thought about it and he never did. It became a source of great contention because when they found out they thought I was trying to impose it on the organisation. It was nothing of the kind. It was just delinquency on the part of the person who was responsible. So the journal never came out of Puerto Rico because I had to back off, which I think was a very bad thing. Anyway, we did it in Montreal instead. We brought out an edition in Montreal, and then when I came to Trinidad we put out one in Trinidad when Millette was there.

AB: I'm trying to get a feel for the structure of the work. Would each group for example, say Puerto Rico, Trinidad, Barbados, decide, well this is a particular issue, we need to put out something on this issue, and we're going to put it out as New World Group or we do it independently?

LB: No. The thing was never so tight. All these structures were structures but they were informal structures. And since we had nothing to offer people in terms of money or office or promotion or anything, this was an informal group seen as a subversive group by the establishment. So anybody who joined it joined because they believed in it and this was all over the region. Millette ran quite a big group here. I have to come to that, because they say that I broke that up. Millette ran quite a good shop here, except that the accounting was very bad.

AB: Who would he have sent records to?

LB: He would send the records to David de Caires. That is for the *New World Fortnightly*. But I tell you something, I don't like to tell these stories, I never told them before but we brought out an edition in Trinidad, I came here, Karl Hudson Phillips, you know who that is?

AB: Yes.

LB: He was my political enemy later on. But he is always my friend. He comes here up to now, regularly, when I was sick he was here every day. Because we were at QRC [Queen's Royal College] together, we were at Cambridge together, we lived in London together. We were real friends and politics has not separated that. I asked him because he was in the government, he was a minister, to raise the advertising for me for an edition of the *New World*. At that time we were not seen as a political party because we were not. *New World* was not yet *Tapia* – although there is a sequel to that – Millette was building a party on the side, but I will come to that. He said yes, of course, no problem and you know a lot of people get on about it and he got all the ads for the journal. Do you know that two months later I think it was, or three months, I came to Trinidad and found that they had printed the journal, sold all the copies, and collected all the advertising money and we didn't have a cent in the treasury? It was a miracle of accountability! They had absolutely no idea of how to run a shop properly. And Eric St Cyr, [the fellow who is working with me here now] and I and a few other people had to pay the printer. So they sold the journals, collected the advertising, didn't pay the printer and they had no money. That is a very bad accounting. For a long time afterwards we were paying off the printer.

BM: Who was in the Trinidad group apart from Millette?

LB: Plenty people, it was big, much bigger than Mona. Well, much bigger than anywhere else, because here Millette was very into the politics without being formally into it. Toward the end it was a vast assembly of people. They used to meet in Port of Spain and the average was about 100. That is a lot of people for a thing like that. It really entered the political life of Trinidad because Millette wrote a series of articles in 1967. That was the year in which the *Express* was founded and Millette got into a dispute with Ken Gordon who had become the head of the *Express* and members of the business community.

NG: Tommy Gatcliffe.

LB: Tommy Gatcliffe also. What is the name of that fellow, Mark something from Canada?

NG: Siegel.

LB: Mark Siegel. He was in Trinidad at the time and he was in the New World Group. He was from Canada and he got a job down here in the University. They had a lot of people. Earl Lovelace was in it and Ivan Laughlin.

NG: Syl Lowhar.

LB: Syl Lowhar, of course.

AB: Let's go on. So you were in Montreal, there was a group found in Montreal, you put out a journal.

LB: We put out a journal and we had meetings there and [Edwin] Carrington was there, O.C. Harewood was there who later became the governor of the [Trinidad and Tobago] Central Bank, Delisle Worrel, Emelda Rennie, Noel Boissiere, there were a lot of people, because Kari had a lot students.

AB: And you were in Montreal in 1968?

LB: I came home in November 1968.

AB: So you were in Montreal at the Black Writers' Conference?

LB: Of course. I was a very controversial figure there.

AB: There was rumour of a conflict between you and Walter [Rodney].

LB: No that is nonsense. The press said that here. They allowed Michael X from England to get up in the meeting and make a speech for ten minutes only in four letter words. I got up and said that that can't dignify us. We can't do that. If we are doing something serious we have to deal with serious ideas, we can't have a man getting up and cussing white people and cussing this and that and only four letter words and 'honkies' and so on. I said we can't do that, we have to stay within dignified limits. They shouted me down, of course. One of the things I said was that look at the people we have here. Kari Levitt, she is one of us, in my organisation and Mark Siegel was there and so on. These are white people and they share what we are doing here. C.L.R. James was in the meeting and he told me that I should not have done that. Anyway, I did it and they shouted me down and they called me an Uncle Tom and that was reported by the newspapers here in Trinidad by my enemies and they said that Walter Rodney called Best an Uncle Tom, which is not true. Even if he thought so he wouldn't do a thing like that, [he was] not that kind of person at all. I have something to tell you about Walter later on. So I was there for the Black Writers' Conference which was very important. In fact I had come home a week before to Trinidad, definitively, to take up my job and one week after I was here, I went back to Montreal for the conference. I can't remember for what reason that I had to come here and I went back to the conference. Stokely [Carmichael] spoke. In one of those articles, I was describing some speeches that were given in a seminar in New Guinea in the Pacific which I attended. And the three main speakers were Ivan Ilyich, René Dumont and I. I said in my report on the conference that other than Stokely Carmichael, I had never heard a speaker with so much persuasion as Ivan Ilyich. I said that other than Stokely in top flight with all the beauty and power of his language I have heard nobody else. So Stokely is my top man for speaking. I have never heard anybody like him, I have never conceived that anybody could speak like that and carry a large assembly. You know, a lot of people were, there – Black Panthers – it was a big meeting. People came into town and we all spoke but Stokely was a different level from everybody else. I came back to Trinidad in October 1968.

Trinidad and Black Power

AB: To do what?

LB: To work at the University. I came back to work at the University
        in the Department of Economics. One week after I was here –
        I came back on a weekend and during that weekend, I think
        it was the Friday – Walter also came back from Montreal. He
        came to Mona and I came here and he was prevented from
        coming into Jamaica.

BM: October 16, 1968.

LB: Yes, exactly and the whole place flared up, not only in Mona
        where some people were killed and the full force of the Shearer
        regime was brought down on the dissenting forces and that
        ignited political protest all over the region, that is, in Barbados,
        the other islands and Trinidad. But the only place where the
        protest endured and never stopped thereafter, was Trinidad
        and that is because Geddes Granger was the leader of NJAC
        [The National Joint Action Committee]. It was called NJAC
        shortly after, but he had some young forces, many of whom
        were my students and almost all of whom were also in Tapia
        at the time. Kafra Kambon [Dave Darbeau] – I had forgotten
        the people who had come to the first Tapia meeting was there
        – Iyagoro, was there, he wasn't called Iyagoro then.

BM: He was still David Murray

LB: David Murray was there. I think 29 people came to the first
        Tapia meeting, but I'll come back to that.

LB: Did I give you one of these? [Passes around a copy of *New World
        Quarterly*] This is the first edition of *New World Quarterly*, March
        1963. It is marked up by Kari's father.

NG: Karl Polanyi.

LB: He read it and he marked it up and he said to me, 'This is the
        first piece of work to come out of the new countries that I find
        has any significance.' He said 'I have looked at all the stuff
        coming out of these countries and this is the first original piece
        of work.' That's what he told me. We became great friends. In
        those days, I don't know if you know that, Kari is now hot on
        him because they have founded an institute for him in Montreal
        and there is a rage about him all over the world now. He is
        assuming the proportions of Marx in Europe. But when I first
        got to know Kari she thought he was milk and water. She was
        then a flaming Stalinist and so he and I got to be friends when

she and he were not friends really, intellectual friends. They were family.

AB: So you come back to Trinidad and what happens?

LB: I come back to Trinidad and immediately, there is a big march from the University to the Jamaican Embassy and to Woodford Square to protest what had happened to Rodney and I was in that march and many of my students, who had gotten very close to me. Now I have to digress for a minute here. What became NJAC was comprised of two sets of forces: the first were forces in the University, most of who were my students and their friends and they had a group called Pivot which was doing the same thing that New World used to do in Mona. This was a younger generation. By this time I was going on 40 and they were 20 or less. And then Granger came out of the public service where he had an organisation of sorts of the equivalent of Black Power. Nobody called it that, but that was the vein in which it worked in the public service and he was the spokesman. There is a long piece in *Tapia*, in fact I think the whole journal was devoted to Granger. It tells that whole history, you can look at it in our archives. Those were the two wings that were brought under the National Joint Action Committee led by Granger, in the first place, informally, but he was obviously the spokesman. He was older and he was a very fine speaker. So you have to follow the fortunes of Pivot and bear that in mind when I am talking to you about NJAC. We go to the Jamaican High Commission and we protest there, it was a Friday and then we go to Woodford Square. The meeting takes off and minor speakers are speaking and then there just comes a point where Granger says to me, your time has come. Fortunately, you can check all of this because an Italian journalist met Granger some years afterwards and this was recounted to him. He wrote me a letter from Italy. To ask me why it is that Granger is so bitter against me and the reason is that I turned it down. I said, 'Look, my time has not come, I don't think in these apocalyptic terms, I think....I am not against coming to the Square.' But I fear that I could see where Granger was going already; of course I have a political eye. I said 'I fear if you go where I think you are going, we are going to bring the pot to a boil when you can't handle it.' Because they were already talking about getting rid of Williams and in that vein. So I didn't speak. I said I will speak at the University on the Tuesday. Millette spoke and [Euric] Bob spoke. And then the meeting wound up. I spoke at the University on the Tuesday and the whole verdict after I spoke...before that, let me tell you something, before I get to that conclusion. In those days you had something called the Guild Hall, which was a meeting place, which was like Grand Central Station. It had activity all the time, all kinds of intellectual activity, students, people from off campus, you could eat there, you could go to the library there. It was really what a university should be. All the speeches in this period after Rodney brought tremendous ferment. All the speeches took place at the Guild Hall at lunchtime. People came from off campus, all over the country to be part of these meetings and I spoke and the verdict after I spoke was that I took the emotion out of the situation. I asked them, 'what the hell you expect, this is a university. I want to take the emotion out. I want you all to understand what you are going in for.' The speech is probably somewhere, it's published. I spoke in a very sombre tone telling them that 'If you bring the pot to a boil, Williams will eat us raw.' This is what happened. Everybody said that is just theory, the usual thing they say about me. They paid me no mind and they went on as usual and they brought the pot to a boil and that was 1968 and they brought the pot to a boil by 1970. The upheaval was February....

BM: February 21.

LB: April 21 was the army rebellion, but February was the time of the court trial, when we knew something was going to happen because they charged them [the demonstrators] with something and brought them to the court on a Monday morning. Thousands of people turned up outside the courthouse. You know something is happening politically when people come to hear a case. The actual State of Emergency which is what people called the revolution was April 21, but I gave it the name the February Revolution because I tell you what was important was not what happened in April when the government declared a State of Emergency, but what happened in February when the population said what they thought. Anyway, I spoke on that Tuesday and they all got very cold with me, though Kafra Kambon, who was the closest to me of the students, he came to me and said, 'I think we could solve this problem if you became the Chairman of Pivot.' I told him, 'How could that be? I am not one of the people there; I am much older; it would really be forcing it for me to become head of this thing.' What they really wanted was a political leader. He said, 'All right, I know what you are thinking, but let us at least have an election for it so that if the people vote for you can't say it is forced.' We had this election with Pivot and all these young fellows and girls assembled there. They voted in my favour but the margin was not strong with a lot of dissent. I told them, 'I know I won the vote but I don't think I want half of this organisation as an organisation so I won't take it.' So I refused the post and they went on their way with Granger, because shortly after that New World would split. Although many of them continued to come to Tapia the bifurcation was irrevocable because they were agitating all the time. Lloyd Taylor and I used to go to all the meetings, we didn't leave anything to chance to find out what the people were saying. For a long time they never had more than two or three people in their meetings and most times nobody; but Granger was a political man and these are political people and they know that it might catch fire one day. They were on the road every night, all over the country, speaking to nobody but getting their message, sending to nobody; you don't know who hearing and so on. And you know what happened to that; it did catch fire later on when the police made the mistake of locking them up.

BM: Lloyd, let me back track a little bit. That decision not to go with Pivot intrigues me. A majority vote: fine, so there is a dissenting minority, there is not consensus. But surely had you accepted that, you would have been in a position to win over that minority or to be able to shift the balance?

LB: But, no, that is not my only option. That was not the only forum in which I operated.

BM: Yes, but it could have been one of a number.

LB: There was too much bitterness there, too many people who were against it and not just the people, but particular individuals. You really can't do that. I really had no credibility there, no validity there, to be chairman of that organisation or to be president; I can't remember what they were calling it. All these people, I had access to them and they had access to me and we had first of all New World and then we had Tapia. I know a lot of people tell me that I am a Hamlet. That is the big thesis; that every time I get a chance to do something I don't do it. But you have to ask yourself what the sequel has been to all these things. These things were really flimsy. No work was going on, no real thought was going on. It was just the idea of moving the Government and protest about poor people and all this kind of thing. I am a poor person. My father is a poor man. You don't have to tell me about poor people. I don't regard them as something different from me. I am part of this. I mean, we have to say how we are going to move this government in a way that we can take control of the country. You can't be speculative about this, although I am not suggesting that you have to have all the answers, but you have to have some reasonable strategy that could work. But all they were doing was agitating on the road, getting people bitter and riling people up and so I went off. Let me tell you what happened. I saw what Millette was doing. He was my very close friend. I say in one of my writings somewhere that people in Tapia have always accused me of being an apologist for Millette. He was my friend, we were real close colleagues – I knew his weaknesses, he knew mine. I would write things and he would read them as if they were his; we were so close. Then one day I discovered that he was running a separate group in San Fernando, that the people in St Augustine didn't know anything about.

BM: A separate New World Group or a separate political group altogether?

LB: Well, I think they were calling it New World. Certainly the people in the group had no doubt of his connection and his national image as the local leader of New World. We were so close that he invited me to San Fernando to see it. I went to two meetings that they had in San Fernando and I was appalled at the way these people were carrying on. They were saying they were New World but they had no connection at all to the ideas. They were just wild people. A lot of dubious people, a lot of cranks as you get into these things if you are not careful and they were carrying the thing in a certain direction. I went to a meeting, I had been to several meetings before of course, coming here all the time, and I realised that we can't have any discussion because Millette was the chairman of the group and he was saying to the group 'We don't need to talk about anything since we all agreed already.' I heard him say with my own ears. He said "Why are we talking about anything, why do we have any contestation here when we all agree already, let's not talk about anything". All he was doing was that he wanted plenty people. And he was afraid to have any discourse because if you have discourse then you are going to have dissent and some persons will go, but you have to have that process of winnowing if you are going to have any serious organisation. I went to a meeting on November 7. I got up and said I didn't think that we were going anywhere and that we better do something different and that I was prepared to do something different and I had a meeting at my house next week Thursday and anybody who wishes to come is free to come. That is where you get that list of people there who came to the first meeting of Tapia. November 14, 1968 is when Tapia was founded. Not long after I came home.

BM: Given the events that had happened in Trinidad, what was happening in Jamaica? Norman has a comment to make.

NG: Let us back up a little bit. I came back to Jamaica in 1966. Around August/September just when Lloyd was leaving to go to Montreal and at that time, a thriving New World group was operating as Lloyd says. G-Beck[ford] became the key figure in the group after Lloyd left and I think that at that point he became the managing editor of *New World Quarterly*. During that time, we had the regular weekly meetings and to answer Tony's question, weekly meetings were organised around articles that were being produced for the journal. So usually, the agenda of the meeting was the discussion of a paper, which had been submitted to the *New World Quarterly*, plus the discussion of topical things. However, from that time, one of the key and a recurring issue was that of thought versus action and there was a constant pressure from the younger New World members and students like Garth White, Peter Phillips....

LB: That fellow from Barbados....

BM: Timmy Callender?

LB: No, I think he is dead now. He was in the government.

NG: I can't remember his name. There was [pressure] about becoming more popular, becoming more rooted, more grounded – going to the people. The argument was that the journal was too 'highfalutin' and intellectual. You need to go to the people. And partly in response to that, we produced a number of pamphlets: the Unemployment Pamphlet, for example, was a key thing. I remember Trevor Munroe was co-writer, co-author and [David] Dabydeen and Derek Gordon – I think his name is listed on it. Then there was the thing about G-Beck's passport and there was a pamphlet about that and you [Lloyd] were still here for that. And there was one about sugar called 'Life and Death.'[22] So we were able to maintain the journal but in a way partly speak to this demand for more grounded stuff in the pamphlets. And then Walter came in '68 and he really took his thing in the direction of grounding with the Rastafarians.

AB: Did he relate to the New World at all?

NG: I remember when Walter came I tried to get him into New World and to bring him into it because he and I had been friends from London and from before that in the West Indian Society for the Study of Social Issues, and I gave him copies of the journal. I remember him saying, 'Well, all this is useful and interesting but I'm really not into all of that. I am going to go into the ghettos and ground with the Rastafarians and this is what we need to do, learn from the masses as well as teach the masses.' So he was not into what he perceived as the more intellectual orientation of the New World. And most of the students followed his line. They tended to be more attracted to what Walter was doing. When the Rodney riots happened, that sharpened the whole issue between being more activist and being more intellectual and that's when *Abeng* was launched and G-Beck and I joined up with it but still maintained connections with New World. By that time, I had been chair of the New World group in Jamaica and around that time, I handed it over to Stephen DeCastro. So New World did continue, but it continued more with the non-Jamaican members of the group [and this is very important]. They became more vital to its functioning because what Shearer's speech had done and what the Rodney incident had done was to say, 'Non-Jamaicans stay out of Jamaican politics and stay out of anything that has to do with activism.' So when *Abeng* was being launched that was Jamaican: Rupert Lewis, Trevor Munroe, Robert Hill, G-Beck, myself with C.Y. Thomas being very low key because the message was if you are not Jamaican, don't even think about going off campus and talking to anybody, because you are going to get kicked out. So more non-Jamaicans stayed with the *New World* and G-Beck and I moved to *Abeng*. At that time, the split happened in Trinidad, so obviously it resonated with what was going on in Jamaica and James Millette allegedly stood for more activist, politically oriented [work].

LB: Yes, he did, without doubt.

NG: Lloyd stood for the more traditional role of *New World*. At the same time, we did not take sides. Obviously, the main thing was that we were very distressed by the split and we figured this was bad for New World. I remember coming to Trinidad on some other business and I believe I had in my mind if there was some way to try for a reconciliation. I might have spoken to both Lloyd and James separately, I am not sure, but I certainly spoke to a number of people on both sides and I came back and reported that there was no chance of this split being healed. This thing has gone beyond anything. But we did not take sides with it as such either officially or unofficially, but we were very distressed with what we perceived to be something that was going to have very negative repercussions.

AB: So when did *New World* finish in Jamaica?

NG: Well *New World* continued for some years but it continued as a journal because by that time people like G-Beck and I were in *Abeng*. It continued with people like Stephen DeCastro, Vaughan Lewis who became editor because George Beckford resigned to go into *Abeng*.

LB: For which I was the agent here.

NG: Vaughan Lewis, Stephen DeCastro and Mervyn Alleyne, I think, for some time and Eddie Green. But it continued as a journal, I don't recall meetings of the group taking place.

BM: You've not called one Jamaican name in that group.

NG: No. The leading Jamaicans in the group before were G-Beck, Jefferson and myself. But Jefferson didn't go into *Abeng* because he was a more reticent type. I don't know if he stayed, attending New World meetings or not because certainly Jefferson and I co-edited the book *Readings in the Political Economy of the Caribbean* in 1970 which was a New World publication but virtually all of the articles in that publication were produced in the period before 1968, which was really the period of greatest [output]. So what happened actually to New World; I think you would have to talk to Jefferson and find out what happened to the journal. I don't even recall when the Journal ceased publication.

LB: It became more of an occasional journal. I think the last one was edited by Vaughan Lewis.

AB: So what happened to the other New World groups then, in the other places?

LB: By this time, the trend that you had noticed earlier had gone very far. Jamaica and Trinidad had gotten independence and the other islands were getting it or had gotten it. Barbados certainly got it in 1966 and Guyana in 1966. Many of the people were drawn to local concerns and the regional idea was dead because all of these people were into independence singularly as Sparrow[23] said.

NG: The other factor was that more and more of the younger radicals, so to speak, were drawn to activism; they were not satisfied with an activity that they perceived as being exclusively intellectual and academic.

LB: And once you are dealing with your own situation at home you must and so did we. I mean we were not inactive, we'll come to that, but it was in a different way.

AB: I am just thinking that I joined, Trevor brings me to the Abeng group as a high school student and it is in the Abeng group that I learn of New World by reading some of the stuff that he gives me. But I first knew of it when he writes the document against bourgeois idealism.[24] That document then leads me to go and look on what the original stuff was, because then those of us who were drawn were drawn more by Walter's activism and the black power thing and then it was almost like a back tracking, to go back and look at *New World*.

LB: Do you remember that we had encounters with the…what you call it…People's something…? Who were the people that wanted to talk to him just before he was banned?

AB: The Unemployed Workers' Council.

LB: Right Ben, Ben Munroe. We were very close to them. We had a lot of meetings with them. I used to go there regularly. I don't think other people's influences are a matter of activism versus non-activism but it is a question of the way that you do it. I think the method is very important. I don't know. I quarrelled with Walter a lot. Just before he died, we were both in California together on speaking tours to the same places – UCLA, Berkeley and Stanford. The first one was at UCLA and I spoke, possibly, for an hour, at the conference about the whole strategy of change in the Caribbean and the differences between what I believed was right and what I thought Walter was doing. I mean we were very good friends. I could talk frankly to him. There was nothing like any conflict or anything, it was just a difference of strategy. When he got up to speak, he said, 'Lloyd Best is my mentor and my teacher and I am not going to answer any of those things he said.' That's how he handled it and he never replied. But I told him quite frankly what I thought. It wasn't something clandestine. I don't see how he expected to bring change in Jamaica by the methods he employed. Even if he were a Jamaican, it would be very difficult and being a Guyanese what happened to him was bound to happen. And you really have to calculate that. You can't say that that is an accident, in politics. It's like Manley saying that the CIA destabilised him. He didn't know they were going to do that before he started? That he had to avert them? You must know that, I mean, are you a child? It's the same with Walter. He was bound to be stopped in his tracks. In Jamaica we had all those options and we did a lot of work, of spade work, without making these agitational claims that draw attention to the authorities. You have to have organisation and he had no organisation really – he was just talking to crowds.

AB: The phrase you mentioned a while ago is 'agitational claims' and I am trying to work through whether or not you have a particular view of politics that has agitational claims as one phase, which is preceded by thought and strategy. How do you see it?

LB: It can't be otherwise, though, if you are serious about anything in human affairs then you know how important accidents are and if you are overcome by accidents then you have to deal with them. So you can't predict that you are going to have some linear interpretation of history by which you are going to progress to this and then to another state, nothing like that. But, insofar as you are able to make sense of your situation, you cannot do things that are certain to fail. No organisation, not NJAC, not the ULF [United Labour Front], not any of the organisations in Trinidad has had as rich a history of popular involvement as Tapia has had. And nobody talks about that. The Tapia House here in Tunapuna, was a beehive of activity, all the better village groups from around here used to come here. All the sporting activities used to take place on this road in front of my house and the headquarters over there. The taxi drivers were here; all kinds of people were here. Theatre was going on here, Rawle Gibbons, all kinds of people. You don't consider that grassroots activity? Because we don't announce it? Not only that, but we were involved with groups all over the country on agricultural projects. We had a project in Arima; Matura; we had a project in Central Trinidad; all over we were doing work with small people. We don't make a political noise about it. What you want is to get people conscious and organised. If you don't do that you are spinning top in mud and it does not matter how many people you get. Look at the situation. We are still here, where are all these groups that were going to have revolution and bring down Williams? Where are they? Beginning with James, where is he now? He fell back on all kinds of turgid stuff from papers from all over the world – from Poland and all kinds of things. He had a paper going and when it couldn't attract anybody it became a scandal sheet – he was rivalling the *Bomb* and all the weekend scandal papers. He was selling 35,000 papers and then he collapsed. How could he be selling 35,000 papers and then collapse? Thirty-five thousand papers is a lot of papers, even today far less then… so I don't understand it.

BM: Accountancy problems?

LB: I don't know if it was purely accountancy problems. And if it is accountancy then it is real too; because you can't be running a serious political operation if you don't have people taking the accounts carefully about how you spend money. Where are all these fellows? Where is NJAC today? They're running calypso. They call themselves a cultural organisation. But if you look at the whole history of what they said they were going to do and what they have actually done and what they are doing now you will see the vast gap. We have said what we are going to do and we are doing that. It might take a hundred years. In fact that is one of the reasons why Millette and I fell out. He asked me 'What do you tell people when they come to join New World?' I said I tell them that we may never win anything, but this is a lifetime of struggle and we have to go on until something happens in our favour. He said, 'You must be mad, I tell them we will be in power next year.' What kind of thing is that? It is something about the Caribbean, a whole cultural problem and they do it in many places. We have to get serious. We have to move these governments. All these governments are useless, especially in Trinidad, but we are not going to move them by agitation. These governments have police, they have army, and they have vast financial resources, especially in Trinidad. You have to persuade people, you have to bring people over and you can't do that in a morning. People must see that you are serious. It takes many years to build institutions and build concepts that people can trust, because they see you perform them and they see you mean it when you live them. If you don't do that then you are just joking. All these political movements that are in Trinidad and Tobago are joking. We are the only ones that are serious – I don't want to say that. I think it's a hell of a thing to have to make those claims and you shouldn't really, but quite frankly, if you look at the empirical evidence we are the only people who were doing what we said we were doing and we are still doing it and it is there, it is implanted, it's not going to go away.

On Philosophy and Political Economy

AB: Let me ask you another question, to do with New World. The Independent Thought[25] essay – why that essay? What exactly were you intervening in, what were the debates at that point?

LB: I was addressing my colleagues because this debate was pregnant; it kept breaking out wherever you went. People would charge us for the things that Norman said, for not being active, for not being serious. We had to write something that could persuade people that what we were doing was reasonable. Reasonable people must see that, and I think it persuaded a lot of people. But it was not airy-fairy; it was meeting a political situation.

AB: Wasn't it a talk you gave in Montreal?

LB: Yes, but I expanded it. I gave that talk in Montreal because that was the place where I was, but the debate was there [at Mona]. Tim Hector and the wicket keeper, West Indies wicket keeper who died, Alfie Roberts. He and Tim Hector were adamant about the necessity of going out to the people, what I call agitation. I was in the middle of that and I had to defend our position. First of all I don't have this notion of the people, this notion that we assume the people are somewhere else and I am here – I am going out to them. I am a poor man, very poor. All my family are taxi drivers and nurses and nursemaids and domestics. That's where I come from; I am seeing them everyday. And I didn't move from Tunapuna to the West. I had the income; I had the status to do that. I am living here and I am living among these people. The other day Jeremy Pantin told me 'you must listen to the people.' I said that is for you,

you have to listen to them because you are somewhere else
and you are somewhere else. I don't have to listen to them; I
hearing them all the time, everyday. My mother is 91; she's
up the road – poor people. So I don't have this notion of
the people as something different from me. I am living my
normal life, I am on the streets like everybody else, I have
gone everywhere in Trinidad, I have campaigned everywhere,
thousands of public meetings in my time. But in addition to
that I write a lot in the papers and we have intellectual life and
we have organisational life as well. As I have told you no group
in Trinidad has done more work among the population of all
kinds, all levels of population as we have. But nobody pays
any attention to that because unless you get it in the papers,
for a confrontation with the police it is not noticed, the press
don't report that. Scholars can't do that; scholars have to look
at the facts.

AB: So you are arguing against Tim and Alfie.

LB: Yes, that debate was going there and I was their main target
in a lot of the things that they were saying. Until very recently,
they were attacking me all the time until we became quite good
friends just before he [Tim Hector] died. I actually met him. I
never really met him before properly. He came to a conference
in Jamaica and his wife was there and so on and we got to know
each other in a social way and that always softens politics. And
then he stopped.

NG: The first draft of the paper as I recall was given at a conference
on West Indian affairs in Montreal in October 1966.

LB: That's what they say. But that was not the first conference. That
was when I gave my paper, at the second conference; they had
a conference on the same thing a year before.

BM: I want to take up an obvious issue that stems from the paper,
which is the issue of Best, New World and Marxism. What
strikes me going through the narrative is the engagement at
almost all stages of your intellectual career with certain kinds
of Marxism, with Joan Robinson, Bettelheim, Kari Levitt, Karl
Polanyi...the list goes on. Why are you not a Marxist or what
are the processes that distanced you from that sort of default
position on the Left?

LB: It's very simple. It is that Marx wrote for a particular place and at a particular time and if you ask me…if I think that much of what he said was valid, I would say yes, for the time and the place. In the newspapers I quote him all the time. I respect Marx, I have read all his works, I know a lot of Marxists, but it does not fit the Caribbean situation, if you just take over the model without modification. The concept of class is vital, for political sociology but you have to understand what Marx means when he uses the term and I say that the Caribbean is classless, because what we have here is stratification. Stratification is not class. You can have stratification by income, wealth, colour, by race and now in all these countries that are pretending to be democracies you have it by education and schooling. People become eminent because of all these reasons. But that is not a sufficient condition to constitute a class. These people are still proletarians. That is the problem of these countries: they don't have a ruling class, which I don't want, or a responsible elite, which I do want. Because either a ruling class or a political elite accepts the responsibility for the countries in which they live. That's the first thing about it: they have an idea of the public good. You may not agree with it, you may not agree with the way they distribute their fruits of the thing, but they don't let it run down. They service it and they take charge of it and they have a theory of how the whole thing works. They may intervene for themselves but they are intervening to do something for the whole place. In the Caribbean these people are just rich, or they just have high colour, or they just have education, and they are getting good salaries, but they have no theory. C.L.R. James said these people live without ideas of any kind. They have no concept of the public good, they don't understand the simplest things about politics, they don't know the difference between politics and the government, they don't know the difference between Westminster and something else – they mix it up. All these people are just going to school, passing exams and getting money. That does not constitute a ruling class. Marx is talking about people who are dealing in property; who own the country and who own the land and they are not letting anybody else get it. They are running it in a certain way – nobody is doing that here. There were elements of it when you had an absentee investor class, which was also resident, that came here for calls of duty; that has come out in all my work. These people did not consider the West Indies their nation or their home but they had property here and they had business interests and as long as they were making money they knew that they couldn't let it run down. They had to service it. But the moment they left after emancipation, you got a society that was essentially classless. It took some time for them to disappear, but now there are very few white people in the Caribbean, there are no business people, there is no serious economics at all. These people are just living on foreign investment whether it be tourism or bauxite. They don't do anything; that's not a ruling class, that's not a serious elite that is going to run the country on behalf of a democratic society; it does not exist. I say that not to denounce anybody but you have to create it. To get these countries viable we have to create people, classes of people who will assume this responsibility and I am not talking about elites of privilege, I am talking about elites of responsibility. You can't ever have a society without eminence. People are going to emerge if colour is the thing, because of that; if education is the thing; if business is the thing; people are going to come to the top and get responsibility for where they work and their location in the scheme of things – you can't avoid that. What you can avoid is making them a privileged class that is going to get a disproportionate share of the product or a disproportionate share of the power. You have to make sure there is enough recycling and democratising so we don't get hereditary systems where people entrench themselves. But you can't escape having political leaders and educational leaders and so on. The left is hostile, in this country, all those who attack me in the papers, to my concept of the elite because they think that the elites are something bad. Elites may be something bad, but we can't avoid them, and what we have to do is to make them something good. You have to circumscribe them.

BM: How do you contrast or compare your position, say, with C.L.R. James's? You know, the kind of sketch James gives in 'Every

Cook can Govern,'[26] in which he is calling for a kind of populist control from below?

LB: I agree with James, except that James is not a practical man in anything that he does and he has not translated this into operations. I have translated it into operations, in that the people who will become the responsible elite have to come from below and they have to be controlled from below. You have to have democratic processes that can change them, that can select them, but every cook can't govern together, everyone can't be Prime Minister at the same time and everybody can't be leader of the university at the same time. You must have eminent elites, you can't escape them, what you have to do is to entrench them in democracy and I think I have surpassed all these fellows including James and Marx. I think my work will come down as serious thinking about the problem. I have rewritten this Marxian sociology; I have rewritten it to suit our case.

AB: How would you respond to a criticism that says that what you are doing is taking the fluidity of the class/social stratification of Trinidad and generalising it to the entire Caribbean? That in places like Jamaica, for example, it is extraordinarily hard, that the stratification used in your definition has evolved to classes.

LB: I think there is validity in that criticism because Trinidad is the extreme case in the phenomenon. But in world terms, Trinidad and Jamaica are not very different. Jamaica and Barbados are at one end of the spectrum where you tend to have ruling classes, where you tend to have elites, because these countries inherited something from the pre-emancipation period. And in the post-emancipation period, when you've got people like Manley, Pen keepers and you've got people with horses and land and public schools that had some concept of the country. But I am afraid that independence has not sustained these things. What we have got is a fake democracy in all these countries and they have regressed in Jamaica. I was telling you that when Sherlock sent me in to the country, I realised it was a serious country. Manley had built real structures all over, there were people who were not just slavish followers of Manley; they had ideas.

And they were thinking about all these things, you could have a real discussion in Clarendon, or in Spaldings, with people, with farmers. In Trinidad you can't have that. In Trinidad you can't get it in the University. Jamaica is different from Trinidad, I agree with that. But, it's not sufficiently different to make a difference to my analysis. If I had to write it down, as I am doing, I'd make the differentiation. I always say that Cuba first, Cuba is a really serious country, then Jamaica, then Barbados; all the rest is just stupidness. All the rest are just playing with democracy and pretending and they don't have the first idea of what they are involved in. Places like Guyana; Burnham and Jagan mash up that country!

BM: Lloyd can we just carry this point a little further? Let us for the moment assume your argument to be the case for the Caribbean; but there is a macro-system of capital, the kind described by various thinkers like Immanuel Wallerstein, Samir Amin etc. which remains and which has certain cycles and ways of operating to accumulate which impinge on us and which requires a macro analysis. How do you position yourself in terms of that analysis? Even if we assume that classes are stratifications to be defined differently here.

LB: I agree that there would still be something called a world system. I know Wallerstein well and worked with him. That's where I met Courtney Blackman, I was giving a lecture at Columbia University to a class by Wallerstein and Terry Hopkins and Blackman was there and he was a flaming Marxist. And now he tells everybody that I saved him from Marxism. All I am telling you now, I told him then. I persuaded him. Anyway, I know Wallerstein very well and I know his work and I think it makes a lot of sense to treat the world as one entity. But I also think that you have to develop typologies within that. It is very important to disaggregate the world into different civilisations and into different systems and sub-systems within the world system. I think I was talking to you this morning about my analysis of America. We bring students here, you'll see that every year during their spring term and I am going to speak next week. I'm speaking on Caribbean civilisation, society and culture. And I think America is a very different place from the rest of the world. The first thing that you have to do is to differentiate America from the rest of the world. Because the most important feature of American civilisations, all of them, is migration. The most important single factor explaining historical development in the last 400 or 500 years is the arrival of the conquistadors and all the things that follow from that, Pizzarro, Cortez and so on. But the point is that America has to be differentiated from the rest of the world because of the patterns of settlement that have emerged over the last 400 or 500 years which are very different from every other part of the world and which is the fundamental difference and which is the basis of our plantation economy work. The Ricardian system of economics assumes a sedentary population is producing for its own consumption and therefore international trade becomes a sub-system of domestic trade when there are surpluses. International investments spring from domestic investments and there are many other things that spring from that. That is true of Asia, it is true of Europe, and it is true of Africa, although Africa has other complications. But in America the systems that have developed since Columbus are based, in the first place, on exports. When people came to America, the first thing they had to do was export. They couldn't live. The length of a crop is too long. In North America, where Europeans went, they were able to change that quite quickly, so they get a pattern of settlement that was not very different from that of the other continents. You have to know how it starts and therefore I call them 'Colonies of Settlement' because people settled there and they go there to own land and run business. In Southern America it is not like this at all. We have a system of *Encomienda and Encomiendados*. The land is divided in a certain way and conquistadors run it in a certain way and there is no question of ownership and settlement, only for the conquistador. It is on very strict terms, first of all by the Spanish monarchy and later on by the captainships and that's a different case again which I know a lot about but I wouldn't consider myself an expert. In the Caribbean, however, we are the extreme case of the phenomenon, where there is no settlement at all. What you have is exploitation. You have a handful of people who come and they bring in populations to work. Everybody that has come to the Caribbean including many of the Europeans in the early days came to work, not to own. They were indentured, Whites before Blacks, then Blacks and Indians and so on, everybody a part from the Syrians who came at the end are not important or are important in a different kind of a way; everybody came here to work. So you have a proletarian civilisation where people have nothing to sell but their labour and you have a whole analysis that springs from that which incidentally runs against Marx, in that they think that the slave system is different from wage labour when in fact it isn't.

The fundamental commonality between the slave system and the other system is that in both cases, the populations have nothing to bargain with but their labour and that is more important than anything else. That is why I am rewriting the sociology to suit our case. So we have a theory of America as a place that is differentiated by settlement and where you have a spectrum at one end of which is the Caribbean where there is no settlement. At the other end is North America where you get settlement after an initial period of exports. So in the Caribbean, which is different from every other part of the world, the economy begins its life with exports. Exports do not spring from domestic activity, exports are the *raison d'être* of the system; the system is set up for export. There is no domestic activity, there is no domestic output, so the population is hanging on to these exports and the whole system turns on the terms of trade; whether you get markets for these exports and what prices you get and so on and our whole theory of the plantation economy is about that. We're not trying to tell people that these countries are exploited, we know that. We are not trying to do what Beckford did, which is [to explain] persistent poverty – we know that. What we want people to know in these countries is how these economies work, differently from what is in the text book and what people are being taught everywhere in the world, so we can deal with it. I am not interested in dependency like Norman. I am interested in the theory of adjustment of these societies where you have export as the only activity in the first place, and where domestic activity comes in only when export activity collapses – the opposite of other parts of the world. We need a whole theory of economy and society that deals with this reality. I've spent all my years writing about these things because you can't read it in a book somewhere; there are no books on the West Indies on all the things I am talking about. You have Marx and the whole pre-history of Locke and Hobbes and plenty things before. We are starting *tabula rasa*. We have to make sense of our own reality in terms of what we learn from what is on the ground. We can't take Marx, we can't take Weber. We have to know them and we have to understand what are the relationships that they use, which are useful to us. I don't throw them out, I am not an anti-Marxist. I am just not a Marxian, in the sense that I know Marx's work and I know how he is different from what I am saying.

And I find that most of the people who are in the West Indies, who are talking revolutionary politics don't know any of these things. How are you going to deal with the situation if – a) you don't know Marx thoroughly and properly and b) you don't know the country you are talking about? The great challenge is to find out about our own place, to know how it works and how it fits into the world system. You can't fit the Caribbean into any straitjacket that Wallerstein sets down. When he says capitalists come here, what capitalists come here? Capitalists came here in a very special form. They are not capitalists because real capitalists take responsibility for the place. What we have are absentee investors and of course because they live here and they are resident here and they have all kinds of interests here there is an impulse towards capitalism, I am not denying that, but it is not serious. The moment you get high prices for sugar for two years and they make a killing, they're gone, and that's empirical, everybody knows that. So you have to deal with the theories of capitalism by Marx or by Wallerstein or by anybody else in terms of their own reality. I think that is what we have been doing in that way for a long time.

AB: How do you respond to the comment that says that that analysis is dated?

LB: Globalisation?

AB: No, not globalisation. The last part of what you said, that in fact the examples of whether it be sugar or bananas, the development of the plantation theory was based up on a certain kind of commodity structure. That in the present conjuncture those are already objectively dying. And that there are services, there is intellectual stuff, there is technology etc. How do you respond to that to say well those structural conditions still remain?

LB: I don't see any difference, I see differences in form. We presented a model, Eric St Cyr and I, to the Central Bank Conference. I presented a model at the St Kitts Conference with Dwight Venner, dealing with these questions. I was asked this question because I said in the paper that the model that we have developed for Trinidad, which is a classic case of the old system – oil and natural resources, a commodity – fits all the Caribbean region *mutatis mutandis*. It is not oil, it is not gas, it is not sugar, it is not bauxite; they are new things. But the important thing about the Caribbean economy is that it is externally propelled and that has not changed. By external I do not mean export-led, the distinction is fundamental. New Zealand is export-led, Australia is export-led, England is export-led, and Japan is export-led in that export demand is by far the largest share of total demand in these countries. They have to sell abroad to live. In the West Indies it is not that they are export-led in that sense. It is that the ownership of land, the direction of all these things that happen here and it does not matter what they are, including all the internet things, the people that are doing it are not Trinidadians or Jamaicans. They are copying things from Miami and Los Angeles. They are not doing the software. They are buying the hardware and getting the software from somewhere else. What we need are conceptualisers. So the whole computer revolution and the whole internet e-revolution requires brains; sitting down here and conceptualising for this country: to see how you can make profits for this country, to see how you could sell exports to this country or how you could keep this country viable. That is not going on; it is worse than ever.

With all this so-called technological revolution and globalisation, I don't buy it at all. First of all, I don't buy the idea that globalisation is anything new, because it started here in the Caribbean. And I feel we could lick the system if we wanted to. We certainly have the brains, we have the people if we wanted and we are also free of a lot of the encumbrances; a lot of the things, which I have described as negatives, can be turned into positives. In this country we should really be the ideology of free. I wrote a piece in which I said I expected 200 years from now that either Port of Spain or Kingston or Havana would be the centre of diplomatic and intellectual life in America. Now I believe that, and I believe it is possible because I see that the [North] Americans are bogged down by an ideology that they can't get out from under. They are going to damnation. They can't get away from a lot of the things there because there is a whole dynamic inside the system, which keeps them on a certain kind of track. Now we don't have that, we are very small countries and we should just stop saying that smallness is a disadvantage. Smallness is our biggest advantage and the division that we have inherited from all these different races and different parts of Africa, this is a real advantage because we have learned to live with each other in a way that few people have. We don't have what you call ethnic mixing of the kind that you have in the United States where you mix and you remain a Greek or you remain an Irish family or a black or that kind of thing. I think that these societies are well poised because they are small and because they are mixed in the way that they are in what I call an ideology free. Nobody is ever ideology free, of course, but I mean the ideologies that dominate the world system, we don't have to get caught up in that. And people are not afraid of us, they think we are not going to do anything. They deride us; they think these countries are useless. I first said it in Cuba. I gave a lecture in Havana and I said that I expect that this part of the world will be the centre of diplomatic and economic life. I said that one of the reasons for it is that North America is going to be speaking Spanish

100 years from now and Cuba better think about that, what it means in terms of relationships and what they can do. So I am saying that these countries are small, they are mixed and they are beautifully placed. People are talking about e-mails and e-this and e-that and computers, but physical location remains important. We had better see how we can exploit these things and stop moaning and groaning about special and differential treatment, begging for all kinds of things. I'm not begging for anything. And I think we should sell intellectual services. What we have to do is to understand ourselves, understand America and understand the world and bring thousands of students from all over the world to study here. I am doing that in my private life. And I feel with a population of six million people that we have here that it is entirely feasible if we wanted to do it. But we have to change our perspective and our orientation from moaning and groaning about what white people do we, and all those kinds of things and see that we can do them back.

BM: I want to take up the question of ideology with a little epistemology. What are the cornerstones of how you think? You present it as a very familiar and obvious thing: you observe things and you look at them and you make assessments and you come to a conclusion. But presumably there is a lot more. Without putting labels on it, what is the underlying, substrate intellectual approach and methodology and what is it informed by?

LB: I think you have to begin from typologies. You have to begin from the hypothesis that although the world appears to be the same in many ways, in fact you have many different systems of society and culture and that the important intellectual task, the first intellectual task is to disaggregate the world system and find out what your own system is about. Of course you need to know other peoples' as well, but that is what drives me. I don't spend much time on other people's things although I do a lot of reading, I travel, and I read paper. My main thing is to find out what it is that has made West Indian society what it is, what drives it and what we have to do to turn it in the directions that we want it to go. So typology is central to my system of thought.

BM: I want to take off on that. Norman makes a point in a paper that he has just written but I don't think you have shown Lloyd yet. He is really quoting a number of different people on their view that the plantation model in particular and your work in general don't really present us with a theory that you can quantify in order to disprove or prove.

LB: I've heard this for 40 years now or more, or 50. I don't buy it at all. There is no need to quantify anything. First of all, ninety nine percent of the conclusions reached by humankind are based on observations by individuals who bring their judgment, their experience and their intuition to what they see and statistical measurement is only a small aid to that. All the econometrics hardly contributes anything, to my mind. Certainly econometrics, I don't pay them any mind at all; the things that they are saying don't add anything. Joan Robinson always taught me that if you can't say it in words, you can't say it in mathematics. I believe that is essentially true. You have to think it very clearly in your head before you can think how you are going to formulate it in a calculus or algebra. I am not worried about that at all. It does provide a theory in the only sense that you can have a theory, in that no theory is provable. It can be disproved, as you know all theories are provisional in the light of what you have seen and what you have been able to assemble as what other people have seen. So that as a theory, the theory that we have is a set of hypotheses about how these systems were founded, what were their essential properties and how they have been moving through time, evolving to where they are now. That's what I am trying to find out about the Caribbean. You can't find it out by any quantitative test and you can't find it out by reading any encyclopaedia or any book. What teaches the present is history and what teaches history is the present. I am reading the philosophy of history all the time. I have a lot of books here on this question. I am reading William Irwin Thompson now about transformations of history.[27] I know that there is nothing that you can find definitively, because you are getting new experience all the time, which throws the past into a new light. He says in this book that you have to rewrite history every 100 years.

AB: Probably less than that because there are new questions that face you...

LB: All the time. But these new questions arise from experience that you have now. You can't read it in a book. Something happens to you, an accident or something and you notice connections. If you are a scientist, if you are noticing. I grew up on my father's farm and I noticed everything because if you are on a farm and you don't notice everything you can't eat. You have to notice everything around you and park it somewhere in your brain, to see how it impinges on all the other things that you are reading and writing and noticing. So work is an ongoing progress, there is no definitive answer to anything. You have to keep on interpreting all the time and making new interpretations.

AB: It might be useful to stop here and come back tomorrow on the plantation economy and more on the theoretical stuff.

BM: Yes, we've had a full day.

LB: I've enjoyed it.

The Following Day

BM: We are back again on day two of our recollections and discussion of New World and there were things that you wanted to remind us of that you didn't mention yesterday.

LB: The first thing was the year that we spent in Georgetown, Dhar and I, with the Jagan government. This was very uneventful in the government itself, because Cheddi was not ready to open up any issues to discussions, but in the country, it is inconceivable the kind of exchange that was going on. I got into a lot of trouble of course, because the PM's wife was attacking me in the papers every day. Can you imagine? I am an international civil servant working in the PM's office and the PM's wife is attacking me in the papers. It was that kind of situation and nobody thought it out of the ordinary. The discussion was open and nobody could stop it. It was just floodgates. And that continued the whole year that we were there and I told you what had happened with the development of the New World itself as a group, but in the country I gave a lot of lectures. We were in great demand to speak on all kinds of things including things we didn't know anything about. During the course of that year, Eric Williams, Errol Barrow and Arthur Lewis came into town, so you could imagine all this added fuel to the fire, so to speak. I think Williams was the first to come. It was an official visit and what I remember most about it is my own part in the thing. At the cocktail party that Jagan had at his house, the Red House, Williams buttonholed me after about five minutes and you know how he is, obsessive. For the whole night he talked to me alone. He is a man like that. He comes to a party and he finds somebody to talk to and he talks to that person, does not even say good evening or anything. And the reason he talked to me is that he apparently had visited the Ministry of Education and found a Greek Cypriot called Germanicus who had been sent there by UNESCO to help them reorganise their education system from top to bottom. Also in town was Harold Drayton and his wife, they were the advisers of the government and Jagan had already taken the decision to bring Lancelot Humben to be in charge of tertiary education and the University [of Guiana]. Those decisions [to break away from the University of the West Indies system] had been taken before I got there. I threw a spanner in the works immediately. I said we can't do this at all. We have to have a much wider discussion about education. The government can't simply do a thing like this without a regional debate of some kind to say what it thinks about the UWI and to say why it's leaving. I was very young and very junior so nobody listened much to what I was saying. They said I made a lot of noise. So I said let us send for Arthur Lewis, if you don't want to listen to me. Lewis was still the Principal of the University, let us send for Lewis and let him make a case for staying in the UWI and for the development of regional higher education and the extremely complex situation with these 12 territories. Lewis certainly came and he outlined to them all the reasons why he thought they should stay in the UWI; not only educational reasons but also the federal question. Then he proposed to them that if they wanted he would establish a campus in Georgetown on the same terms as the campus had been established in St Augustine; the liberal arts college and all that went with that. Lewis was very arrogant, I must tell you that. Lewis is a man, he is like Jimmy Carter. I briefed Jimmy Carter on three occasions when he came to Haiti. I tell you, I have never met anybody who does not listen like that, listens only to himself. Lewis is like that. Of course he is very bright, has a lot of statistics and he's a man that could crush you with arguments. He was not *sympathetique* with them. He was kind of standoffish; you take it or leave it. That was his attitude.

Jagan was talking a lot of foolishness, really, about 'People's University' and so on. It may be desirable, but how are you going to get there from where you are now? You have to answer that question – Lewis had no time for that at all. So he said, 'Alright, if you don't want to listen to me, I will suspend these meetings and I will go and talk to the American ambassador to see if we can get a commitment for them to pay for it,' and he did. They got American money to establish a liberal arts college in Georgetown and he came back triumphantly and he said its right there, I mean let's do it. And, of course, Jagan put his back up right away, nothing of the kind. He said 'I want a people's university and I want Humben there.' Humben was from England, he was a well-known natural scientist. Humben wasn't there in Georgetown at the time, but he was the *eminence grise* behind all their thinking. Lewis just left in a huff. He said if you all don't want it, okay. He never really tried to bring them across with persuasion; he was just bullying them with argument. So they went ahead and had their university and the great irony about it is that Jagan established the university and Burnham inherited it and it became not only a government department but a kind of KGB. Rodney couldn't get the job up there and there were absolutely no rules. He put his wife to head it and he brought a fellow who was at Cambridge with me, Dennis Irvine. He was the Vice Chancellor, but he was largely nominal. He was a reasonable, very capable fellow, but nobody really listened to him. He was largely titular and they went ahead and did what they wanted, violated every conceivable academic rule. That was the Lewis episode and that helped to stir the pot in Georgetown and then Williams came. Lewis really came first and this discussion was raging when Williams came and he went to the Ministry of Education and found this discussion going on. He wanted a neutral person to give him a brief on what was really happening, so he got Germanicus to brief him and lo and behold Germanicus told him that, 'I don't really know anything about this, the man who is behind all this is Best. Best is stirring up the trouble, confronting the government.' That is why Williams buttonholed me, as soon as he got to the party. He kept me there the whole night talking about all aspects of education – primary education, secondary education, university education and he was talking most of the time even though he was supposed to be talking to me. He subsequently left and went back to Trinidad, but before he left, he asked me whether I would come and advise Donald Pierre, who was the Minister of Education at this time, about what they were doing in Trinidad. My colleague from QRC and Cambridge, Ralph Romaine was then the Permanent Secretary, and he was the factotum of Williams, he did anything he wanted. He was subsequently decapitated. You know, Williams uses you and then he spits you out. But at the time he was riding high, very arrogant and I went to see Donald Pierre, I think it was a Saturday morning. We got to talking and after exchanging pleasantries he asked me 'Why did Williams ask you here; how many degrees have you got?' So I just exchanged a few more pleasantries with him and I left, didn't waste the time. He has no idea of education. He was a very foolish man. If you look at the early editions of *Tapia*, you will see that in one of the headlines of the paper, the headline writer in the Tapia office wrote 'The Agony of Donald Pierre,' it was some big issue in the Ministry of Education and the headline maker in the press who made the headline made a mistake and put 'The Asony of Donald Pierre.' We kept the headline. In any case I don't know how Williams ever expected that to work and I certainly couldn't work with Romaine. The Ministry of Education's senior technical officers were O. Braithwaite, Lloyd's brother and C.B. Gocking, he was very close to me and still remained close until his death. Romaine was just chewing them up, saying that when he was a boy at

QRC they discriminated against him. He is a very pathological
case. So much so that Roddy Robinson, [the first professor
of mathematics in St Augustine – he was a fellow of Trinity
College Cambridge when I went up there first] when he came
down here as professor, Williams appointed him as the head
of a commission to investigate Queen's Royal College, our old
school, which everyone was complaining about had fallen as
a school. Romaine was on this commission and Roddy told
me that one day while the commission was in full swing he
[Romaine] said 'Mr Chairman, excuse me, I would like to go
down in the audience and talk about my experience at QRC.'
And he went down and he harangued the commission about
when he was there and how they kept him back as a black
man, and all kinds of things. He was a very sick fellow. I mean
you can't be in a commission and say you are going down on
the floor to address the commission. That's the kind of man
Romaine was. So there was no chance of my ever working with
them. I wasn't looking for a job. I told you I was very rich at
the time. And that was Williams.

The third thing was Errol Barrow. Barrow came there not
too long before I left, maybe two or three months. And I was
detailed to take him around the country. It was a wonderful
and enchanting experience because Guyana is such a beautiful
place and most Guyanese not only don't know about it, but
can't know about it, they don't have the money, and the roads
are not there. You have to be a UN expert or a foreign Prime
Minister coming in to get all the vehicles and amphibious
planes, you have to pull out all the stops. We went everywhere
in the country, up in the old North West, up in Rupununi, all
up in Essequibo, in the tributaries and the Venezuelan border.
For me it was such an eye-opener, such an experience. We were
sitting all the time together, whether we were in planes or in
boats, I sat next to him and we talked. That is how Barrow and
I got to be very great friends. I wrote a piece which I think that
fellow Tony Payne in his book that he wrote about Caribbean
integration, quotes a bit from me, a manuscript in which I
proposed a way the Federation could be organised. At that
time he was considering alternative ways of approaching the

federal question. Barrow and I talked about it a lot while we were in the plane or the boat and we came to share a common position. I think that is why ultimately Barrow and the other two prime ministers, Burnham and Bird of Antigua came together to restart the federal movement through CARIFTA. Barrow was very profoundly influenced by those talks we had and we became very great personal friends. He would come to Trinidad anytime, stay at the Hilton and he would call me and I'd go down there, chat and meet people and whenever I went to Barbados I would go and see him. He actually asked me to give the feature address at one of his party conventions in the early 1970s. I don't remember which year it was, but the interesting thing about that occasion was that it was a big thing in Barbados. We talked a lot about what I should say and I proposed something like the Indian Civil Service for CARICOM then and certain institutions, central institutions that we needed to start off this thing. It was the lead in the Barbadian newspapers, it went on the wire services but it never came to Trinidad. The reason for that was that there was a man called, I won't tell you his name, who worked for [Eric] Williams in the *Guardian* who would systematically block any story by anybody not in the interest of Williams. Nobody wanted to give me any exposure. I was just coming up. I couldn't understand this at all and I asked someone and they said well you are really naïve to think that that is a story that could ever get into Trinidad's papers. Williams does not want anybody to see. So those are three episodes from my year in Guyana that add a little spice, and kept the pot boiling at every stage.

Origins of the Plantation Model

Let me tell you the other one, which was after I went back to Jamaica in 1964 and on my way spent the summer school in Puerto Rico. I then went back to campus, you know, and within weeks I was asked by McIntyre to come back to Port of Spain, to teach the course named Caribbean Economic Problems. That is when McIntyre, Kari Levitt and myself sat down in my flat in St Johns Road. It was a kind of transit camp. We stayed there, we spent a couple of weeks really, brainstorming and we began the whole exercise with something we called 'Model 2.'[28] The point of departure was Arthur Lewis, because Lewis had said that the colonial office and Benham and all them, regarded the black population, especially in Jamaica, as lazy and that if you raised wage rates that they would stay home; if they got more money they would stay home. Lewis said that this was absolute nonsense. The problem was that these people had their own stake in their own businesses and their own land. As soon as they got enough cash to meet their needs, they made all their investments, sweat equity, on their own properties. So this whole business of a backward sloping supply curve of labour, which was so prevalent in the discussions of so-called development economics in those days – we squashed it completely by showing perfectly rational reasons why labour should stay home. We started with that and we had a lot of diagrams and notes. One of the great tragedies of the fire that we had in Port of Spain in 1982 was that all of those things were burnt up; the original foundation of the plantation [model] in which people didn't know that McIntyre was involved at that early stage. That is what ultimately led, before I went to Montreal, to the piece I wrote that appeared in *Social and Economic Studies* as 'Working Notes Towards a Model of Pure Plantation Economy.'[29] That was the first thing to appear in print. It really had its origins there. That is what I was doing when I got back to Mona, although I had to leave again for several reasons. That was the time when I was working in Suriname – I was up and down as usual. But while I was in Mona, that is what we worked on and that produced that paper. It wasn't published until 1968. It was obviously there before.

AB: What were the intellectual influences that led you guys to begin to think about questions of the Caribbean as a plantation, the plantation economy?

LB: Well, the historical facts. My first three years in Mona I spent reading West Indian history in William Demas's office – really fascinating – and I had already had this inspiration from Demas's thesis that made me see right away that the Ricardian model that we were being taught in Cambridge didn't make any sense in the Caribbean. And there is a thing that I should tell you, although I had said that Demas was the real father of those ideas and he developed them, yet in some ways in the early stages, he was very hostile to them. I must have told you that Demas told me that the only thing important about New World was that the Latin American fellows thought it was important.

NG: What?

LB: I'm telling you. It was incredible. He thought I was wasting my time and that I could do better work. It was only later on that Demas became persuaded about it and persuaded only intellectually. He never translated it into his own work. People don't know that, I don't want to say that – see you have to be very careful about how you say these things. But he was the real father because that is where I first learnt about....

NG: What was his thesis about?

LB: His thesis was about the West Indies economy after emancipation, the case of Jamaica, Barbados and Trinidad. That was the first thing in my whole life that I ever learned about the West Indies.

AB: And his model was about the plantation?

LB: It was economic history. He described what happened. It was my very first exposure.

AB: Was that a PhD Thesis?

LB: It was a PhD thesis, but they only gave him the MPhil. They didn't give him the PhD. Both he and McIntyre did not get the PhD thesis and that tells you something. Because in those days, as Kari has written somewhere, and Sunkel has written, people sneered at anything called 'development economics,' anything about the colonies or the poor countries. They said 'what is that?' The professor at Cambridge said, 'Development economics – what is that?' So they were swimming against the stream in those days. To write about these countries – nobody considered that economics.

BM: The stream is back.

LB: The stream is back again, eh? Yes, a perfectly good piece of work and I gave a copy of it last year to Susan Craig, who is writing a book on Tobago and she is drawing very heavily on

Demas's analysis of Barbados. So Demas is really the spiritual father of the work but I believe that the reason he never took it up afterwards and thought that I was wasting my time was that he never recovered psychologically from the fact that they never gave him the PhD. If you read his work in that perspective you will see that he was hurt, very hurt, quite rightly, I think. The same thing with McIntyre. McIntyre was a very bright man, but he never showed any interest in serious work. He became an administrator very quickly and he would write things – policy things – but not fundamental academic things McIntyre showed no interest in it. I think it is the same thing, after the thesis thing he turned off and he went into another stream, which he was very successful at and so on. We have talked about it.

AB: So you have Demas and the first iteration is...

LB: [Lloyd] Braithwaite, [Elsa] Goveia, [Roy] Augier, especially Goveia.

AB: In what sense?

LB: Well, she was Professor of West Indian history and she brought out the book on the Leeward Islands and subsequently the other one, the historiography one.[30] Elsa was absolutely seminal, not only to me though, but she was such a good looking woman to start with. We were all in love with her.

NG: Charismatic.

LB: Yes. I used to go to her lectures and I wasn't a student in her class. A lot of people went to her lectures just to look at her the whole time. She was lecturing in West Indian history.

BM: You certainly kept this away from us. Lloyd has revealed this now.

LB: Elsa Goveia and Lloyd Braithwaite – those are the main ones and of course ISER was a hotbed of discussion of West Indian social scientists Raymond Smith, Braithwaite and Jayawardena and that is all we talked about.

AB: We've spoken of Raymond Smith, Elsa Goveia and Lloyd Braithwaite so there must be discussions about questions of social stratification, of Elsa's thing that crime comes out of the social framework; Raymond's thing on race and the family in Guyana. I'm trying to work through now: how does the plantation come up in these discussions?

LB: I am an economist and therefore I'm interested in economic aspects and fortunately the plantation economy, the plantation, is a microcosm of the economy. In fact, we argue that there was no society at the beginning because the plantation was a total institution. You had several societies alongside; there was no contact between them and no economic contact in terms of interdependence. So it made a bridge very easily from the microeconomics of the plantation to the macroeconomics of the society. What we did was to develop a general view of the whole region both in space and in time, so-called 'Models One, Two and Three,' and they constituted the four volumes that we finished in 1968 from which we have selected for this forthcoming volume.

AB: What was the reaction of people to the ideas that they were developing?

LB: Oh, it was tremendous excitement

AB: Like Elsa's reaction, Braithwaite's Raymond's?

LB: Elsa didn't know very much about it. We went to her thing as a kind of goddess. She would come to seminars in the evening of the kind we had, but there wasn't very much exchange with her personally. Lloyd was the most voluble person and Ray. Lloyd was very excited by it, very interested in it and very helpful in every way. M.G. [Smith] remained more or less aloof because in those days he and Lloyd were at loggerheads. Lloyd subsequently conceded that he [M.G.] was correct, in that Lloyd in his social stratification thesis failed to see the importance of the East Indian community. He treated them as outside the system and didn't see that he couldn't do that. He subsequently conceded that point, explicitly in an article, that M.G. was right. But M.G. was like Lewis. He was always triumphantly right.

AB: One of the things that fascinates me is that by that time he's into cultural pluralism so how does he relate to the plantation model?

LB: I read all the things that M.G. talked about beginning with Furnivall.[31] That was important, that was our seminal idea although both Ray and Lloyd at that time, and I think probably still, never abandoned, their position. Ray [Smith] thought that M.G. selected a piece of Furnivall that was not representative of the whole work and built a whole superstructure that couldn't carry and there's some truth in that. If you read Furnivall, it is almost in passing that he talks about plural societies. M.G. sounded very rich, though he had a too simple idea of political systems that were held together only by power. M.G. argued that as soon as the imperial power left you would get political violence and breakup of these states and the experience in Guyana seem to support it. I think with that it was unfortunate because even in Guyana, there's a much larger Guyanese culture and Caribbean culture that holds this thing together and the violence really is more a political phenomenon than you would think. I'm not saying it is not important, but Lloyd could not buy it at all in the early years. He probably mellowed later and conceded something to MG. I lost contact with him in those later years after he came here as principal [of UWI St Augustine].

AB: I'm trying to almost trace a genealogy, quite frankly, of the plantation. There's a 1958 conference in Columbia?

LB: I know it yes, with Vera Rubin.

AB: Published by The Institute for the Study of Man.[32] So what I am trying to work through now is, this is 1957, 1958 where there is a discussion of plantation, there's a discussion of stratification by Braithwaite, there's discussion of cultural pluralism by M.G., Franklin Frazier...

LB: Franklin Frazier.

AB: The American sociologist, he is talking and he is against Herskovits' argument of African survivalisms among African Americans.

LB: I know these materials very well.

AB: Is there a link; is there a kind of intellectual link?

LB: I read them very copiously, I read them all and we were very friendly with Vera.

LB: She came regularly; she was on the commission that they set up to evaluate the University, the Cato Commission. It was set up to evaluate the University of the West Indies sometime about that time in the late 1950s, just before I got there. Lloyd was very close to her, Ray was very close to her, M.G. and we all went to New York. So we knew the work very well and you could see that we have drawn on it. This business of African America, European America, and American America are [Charles] Wagley's concepts, you know?

BM: What about the Department of Economics at Mona? It is still very much dominated by a sort of mainstream – oriented neo-classicism. People like Cumper, I imagine, are there at this time?

LB: Yes, but Cumper was not like that. Cumper was a man grounded in Caribbean reality in my view. He was a weak personality. In a meeting, he would go with [Head of Department] Charles Kennedy. He would scarcely dissent, but really, Cumper's work is grounded in Caribbean reality.

BM: What were the reactions from the mainstream to what you were doing? What were the critiques and the social interactions?

LB: Cumper had an important piece, in which he was very critical of us, though, less of me than of anybody else. He said 'Best might be an exception to his criticism,'[33] not in those words but it was very intelligent. It wasn't a wild ideological critique. It was grounded in serious theoretical argument. I take it very, very seriously. I'm answering it now as a matter of fact. Cumper can't be said to be an unrepentant neo-classicist at all. Kennedy was. Kennedy didn't understand anything. He tried to tell us that the Keynesian model, once you could open it up, and let exports rather than investment be the driving force of the economy, no problem. He said 'no problem.' What? What you talking about? He couldn't see that this was a whole social system that had different origins, a different evolution a different orientation from the Keynesian economy. He was unrepentant. He left there thinking the same thing in spite of so much argument in the country. But I don't think he read very much outside of economics, did he?

NG: I doubt it.

NG: Keynesian and Domar type theory for the open economy. I'll tell you something though, about that, which is how Kennedy got to be there in the first place. When Lewis came, he was appointed as Professor of Economics and before he took the job up, he was kicked upstairs – that's not a good phrase for it – he was recruited to be Principal of the University and to manage the transition, from the University as a college of the University of London to becoming a fully independent national university. He immediately got into conflict with the West Indians, all of them. Although Roy Augier would not admit it, I always tell him that. He never admits it, or Rex [Nettleford], I don't know why the two of them hold to this thing. But I was there and I'm sure it's correct that Lewis was very hostile to West Indians and very disdainful of them. He thought that West Indians were expecting special treatment for being black and for being West Indian; that the only way they could advance was to perform. He kept telling people how he had nobody to talk to. He didn't [talk] with Braithwaite, and certainly not me, or any of the people there that he could talk to. He never came to the seminars at ISER, he never came once. And therefore, he said openly, he sent to Oxford and told them he wanted a young, British economist that he could talk to. He wanted a young British economist to whom he could talk, and that's how Kennedy came, to talk to Lewis. Lewis was real Afro-Saxon you know [laughs]. Lewis was a complete Afro-Saxon. Although he was unquestionably a West Indian, the orientation of his work in so far as it wasn't done in Britain and when he came here he was a very serious scholar. He wrote a lot very quickly, but he had this problem of not having West Indians with the right qualities to talk with and of all people to get, he gets Kennedy. Kennedy was inarticulate [laughs], you know. Nobody could follow what he was saying. He landed up with Kennedy saying he wanted somebody to talk to. Did you know Kennedy?

BM: I didn't know him personally.

LB: Smoking his pipe and nobody really knew what he was saying. He never finished his sentences and that's a very sad story. I had written that Kennedy set back the Department of Economics thirty or forty years, because he held up the changes at the time when it was fertile, when it could be done. And of course, it hardened, it became more and more difficult to bring change in the Faculty of Social Sciences as it expanded and it was a going concern. It is hard to change a going concern; it's much easier to go on, as you are going on. But it was a small outfit when Kennedy came and we could have changed it. Beckford and I agitated for it and they never thought that they could introduce a course in Caribbean economics as bad as it was. Kennedy said there is not material to teach Caribbean economics, none at all. This was rhetorical of course, [he said] 'You all go and bring material, show me what you can teach from.' And Beckford and I brought a whole lot of stuff, a whole concept of what was possible. Beckford ultimately published [this episode] called the 'Struggle for Relevance' out of that debate. He [Kennedy] didn't intend at all to concede it, he never thought we would be able to deliver something cogent and rational, that we could teach about the West Indies. They conceded something called 'Caribbean Economic Problems.' What we wanted was that the main macroeconomic course should be taught in terms of Caribbean institutions, which is quite different from bits and pieces from Jamaica and Trinidad. We have not recovered from that yet. Up to now, it's going on; we are teaching the same thing. Of course, it's very hard to change it now. You have to have a very strong Principal and a council to take a stand and say let us take a year off. You would need to take a year off to retool and restructure if you were to turn it around, because the exams are coming on you and students are coming on you and you can't stop it.

The Cuban Revolution

AB: Can we shift focus a little to ask your view of the Cuban revolution?

LB: I've been a great supporter of it, though I'm also quite a critic of it, less of a critic than a supporter. It is for this reason, which follows directly from the work that I'm involved in: I don't think Castro had any idea when he came to office that Cuba was a Caribbean country. He had this fanciful idea from Guevara that Cuba was a Latin American country and he didn't understand that the most important, single thing about Cuba was that it came to be dominated by Afros, and the sugar plantation, in

304

the nineteenth and twentieth centuries and became like one of the other islands. He expended vast energies and resources trying to make the revolution in Latin America. This is what I said when [Castro] said he was a Marxist-Leninist and I told you about that meeting in Warsaw, which people thought was such a major statement. I told them in very simple terms that Cuba was a Caribbean country and the term I used in the meeting, was that the soft underbelly for them is that we are all sugar countries in the region. Although it looked very difficult, because there are the British colonies and so on, I thought he [Castro] could have made a vital connection because all these people understood sugar, understood the exploitation of sugar. He had to make a field for them and it would have upset all the politics in the region, which he couldn't do in Latin America where he didn't know anybody and nobody paid him any mind. In fact, when I was in Chile, [Salvador] Allende was in office and I spent a week and a half or two weeks there working at the University of Santiago and the Catholic University as well. Good friends, Kari and Norman were there. Everybody was obsessed with Allende and the CIA. We expected him to fall; they were all over him; it was only a matter of time. It was a test case and we knew he would lose. But I asked them; everywhere I went I asked them, what do you think of Fidel? Because Fidel was of course the other test case of a Marxist regime in this hemisphere. They said Fidel is a very good boy but he is *mas tropical*, he's too tropical for us.

NG: That was exactly the phrase they used, *tropical*.

LB: What they meant was 'Caribbean.' They saw that about him, but he didn't see it about himself. He learnt of course, because he subsequently turned the revolution towards Africa. When I was there I met many people in Equatorial Guinea, in Congo where he sent a lot of medical people and, and of course, he sent a lot of troops to Angola, which is right next door to Congo. I met a lot of people who knew the Cuban troops, and knew about the debate and they fully understood that Castro had become converted to say what he said, that Cuba is an Afro-Latin country. He made the shift. Many people wouldn't have the honesty to do. He made a fundamental error from the start and because of this, I think, he fell back on the Soviet Union. He didn't have the information. I won't say he didn't have the courage because I don't think he knew. He had two choices. He had a choice between going with the Caribbean and going with Latin America, which really meant going with the Soviet Union and he took the second choice. You could see why in terms of immediate material considerations, it was hard not to, with the United States breathing down his back, but he had to take the chance because they would never have suspected the revolutionary potential of the Caribbean. Nobody would have suspected it, but I think it would have been there, because the objective conditions, if I may use that Marxist term, were there in the region. He had the authority, certainly, because he made everybody sit up, everybody in the world, far less in the region. And he had to make a bid really, to make some kind of permanent alliance with countries that could endure, that could last in the alliance. He didn't and that had a lot of consequences including the state of siege. The thing about the Cuban revolution is that the state of siege has continued all along. The kind of government, democratic government you can have when you don't have a siege, you can't have when you have a siege. I still think that he's gotten the habit of, he's drunk with central power and that he could have decentralised and devolved a lot more than he has, and I've said so when I was in Havana the second time. I saw two weeks of the National Assembly, they were televising it and Fidel would always talk about the revolution as if it took place yesterday. He always talked about what we are going to do and what we will do, all in future tense. It was quite remarkable, but the thing about that assembly that struck me most was that he gave everybody else three minutes to speak, and every time he spoke, he spoke for an hour and a half at least, sometimes three hours. It really is the voice of one. I think that's a Caribbean pathology, a Caribbean disease. We have the same thing. Williams was just like that, and Manning is very low quality but he's just like that. I'll not mention Burnham and Bird and Gairy and Bradshaw and that's why Archie's book [*The Hero and the Crowd*] is important. That's why Archie's book was important because he had the paradigm there and you have to apply it all these other places, *Mutatis Mutandis*, their differences and so on. But I think Castro has made some fundamental errors and those two are the main ones, which is his failure to see how important the Caribbean was, though he sees it now. Did you see in my piece last week, I said that when he was in Barbados and he was passing by, [Michael] Holding was there and they were playing cricket. And like W.G. Grace he said he wanted to bat and he said on that occasion that the main links between Cuba and CARICOM should be Cricket and the University. You know that I'm involved in a big cricket movement in Cuba? I sent them a ton and a half of materials – bats, bails, stumps, clothes, boots, everything. There is a league going there, all West Indian. I have a cousin who is in the National Assembly, her name is Alelia Best.

AB: Just how did New World relate to *Savacou*, which came a little later?

LB: We were very friendly, because of Eddie [Kamau] Brathwaite and Ken Ramchand. They saw themselves more and we saw them too as a literary journal. We were more in social sciences so there wasn't any conflict, although I think there was internal conflict in their journal.

AB: Brathwaite has a piece on Caribbean studies where he argues that the problem with the plantation economy is that you guys did not look at look at what he calls 'the inner plantation.'

LB: I know that argument but I don't buy it. I mean what is the substance of his argument?

BM: That the sort of cultural and psychological inner workings of people...

AB: What he calls the subjectivities...

BM: ...are not sufficiently appreciated.

LB: No. At that time this was a first reading of the situation that was new, which we never knew. We were economists, so we were doing our jobs as economists in the first instance. But I certainly have done that since. All my writings in, in the newspaper which are academic writings, I've dealt with the sociology, I've dealt with the psychology, I've dealt with the culture, every aspect; developing a whole theory of Caribbean civilisation.

AB: What is the distinction you're making, if at all any, between a theory of Caribbean civilisation and a theory of Caribbean society?

LB: No, there is no difference. I showed you last night, Huntington has a long list of things, about cultures and societies and civilisations and these are just tools. You have civilisations. If you think in terms of concentric circles, that's the outer circle. Then within a civilisation you have societies. The thing that distinguishes one civilisation from another is that the participants in the civilisation share the culture. There are differences of course compared to other societies, but compared to the rest of the world there are similarities which are more important. I use these terms interchangeably. When I am talking about a specific society, dare I say, Jamaican society, or I may say West Indian society, depending on the scale of my canvas, I am talking about a specific set of arrangements. When I say culture it is much wider, it's a wider reference. And when I say civilisation it is a much wider reference still.

The Legacies of New World

BM: If you were to try to trace the living legacies of New World what would you say that the main institutional as well as theoretical ones are in the contemporary Caribbean?

LB: Well I will start with the institutions first, because we dealt with it cursorily yesterday but we should have dealt with it a lot more. I think that in 1968 what happened was that we simply changed the name of the *New World* to *Tapia*. We rescued it from something that had very little to do with what we really stood for in terms of method in terms of this whole epistemic thrust and we carried on our work. You can see what the consequences are now. When Walcott, for example, got his Nobel Prize, we could go back to our *Tapia* newspaper and find dozens of articles about his life and work and people thought this was a political paper, a party organ, that this was the high point of our involvement in political competition for control of the state. They told you what our preoccupations were and even when the elections were over we founded the Institute and we founded the *Trinidad and Tobago Review*. These, I think, are some of the more farsighted decisions I have ever made, to keep us in a kind or orientation, a certain kind of work, a certain kind of community. So in terms of institutions, I will say without any boastfulness, but at the same time without any fear of contradiction that the Tapia House Group has continued the work of the New World seamlessly, without fuss, institutionally. Because of that we have retained a lot of relationships with people who have gone in other directions politically and explicitly, and that didn't make any difference to us because of the kind of organisation we are. We are not competing for anything, not even for political office. I think we made a miscalculation [in contesting Trinidad and Tobago general elections] in 1976, not a mistake. We didn't fully understand how the political system worked. We knew a lot about it but we never thought we would get so few votes. We didn't understand that unless you're within one of the two ethnic parties it does not matter how good you are or how much support you have, you are not going to get votes because people don't see it as an option. We had to break that up and I broke that up because I conceived of what became the National Alliance for Reconstruction [NAR]. As soon as we lost the election in 1976 I wrote a paper in the no.75 edition which I numbered and circulated to a whole lot of political people in the country suggesting that we have to form a 'party of parties' – this became a household word in this country – to move the PNM. I set out a whole structure as to how it could be done. We gave up the idea of participating in the competition for power after the election of 1976. We ran in 1981 but only as a bridge to help the creation of the party of parties. I didn't run in 1986, for example because they weren't doing what I thought they should be doing. I was one of the four leaders. Both Leroy and Lincoln Myers and other [Tapia members] ran. We had several ministers in the government, four ministers I think, but I didn't go nor did the core of Tapia, because we didn't think that they were fulfilling anything like the requirements to build a 'party

of parties.' They wanted to move Williams and that was all
and they never evolved beyond that. So institutionally I don't
think there is any problem. Epistemically, it is more complex
and it is bound to be because New World in the first instance
was not a political party to begin with. It was a very broad
front of different conceptions and perceptions. Because it was
manifestly a university institution and not a political institution
outside the university it could handle all these differences, as
nobody was competing for anything then. Ideas, simply ideas
contested – that's all. I don't think we can lay claim to be the
only inheritors of New World. We are certainly the main one
and we are the vector on which it continues, because we have
an institution, we have a journal and so on. But the ideas were
spread all over and even those people like C.Y. for example,
or Brewster or McIntyre in their different ways who were not
fully New World, were partly New World. A lot of their ideas
crossed with us and they have carried these things. Brewster
in particular, I find has been one of the most intelligent
interpreters of the Caribbean condition I could wish to hear
or see. After he left the university he continued to write very
sensible stuff of the kind that I support myself. But he is not
in New World or Tapia or anything like it. So there is a wide
spread of the ideas all over the region in different people, in
different ways and they are doing what they see to be the right
thing. It is a much wider front of New World discourse.

Integration and Regionalism

BM: You spoke specifically of the connection to CARIFTA with
      Barrow etc. In the contemporary moment, a month before the
      signing of the CSME, how do you see the New World influence
      on Caribbean integration?

LB: It is having very little influence. All it did was to midwife it, to
      bring it into existence but this is a whole other discussion that
      we have to have and we can't have it here. We need a whole
      conference on CARICOM and I will tell you what my
      interpretation has been and it is all written down. My argument
      is that at no stage was CARICOM itself able to evaluate the

real significance of the break up of the Federation. Because they haven't done that they have gone entirely in the wrong direction. They are still on that wrong path, not going anywhere really, just *ad hoc* with no conception of what the task is and what the requirements, the measures are to bring a regional integration movement into being, of the kind that we had in mind when we midwifed it in 1966. I think that the real impact of the break up of the Federation was that it created 12 jurisdictions where there had only been one before. Nobody in the West Indies ever thought that the British would allow any of the islands singly to become independent. The whole mindset of the region was of a dominion with one government to face the outside world and to face the decisions inside. We were just thrown into confusion by the fact that we now had to get twelve entities to agree to everything. It required a completely different institutional framework and different approaches. We didn't do that. We kept thinking that these things would be easy. Demas came along after the early years when nothing much happened and he designed the Treaty of Chaguaramas and tried to bring the thing back on the rails. Nobody ever took it seriously until 1989. Nobody could tell you what the Treaty of Chaguaramas was. It was paper transaction. But what happened was that in order to make it work, Demas did what Lewis had done before which is to make CARICOM itself, the thirteenth state or whatever number, be it ten or twelve. He made CARICOM a state of which he was the prime minister. When Lewis had been there with the federation, Lewis made the university the eleventh state and he was the prime minister and he dealt with prime ministers on an equal basis. Therefore, the person became more important than the institution and Demas recreated this with CARICOM. He could call any Prime Minister anytime in the middle of the night. Demas could call any Prime Minister or turn up in the country and knock at the Prime Minister's door 'I want to see you,' and they developed a whole decision making structure that did not depend on institutions. It really depended on being able to persuade any given prime minister on any given thing at any given time. CARICOM has continued in this way. It has never set up any machinery for decision-making that could commit countries institutionally above the persons. It is all about the head, the heads, everything is the heads. You never hear of another minister making a statement out of CARICOM and you never hear anybody making a statement out of CARICOM in their own country. There is no discussion in the party, there is no discussion in the parliament and there is no discussion in the public. It is only now that they are getting frightened over the future, especially the business community. They have not brought the population in at all. The population does not have the foggiest idea of what CARICOM is about, or the ACS [Association of Caribbean States] is about or the CSME [Caribbean Single Market and Economy] is about. They read these things in the papers and they don't think it has anything to do with them. It was not brought into active consideration in any important place. Until they understand this and see that it requires two things, they are not going to make any advance. The first thing it requires is all this talk about implementation, this business of having a commission. Now I am not against a commission, I think we need executive mechanisms to carry things on. Obviously you need that, but Ramphal, Demas and McIntyre, never brought to the fore that the problem of implementation was *not* a problem of implementation. You can't have for 20 or 25 years Prime Ministers meeting twice a year and taking decisions about all kinds of things and they don't implement one. That is not an implementation problem. If the Prime Minister can't get the passport things that they agreed on about a hundred times now and it never happens, that can't be, it must be something much deeper. The real problem is that all the political leaders are mortally afraid of being a Manley, Norman I mean; of making decisions that are altruistic and good for the region, but will kick them out of power. Nobody is taking that chance. Unless you get mechanisms inside the country for building consensus – a very crucial thing – you are not going to get anything implemented because nobody is going to take a chance. You hear a lot of talk about this CCJ [Caribbean Court of Justice], that's not going anywhere, because Panday is not going to allow Manning to do it. The ones that they can get without a majority or with a simple majority [they will do]. Anything that requires constitutional change, where the opposition can block it, they are going to block it. In every country, it does not matter what they are saying before, because that means that they are going to get into office. If you want to put your head on a block, that is your business. I think we made a very big mistake in devoting so many resources, expending so many energies in trying to bring down governments or change governments and I feel that the educated elites especially in social and political science should have devoted much more attention to creating mechanisms of consensus-building inside countries and within the region. That is what New World did in a very microcosmic kind of way. It has made what turned out to be possible, possible. In my article I mention two institutions that have achieved this in the history of the modern West Indies, the first is the Caribbean Labour Congress. It did this in the 1930s and 1940s. That made it possible to have the Federation because there is a whole fraternity of people in all the islands talking to one another, conferences, all kinds of things about the question of integration. When the time came they broke up, of course, for reasons that we can't explore. But they 'midwifed' that and then with CARIFTA, again, we put these ideas about and it gave certain prime ministers the will to start something. I think that we need much more of this. Now I am not saying this as a critique, because I understand that one of the reasons why it didn't happen was that centrifugal forces were set in train by the mere factor of independence and people looked inward. Plus the fact that the upheaval of 1970 induced all these governments to prevent people from speaking in other countries. Williams actually put people out of here. He refused to let C.Y. Thomas come to work, [Bill] Riviere and [Pat] Emmanuel. There was a state of terror in the university among the intellectual classes; people were afraid to speak. The kind of cross talk that you needed across the region to create a climate for consensus on certain seminal questions never happened. I think part of the reason for that was that the educated elites of the university including yourself did not see the importance of this and too much time was expended with the whole Marxist approach of trying to get governments out of the way too quickly – what I call the Rodney approach and the Bishop approach, which I never supported although I was very friendly with both men. I told Bishop so when I went to see him. I quoted a piece yesterday from Allan Harris which he said one week after the takeover, it is not something on reflection that we stood for. I was teaching in Martinique and I came home after what happened in Grenada and I found a *Trinidad and Tobago Review* ready to go to press. I changed it and I put Allan Harris' article in the front-page editorial. I thought it was so important for what we stood for in the midst of all the other things. So many people supported Bishop and I think it destroyed him because I don't think he had any concept of what was required anywhere in the Caribbean and certainly not in Grenada. As Allan Harris said, what the West Indies required was a revolution and what we got was a coup. You change the government but where is the architecture, what was the idea? These fellows were reading Plekhanov and Lenin in the cabinet. They were playing the ass. You have a country to run, you have a real Caribbean situation here and they had no theory of the society, they had no theory of the economy; all this rhetoric about the people and the masses. You have to get rid of that. That does not make any sense. We want concrete analysis where we are situated. I hold the position that we made a mistake as a class, not as a social class in the Marxian sense but as a core of people, of elites being put out by the university who are to choose how they are going to intervene in the political system. I think we intervened in the wrong way and we have set the West Indies back 30 or 40 years because we have entrenched all these one-man regimes. In every country in the Caribbean it is like that. Nothing is going on in the Caribbean, nothing is going on. Patterson is not doing anything, never did. And Manning is doing nothing, he is just spending money; he has huge sums of money. [Owen] Arthur was the only man with any promise, I certainly thought so. He is the first Caribbean politician that

I ever endorsed. I really thought that he had the wit and the skill, the energy and the courage to do something different and he did start out that way. He did try to bring Barbados together, but what scuttled Owen Arthur was the opposition in his own party, all his colleagues in the BLP opposed him. 'What the hell are you doing?' They were anti-Federal really; they didn't want to incur the cost. He was prepared to incur the cost. He said a lot of very seminal things in a short period of time and he wrote a very important piece that is published in that book by [Kenneth] Hall.[34] He was a good Prime Minister but he is dead now you know. He became quite a tyrant.

Reflections on a Caribbean Life

I consider myself to be the luckiest man in the modern West Indies because of when I came back to Mona the first time and how I came back. I gave up all that graduate work and then I came back. I was *tabula rasa*, I was clean, unsullied and I started to work in a completely different direction from what was expected of me. I came to understand very early, because of the luck of the draw with the open lectures and the seminars that the thing was to build intellectual institutions. Without that nothing is going to work. You have to build elites in this country who believe in this country and who put the country first. You can't build that by rhetoric. You have to have concrete things that people can believe in and see that these things mean something over a long period. I was lucky to have been thrown into that pot as soon as I came back and I was young. I was lucky to be young. I was 22 when I came back. So there you have a situation in Jamaica, you have a very young fellow, coming back. I am not a fool also and I was really set on the right track from the beginning and then only by accidents thereafter. The fact that my contract was not renewed and I went back to Europe or to the tremendous education I had from being in Europe and from there going to Guiana, these had a momentum of their own right up to the present. But I think that if you ask me what the most important thing about me is, I would say that it was what I learned on my father's farm. I am the second of eleven children, real poor people, you know? People don't know that – they call me a *petit bourgeois*, just because I went to Cambridge and Oxford. But I am poor people. I grew up where you only had one meal a day. You get one meal a day at about 4:00. We had coffee in the morning or cow's milk. I was the second of eleven children and my father was working here on campus in the Imperial College of Tropical Agriculture. He was an artisan there, a carpenter. He also had a cane farm at the same time, because it was close by. Being the first boy and the second child I immediately became the leader of all these people whether I liked it or not. I had to make decisions every morning: what we going to do, and every time we go out in the garden, are we going to plant cassava, are we going to plant sweet potato, are we going to reap this, reap that. We had cows, we had pigs, we had ducks and I was the decision maker in all of this. So I started my life very early as a decision maker and a manager of money.

These are the resources I brought into New World. I never told anyone of my early life. The most important thing is that I learned to observe empirical things. You could plant all the cassava you like, and all the sweet potato you like and have it flourishing and one day a cow come in and mash down the whole blasted thing and eat up the whole thing and you have to start over. You have to guard against that and that was confirmed when I came to Jamaica to work for the FAO. The Jamaican concept I got, I knew, but didn't have the concept for, was 'every little thing.' If you so foolish as to plant only one thing and a cow come and bite all that down or drought get it or rain, you starve. So you have to plant 'every little thing' in case. You never know. Growing up on my father's farm, I learnt that; to observe all these things and plan. You take account of every little thing, and you are looking at the whole picture; every time you see where you stand. So you could eat, because we never had any money. We got money once a year – real money – which was when we got the money from the cane. A good capital sum, we just used it to buy flour and oil and so on, every week with the salary. You know we used to 'trust' and pay at the end of every month. You know what trust is? And we never had any cash except at the end of the sugar year. You have to have corn drying inside somewhere. You have to have sweet potato. You have to have dasheen, tania and all these things would be coming in at a different time. They were ripening at a different time and ready to eat. I learnt these things and when I went to QRC at age 11, I was a big man. Other fellows that went to that school were little boys because they didn't have those experiences. They were very sheltered. But I had a very clinical eye about QRC and I never paid much attention to what they were doing. While I was there I would stay with a company and do well academically, but I wasn't really a school man at all. I had a whole life outside of school. I had women already by the time I started going to school – you know our culture. You had a club called the Flamingos and it was made up of boys from the two main schools in the country, in Port of Spain – St Mary's and QRC. We didn't see why we should be playing against one another and not playing with each other on the same team. So we founded this club. And the reason I could invent this concept of 'doctor politics' was because I lived it. In one year I was elected as captain, president, secretary and treasurer – real centralised power. That rescued me to be a democrat. Because all I found out from total power is that when you have total power you have no power. Sometimes these fellows tell you 'do what you like,' they say 'alright, you do what you want, you are in charge.' You know, you will never find out anything. You will never find out the truth, they will never tell you what they are thinking. As soon as you leave, they are having a different discussion going on about you. I learnt the only way to do anything was to be a democrat. I did not play the role of a maximum leader although I had the position. I was very energetic, I was not much older in age than these fellows, but I was a much bigger man. My house was the centre, where they kept all the gears. I would wake up everybody on Monday morning at half past five to go and fix the pitch and put down the matting. The game started at nine o'clock and then we played from nine to one. Then we played in another competition from two to six. I am in charge of all these processes. That was my life outside of the school. It was quite a learning experience. If I didn't, because of the luck of the draw, understand that you cannot have total power and if you have it already that you will find out nothing, I would not have succeeded in building organisations and institutions thereafter in my life. Wherever I go I start something immediately. And it has to be democratic or else it can't work. If people don't feel committed to it, that it is theirs, you split up in months.

BM: Lloyd, you speak about learning methods of operation; learning leadership and democracy, but is there a dimension having to do with self-confidence, a psychological dimension? You allude to it in relation to McIntyre and Demas and their self confidence being shattered by a particular experience. But what is it about your life experiences that obviously gave you this sense that you can form institutions; that you can rethink Marx or whatever it may be? Is it just you or is it a setting?

LB: Both. It can't be one or the other because you always have a degree of subjectivity. It does not matter what you are thinking; there must be dialectical relationship between the two. I think the important things, and I've said it many times here and before, are accidents and luck. Things have to happen to fall your way. Some people are like that and some people are not like that. Until I got sick, since 1996, and my health began to flag, everybody used to think that I was immortal. I never got sick; I never went to hospital even one time in my life. Nothing ever happened to me; I was well. When we brought out the *Tapia* newspaper I was coming back from abroad, I can't remember where, on a Sunday night and the PNM were having their annual convention in Tobago. It occurred to me that this was the time when we should start our paper, that this was the moment to do it. I came back on the Sunday and we had our regular executive meeting on the Monday night and I put it to the Tapia people that we should start our paper. They agreed to it and by Friday the paper was on the streets. I raised the money, got the copy, got the advertising, supervised the publication, the printing, everything in one week and Lloyd [Taylor] can tell you that I did not sleep for three days. We just went from beginning to end. Now that kind of behaviour you could only do if you were really fit and well. You pay a price for it and I am paying the price for it now. But you have to have the luck of being healthy. Demas told me that before he died. I went to see him at the hospital and I held his hand. Roy Thomas was there and a few other fellows and you could see that he knew it was the end because so many of his friends came to see him at the same time. I held his hand for a long time, for about an hour and we talked and joked. He said 'Lloyd I want to tell you something. People say a lot of things about me but what they don't know about me is that all my life I have been struggling against ill-health, all my life I have been struggling against ill-health.' I am just the opposite. I never had a cold for years. You know luck has a lot to do with it, constitution has a lot to do with it, and accidents have a lot to do with it. If you are able to take advantage of the opportunities that you get and you have the courage to believe in what you are doing and don't let anybody tell you what to do, then you have a chance to do something different. Of course, there is no law that says that you are going to succeed. We cannot talk, even to think that we have succeeded yet. We have endured, certainly and we have done certain things and we are still here to pose certain vital questions, including questions of power, but you don't know what is going to happen tomorrow.

You know we had that fire in Port of Spain in 1982 that set me back? I can't imagine. I lost all my books of 25 years of collecting. I lived in all these Caribbean countries and I was a big collector of world documents. I had a vast archive and library. All the newspapers I had bound. Lennox Grant who had been the editor of *Tapia*, said it was a great irony for an organisation like the Tapia House Group which was so scrupulous about collecting materials and archiving them and ordering them, should have a fire like that. We lost everything – three floors, three floors. So much so that I could not look at it, I could not look at it. I would stand up outside at the place next door, one of the houses on the property that was not caught in the fire and I would feel weak, my knees would just buckle just to think of what had happened. That was January 24, 1982 and I decided to go away; to leave the country for a while and do some international work. I wrote to McIntyre who was in UNCTAD at the time, to tell me what jobs were on offer, to make me an offer of those things they had available. He sent me about half a dozen jobs which were going in UNCTAD and one of them that they offered me definitively. I spent five years in Africa, three years and then I came back in 1986 for three months and then I went back for another year and three quarters. That was also a part of my life that people don't know anything about. It was a great experience. I would like to go back now. I was able to bring a lot of my experience, a lot of my skills to bear on that job that I did, the *Chef de Mission*. When I got there, the secretariat where I worked was in such a state of disorder that most of the technocrats never came to work, all had jobs somewhere else. No work was done and I beat it into shape very quickly. I organised a programme of work and by the time I left, everybody was coming to work in the nights, Saturdays, Sundays, you can't imagine. One thing I remember about it is that when I was leaving they had quite a lot of parties for me. Then they had the big one at the end and all the secretaries spoke and all the big wigs and so on spoke. Then at the end of it a small secretary, a very junior man – he was 35 – said 'I want to say something about Mr Best' And of course all these people talking and they butter you up – you're bound to, that is what this whole thing is about. He said, I want to say something of Mr Best [in French] 'He is a real leader, he's very tough as nails, he's very demanding and he always forgives – *Il pardon.*' That is the best thing that happened to me in Africa. Nobody asked him to say it. After all the buttering up and plenty lies, he came out and said what he really thought. I really cherish that. I came home very happy.

BM: I noticed that you left out 1970–73 and I want to say that you were my first economics lecturer, indeed, one of very few economics lecturers, because I then went on to do other things which did not involve the formal discipline of economics. On the question of energy: I recall you had a very early morning class that you insisted that we come to at six o'clock. As you know a young undergraduate at the age of 17 when I came, getting up at six, having a class at six after a hectic night is a very difficult task. I also want to say for the record that by far, you had the most profound influence on my young mind. It's true that I did not necessarily follow your recommendations politically, but at this more advanced age the legacy of that influence on my own thinking and my ability to move beyond a certain frame of reference is profound.

LB: Well I am very happy to hear that. You can only really find out about yourself from your students. You can fool yourself that you know, that you have self-knowledge and all that, but your students see things in you that you don't know are there. Like this young secretary.

I am happy to have been able to serve and to still be here. Last year at this time they thought that I wouldn't be here at this time, a year later. They had a cocktail party, a birthday party for me. There were 250 people there. They all rallied because they thought they wouldn't see me again. I was very, very sick with the prostate. For two months it was driving me mad. But I've put on a lot of weight and I am much better at the end of the year than I was at the beginning. Nobody knows how long this Indian summer might last, but I am glad we were able to do this. It is long over due.

AB: Could I just ask one last question, Lloyd. One thing that has always struck me about your work is your optimism, in spite of what has happened in the Caribbean region.

LB: That is what they say – I am the eternal optimist.

AB: And I just want to ask you, what drives that optimism and how do you see the Caribbean?

LB: Well I wouldn't call it optimism. People say that and I notice it of course, I hear it everywhere. I call it faith really, although I am not a religious person. I think it springs from insight and information about what this place is really about. I think that most of the people who behave as if they are important don't know anything about the place. If you see how we have transcended all the difficulties, all the hurdles that we were confronted with in the four hundred years. I mean 250 years of slavery or whatever it is. We have emerged from this, ready to pose all kinds of awkward questions for people. Once you understand that and how Wilson Harris said we have parked what he called our sleeping resources.[35] We weren't able to use all our talents, we weren't able use them because they were owned by other people. We had to do what they said. We parked all those ancestral resources somewhere else and we have been able to activate them under conditions of freedom. The time has been very short of course – people don't know that emancipation was only yesterday, in historical time. That's like a morning. I mean how many generations since 1838? Six generations? That's nothing! We had the strength to fight. I wrote a piece the other day about the household. People say that the West Indians have no family life. Nonsense! We couldn't have family life in the biological sense because there were no families in that sense. They were owned by people and they broke up the biological family. But we constructed the household so that your brother is not your biological brother; your brother is the man who comes up in the household with you. And your sister is the same. Your mother is not the woman who bore you; but the woman who gave you her breast to suckle and brings you up. And everybody who lives in the West Indies, especially a poor man like me, that is normal. I set out how this continued after emancipation when there was so much migration because there were no jobs. So that is why they went to Cuba and that is why they went to Panama and that is why they went to New York and all over and that broke up families. It didn't break up households. Your mother would go to Panama and she would send back home the money to your aunty and your aunty would bring you up and your grandmother or just a woman, not necessarily family at all, she brings you up. All this damn foolishness that they borrow from a sociology that is not relevant here, they won't describe the facts of the day. They keep talking about our families in a way that didn't make any sense of the empirical facts. They are saying that the family is broken up. It is not so. What I put forward in my view is that the educated elite in the Caribbean does not understand it, anything about us. They have broken up communities, broken up yards. All this so-called economic development, which is building housing and so on [is occurring] without any sensitivity to how we came to be. I see [Selwyn] Ryan is trying to deal with me....You saw his piece this morning in the paper?

AB: No I haven't.

LB: It's talking about 'Social Capital.'[36] I won't use that concept because it is Putnam's from North America[37] and I don't want any confusion with what he is saying. Because I wrote about ten pieces in the *Express* running, he is answering me, I am sure. His piece is continuing next week. He is talking about social capital and he is referring to some of the things to which I am referring which is that we constructed a whole set of community relationships in which, although families in the biological sense didn't function, people were circumscribed by community. You couldn't do what you like. A man in your village would tell you 'What the hell are you doing?' and he's not your family. There is a whole West Indian way to be properly described which we have not yet done. There is a little bit by Edith Clarke and Madeline Kerr, but in terms of systematic macro interpretations of Caribbean society, it has not been done. I am trying to do it in the way that I can here, in relation to ongoing discussion. My editors have to go through my work, and select and put these things together. I am dealing with them, [in] the only way I can deal with them, given my circumstances as somebody who does not work anywhere; I have to write to live. All my work has to come out in a form that's appropriate to my circumstances. I don't take grants from people. To start with, the first grant I took from anybody was recently from Ford and the Caribbean Development Bank and I had to earn that. C.L.R. James was saying that Best was a CIA man. Can you imagine that? You know, James was a man with no judgement at all. He was my very good friend but he had no judgement of people or situations. That is what I said at the conference. He is always right on the algebra, but when you come down to brass tacks and fair assessment of concrete situations he is a very muddled thinker. That's something about Best and James for some other time. We had to earn very cent.

So I have come to understand the West Indies in a certain way partly because of my study of the history of the place and partly because of my personal experience and that has made me who I am. I have a lot of faith in what is possible here. I told you yesterday that I am saying that 200 years from now we should envisage ourselves being the centre of diplomatic and intellectual life in the region; being a greater power in the world than the United States. What is to stop it? They don't have any better people than we have. And their numbers are going to work against them. Our small numbers are going to work for us if we have any sense. You can't build any civilisation unless you have elites, in the sense that I have talked about it; who have a concept of what is required and who can mobilise people who are working to get it done. You have to have a group of people in the society who can see very far ahead. And I am saying given the nature of the configuration of Caribbean society, where we have come from, the shortness of our history, the multiplicity of our peoples; all these things are positive things, if we could only see that. We have to deal with the Americans. You don't see me getting up cursing the Americans. I don't because it does not make any sense to rile them. The Americans don't think I am a radical; they are not afraid of me. I am the man you should be afraid of most. You don't know that? What I am doing is a dagger at their heart. But what is the point of saying 'What we're really going to do with the United States?' There is no point in saying that. We have to do the work and get ready for subsequent generations to mobilise themselves and take charge of the world. What is to stop us to do that? People think that big countries have a better chance than small countries but there is no evidence in history to suggest that, none at all. It is when you triumph and your ideas come on top that you become a big country. You attract populations and you get territory, but you have to start small. England was a very small country. By the eighteenth century England was in charge of the world with no resources to speak of. So I have a lot of faith in our possibility. I think we are going to break stride, I don't know how or when, but I am feeling that in Trinidad the population is very restless.

BM: I think that is Caribbean-wide.

LB: Because this independence thing: people have seen 40 years of independence and more and they can't see any difference in their condition, really. These governments give away millions of dollars for foreign experts for all kinds of stupidness. They have no self-respect at all. This government has all this money in Trinidad and I don't know if you know about the consultants they have here from everywhere. How long will the population take that? I believe we are going to have an accident. I believe we are going to have an accident, something that nobody anticipated, nobody planned. It will be an opening for fresh ideas and new people. Unfortunately for me I will not be there for it. But you all are still here and a lot of the younger generation is coming up. That's alright with me; alright with me.

Notes

1. The interview was held at Lloyd Best and Sunity Maharaj Best's home at 91 Tunapuna Road, January 15–16, 2005.
2. The Institute of Social and Economic Research [ISER] was the antecedent and research arm of the Faculty of Social Sciences at the University of the West Indies, Mona campus. It has now expanded to include centres at St Augustine in Trinidad and Cave Hill in Barbados and has been renamed the Sir Arthur Lewis Institute of Social and Economic Studies (SALISES).
3. Queen's Royal College (QRC) is the alma mater of many leading Trinidad and Tobago scholars, politicians and activists including, notably, C.L.R. James, Eric Williams, Karl Hudson Phillips, V.S. Naipaul and Best.
4. See William Demas, *Trends in the West Indian Economy, 1870–1913: A Comparative Study of Some Aspects of Economic Development in Jamaica, Trinidad and Barbados, 1870–1913*, MLitt thesis, University of Cambridge, 1956.
5. See, among others, C.L.R. James, 'The Artist in the Caribbean' in *C.L.R. James: The Future in the Present: Selected Writings*, (London: Alison and Busby Ltd., 1980), 183–90.
6. The break between James and Williams took place in October, 1961. See Selwyn Ryan, *Race and Nationalism in Trinidad and Tobago*, (ISER, 1974), 230–2.
7. C.L.R. James, *Party Politics in the West Indies*, Port of Spain, 1962.
8. Reference here is to the mythic full moon, rising over the Mona campus. Background to many a student romance.
9. Sealy was then Editor of the *Daily Gleaner.*
10. Alister McIntyre was then a researcher at the ISER. He later went on to distinguished careers at the UNDP and as Vice Chancellor of the University of the West Indies from 1988–98.
11. Archie Singham taught in the Department of Government at Mona in the 1960s.
12. Jagan was then Premier of British Guiana.
13. Clive (C.Y.) Thomas, the noted Guyanese economist, still teaches at the University of Guyana.

14. See Cheddi Jagan, *The West on Trial*, (London: Michael Joseph Ltd, 1966), 248–66 and Maurice St Pierre, *Anatomy of Resistance, Anti-Colonialism in Guyana, 1823–1966*, (London and Basingstoke: Macmillan Caribbean, 1999).
15. David de Caires, Managing Editor of the Guyanese newspaper *Stabroek News*, died in 2008.
16. Indian economist who worked with Best on a study of the economy of British Guiana for the Jagan government.
17. See Ray Kiely, *The Politics of Labour and Development in Trinidad*, (Kingston: UWI Press, 1996), 99.
18. See Philip Sherlock, and Rex Nettleford, *The University of the West Indies: A Caribbean Response to the Challenge of Change*, (London and Basingstoke: Macmillan Caribbean, 1990).
19. George Beckford's passport was seized by the Government of Jamaica after he travelled to Cuba in 1966. See Obika Gray, *Radicalism and Social Change in Jamaica: 1962–1972*, (Knoxville: The University of Tennessee Press, 1991), 137.
20. See Stephanie Black, *Life and Debt*, Tuff Gong Pictures, 2001.
21. See Archie Singham, *The Hero and the Crowd in a Colonial Polity*, (New Haven: Yale University Press, 1968).
22. See Havelock Brewster, 'Sugar: Our Life and Death' in *Readings in the Political Economy of the Caribbean*, edited by Norman Girvan and Owen Jefferson (Kingston: New World, 1971).
23. See Mighty Sparrow, 'Federation,' *Mighty Sparrow Volume 1*, Ice Records, 2000.
24. See Trevor Munroe, 'New World Philosophy and Marxist Ideology' in *Jamaican Politics: A Marxist Perspective in Transition*, (Kingston: Heinemann Caribbean, Lynn Rienner Publishers, 1990), 204–30.
25. See Lloyd Best, 'Independent Thought and Caribbean Freedom' in *New World Quarterly* 3, no. 4, (Cropover, 1967), 13–34.
26. See C.L.R. James, 'Every Cook Can Govern: A Study of Democracy in Ancient Greece' in *C.L.R. James: The Future in the Present: Selected Writings*, (London: Allison and Busby Ltd, 1977), 160–74.
27. See William Irwin Thompson, *Transforming History: A Curriculum for Cultural Evolution*, (Massachusetts: Lindisfarne Books, 2001).
28. See Lloyd Best and Kari Polanyi Levitt, *Essays on the Theory of Plantation Economy: An Institutional and Historical Approach to Caribbean Development*, (Kingston: The University of the West Indies Press, 2009).
29. See Lloyd Best, 'Outlines of a Model of Pure Plantation Economy,' *Social and Economic Studies* 17, no. 3 (1968).
30. See Elsa Goveia, *Slave Society in the British Leeward Islands at the end of the Eighteenth Century*, (New Haven: Yale University Press, 1965) and Elsa Goveia, *A Study on the Historiography of the British West Indies to the end of the Nineteenth Century*, (Washington, D.C.: Howard University Press,[1980]).
31. See M.G. Smith, *The Plural Society in the British West Indies*, (Berkeley, Los Angeles and London: The University of California Press, 1965).
32. See Vera Rubin ed. *Caribbean Studies: A Symposium*, (Mona: ISER, 1957).
33. See G. Cumper, 'Dependence, Development and the Sociology of Economic Thought,' *Social and Economic Studies* 23, no. 2 (1974): 465–82.
34. See Owen Arthur, 'Economic Policy Options in the Twenty First Century' in *Contending with Destiny: The Caribbean in the Twenty First Century*, edited by Kenneth Hall and Denis Benn (Kingston: Ian Randle Publishers, 2000), 12–25.

35.	See, for instance, Wilson Harris, 'History, Fable and Myth in the Caribbean and Guianas,' in *Wilson Harris: The Unfinished Genesis of the Imagination*, edited by Andrew Bundy (London: Routledge, 1999), 152–66.

36.	See Selwyn Ryan, 'Assessing our Social Capital,' *Trinidad and Tobago Express*, January 9, 16 and 30, 2005.

37.	Reference is to Robert Putnam, *Bowling Alone: The Collapse and Revival of American Community*, (New York: Simon and Schuster, 2000).

Contributors

Lloyd Best, scholar, journalist and Caribbean *homme de lettres*, was the founder of the New World movement, the *New World Quarterly* and the *New World Fortnightly* journals. Best left *New World* to found the Tapia House Movement, which published the journal *Tapia* and evolved into a political party with the same name. He later founded the Trinidad and Tobago Institute of the West Indies (now the Lloyd Best Institute of the West Indies) as a research and teaching institution for Caribbean affairs and edited for the rest of his life the *Trinidad and Tobago Review*. He published numerous articles in journals, magazines and newspaper columns, including the iconic piece 'Independent Thought and Caribbean Freedom' first published in *New World Quarterly*. His seminal study with Kari Polanyi Levitt, *Essays on the Theory of Plantation Economy* was recently published by the UWI Press. Lloyd Best died in 2007.

Anthony Bogues is the Harmon Family Professor of Africana Studies at Brown University where he is an affiliated faculty member of the departments of Political Science and Modern Culture and Media, as well as the Centre for Latin American and Caribbean Studies. The author of four books and over fifty articles he is a Honorary Professor at the Centre for African Studies, University of Cape Town, South Africa and a member of the editorial collective of the journal *Boundary 2: An International Journal of Literature and Culture* and an associate editor of the journal *Small Axe*.

Michaeline Critchlow teaches at Duke University, and is affiliated with the departments of African and African American Studies, Sociology and the Centre for Latin American and Caribbean Studies. She is the author of *Negotiating Caribbean Freedom: Peasants and State in Development* (2005) and *Globalization and the Post Creole Imagination: Notes on Fleeing the Plantation* (2009) and co-editor of *Informalization: Process and Structure* (2000).

David de Caires, lawyer, publisher and writer, was founder and Editor-in-Chief of the *Stabroek News*, one of the Caribbean's leading daily newspapers published in Georgetown, Guyana. Together with Lloyd Best he founded the *New World Journal* in Guyana in 1963, and went on to publish *New World Fortnightly* during the 1960s. He practised law in partnership with Miles Fitzpatrick from 1960 to 1988. David de Caires died in October 2008.

Norman Girvan is Professorial Research Fellow at the UWI Graduate Institute of International Relations at the University of the West Indies in St Augustine, Trinidad and Tobago. He has been Secretary General of the Association of Caribbean States, Professor of Development Studies and Director of the Sir Arthur Lewis Institute of Social and Economic Studies at the University of the West Indies, and head of the National Planning Agency of the Government of Jamaica. He received his Bachelor's degree in Economics from the University College of the West Indies and his PhD in Economics from the London School of Economics. He has published extensively on the political economy of development in the Caribbean and the Global South. He is the recipient of several honours and awards.

Paget Henry is Professor of Sociology and Africana Studies at Brown University. He is the editor of the *C.L.R. James Journal* and the co-editor of *C.L.R. James' Caribbean*. He is also the author of *Peripheral Capitalism and Underdevelopment in Antigua, Caliban's Reason: Introducing Afro-Caribbean Philosophy*, and the forthcoming book, *Shouldering Antigua and Barbuda: the Life of V.C. Bird*.

Kari Polanyi Levitt is Professor Emerita of Economics, McGill University. She has been a Visiting Professor at the Institute of International Relations in Trinidad and the George Beckford Professor of Caribbean Political Economy on the Mona campus of the University of the West Indies. Recent publications include, *Reclaiming Development: Independent Thought and Caribbean Community* and, jointly with Lloyd Best, *Essays on the Theory of Plantation Economy: a Historical and Institutional Approach to Caribbean Economic Development*.

Vaughan A. Lewis, now Professor Emeritus, Institute of International Relations, the University of the West Indies St Augustine, has been an academic for most of his professional life, specialising in, and writing on the international relations of small states, small state-major power relations, regional integration, and the role of developing countries in international relations. In between his academic activities, he has served as founding Director General of the Organisation of Eastern Caribbean States (OECS) between 1982 and 1995, and Prime Minister of St Lucia 1996–97. He was a member of the West Indian Commission on Caricom integration, Chairman of the Technical Working Group on Governance of the Caribbean Community 2006–7, and most recently Chairman of the Task Force on Integration between Trinidad and Tobago and countries of the Eastern Caribbean.

Brian Meeks is Professor of Social and Political Change, Director of the Sir Arthur Lewis Institute for Social and Economic Studies, UWI Mona and Director of the Centre for Caribbean Thought in the Department of Government at Mona. He has also taught at Michigan State University and Florida International University. His books include *Envisioning Caribbean Futures: Jamaican Perspectives* (2007) *Narratives of Resistance: Jamaica, Trinidad, the Caribbean (2000)* and *Caribbean Revolutions and Revolutionary Theory: An Assessment of Cuba, Nicaragua and Grenada (1993 and 2001)*. His first novel, *Paint the Town Red* was published in 2003.

Kirk Meighoo is author of *Politics in a 'Half-Made Society:' Trinidad and Tobago, 1925–2001* and (with Justice Peter Jamadar) *Democracy and Constitution Reform in Trinidad and Tobago*. He was a close collaborator of Lloyd Best's from 1997 to 2005. Meighoo was a Contributing Editor of the *Trinidad and Tobago Review* during that period, a Director of the Trinidad and Tobago Institute of the West Indies, and the Institute's first fulltime Research Fellow. Before Best's death, the two jointly produced a first draft of a full-length manuscript *Government and Politics in the West Indies: the Case of Trinidad and Tobago*. Meighoo is a founder of the Democratic National Assembly and contested the 2007 General Elections as part of the UNC/Alliance. He is also CEO of ELGE, Ltd.

James Millette is Professor of African American studies at Oberlin College. He was among the founding members of the New World Group in Trinidad and went on to found the United National Independence Party (UNIP) which published the newspaper *Moko* and functioned in Trinidad and Tobago in the early seventies. Millette has published numerous articles on Caribbean history and politics and two books, *The Genesis of Crown Colony Government: Trinidad, 1783–1815* and *Freedom Road,* a study of the post-emancipation period in Caribbean history.

Pat Northover is a Fellow at the Sir Arthur Lewis Institute of Social and Economic Studies (SALISES, UWI, Mona) where she lectures in development studies and microeconomic policy. She is the author and co-author of several publications in the philosophy of economics and development studies, including an edited double volume issue of the journal, *Social and Economic Studies*, (2005) on Arthur Lewis's 'Theory of Economic Growth.' Her forthcoming books are *Growth Theory: Critical Philosophical Perspectives* (Routledge) and *Globalization and the Post Creole Imagination: Notes on Fleeing the Plantation*, Michaeline Crichlow with Patricia Northover, (Duke University Press).

Dennis A. Pantin is Professor and current Head of the Department of Economics, UWI, St Augustine and also Coordinator of the Sustainable Economic Development Unit (SEDU) based within this Department. He also has conducted policy oriented research on sustainable development related issues in several countries of the Caribbean including Belize, Jamaica, St Lucia, Grenada, Guyana and Trinidad and Tobago. He has published in regional and international journals and is editor of *A Reader in Caribbean Economy* published by Ian Randle Publishers. He also is co-author of the recently published *Economics of an Integrated (Watershed) Approach to Environmental Management in Small Island Developing States (SIDS).*

He also is a founding member of the Trinidad and Tobago Economics Association (TTEA) and the Association of Caribbean Economists (ACE) and of the Constitution Reform Forum (CRF) of Trinidad and Tobago.

David C. Wong is a Jamaican. He obtained a BSc (Special Honours) in Mathematics (1970) and a MSc in Mathematics from UWI (Mona)

(1974) and a PhD in Economics from University of California, Santa Barbara (1984). He currently resides in Fullerton, California where he is a Professor of Economics at California State University, Fullerton. His scholarly publications have appeared in *The Economic Journal*, *Journal of Human Resources*, *Journal of Comparative Economics*, and other professional journals.

Index

www.ingramcontent.com/pod-product-compliance
Lightning Source LLC
Chambersburg PA
CBHW020603270326
41927CB00005B/152